The

County Courts

of Medieval

England

The
County Courts
of Medieval
England

1150-1350

ROBERT C. PALMER

Princeton University Press

Princeton, New Jersey

Published by Princeton University Press, 41 William Street,
Princeton, New Jersey
In the United Kingdom: Princeton University Press,
Guildford, Surrey

Library of Congress Cataloging in Publication Data will be
found on the last printed page of this book

Publication of this book has been aided by a grant from
the Paul Mellon Fund of Princeton University Press

This book has been composed in Linotron Aldus

Clothbound editions of Princeton University Press books are
printed on acid-free paper, and binding materials are chosen
for strength and durability

Printed in the United States of America by Princeton
University Press, Princeton, New Jersey

TO MY PARENTS
Albert F. and Josephine E. Palmer

Contents

꙰

Tables

꽃

Preface

꒜

THIS BOOK is an examination of the constitutional and legal aspects of English county courts, primarily from the mid-twelfth to the mid-fourteenth centuries. During that time county courts declined drastically in importance while the king's court became a normal court of original jurisdiction. The decline of the county courts, along with the decline of the seignorial courts, was the obverse side of the increasing functions of the king's court. The history of the county courts during these years is thus of central importance to legal and constitutional history.

It might therefore be expected that this book would be only the latest in a long series of works to deal with the subject; on the contrary, however, it is the first book-length study. Other writers, primarily F. W. Maitland, W. A. Morris, and Helen Cam, have dealt with county courts, but only in the form of chapters in a more general work, introductory essays, or articles. It was thought that there was inadequate evidence for a book-length study. This book, however, is based largely on new sources which only came to light while I was researching a completely different topic. The fortuitous nature of the discovery and the novelty, extent, and quality of the sources explain the way in which this book is structured.

Although the chapters seem to fall into a rational arrangement, this book is not the result of a rationally preconceived research project. It grew from an aborted short note to a published article, from the article into a dissertation, and from the dissertation into the present book and a future edited volume of sources. The topics treated are solely those topics relevant to the county courts on which I was able to garner new information during four years of uninterrupted research in London and two and a half years of almost uninterrupted research and writing at various venues in the United States and Canada. As it happens, I have come across valuable new evidence on every topic of importance. Nevertheless, while these materials are much fuller than those previously available, they are not so complete that

I could follow a chronological format; and the arguments in some of the chapters involve the whole period. The state of the evidence will allow nothing more until these arguments have been accepted; thereafter some simplification may be possible. Thus the first part is concerned with institutional framework and personnel; the second, with jurisdiction. These are the topics most accessible to a nonspecialist audience. The third section, a treatment of the legal procedure used in county courts, is reserved for the Selden Society volume which will contain the documents at length, as mentioned below.

This book makes little attempt to deal with bibliography. I have not felt called upon to refute explicitly everyone with whom I disagree except insofar as that has helped me frame my arguments. This approach is justified by the vastly larger base of documentation used here, both sources that were unknown before, such as the county court year book reports and the writ file records, and sources that had not been closely examined for evidence on the county courts, such as the king's court plea rolls of Edward I, the unedited Cheshire plea rolls, and the early close rolls. The footnotes here are therefore relatively useless for bibliographic purposes. They are usually excerpts of documents or references to documents. Where the documents support a particularly new approach, I have tried to include at least one important excerpt in the notes; other references, those which are followed by the designation "[S.S.]" are documents that will be printed in the volume of sources I am preparing for the Selden Society. This book and the edition—both the sources and the introduction—must be seen as companion volumes. Since this book will appear rather in advance of the Selden Society volume, however, I have tried to reproduce at least sufficient evidence in the notes here.

Much of the work below concerns procedure, and the argument often proceeds upon a discussion of texts. This may seem tedious, but I have tried at least to avoid unnecessary technical language and to omit those technicalities that are inessential for the argument. Knowledge of the procedure, however, is often simply not dispensable. It is, for instance, precisely the procedure that determines the relationship of the county courts to the king's court and to the liberties. Moreover, without some knowledge of the procedure, much of the evidence would lose its force. Since the conclusions vary widely at times from current historiography and are based at times so heavily on procedural arguments, there is simply no way around dealing with procedural questions at length. Besides, there is no other way, particularly for a beginner, to ascertain the sophistication of a legal system than to become familiar with the inner workings of the law.

One might also have wished that I had merely stated conclusions drawn from documents and included the excerpts in the notes, rather than parsing documents in the text. This was not possible for three reasons. At times my arguments depend greatly on a feel for the documents and the language they use. One has to demonstrate that a document is a paraphrase, that a seemingly clear reference contrary to the argument is either not clear at all or mere form, that a passage from a treatise—although often cited—has been misunderstood. The proper interpretation of a document, in short, is often not at all obvious. Moreover, it is desirable in itself that such a feeling for the documents be conveyed. New references can thus be properly evaluated in regard to the argument; these materials may also be better used for investigation of subjects other than the county courts. Most importantly, however, when dealing with such an important topic and arriving at conclusions that are not consistent with current historiography, it is absolutely necessary to expose both the evidence and the reasoning process. If the arguments are false, they can be more readily rejected. If the arguments are true, they can be more readily accepted; and the fuller exposition will make others relatively as comfortable with the research as the author. Only in that way can the conclusions be applied to related areas.

As much as possible this book is directed to a treatment of the county courts as institutions and as they related to the other courts, not to an ultimate explanation of Parliament or the increasing importance of the king's court. That choice has dictated that several themes around which the material could have been organized appear only here and there. There is, for instance, an important argument to be made concerning the legal profession. Part of that argument I have put into print already; part appears only here; part I shall return to in a later piece. Another important argument concerns the integration of the courts of England. I have previously put forth the proposition that the king's court, the county courts, and the hundred liberties constituted a legal system in the thirteenth century. The various elements of that argument are scattered through this book. While that is not the organizing theme of the book, the argument is made again in the conclusion. Likewise, the material could have been ordered around the rise of the king's court. It is not, but the book can almost be read in that way. Despite the importance of these themes, in short, the book by and large takes the form of an examination of the county courts; that approach is justified by the range of interesting problems it has necessitated answering.

Portions of this book have already been presented elsewhere. A good part of chapter 4 appeared in the *English Historical Review* in 1976 in a similar form. The version here printed is slightly condensed, but it also contains new information which greatly reinforces some of my previous conclusions. Chapter 8 was delivered first in Edinburgh at the Third British Legal History Conference, then at a branch meeting of the American Society for Legal History in Philadelphia. Although the argument has remained the same, it has undergone several revisions and, of course, can be presented in fuller detail in print. The recurrent insistence in this book that the nonmanorial and non-borough territorial courts formed a legal system was the subject of a paper delivered to the American Society for Legal History at Williamsburg in 1979. Finally, chapters 3, 4, and 5 are a somewhat condensed version of my dissertation, submitted to the University of Iowa in 1977; the dissertation also had a large section of edited documents.

Two items of terminology must also be mentioned. The word "seneschal" is equivalent to "steward," and the latter is perhaps more frequently used than the former. I have followed Sir Frank Stenton's lead, however, in using the former. The reason for the choice is the connotation for "seneschal," which is more legal than household in nature; I realize that that distinction between "seneschal" and "steward" may only be my own. My distinction between "justice" and "judge" has a better foundation. I use "justice" to indicate one who is a presiding officer of a court who is likewise the person who renders the judgments. "Judge" is used to indicate one who renders judgments, without any reference to the function of presiding over a court. That distinction has no basis in modern usage, but some such distinction had to be made to deal with those who rendered judgments in county courts once I discovered that it was not possible to maintain that the suitors always rendered judgment. "Doomsmen" seemed inappropriate, because it has normally been used in connection with people who could not be considered lawyers. I have also used "judge" instead of "judger" to refer to the Cheshire *judicator*, because the latter form seems to have been produced to rival the verbal flavor of "doomsman." Such terminological problems should not prove burdensome.

The research for this book was made possible by grants of fellowships from various institutions: the American Bar Foundation (1976-1977); the Andrew W. Mellon Foundation through the City University of New York (1977-1978); the Izaak Walton Killam Memorial Fund for Advanced Studies though the University of Alberta at Edmonton (1978-1979); and the Michigan Society of Fellows together with the Law School of the University of Michigan at Ann Arbor (1979-1980). I hope that this and other works resulting from my research during these fellowships will justify their expectations and generosity.

I would also like to express my gratitude to all who have helped me in this project. In particular I would like to acknowledge the great assistance of Professor Donald W. Sutherland of the University of Iowa, who introduced me to legal history and supervised my dissertation; of Mr. G.D.G. Hall, late president of Corpus Christi College, Oxford, who persuaded me to study the county courts seriously; of Paul A. Brand of University College, Dublin, and of Professor Charles Donahue of the Harvard Law School for their critical appraisals of parts of the book. I also must thank Edward Powell for his careful reading of the typescript, Lorna E. M. Walker for permission to cite her thesis, and the editors of the *English Historical Review* for permission to reprint here in large part the article published there. I am also indebted to the staffs of the British Library and the Public Record Office. No one, however, was more instrumental in promoting my research than my wife, Patricia Rochford Palmer. She worked as a social worker for three years in London and thus largely financed the initial research. Since our return from England she has endured the hard and insecure life dictated by marriage to a transient postdoctoral fellow. Despite both the personal hardship and her seeming immunity to the contagious joys of medieval English law, she has remained a steadfast and encouraging friend.

Common
Abbreviations

۞

AHR	*American Historical Review*
BIHR	*Bulletin of the Institute of Historical Research*
Brit. Lib.	The British Library
CCR	*Calendar of Close Rolls*
CFR	*Calendar of Fine Rolls*
CIM	*Calendar of Inquisitions Miscellaneous*
CLR	*Calendar of Liberate Rolls*
cp	the crown pleas folios of the king's bench plea rolls
CPR	*Calendar of Patent Rolls*
CR	*Close Rolls*
CRR	*Curia Regis Rolls*
EHD	*English Historical Documents*
EHR	*The English Historical Review*
EPNS	The English Place Name Society
IPM	*Calendar of Inquisitions Post Mortem*
PQW	*Placita de Quo Warranto*
PR	Pipe Roll
RH	*Rotuli Hundredorum*
SS	a document which will appear in the future Selden Society volume *Medieval County Courts*
VCH	*The Victoria History of the Counties of England*

NOTE: Document abbreviations for Public Record Office documents are in the Bibliography.

PART I

Institutional
Framework and
Personnel

1

Venue and
Scheduling

Venue and scheduling constitute the most basic elements of the institutional structure of the county courts. Since these courts met normally once a month for only one or two days and not daily, it was important that the time and place of meeting be known in advance. The damage to litigants which would otherwise ensue would dictate that much. In matters of scheduling, however, the courts went beyond a schedule known in advance to one that was nearly predictable which endured for centuries. That rigidity was maintained by the demands of process built up around and in the courts. In matters of venue the county courts likewise tended toward rigidity, with only a few exceptions. Since a town which was a county venue reaped benefits from the patronage of litigants, it behoved the king to fix the venue in a royal borough. Both venue and schedule thus were fixed during the thirteenth century and were rarely subject to alteration in the succeeding centuries.

These aspects of the institutional structure of the county courts are only hinted at prior to the thirteenth century. In the late tenth century, county courts—then and through much of the twelfth century called shire courts[1]—met regularly only twice a year.[2] During the eleventh century at least some additional sessions were assembled to

---

[1] The word "shire" appears in official documents of the thirteenth century only when the terms of a previous document were cited, such as in the confirmation of a charter. With "shire" one can speak of a shire court: "scirgemot." With "comitatus" the designation of the geographical unit and the designation of the court are identical. The phrase "curia comitatus" was not used.

[2] Edgar's Ordinance, 5:1; II Cnut 18. Helen Cam, *The Hundred and the Hundred Rolls* (London, 1930), p. 10, hypothesizes that there were regular monthly sessions prior to 1066, but it would not seem impossible that most business could have been handled at the local and hundred level.

decide particular cases; such sessions were often irregular both in schedule and in venue.[3] By the reign of Henry I the frequency of county sessions had become a matter of concern. Henry ordered that counties return to the practices of the reign of Edward the Confessor in matters of both place and times of meeting.[4] The effect of this ordinance in practice—and even Henry's interpretation of ancient custom—cannot be determined, but it is clear at least that frequent sessions were and continued to be a problem.

County sessions were regulated in the early thirteenth century and soon thereafter settled into a fixed schedule. Magna Carta, c. 42, provided that county courts should meet no more frequently than monthly, and this soon came to mean a one-day meeting every twenty-eighth day, so that county courts met thirteen or fourteen times a year. Longer intervals could be maintained by the terms of the charter only if they were customary. Compliance with the charter was not immediate. Wiltshire in 1222 was still meeting irregularly at intervals of three, four, five, or seven weeks.[5] Such aberrances, however, died out fairly quickly. As early as 1218 Devon was normally meeting monthly, and a defendant was able to challenge successfully the legitimacy of continuing process after only a three-week interval.[6] In 1220 the sheriff of Surrey was amerced for allowing his county court to meet after a three-week interval.[7] Such enforcement by the king's court soon subdued most counties to the twenty-eight day schedule.

The longer interval mentioned and permitted by Magna Carta was normally six weeks. The number of counties that originally used the six-weekly schedule is unknown. In 1219 Somerset county court was meeting six-weekly,[8] as was Oxfordshire in 1222.[9] By the reign of Edward I, the only normal counties to follow the six-weekly session were Lancashire, Lincolnshire, Yorkshire, and Northumberland.[10] They

---

[3] II Cnut 19.

[4] *Select Charters Illustrative of English Constitutional History*, ed. William Stubbs, 8th ed. (Oxford, 1900), p. 104.

[5] *CRR*, 11:348. The reference that Lady Stenton interpreted as meaning that the Staffordshire court was meeting fortnightly (*Rolls of the Justices in Eyre for Gloucestershire, Warwickshire, and Staffordshire, 1221, 1222*, ed. D. M. Stenton, Selden Society, vol. 59 [London, 1940], p. 244) probably does not refer to the county court.

[6] JUST. 1/180, m. 7, quoted in Lorna E. M. Walker, "Some Aspects of Local Jurisdiction in the 12th and 13th Centuries, with Special Reference to Private and County Courts" (Master's thesis, University of London, 1958), pp. 286-89.

[7] *CRR*, 8:223.

[8] *CRR*, 9:134.

[9] *CRR*, 10:345.

[10] J. J. Alexander, "The Dates of County Days," *BIHR* 3 (1925-1926):89-95.

maintained that schedule until 1548, when it was abolished by statute.[11] Cheshire county court, not affected by Magna Carta, had an extremely variable schedule—sometimes six-weekly, sometimes fortnightly—into the fourteenth century, when it finally adopted the six-weekly schedule.[12] In 1540 Parliament reduced the sessions to two each year, in accord with a practice that seems to have become customary in Lancashire when it became a palatine court,[13] but the following year the problems of such infrequent sessions were recognized and Cheshire was made to meet every month.[14]

Different county courts met on different days of the week. Devon, for instance, met every fourth Tuesday, while Lincolnshire met every sixth Monday. No county normally met on Fridays or Sundays, although rare irregular sessions or sessions of the rere-county were held on those days. In 1319 Devon even met on Christmas day,[15] but such incidents were not common. In medieval England Monday was often the customary day for the county session, but in 1696 more rigorous religious ideas prevailed. Because people were forced to travel on Sunday to attend a Monday court, all county courts which had been meeting on Monday were ordered to meet thereafter on Wednesday.[16] Furthermore, contiguous counties normally did not meet on the same day, even though Derbyshire and Staffordshire did so regularly from the thirteenth to the seventeenth century; for shorter times Buckinghamshire and Surrey as well as Northamptonshire and Oxfordshire met on the same day, while Lincolnshire met alternately on the same day with either Norfolk or Nottinghamshire.[17] Nevertheless, county schedules were usually so arranged that litigants with suits in more than one county would not suffer hardship nor violate religious prohibitions.

County schedules, once determined, were carefully maintained. County courts adhered not only to their fixed day of the week, but

[11] 2 & 3 Edward VI, c. 25.

[12] The thirteenth-century rolls of Cheshire calendared in *Calendar of County Court, City Court, and Eyre Rolls of Chester*, ed. R. Stewart-Brown, Chetham Society, n.s., vol. 84 (Aberdeen, 1925) still show a variable schedule. Chester 29/7 gives eight sessions for 1292-93 with a six-week interval; KB. 27/158, m. 36 shows process every two weeks in 1298; Chester 29/13 (1300) has sessions with intervals of four, five, six, and eight weeks; Chester 29/30 (1316-17) has intervals of four, five, six, seven, and eight weeks.

[13] 32 Henry VIII.

[14] 33 Henry VIII, c. 13.

[15] CP. 52 octave Hilary, 13 Edward II.

[16] 7 & 8 William III, c. 25.

[17] Appendix I.

also to their position in the twenty-eight day cycle with regard to the other counties. Thus, if a county allowed a five-week interval between sessions once, it would soon compensate with a three-week interval to regain its position on the archetypical lunar calendar. Variations from the proper day normally occurred as variations of a whole week instead of a displacement by one day only. During the reign of Edward I variations from the proper schedule amounted to less than 10 percent of the total sessions examined. This figure coincides with J. J. Alexander's results for the fourteenth, fifteenth, and sixteenth centuries.[18] Permanent alterations in county schedule happened very infrequently and at times of crisis, seemingly no more than seven times from the thirteenth to the seventeenth century. This regularity lasted until the county courts were reformed in the nineteenth century.[19]

The arrangement of county days indicates control from the king's government. Fourteen counties met on Mondays; thirteen on Thursdays. These two days were the ones most heavily used. In all, nineteen counties met in the first part of the week, on Mondays or Tuesdays; nineteen on Wednesdays, Thursdays, or Saturdays. Furthermore, fifteen of the counties meeting early in the week were on the coast, while seventeen of the nineteen counties meeting later in the week were inland counties.[20] That fact is convenient mnemonically, but so far cannot be ascribed any rationale. The division of the counties, however, together with the correlation between day of the week and geographical location, would not have happened without control from the central government at some time earlier than the 1270s.

Venue was as important to litigants as was the scheduling of sessions; to shopkeepers and innkeepers, it was more so. The regular influx of officials, lawyers, and litigants was profitable, and in some

[18] J. J. Alexander, "Dates of Early County Elections," *EHR* 40 (1925):1-12. The figure for the reign of Edward I was obtained from the examination of over 1,500 county sessions recorded in exigent procedure and returns to *recordari* writs.

[19] J. J. Alexander, "Dates of Early County Elections," p. 10, maintained that county sessions began to depart from the schedule in the late seventeenth century. His figures came solely from returns of members of Parliament and were thus the result of the adjournment of elections to a more convenient place and day, process which became normal in the late seventeenth century (7 & 8 William III, c. 25). See Cam, *Hundred*, p. 109.

[20] Appendix I. For this purpose Gloucestershire has been treated as a county with a seacoast because of the Severn estuary. It is possible that Durham met on Wednesday, but that is based on only one date; the county was not strictly under the king's control. Cheshire, despite its standing as a liberty, is included in the figures.

counties there were prolonged disputes as to the proper or most profitable place for the county venue.[21] In most counties, however, a single borough had, with the advantages of a royal castle, gaol, and tradition, no trouble in maintaining its position as sole county venue. In any case it became established that only royal authority could permanently change the venue. For the majority of counties, the venue has been listed in Appendix II, with minor deviations or permanent changes noted. For a smaller set of counties, however, there was no dominant county venue. In these counties the change of venue can often be related to early traditions and to differences in the kind of session. The counties that were not restricted to a single venue were Kent, Sussex, Middlesex, Essex, Hertfordshire, Berkshire, Buckinghamshire, Rutland, and Cornwall.

In multiple-venue counties, one venue was associated particularly with the twice-yearly sessions of the general or great county court. In Hertfordshire, for instance, the county court met regularly at Hertford every twenty-eighth day. The only exceptions were the sessions that met immediately after Easter and immediately after Michaelmas. These two sessions were normally held at Cheshunt and were occasionally described as sessions of the general county court.[22] Essex similarly, up until the 1260s, normally met at Writtle,[23] although soon after the 1260s the normal venue was transferred to Chelmsford.[24] Even though the sheriff's office was at Colchester,[25] no meeting of the county court was ever mentioned as assembling there. Both before and after the transfer to Chelmsford, however, the sessions after Easter and after Michaelmas were held at Stratford

[21] Below, chapter 1, at nn. 29-34 and 49-57.

[22] E. 370/5/30 (printed in W. A. Morris, *The Early English County Court*, University of California Publications in History, vol. 14, no. 2 (Berkeley, 1926), pp. 204-6). The meeting of 17 Oct. at Hertford is somewhat exceptional, but two other such instances can be cited: 9 Apr. 1355 (C. 88/48, m. 3) and 3 Oct. 1370 (C. 88/43, m. 16). Normally, meetings after Easter and Michaelmas were at Cheshunt: 27 Oct. 1306 (C. 88/5, m. 1), 13 Oct. 1317 (CP. 52 octave Purification, 11 Edward II), 25 Oct. 1330 (KB. 27/283, m. 13d, c.p.), 7 April 1334 (KB. 27/297, m. 5d, c.p.), 12 Oct. 1340 (C. 88/13, m. 9), 10 Oct. 1364 (C. 88/47, m. 36), 9 Oct. 1365 (C. 88/40, m. 40), 5 Oct. 1368 (C. 88/40, m. 46). I have not seen any evidence that Hertfordshire met at Cheshunt other than at the sessions after Easter and after Michaelmas. The sessions of 17 Oct. 1258, 1 May 1259, and 13 Oct. 1317 are specified as sessions of the general county court.

[23] E. 370/5/30 (Morris, *Early English County Court*, pp. 201-4).

[24] CP. 52 octave St. Martin, 24 Edward I: five successive sessions at Chelmsford in 1296.

[25] Mabel H. Mills, "The Medieval Shire House," in *Studies Presented to Sir Hilary Jenkinson*, ed. J. Conway Davies (London, 1957), p. 255.

Langthorne, and those sessions were the only ones ever designated as sessions of the general county.[26] This pattern of venue continued through the fourteenth century, but at least by the end of the sixteenth century such regularity of venue was deteriorating.[27] Since both Cheshunt and Stratford Langthorne are geographically eccentric, situated in the corner of their respective counties closest to London, these venues would have been inconvenient for most litigants. It is conceivable that the customary two meetings each year at such venues were fixed by the preferences of Geoffrey de Mandeville when, in the early 1140s, he managed to become both sheriff and justiciar in Essex, Hertfordshire, Middlesex, and London.[28] There is no proof for that hypothesis, but it would have made his duties rather easier.

The history of the venue of the county court of Cornwall is particularly tortuous, involving both a great county venue and a dispute over the venue of ordinary sessions. Twelfth-century county court sessions are mentioned both at Bodmin and at Launceston,[29] but during the second quarter of the thirteenth century Launceston was granted the privilege of being the venue for eight sessions in the year, beginning with the first county session after Easter and continuing through the specified number of sessions.[30] Richard, earl of Cornwall and sheriff-in-fee of the county of Cornwall, thereafter removed all but three of the sessions to Bodmin, leaving Launceston with only the sessions after Easter and Michaelmas and a January session.[31] Edmund, earl of Cornwall, further altered arrangements by removing the Bodmin sessions to Lostwithiel late in 1286 or early in 1287 and then constructed a county house there at reputedly great expense.[32]

[26] Sessions at Stratford Langthorne specifically designated as sessions of the general county: 8 Oct. 1258, 22 April 1259 (E. 370/5/30; Morris, *Early English County Court*, pp. 201-4), 20 Oct. 1299 (CP. 52 octave Hilary, 38 Edward I). Other sessions at Stratford Langthorne: after Easter 1303 (*IPM*, Edward I, 4:81), 2 Oct. 1313 (C. 88/5, m. 15), 30 Sept. 1315 (C. 88/5, m. 26), 25 Oct. 1316 (C. 88/6, m. 17), 14 April 1338 (C. 88/12, m. 1), 13 April 1339 (C. 88/12, m. 22), 26 Oct. 1339 (C. 88/13, m. 19), 9 May 1340 (C. 88/13, m. 11).

[27] C. 88/223, m. 7: 1 July 1600 at Chelmsford, 29 July at Fyfield, 26 Aug. at Dunmow, 23 Sept. at Chelmsford, and 23 Oct. at Stratford Langthorne.

[28] For his offices: Doris M. Stenton, *English Justice between the Norman Conquest and the Great Charter* (London, 1965), p. 66.

[29] *British Borough Charters*, ed. Adolphus Ballard and James Tait, 2 vols. (Cambridge, 1923), 2:379; *The Cartulary of St. Michael's Mount*, ed. P. L. Hull, The Devon and Cornwall Record Society, n.s., vol. 5 (Torquay, 1962), p. 42.

[30] *British Borough Charters*, 2:239.

[31] *The Caption of Seisin of the Duchy of Cornwall (1337)*, ed. P. L. Hull, The Devon and Cornwall Record Society, n.s., vol. 17 (Exeter, 1971), p. 4.

[32] CP. 52 morrow John the Baptist, 14 Edward I: Cornwall meeting at Bodmin 26 Nov. and 24 Dec. 1285, at Launceston 21 Jan. 1286, and at Bodmin 18 Feb. 1286. CP.

Later, both Launceston and Bodmin attempted unsuccessfully to regain the migratory sessions.[33] Although no mention of the three sessions that remained at Launceston was made in any of the parliamentary petitions concerning the Cornwall venue, specific dates make clear that those sessions did remain at Launceston, and the sessions after Easter and after Michaelmas were designated as sessions of the great county.[34] Lostwithiel became the normal venue of the Cornwall county court in the fourteenth century, but the site of the great county sessions was so fixed by tradition that those sessions were automatically excluded from all debate concerning change of venue.

Middlesex had the most regular and complicated pattern of shifting venue. Three places were involved: Brentford, Stonecross, and Ossulstone. Brentford was at the intersection of the Roman road to Bath with the river Brent near the Thames.[35] Stonecross was located near the present-day church of St. Mary le Strand, midway between London and Westminster, formerly marked by a stone cross said to have been erected by William Rufus.[36] The location of Ossulstone has presented some difficulties, but the most recent analysis puts it approximately at present-day speakers' corner, near the site of the Tyburn hanging tree.[37] County venue alternated regularly between Brentford and Stonecross, with the sessions after Easter and after Michaelmas meeting at Ossulstone. The Ossulstone sessions, however, did not disrupt the alternation between the other sites; if the county met at Brentford before the Ossulstone session, it met at Stonecross afterwards.[38] This pattern persisted rigidly into the sixteenth century. Records of outlawries from 1574 and 1585 show the

---

52 3 weeks Easter, 15 Edward I [S.S.]: Cornwall meeting 13 Jan. 1287 at Lostwithiel. See *Caption of Seisin*, p. 4; *Rotuli Parliamentorum*, 6 vols. (London, 1767), 1:296.

[33] *British Borough Charters*, 2:239; *Caption of Seisin*, p. 4.

[34] E. 370/5/21, 22: the dates of the sessions for the county and hundred courts of Cornwall from Mar. 1331 to Sept. 1333. All the county sessions were held at Lostwithiel except the sessions of 15 Apr. and 30 Sept. 1331, 20 Jan., 11 May, and 2 Nov. 1332, and 18 Jan. and 12 Apr. 1333, all of which were held at Launceston. It is interesting to note that these dates for the county court of Cornwall relating to Launceston are the approximate schedule prescribed for Parliament by the Provisions of Oxford.

[35] EPNS, *Place Names of Middlesex*, vol. 18 (Cambridge, 1942), p. 31.

[36] Ibid., p. 173.

[37] *VCH, Middlesex*, 6:1.

[38] Sessions at Ossulstone: 19 April 1296 (CP. 40/113, m. 148d), 26 Oct. 1301 (CP. 52 month Michaelmas, 29 Edward I), 23 Oct. 1326 (KB. 27/284, m. 23d), 17 Oct. 1331 (C. 88/10, m. 14), 15 Oct. 1332 (KB. 27/290, m. 41d, c.p.), 27 April 1340 (C. 88/13, m. 22), 5 Oct. 1340 (C. 88/12, m. 32), 4 Oct. 1341 (C. 88/14, m. 1), 3 Oct. 1342 (C. 88/15, m. 8), 17 April 1343 (C. 88/16, m. 13), 2 Oct. 1343 (C. 88/16, m. 19), 15 Apr. 1344 (C. 88/16, m. 44), 23 Oct. 1460 (C. 88/150, mm. 30, 52), 27 Oct. 1457 (C. 88/150, m. 55). These references also show the complete venue pattern.

same pattern.[39] In 1599, however, a session which should have been at Stonecross was held instead at the Castle Inn in St. John Street, well to the north of Stonecross. The next session (1 February) was held at Ossulstone, followed by a session at Brentford. The next session was the session before Easter, and it was held again at Ossulstone.[40] The meeting at the Castle Inn and the irregular sessions at Ossulstone are the first documentable deviations from the medieval pattern. By 1738 the county was meeting consecutively at the sign of the Elephant and Castle, in the parish of St. Andrew, Holborn, perhaps the same inn mentioned in 1599.[41] By 1814 the county was meeting at the sheriff's office, at that time on Bedford Street in Bedford Row in the parish of St. Andrew, Holborn,[42] and by 1833 located in Red Lion Square.[43] No medieval session at Ossulstone was called a meeting of the general county, perhaps because the earliest Ossulstone session discovered was in 1296. That date is rather late for any southeastern county to describe a county session in such a manner. The treatment of Ossulstone sessions in the venue pattern nevertheless leaves no doubt that that site was particularly associated with meetings of the general county.

Any settled venue that Kent had ever had had already deteriorated badly by the late thirteenth century. Most of its venues were along Watling Street: Rochester, Newington, Sittingbourne, Chestnut Street (Castinarios?), and Canterbury. Of these, Canterbury was the most frequent venue, but only the meeting at Sittingbourne was unusual. Kent, however, had retained its traditional general county meeting place: Penenden Heath or, at times, nearby Maidstone. Although the county met at Maidstone and Penenden Heath at other times, it invariably met there at the session after Michaelmas.[44] The session

---

[39] C. 88/210, m. 31; C. 88/219, m. 32.

[40] C. 88/223, m. 2.

[41] KB. 17/1.

[42] Ibid.

[43] Ibid.: "At my open county court of Middlesex holden in and for the county of Middlesex at the House known by the name of The Sheriff's Office in Red Lion Square."

[44] Sessions at Rochester: 8 Dec. 1253 (JUST. 1/361, m. 51), 29 Sept. 1259 (E. 370/5/36), 12 Nov. 1291 (JUST. 4/1, Kent Eyre 1293), 21 Nov. 1306 (KB. 27/187, m. 21, c.p.), 11 Nov. 1314 (CP. 52 octave Hilary, 8 Edward II), 10 Nov. and 8 Dec. 1315 and 5 Jan. 1316 (C. 88/5, m. 23), 3 Feb. and 31 Mar. 1315 (C. 88/5, m. 20), 5 Nov. 1319 (C. 88/6, m. 22), 19 Apr. 1321 (C. 88/7, m. 14), 18 May 1321 (C. 88/6, m. 31), 25 Jan. 1367 (C. 88/43, m. 79), 2 May 1513 (C. 88/194, m. 4).

Sessions at Newington: 5 Jan. and 3 Feb. 1254 (JUST. 1/361, m. 51), 17 Jan. and 14 Feb. 1306 (C. 88/4, m. 11), 6 June 1306 (C. 88/2, m. 40).

Session at Sittingbourne: 29 Jan. 1274 (CP. 40/9, m. 51).

Sessions at "Castinarios" (Chestnut Street?): 1153 (Walker, "Some Aspects," pp.

after Easter was not associated with any venue. Kent was thus different from the other counties, but it had itself long been a divided
county. The River Medway divided the men of Kent from the Kentish
men. In Domesday Book the men of Dover had even claimed that
they were not obliged to travel farther than Penenden Heath to attend
the county court, and Penenden Heath is situated just to the east of
the River Medway.[45] It is unlikely, therefore, that the whole county
would have attended a general county at a single venue. This fact
lends some color to the inconclusive evidence that the second session
after Michaelmas met at Rochester, situated just west of the River
Medway.[46] A schedule that allowed a general county at Penenden
Heath for East Kent and thereafter at Rochester for West Kent, both
after Michaelmas, would at least account for the lack of importance
given the session after Easter, but the evidence for the Rochester
general county meeting is only suggestive, not conclusive.

The county of Rutland is the last county in which a specific venue
can be associated with a particular session. Most of the Rutland sessions convened at Oakham, although the county very rarely met also
at Wing and Weston Thicket. Although the evidence is meager, it
seems that there was also a custom of meeting at Bradecroft at the
session immediately prior to Easter.[47] Bradecroft was a Rutland ham-

346-47, a single session), 3 March 1260 (E. 370/5/36), 26 Aug. 1286 (JUST. 4/1, Kent
Eyre 1293), 2 Aug. 1305 (C. 88/2, m. 6), 22 July 1314 (C. 88/5, m. 16), 21 June and
16 Aug. 1316 (C. 88/6, m. 6), 15 June 1321 (C. 88/6, m. 31), 4 April and 27 June
1334 (KB. 27/298, m. 9d, c.p.).

Sessions at Canterbury: 10 Nov. 1253 (JUST. 1/361, m. 51), 7 June, 5 July, 30
Aug., 27 Sept. 1305 (C. 88/2, m. 6), 16 Feb., 16 Mar., 13 Apr., 11 May 1349 (C.
88/21, m. 12), 10 Dec. 1291 (JUST. 1/4, Kent Eyre 1293); 22 Feb., 22 Mar., 19 Apr.,
17 May 1367 (C. 88/40, m. 20), etc.

Sessions at Penenden Heath: special session ordered by William the Conqueror
(EHD, 2:449-51), 13 Oct. 1315 (C. 88/5, m. 23), 11 Oct. 1316 (C. 88/6, m. 7), 8 Oct.
1319 (C. 88/6, m. 22), 13 July 1321 (C. 88/6, m. 31), 22 March 1322 (C. 88/7, m.
14), 13 Jan. 1332 (KB. 27/298, m. 33d, c.p.), 9 Oct. 1587 (C. 88/221, m. 16), 14 June,
12 July, 9 Aug., 6 Sept., and 4 Oct. 1809 (KB. 27/187, m. 21, c.p.).

[45] Domesday Book seu liber censualis Willelmi Primi Regis Angliae, ed. A. Farley,
2 vols. (London, 1783), 1:1.

[46] Above, n. 44.

[47] There are several good series of dates from Rutland: (a) CP. 52 three weeks Easter,
15 Edward I: 27 Mar. Bradecroft (Easter was 6 Apr.); 24 Apr. 1287, Oakham; (b) CP.
52 quindene Hilary, 21 Edward I, three weeks Easter, 21 Edward I, and quindene
Trinity, 21 Edward I: 30 Oct., Oakham; 27 Nov., unknown venue; 18 Dec. 1292,
Oakham; 22 Jan. and 19 Feb., Oakham; 19 Mar., Bradecroft (Easter was 29 Mar.);
16 Apr. and 14 May 1293, Oakham; (c) CP. 52 octave Trinity, 28 Edward I: 10 Mar.,
Oakham; 31 Mar., Bradecroft (Easter was 10 Apr.); 5 May and 2 June 1300, Oakham;
(d) C. 47/75/1/27, CP. 52 quindene Michaelmas, 25 Edward I: 14 Mar., Oakham; 11
Apr., Bradecroft (Easter was 14 Apr.); 9 May, Oakham; 6 June, Wing; 4 July, 1 Aug.,
29 Aug., 26 Sept., 24 Oct., and 21 Nov. 1297, Oakham; (e) KB. 27/285, m. 9d: 28

let within the parish of Stamford, Lincolnshire; and Stamford was the only one of the ancient Five Boroughs of the Danelaw that had not obviously been the nucleus of a county. It is theorized that the county that had been forming around Stamford was subordinated to Lincoln in the tenth century to defend against the Yorkshire Danes.[48] It would still be premature to maintain that Bradecroft was the venue for sessions of Rutland's general county court, but it is safe to say that because of Bradecroft Stamford was not wholly excluded from its position as a county town.

The venue for Sussex was altered several times by royal mandate. In 1254 a royal writ recounted that the sheriffs of Sussex had been convening the county at Lewes and Shoreham—there is at least one recorded session at Lewes in 1235[49]—and not at the accustomed venue of Chichester. The king ordered that the county should meet as custom dictated at Chichester.[50] This order was apparently instigated by Richard, earl of Cornwall, because a complaint relating him to such actions survives in the Hundred Rolls, a complaint that he had caused the county to be moved from the fixed place in the towns of Lewes and Shoreham to Chichester and that this was to the detriment of the county.[51] It cannot be determined whether or not Chichester had been the customary venue earlier, and the earl indeed had not shown himself terribly concerned about customary venues in Cornwall. The transfer, at any rate, was not completely effective. Sussex did meet at Chichester, but frequently also at Lewes and Horsham, as well as at Shoreham, Arundel, and Crowley.[52] The uncertainty of venue,

---

Mar. 1331, Bradecroft (Easter was 31 Mar.); (f) C. 88/10, m. 34a, KB. 27/294, m. 12d, c.p.: 25 Mar., Bradecroft (Easter was 4 Apr.); 22 Apr., 20 May, 17 June, 15 July 1333, Oakham; (g) CP. 52 quindene Michaelmas, 19 Edward I: 6 Sept., Wing; 9 Aug. 1291, Weston Thicket.

[48] H. R. Loyn, "Anglo-Saxon Stamford" and Alan Rogers, "Medieval Stamford," both in *The Making of Stamford*, ed. Alan Rogers (Leicester, 1965), pp. 22, 28-31, 49-50.

[49] *The Chartulary of the Priory of St. Pancras of Lewes*, ed. L. F. Salzman, Sussex Record Society, vol. 40 (Lewes, 1934), p. 43.

[50] *CR, 1253-1254*, p. 18.

[51] *RH*, 2:202, 215.

[52] Sessions at Lewes: 22 July 1288 (CP. 52 octave Trinity, 19 Edward I), 5 May 1306 (C. 88/2, m. 29), 6 Apr. 1307 (CP. 52 month Easter, 35 Edward I), 5 Mar. 1331 (C. 88/9, m. 19), 6 Jan. 1334 (KB. 27/297, m. 9, c.p.).

Sessions at Horsham: 22 Apr. 1316 (CP. 52 five weeks Easter, 9 Edward II), 19 Apr. 1319 (C. 88/6, m. 19), 3 Feb., 31 Mar. 1334 (KB. 27/296, m. 20d, c.p.).

Sessions at Chichester: 10 Mar., 2 June, 30 June, 28 July 1306 (C. 88/2, m. 29; C. 88/3, m. 1), 26 Apr. 1291 (CP. 52 octave Trinity, 19 Edward I), 28 Apr. 1334 (KB. 27/296, m. 20d, c.p.).

Occasional Venues: Shoreham, 7 Apr. 1306 (C. 88/2, m. 29); Arundel, date damaged,

reminiscent of the situation in Kent, proved unsatisfactory; the residents of Sussex petitioned for a set venue. The sheriff was thus ordered to inquire where the county could best be held, to inform the chancery, and to hold sessions there henceforward, provided only that the place be a royal borough.[53] By 1331, however, the situation had not changed, since the county met on 5 March 1331 at Lewes and on 2 April 1331 at Horsham.[54] Finally, in the 1340s Chichester seems to have established itself as the primary county town.[55] Even that, however, was not to be a permanent arrangement. In the reign of Henry VII it was provided by statute that the venue should alternate between Chichester and Lewes.[56] As late as 1627, at least, that alternation still determined the venue of Sussex county court.[57]

Neither Berkshire nor Buckinghamshire had a set venue either for normal sessions or for sessions of the general county. Berkshire met at Grandpont nearly half of all sessions, undoubtedly because the same person was the sheriff of both Oxfordshire and Berkshire; Grandpont was situated very near Oxford, the county town of Oxfordshire. Approximately one in five sessions met at Wallingford, while both Newbury and Ockbridge were the venue of about one session in ten. Nevertheless, seven other venues are recorded, and there was no pattern in the determination of the venue for any particular session.[58] In Buckinghamshire Aylesbury was by far the most

---

probably June 1319 (C. 88/6, m. 19); Crowley, 9 Dec. 1333, 3 Mar. 1334 (KB. 27/297, m. 9, c.p.).

[53] *Rotuli Parliamentorum*, 1:379.

[54] C. 88/9, m. 19.

[55] C. 88/16, m. 32 (1344) and C. 88/21, m. 7 (1348), each with five successive sessions at Chichester.

[56] 19 Henry VII, c. 29.

[57] C. 88/227: at Chichester 7 Dec. 1626, 10 Feb. and 29 Mar. 1627; at Lewes 4 Jan. and 1 Mar. 1627. Note also the entry in British Museum *General Catalogue of Printed Books*, 263 vols. (London, 1959-1966), 232:col. 813: "Reasons humbly offered, why the Sheriff of . . . Sussex at an election . . . should be enabled to adjourn the poll at the desire of one or more of the candidates, from Chichester to Lewes, or . . . vice versa [London?, 1720]."

[58] Sessions at Grandpont: 8 Apr., 4 May 1304 (CP. 52 octave Michaelmas, 32 Edward I), 9 Mar., 29 June 1306 (C. 88/2, mm. 21, 35), 6 June, 4 July, 1 Aug., 21 Nov. 1324 (CP. 52 quindene St. Martin, 18 Edward II), 11 Nov., 9 Dec. 1377, 6 Jan., 28 Apr., 18 Aug. 1378 (SC. 2/153/62), etc.

Sessions at Wallingford: 1 July, 26 Aug. 1304 (CP. 52 octave Michaelmas, 32 Edward I), 4 May 1306 (C. 88/2, m. 21), 10 Aug., 7 Sept., 5 Oct. 1295 (CP. 52 morrow St. Martin, 23 Edward I), 24 Oct. 1324 (CP. 52 quindene St. Martin, 18 Edward II), etc.

Sessions at Ockbridge: 10 Dec. 1309, 4 Mar. 1310 (CP. 40/181, m. 193d), 9 May, 29 Aug. 1324 (CP. 52 quindene St. Martin, 18 Edward II), 1 June 1306 (C. 88/2, m. 21), 21 July 1378 (SC. 2/153/62).

Sessions at Newbury: 18 July 1291 (CP. 52 quindene Michaelmas, 19 Edward I),

frequent meeting place, but two or three sessions each year—with no regularity related to Michaelmas or Easter—met at Newport Pagnell. Occasionally a session met also at Buckingham, Stony Stratford, or Wycombe, but no pattern in the venue can be found.[59] If Berkshire or Buckinghamshire had ever had a customary meeting place for general county sessions, that custom had completely disintegrated by the 1290s.

County venue, then, was a matter which could be altered by royal mandate, but was more frequently determined by long-standing custom. Royal boroughs were preferred sites, but were not the invariable

---

13 July 1295 (CP. 52 morrow Martinmas, 23 Edward I), 29 July 1304 (CP. 52 octave Michaelmas, 32 Edward I), 24 Oct. 1324 (CP. 52 quindene St. Martin, 18 Edward II), 24 Oct. 1460 (C. 88/150, m. 70).

Occasional Venues: Hungerford, 6 Apr. 1306 (C. 88/2, m. 21); Wantage, 31 Dec. 1292 (CP. 52 octave Hilary, 21 Edward I); Faringdon, 31 Aug. 1328 (C. 88/9, m. 32); Matingdon, 12 Sept. 1291 (CP. 52 quindene Michaelmas, 19 Edward I); Orlee (Earley?), 3 Mar. 1378 (SC. 2/153/62); Remenham, 3 Feb., 26 May, and 23 June 1378 (SC. 2/153/62); Abingdon, 22 Oct. 1460 (C. 88/150, m. 47). Some twelfth-century venues, not necessarily indicative of normal county venue: Sutton, 17 Nov. 1119; Farnborough, sometime in the 1160s (*Chronicon Monasterii de Abingdon*, ed. Joseph Stevenson, 2 vols. (London, 1858), 2:160, 228.

[59] The schedule for 1290-93:

1290		8 Aug. Aylesbury		3 Sept. Aylesbury
27 Dec.	Newport Pagnell	5 Sept. Aylesbury		1 Oct. Aylesbury
1291		3 Oct. Aylesbury		29 Oct. Newport Pagnell
24 Jan.	Aylesbury	31 Oct. Aylesbury		26 Nov. Aylesbury
21 Feb.	Aylesbury	28 Nov. Aylesbury		24 Dec. Aylesbury
21 Mar.	Aylesbury	26 Dec. Aylesbury	1293	
18 Apr.	Newport Pagnell	1292		21 Jan. Aylesbury
16 May	Aylesbury	23 Jan. Aylesbury		18 Feb. Aylesbury
13 June	Stony Stratford	20 Feb. Newport Pagnell	18 Mar. Aylesbury
11 July	Newport Pagnell	(unknown)		

(CP. 52 quindene Michaelmas, 19 Edward I; octave Hilary, 20 Edward I; quindene Trinity, 20 Edward I; octave Hilary, 21 Edward I; quindene Trinity, 21 Edward I.)

Other sessions at Newport Pagnell: 19 Dec. 1296, 16 Jan., 13 Mar. 1297 (CP. 52 quindene Easter, 25 Edward I); 24 Sept. 1298 (CP. 52 octave Michaelmas, 26 Edward I), 1 July 1299 (CP. 40/124, m. 73), 31 Oct. 1380 (E. 370/9/15).

Sessions at Aylesbury: 29 July, 26 Aug., 21 Oct. 1299 (CP. 52 octave Michaelmas, 27 Edward I); 17 Oct., 12 Nov. 1324 (CP. 52 quindene St. Martin, 18 Edward II), 24 Mar., 21 Apr., 19 May, 16 June, 7 July 1333 (KB. 27/296, m. 20, c.p.). In 1475 eleven of twelve consecutive sessions were held at Aylesbury (E. 370/5/1).

Sessions at Buckingham: 11 March 1299 (CP. 52 quindene Easter, 27 Edward I); 10 June 1299 (CP. 40/124, m. 73); 6 Dec. 1329 (E. 370/9/1); 25 March 1355 (E. 370/9/3); 19 Nov. 1320 (*Luffield Priory Charters*, ed. G. R. Elvey, 2 vols., Northamptonshire Record Society, vols. 22, 26 [Oxford, 1968-1975], 1:67).

Sessions at Stony Stratford: 13 Feb. 1297 (CP. 52 quindene Easter, 25 Edward I); 9 Nov. 1306 (CP. 52 quindene Hilary, 35 Edward I); 9 Sept. 1355 (E. 370/9/3).

Sessions at Wycombe: 19 Feb. 1315 (CP. 52 quindene Easter, 9 Edward II); 12 Aug. 1355 (E. 370/9/3); 20 Feb. 1381 (E. 370/9/15); 29 Mar. 1475 (E. 370/5/1).

venues. Most counties met consistently in only one place, usually in the borough that had given the county its name. Most of the multiple-venue counties had established a clear and unalterable pattern, leaving the general or great sessions of the county—like the venue of the sheriff's tourn—at the tradition-hallowed locations, while the other sessions met at more convenient and preferred locations. A few counties had no discernible pattern for the venue, and in these counties it is necessary to think that the venue was announced at each session for the following session and that the information was further conveyed to the populace both in marketplaces and in the hundred courts and the courts of liberties. Such publication of information concerning venue would necessarily operate anyway in all counties when some variation from the normal twenty-eight or forty-two-day schedule was required.

The schedule, venue, and attendance of the general county sessions suggest that they are the institutional remains of the twice-yearly sessions required before the Norman Conquest. Such sessions typically took place after Easter and after Michaelmas, if allowances are made for the possible exceptions of Rutland and Kent. The only other clearly aberrant meeting was a single session of the general county of Northamptonshire on 20 July 1264.[60] That session, however, could well have been necessitated by the disruptions of the Barons' Wars and, in particular, by the Battle of Northampton only a few months prior to the session. Meetings of the general county were at times associated with abnormal venues, but in most counties the same venue served both the general and the normal sessions. When there was an abnormal venue connected with the general county, however, that place seems to have been long-used by the time of Edward I, particularly in the cases of Penenden Heath and Ossulstone. Furthermore, normal sessions of the Anglo-Saxon counties must have been better attended than the ad hoc sessions. If the Anglo-Saxon normal session did become the general county sessions, it would explain why greater attendance became required in such sessions than in normal sessions. In Oxfordshire, for instance, most people obliged to attend county court were obliged to attend only the sessions of the great county.[61] In Lancashire in the fourteenth century the session after Michaelmas saw a larger attendance because individuals obliged to attend county attended then to make fine for relaxation of that obligation for that

[60] E. 370/5/3.
[61] *RH*, 2:724, 730-34, 738, etc.

year.[62] The same situation probably prevailed in Yorkshire.[63] In Lincolnshire the session after Michaelmas was called the day of the leet; the rere-county, in private hands, then held its view of frankpledge; and on such occasions no pleas were heard.[64] The precise purpose of the great county, however, is nowhere stated. In earlier times it would have provided a convenient opportunity for the final settlement of the most difficult disputes that came before the court. By the reign of Edward I, even allowing for the occurrences in Lincolnshire, Lancashire, and Yorkshire, it is probable that great county sessions were little different from the normal sessions of the county.

When the county court was assembled, whether in a great county session or in one of the normal sessions every twenty-eighth or forty-second day, business was said to be conducted *in pleno comitatu*. It does not seem that any precise constitutional significance can be read into the phrase. Early in the thirteenth century it may indeed still have referred to attendance. There are two instances—one in 1212, one in 1225—in which a county court felt capable of performing routine activities—accepting unchallenged essoins[65] or replevying lands upon the sufficient testimony of the sheriff[66]—but not of determining pleas. Such routine activities, of course, could well have been disposed of either very early or very late in the day, well before everyone could be present or after people had begun to leave.

Later in the century, however, there are no more comments about when a county was full or fully attended. Even in situations in which the county was not fully attended, there is no indication that transactions therefore were not done *in pleno comitatu*.[67] By the latter half of the thirteenth century that had become a stock phrase without

---

[62] Below, chapter 3, n. 90.

[63] E. 370/6/27.

[64] CP. 52 quindene Easter, 13 Edward I: "Et habuerunt diem per essoniatores suos ad proximum comitatum sequentem, qui tentus fuit die lune proxima post festum sancti Michaelis anno predicto, ad quem comitatum ambe partes comparuerunt set non placitaverunt quia non fuit dies placiti, set habuerunt diem." E. 370/5/45 (43 Henry III): "Amerciamenta comitatus. De magno comitatu tento die proxima post festum omnium sanctorum: nichil, quia nulla placita tenta fuerunt." E. 370/9/20 (1342): "De amerciamentis: nulla, quia omnes comites, barones, milites, et serjantes apparuerunt per senescallos et in propria persona et nichil factum fuit de placitis etc." E. 370/9/21 (1363): "Die lune proxima post festum sancti Michaelis anno regni regis Edwardi tercii post conquestum xxxvij: Placita nulla nec amerciamenta quia dies leti secundum usum comitatus tenta apud Lincoln'." Below, at n. 71.

[65] CRR, 6:229. For the phrase in general, see Helen Cam, *Law-Finders and Law-Makers* (London, 1962), p. 123.

[66] CRR, 12:220.

[67] JUST. 1/4, Staffordshire Eyre 1293, Abbot of Rocester v fitzRichard [S.S.]: a case adjourned for judgment *"pro defectu sectatorum"*; below, chapter 3, at n. 133 ff.

any necessary reference to the obligatory attendance of certain individuals. It connoted rather that business was being conducted publicly and without secrecy or fraudulent maneuvers. When business was conducted *in pleno comitatu* everyone who had an interest had the opportunity to attend. This sense is not far from describing the usage in the cases in 1212 and 1225, even though it seems that then *plenus* referred also to actual attendance. When in almost modern times English replaced Latin in the endorsement of writs, sheriffs translated the phrase as "in open county" rather than "in full county."[68] Openness seems to have been the primary sense of the phrase even in the latter half of the thirteenth century.

Following the regular session of the county court, presumably always on the succeeding day, was a session called the rere-county. Business conducted in the rere-county was not, as far as can be determined, described as done *in pleno comitatu*. The purpose of the rere-county was mainly administrative: the collection of money due the king (collection of money should be carefully distinguished from accounting for money) and the submission of writs.[69] Since the sheriff's bailiffs were required to be present at the county sessions, the rere-county was probably also used in an informal way for handling problems in the execution of writs and judgments. The rere-county of Lincolnshire was anomalous in that it had become a court in itself and had fallen into private hands. It first appeared in the hands of Joan, princess of Wales, in the mid-fourteenth century,[70] then as part of the duchy of Lancaster. As such it was appendant to the manor of Brocklesby and concerned itself with business arising in the north trithing of the county. It met at Lincoln the day after the county court session and determined pleas throughout the year; after Easter and after Michaelmas it had the view of frankpledge for the north trithing, held at Lincoln.[71] It is unlikely, however, that Lincolnshire rere-county was typical of the range of activity in other rere-counties, which remained administrative meetings.

The traditional duration of the normal county session was one day, probably lasting until vespers at times, and at times terminating with a meal.[72] Longer sessions, however, were known and eventually be-

[68] Above, n. 43.

[69] 13 Edward I (Westminster II), c. 39; Mills, "Medieval Shire House," p. 259.

[70] *IPM, 7-15 Richard II*, p. 117.

[71] DL. 30/88/200; DL. 30/92/1270; DL. 30/93/1271-74, etc. A rere-hundred in Wiltshire was determining pleas even as early as 1261: SC. 2/208/1.

[72] *CRR*, 6:229; *Somersetshire Pleas from the Rolls of the Itinerant Justices*, ed. Charles Chadwyck-Healey, 2 vols., Somerset Record Society, vols. 11, 36 (London, 1897, 1923), 1:61-63.

came regular. The three-day session of Kent county court at Penenden Heath ordered by William the Conqueror was certainly irregular and is more indicative of royal power than of normal county schedule.[73] The ordinary press of litigation, however, came to prompt sheriffs to extend the county session. In York in 1212 the county could not hear all the suits before it on the county day. The sheriff therefore ordered certain of the knights to appear at the castle the next day "to hold the remaining pleas of the county." At least four of the knights came, but they proceeded to give a dubious judgment in a totally new case, one that had not been before the county the previous day. That judgment was overturned on technical grounds, but no mention was made of the irregularity of the second day of pleas.[74] Magna Carta, in both 1215 and 1216, referred only to the "county day" in providing that justices of assize could cause a sufficient number of knights and freeholders to remain a second day if the county day did not suffice to determine the assizes.[75] In 1225 the sheriff of Lincolnshire attempted to continue the county session a second day to determine the 140 suits left after the end of the county day. Those who appeared the following day, however, objected that the county should only be held for one day, and there was reference made to the 1225 version of the Magna Carta which specified the one-day session. The extended session was terminated.[76]

By mid-century, however, the one-day session clearly placed too many limitations on the county courts. In Lincolnshire the sheriff was often in danger when he adjourned his county court as usual after the meal. Because of these dangers—"plura pericula" apparently presented by frustrated litigants—the king in 1252 granted the sheriff of Lincolnshire permission to hold pleas for two days when necessary.[77] This grant to Lincolnshire was apparently taken to have general implications. In 1286 a dispute in the county court of Devon focused not on whether the county could be held for one day or two, but on whether the litigation on the second day should have been interrupted by a meal instead of continuing straight on into the night, even if by candlelight.[78] By 1336 Cheshire was customarily meeting for two

[73] Melville M. Bigelow, ed., *Placita Anglo-Normannica* (London, 1879), pp. 4-6.
[74] *CRR*, 6:214-15.
[75] cc. 18, 19.
[76] *CRR*, 12:434-35, 461.
[77] *CR, 1251-1254*, p. 168.
[78] E. 13/12, m. 24d, Pyn v le Pruz [S.S.]: "consuetudo dicti comitatus talis est quod comitatus debet teneri per diem martis; et, si placita ad plenum eo die placitari non possunt, tunc comitatus debet teneri per diem mercurii sequentem continue sine in-

days, and a dispute there centered once again on the validity of actions taken after sundown on the second day.[79] Even the volume of litigation shown by the plea rolls of Cornwall, Berkshire, and Somerset seems to dictate a two-day session, although the rolls from Oxfordshire and Bedfordshire indicate a caseload that might have been handled in a single day.[80] In no case, however, was litigation listed as occurring on the second day, even in the plea rolls. All litigation was fictitiously appropriated to the first day. Finally, it cannot be determined whether the rere-county session merged into the second day of pleading or took place on the third day. At any rate, it is certain that many county courts by the end of the thirteenth century were meeting rather longer than the single day.

The surroundings in which county sessions were held varied. Some met in the open air; some, in castles and shire houses. The open-air meeting is most renowned. Such meetings, not conducive to the handling of parchment and ink in a damp climate, were not frequent. When general county sessions were still sessions substantially larger than others—that is, it seems, prior to the fourteenth century—the county might have had to meet outdoors. The *Summa Magna* refers to counties meeting in forests and fields, but, since the author was probably from Kent and the description fits that county most closely because of the meetings at Chestnut Street and Penenden Heath, little of general significance can be drawn from it.[81] Already by the time of the Hundred Rolls individuals had begun building on the green place in Essex where the county court should have been meeting— presumably either at Stratford Langthorne or at Writtle.[82] Likewise, when counties met together, a phenomenon already ended by the mid-thirteenth century, they may well have had to assemble outdoors. Special business could also easily prompt counties to meet outdoors. In the late seventeenth century at least Middlesex county court adjourned to a special session, still called a session of the open

---

tervallo et per candelam si dies ad hoc non sufficiat. Et quia dictus vicecomes dictum comitatum tenuit postquam ipse et alii sectatores comederunt contra consuetudinem hactenus usitatam, dictus Hugo de assensu tam militum quam aliorum liberorum de predicto comitatu tamquam nuncius eorundem inhibi comitatum dicto vicecomiti fecit ex parte domini regis ne dictum comitatum post prandium teneret et hoc ne in consuetudinem converteretur et pro periculo quod inde posset evenire."

[79] Below, chapter 3 at n. 30.

[80] Below, Table 8.1.

[81] *Radulphi de Hengham Summae*, ed. W. H. Dunham (Cambridge, 1932), p. 10; Paul A. Brand, "*Hengham Magna*: A Thirteenth-Century English Common Law Treatise and Its Composition," *Irish Jurist* 11 (1976):147-69.

[82] *RH*, 1:142.

county, for the election of representatives to Parliament; that special session was held in an open area, such as New Brentford or Hampstead Heath.[83] I have seen no similar special sessions for elections prior to that time, but there is a possibility that in special circumstances county courts might have met outdoors for at least a part of their business. Even given these exceptions, by the middle of the thirteenth century at latest, outdoor sessions must have been uncommon.

Even in the twelfth century there are indications that county sessions were held indoors. Cornwall met at least once in Launceston castle in the middle of the twelfth century.[84] In the 1160s and again between 1175 and 1186 Norfolk met in Norwich in the monastery of St. Giles.[85] Yorkshire met in the crypt of York Minster in 1166,[86] although as early as the reign of Henry I there was a house in which the county met, the upkeep of which was a serjeanty held by the Malesoure family.[87] There is thus no reason to think that meetings indoors were uncommon in the twelfth century.

In the thirteenth century, county sessions were typically held indoors: in churches, castle halls, or halls specially built for the county court. Thus Dorset in 1266 met at the Chapel of St. Nicholas,[88] and in 1293 Huntingdonshire met in Huntingdon castle in the aisles of the chapel: *sub alis capelle*.[89] Lincolnshire was meeting in some kind of house by 1225.[90] Somerset met at the king's house in Ilchester after the county venue had been removed from Somerton.[91] In 1275 Oxfordshire still met in the king's manor hall at Oxford.[92] Edmund, earl of Cornwall, erected a hall specifically built for the county court of Cornwall in Lostwithiel.[93] In 1271 the sheriff of Norfolk was or-

---

[83] C. 219/60: a two-day election held at New Brentford by adjournment on 4-5 Sept. 1679; C. 219/64: held by adjournment at Hampstead Heath, 3 Mar. 1681; C. 219/76: held at New Brentford by adjournment, 7 Mar. 1690; C. 219/80: held by adjournment at Hampstead Heath, 15 Nov. 1695; 7 & 8 William III, c. 25.

[84] *British Borough Charters*, 2:379.

[85] *St. Benet of Holme, 1020-1210*, ed. J. R. West, 2 vols., Norfolk Record Society, vols. 2, 3 (London, 1932), 1:100, 120.

[86] *Early Yorkshire Charters*, ed. William Farrer, 4 vols. (Edinburgh, 1914), 2:64. See John Broune, *The History of the Metropolitan Church of St. Peter, York*, 2 vols. (York, 1847), 1:14-18. The Norman choir was about 174 feet long, 89½ feet wide.

[87] *Early Yorkshire Charters*, 1:525; *VCH, City of York*, p. 522.

[88] *CLR*, 5:212.

[89] *Registrum Antiquissimum*, ed. C. W. Foster and Kathleen Major, 10 vols., Lincoln Record Society, vol. 32 (Lincoln, 1935), 3:177.

[90] *Bracton's Note Book*, ed. F. W. Maitland, 3 vols. (London, 1887), no. 1730.

[91] *Registrum Antiquissimum*, 3:121.

[92] *CPR, 1272-1281*, p. 127.

[93] *Rotuli Parliamentorum*, 1:296.

dered to release ten pounds for the building of one house at Norwich and another at Ipswich for the holding of county courts.[94] The sheriff of Cumberland shortly thereafter complained that he had no hall either in Carlisle castle or in the town in which to hold the county court.[95] When the king ordered Hereford castle repaired in 1265, the hall in which the county court was held received special mention.[96] As late as 1460 there is a mention of Cambridgeshire county court meeting in Cambridge castle.[97] In 1458 Huntingdonshire was meeting in the castle at Huntingdon still,[98] and at about that same time both Worcestershire and Northamptonshire were meeting at the castle in their respective county towns.[99] In 1311 Northumberland was meeting at the castle in Newcastle-upon-Tyne.[100] Indoor meetings, whether in churches, purpose-built accommodations, or the halls of a royal castle, were probably typical as soon as the county courts began meeting more than twice a year in a regular fashion and at a specific place.

The royal courts subject directly to the sheriff in any given county were carefully coordinated, but only during the fourteenth century were they regularized into three-weekly courts. Three early schedules are available for Lincolnshire. In that county the sheriff or his undersheriffs presided over the county courts and the five regional courts: the three trithings that composed northern Lincolnshire (as a unit, known as Lindsey) and Holland and Kesteven, which composed southern Lincolnshire. There is little evidence that the individual wapentake and hundred courts in Lincolnshire continued to function to any extent through the thirteenth century.[101] In 1258-59 sessions of the regional courts were held approximately but not exactly three weeks apart. Sessions for any given court could occur on different days of the week. Usually, but not always, the sessions of different courts

---

[94] *CLR*, 6:178.

[95] Mills, "Medieval Shire House," p. 255.

[96] *CLR*, 5:175.

[97] C. 88/150, m. 49.

[98] C. 88/150, m. 50.

[99] C. 88/150, m. 59; C. 88/151, m. 17. The shire hall could, of course, be located within the castle walls, as in Lincolnshire.

[100] CP. 40/184, m. 295d.

[101] I have seen no disputes in the king's court concerning distraints made by order of an individual royal hundred or wapentake court of Lincolnshire, as might have been expected if the courts had been functioning. Furthermore, the accounts of Lincolnshire sheriffs detail profits only from the county and regional courts, not from the wapentake and hundred courts. See, for instance, CP. 52 quindene Easter, 24 Edward I, for an *accedas recordari* for the wapentake of Kirton which was answered by a record made in the court of Holland.

were kept from being held on the same day. Once it even seems that the session of the south trithing was cancelled, because it would have coincided with the county session. Nor was there, at that time, a clear order in which the regional courts were held. Table 1.1 shows that two cycles took place in a counterclockwise order, beginning with the south trithing and ending with Holland; two other cycles, however, exhibited a more random schedule. This lack of rigid scheduling was not caused by the disorder in the countryside in 1258-59. Scattered dates of sessions from the reigns of Edward I and Edward II demonstrate that even then a given court could meet on different days of the week and not at precise three-week intervals.[102] Through the reign of Edward II, then, the sheriff retained a great deal of discretion in determining the schedule of the lower courts. Tables 1.2 and 1.3 show that by 1326, and even more by 1337, the regional courts exhibited the order that became typical in Lincolnshire: a clockwise holding of sessions beginning with the west trithing and ending with Kesteven, with the sessions of any given court precisely three weeks apart and always occurring on the same day of the week. The meetings of one court and the next court in the cycle were spaced well apart for the tourns, but for ordinary sessions the complete cycle took only about ten days.

The courts of the county of Cornwall demonstrate the possibility of even more extensive coordination. The county court of Cornwall,

TABLE 1.1
Lincolnshire Courts in 1258-1259

Court	Tourn*	Normal Sessions		
County Court	Mo 4 Nov	Mo 16 Dec		[Mo 27 Jan]
South Trithing	Mo 25 Nov	—	Sa 18 Jan	Sa 8 Feb
North Trithing	Tu 26 Nov	We 18 Dec	Fr 17 Jan	Tu 11 Feb
West Trithing	Th 28 Nov	Fr 20 Dec	Sa 18 Jan	Tu 4 Feb
Kesteven	Tu 3 Dec	Mo 23 Dec	Th 23 Jan	Sa 15 Feb
Holland	Th 5 Dec	Mo 30 Dec	Tu 21 Jan	Sa 15 Feb

SOURCE: E. 370/5/44, 45

* Note that the tourn was taken a month late in this year; the reason for this is unknown.

[102] CP. 52 octave Hilary, 33 Edward I: the north trithing met Th 29 Oct. and Th 10 Dec. 1304; CP. 52 quindene Easter, 9 Edward II: the north trithing met on Mo 5 Jan., Sa 7 Feb., Mo 1 Mar. 1316; CP. 52 quindene Easter, 9 Edward II: Kesteven met on Sa 24 Jan. and Mo 1 Mar. 1316; CP. 40/102, m. 21: the south trithing met on Mo 26 Nov. 1291, Mo 18 Aug., and Sa 13 Sept. 1292 (there was here an accusation of false judgment based partly on the three-weeks rule [S.S.]).

TABLE 1.2
Lincolnshire Courts in 1326

Court	Normal Sessions			
County Court	Mo 1 July		[Mo 12 Aug]	
West Trithing	Th 10 July	Th 31 July	Th 21 Aug	Th 11 Sept
North Trithing	Sa 12 July	Sa 2 Aug	Sa 23 Aug	Sa 13 Sept
South Trithing	Mo 14 July	Mo 4 Aug	Mo 25 Aug	Mo 15 Sept
Holland	Th 26 June	—	Th 14 Aug	Th 28 Aug Th 18 Sept
Kesteven	Sa 28 June	Sa 19 July	Sa 9 Aug	Sa 30 Aug

SOURCE: E. 370/5/57

TABLE 1.3
Lincolnshire Courts in 1337

Court*	Tourn	Normal Sessions			
County Court	Mo 6 Oct		Mo 17 Nov		Mo 29 Dec
West Trithing	Th 9 Oct	Th 6 Nov	Th 27 Nov	Th 18 Dec	
North Trithing	Sa 11 Oct	Sa 8 Nov	Sa 29 Nov	Sa 20 Dec	
South Trithing	Th 16 Oct	Mo 10 Nov	Mo 1 Dec	Mo 22 Dec	
Holland	Th 23 Oct	Th 13 Nov	Th 4 Dec	We 24 Dec	
Kesteven	Mo 27 Oct	Sa 15 Nov	Sa 6 Dec	Sa 27 Dec	

SOURCE: E. 370/9/19

* Venue for the regional courts was normally Spital in the Street, Caistor, Louth, "Lamcotholm," and Ancaster, respectively. Kesteven, during the tourn, met at Threckingham.

together with the nine hundred courts, the four stannary courts, and the borough court of Lostwithiel, were normally in the hands of the earl of Cornwall. In 1333, however, they were in the king's hands because of the minority of the heir, and thus the accounts and schedules of the courts have survived. Early in the year only the schedules for the county and hundred courts remain. The county court met regularly on Monday every twenty-eighth day. The hundred courts, however, did not meet every twenty-first day. At times, as Table 1.4 shows, the period between the sessions of a given hundred court could be more than a month, and none of the hundreds met consistently on the same day of the week. There was some regularity in the order in which the hundreds met, but not enough even to describe it as a pattern. Later in the year, however, the schedules for all fifteen of the courts which were in the sheriff's charge are preserved. While the hundred and stannary courts were still not meeting three-weekly, they had been put into a set order. The county court met first, and the other courts were fit into the county schedule, beginning with

TABLE 1.4
Cornwall Courts in 1332-1333

Court	Normal Sessions				Tourn
County Court	Mo 21 Dec	Mo 18 Jan	Mo 15 Feb	Mo 15 Mar	Mo 12 Apr
Powder Hund.	We 30 Dec	Tu 26 Jan	Mo 22 Feb	Mo 29 Mar	Mo 19 Apr
Kerrier	Th 31 Dec	Th 28 Jan	We 24 Feb	Tu 30 Mar	We 21 Apr
Penwith	Sa 2 Jan	Fr 5 Feb	Th 25 Feb	Th 1 Apr	Th 22 Apr
Pyder	Mo 11 Jan	Th 4 Feb	Sa 27 Feb	Th 1 Apr	Sa 24 Apr
Trigg	Tu 5 Jan	Th 4 Feb	Mo 1 Mar	Th 1 Apr	Tu 27 Apr
Lesnewth	Sa 9 Jan	Th 4 Feb	Tu 2 Mar	Tu 6 Apr	We 28 Apr
Stratton	Fr 8 Jan	Fr 5 Feb	We 3 Mar	Fr 26 Mar	Th 29 Apr
Eastwevel	Mo 11 Jan	Mo 8 Feb	Th 4 Mar	Mo 5 Apr	Sa 1 May
Westwevel	Tu 12 Jan	Tu 9 Feb	Fr 5 Mar	Th 8 Apr	We 5 May

SOURCE: E. 370/5/22

TABLE 1.5
Cornwall Courts in July-September 1333

Court	Normal Sessions			
County Court	Mo 5 July	Mo 2 Aug	Mo 30 Aug	Mo 27 Sept
Powder Hund.	Th 13 July	Th 5 Aug	Tu 7 Sept	
Tywarnhaile Stan.	Fr 16 July	Th 5 Aug	We 8 Sept	
Kerrier Hund.	Sa 17 July	Fr 6 Aug	Th 9 Sept	
Penwith Hund.	Mo 19 July	Sa 7 Aug	Fr 10 Sept	
Penwith & Kerrier Stan.	Tu 20 July	Fr 30 July	Mo 13 Sept	
Pyder Hund.	We 21 July	Mo 9 Aug	Mo 13 Sept	
Trigg Hund.	Th 22 July	Mo 9 Aug	We 15 Sept	
Lesnewth Hund.	Fr 23 July	We 11 Aug	Th 16 Sept	
Stratton Hund.	Sa 24 July	We 11 Aug	Fr 17 Sept	
Foweymore Stan.	Sa 24 July	Th 12 Aug	Mo 20 Sept	
Eastwevel Hund.	Mo 26 July	Th 12 Aug	Tu 21 Sept	
Westwevel Hund.	Tu 27 July	Fr 13 Aug	We 22 Sept	
Blackmore Stan.	We 28 July	Fr 27 Aug	Th 23 Sept	
Lostwithiel Borough	Fr 30 July	Sa 28 Aug	Mo 27 Sept	

SOURCE: SC. 2/161/74; SC. 2/161/5; E. 101/260/1

Powder hundred and working around the county in a clockwise direction, finishing with the borough court of Lostwithiel, which could coincide with the next county session. This schedule appears in Table 1.5. In Cornwall as in Lincolnshire, the sheriff retained into the fourteenth century the responsibility for scheduling the various courts entrusted to him within his county; only the county court had become fixed to a nearly immutable schedule.

Two other schedules—both from the thirteenth century—indicate the complications involved in scheduling and the freedom with which sheriffs dealt with their courts. In 1264 the sheriff of Wiltshire held the hundred courts in a fairly regular circuit; but, as shown in Table 1.6, at times he followed the circuit in reverse order, so that the sessions of a given hundred were at times only a week apart, at times almost two months apart. Somerset and Dorset present quite another difficulty, since they were traditionally presided over by only one sheriff. As in many counties, many of the hundred courts in either county were held by private individuals, so that the sheriff was not responsible for scheduling them or presiding over them. Nevertheless, the sheriff was responsible for holding two county courts, which met every twenty-eighth day, and eleven hundred courts scattered over the two counties. In general, it seems that the sheriff presided over the county court of Dorset and then proceeded with the Dorset hundred courts. He then turned to the Somerset hundred courts and tried to dispatch them prior to the determined date for the Somerset county court, ideally leaving him a week or more before the next meeting of the Dorset county court. Table 1.7 preserves his harried routine. In every instance examined, then, the county courts had fixed schedules, whereas the royal hundreds into the fourteenth century were subordinated to the county schedule and had not achieved a regular three-weekly schedule.

The county courts after Magna Carta thus rapidly settled into a schedule whereby they convened about thirteen times a year, except for several northern counties which assembled every sixth week up

TABLE 1.6
Wiltshire Courts in 1264

Court*	Tourn	Normal Sessions		
Kingsbridge, Blackgrove, & Thornhill Hundreds	Mo 6 Oct	Fr 14 Nov	Mo 1 Dec	Fr 9 Jan
Swanborough, Studfold & Rowborough Hund.	Tu 7 Oct	Th 6 Nov	We 3 Dec	Th 8 Jan
Branch & Dole Hund.	We 8 Oct	We 5 Nov	Fr 5 Dec	Th 8 Jan
Cawden & Cadworth Hund.	Th 9 Oct	Tu 4 Nov	Sa 13 Dec	Fr 9 Jan
Frustfield Hund.	Fr 10 Oct	Fr 31 Oct	Mo 15 Dec	Tu 13 Jan
Dunworth Hund.	Mo 13 Oct	Mo 3 Nov	Tu 30 Dec	We 7 Jan

SOURCE: E. 370/6/14

* The dates for the county court do not survive; had Wiltshire met according to schedule the dates would have been Tu 23 Sept, Tu 21 Oct, Tu 13 Nov, and Tu 16 Dec. From the dates of the hundreds, however, one cannot tell when the county sessions were held. The grouping of these hundreds in this way is very early.

TABLE 1.7
Dorset and Somerset Courts in 1294

Court	Tourn*	Normal Sessions		
Dorset County	Mo 19 Apr	Mo 17 May	Mo 14 June	Mo 12 July
George Hund., Dors.	—	Tu 18 May	Tu 15 June	Tu 13 July
Whiteway Hund., Dors.	—	We 19 May	We 16 June	Sa 10 July
Redlane Hund., Dors.	—	Th 20 May	Th 17 June	Fr 9 July
Tollerford Hund., Dors.	—	Fr 21 May	Sa 19 June	We 14 July
Uggscombe Hund., Dors.	—	Sa 22 May	Su 20 June	Th 8 July
Godderthorne Hund., Dors.	—	Mo 24 May	Fr 18 June	Fr 9 July
Eggerton Hund., Dors.	—	Tu 25 May	Tu 22 June	Sa 10 July
Williton Hund., Som.	—	We 2 June	Mo 28 June	Fr 23 July
Stone Hund., Som.	Th 13 May	Fr 4 June	Th 1 July	Mo 26 July
Catsash Hund., Som.	Fr 14 May	Sa 5 June	Fr 2 July	Fr 30 July
Andersfield Hund., Som.	Th 29 Apr	—	Tu 6 July	
Somerset County	Mo 10 May	Mo 7 June	Mo 5 July	

SOURCE: E. 370/6/9. Helen Cam in *The Hundred and the Hundred Rolls*, p. 169, dealt with this document by counting the number of sessions per year; producing a schedule from the document makes it much more interesting.

* The sessions of the tourn are not listed for the Dorset hundreds; the sessions of the hundreds previous to the tourn were listed: St George Hundred, 23 March; Tollerford Hundred, 27 March; Redlane Hundred, 2 April; etc. The reason for their absence is not known.

until 1548. Twice a year there were sessions of the general county, and these general or great sessions coincided with the ancient schedule of shire meetings. Well into the thirteenth century these general county sessions were characterized by a larger attendance, in some counties by a special venue, and conceivably by more important business. As soon as one can trace litigation in the county courts, however, the general sessions seem to be no more important than the other regularly scheduled sessions. Business conducted in either kind of session was done in open county, that is, publicly and by the county as a whole. Regular sessions, by the middle of the thirteenth century, might last either one or two days, depending on the amount of business that came before the court. Following the session there was an administrative meeting called the rere-county, which served as a time for the collection of money, the reception of writs, and coordination of the sheriff's bailiffs. In at least one county, litigation was anomalously put before the rere-county session. For most counties the venue for the county session was absolutely predictable and could be permanently altered only by royal mandate. Likewise, county courts were firmly established in their schedules, but variations could occur and the date for a session would have been publicized in advance. In between the county sessions the royal hundreds met. These courts were subordinated to the county schedule and did not adhere to the three-weekly schedule prescribed in Magna Carta and followed by privately held hundred courts. The sheriff was fully in charge of the royal hundred courts and, at least through the reign of Edward II, ordered them so as to complement the county schedule. The county court, then, judging merely by matters of schedule and venue, was the primary royal court in any county. The coordination of county business with the business and schedule of all the royal courts entrusted to a sheriff inevitably required a high degree of planning and a sophisticated staff of competent bailiffs.

2

The Sheriff and His Staff

෫ඁ

THE SHERIFF was the most important local official in English government. His duties cannot be classified solely as financial, executive, or judicial. He was, for instance, the primary agent of the Exchequer in its collection of money due the king, and in this capacity the sheriff appeared each year to render his account in the Exchequer. He was, furthermore, responsible for executing the royal will. He was the most frequent recipient of royal writs and saw to the performance of all the orders for summons, distraint, attachment, and execution of judgment which issued from the king's court. The royal will, of course, was not expressed merely judicially, so that the sheriff at times also found himself responsible for raising military forces and supplies, in addition to the provisions needed more immediately by the king. Prior to 1236, sheriffs had also been responsible for the supervision of royal estates, and this had constituted the single most profitable aspect of the office. Finally, by the very fact that he had been appointed sheriff, he was responsible for convening, presiding over, and executing the judgments of the county court and the royal hundreds within his county. In most counties, the duties concerning the hundreds also included the making of a twice-yearly circuit at which the sheriff functioned as a judge over minor trespasses. During this circuit, called the sheriff's tourn, the sheriff also saw to it that felonies were recorded by a coroner for the information of the royal justices. Thus the operation of the central government as well as that of the local government depended to a great extent on the sheriff and his subordinates.

Sheriffs were appointed in the Exchequer[1] and normally presided

[1] It must be noted that there was a persistent practice of appointing sheriffs as of fee, so that the office could be inherited. In 1300 there were five such sheriffdoms (Cornwall, Rutland, Westmorland, Worcestershire, and Lancashire), but these counties

over a single county. It became customary, however, for certain counties to be administered jointly by one sheriff. These were the so-called twinned counties. Bedfordshire and Buckinghamshire were twinned early in the twelfth century, as were Nottinghamshire and Derbyshire. Near the beginning of the reign of Henry II ten other counties were twinned: Cambridgeshire and Huntingdonshire, Essex and Hertfordshire, Norfolk and Suffolk, Somerset and Dorset, and Warwickshire and Leicestershire. Oxfordshire and Berkshire were twinned only in the thirteenth century, as were Shropshire and Staffordshire and Surrey and Sussex.[2] The most unusual and the earliest instance of twinning is that of London and Middlesex. London had the privilege of electing two sheriffs, and they were responsible also for the county of Middlesex. In all twinned counties it seems that one was usually subordinated to the other. London is the best example of this tendency in its domination of Middlesex.[3] Derbyshire, however, was at one point so joined to Nottinghamshire that it was necessary to mandate that Derbyshire should have its own county court.[4] As late as 1291 a custom whereby the sheriff could take animals seized in Derbyshire outside the county to Nottingham for evaluation and sale was still alleged, an extraordinary disregard for county boundaries.[5] With Norfolk and Suffolk, the sheriff's office was located

---

were not removed from Exchequer supervision. Furthermore, there was great interest in electing sheriffs in the early and mid-thirteenth century, but when it was decided in 1300 to allow election generally, little interest remained. See Helen Cam, *The Hundred and the Hundred Rolls* (London, 1930), pp. 59-62. Election would have been difficult in twinned counties; and the growth in the king's court, the unification of law and process, and the clarification of franchises and royal rights during the thirteenth century would have lessened the desire for election anyway.

[2] The duration of twinning (taken from *List of Sheriffs for England and Wales* [New York, 1963]): Beds. and Bucks.: from before 1129 to 1575; Cambs. and Hunts.: from 1155 to 1636 and from 1644 to 1832; Essex and Herts.: from 1100 to 1147, from 1155 to 1216, and from 1217 to 1567; Norf. and Suff.: from 1116 to 1129, from 1153 to 1155, and from 1156 to 1575; Notts. and Derbs.: from 1091 to 1567; Oxon. and Berks.: from 1248 to 1258, from 1259 to 1567; Salop. and Staffs.: from 1204 to 1345, from 1377 to 1378; Som. and Dors.: from 1123 to 1129 (possibly to 1155), from 1155 to 1217, from 1217 to 1223, and from 1226 to 1567; Surrey and Sussex: from 1242 to 1567 and from 1571 to 1636; Warw. and Leics.: from 1155 to 1159, from 1159 to 1163, from 1164 to 1193, from 1194 to 1567. Other counties at times had the same sheriff, but were not necessarily twinned.

[3] While Middlesex county court kept meeting and the records of outlawries proclaimed there often survive, the survival of records concerning other litigation is well below what would otherwise have been expected. See below, at n. 100.

[4] *PQW*, p. 158.

[5] E. 13/18, m. 25d: "Mos est et consuetudo in partibus illis quod averia capta in comitatu Derby' fugari debeant usque ad villam Nottingham et ibi debeat appreciari et vendi."

in Norwich, so that anyone who wished to consult the sheriff's rolls for Suffolk had to make the journey to Norwich.[6] As early as the 1230s the sheriff's rolls concerning Huntingdonshire were in a similar manner kept at Cambridge castle.[7] Despite the subordination, however, twinned counties normally remained quite distinct and were capable of being separated in later times.

Between 1180 and 1340 there was a decided change in the kind of people who were appointed sheriffs. In the late twelfth century there was a remarkable overlap between the officials of the central government and the sheriffs. The Inquest of Sheriffs in 1170 effectively asserted royal control over sheriffs and was succeeded by commissions of itinerant justices inquiring into royal rights and punishing the corruption and usurpations of royal officials. In the 1180s and 1190s counties were increasingly coordinated with the central government by the appointment of men like Geoffrey fitz Peter and William Brewer (a justice as well as a financial expert) to a succession of counties as sheriff.[8] The proper functioning of the county was too important for such appointments to have been mere financial perquisites of high office; the fact that the appointee held the office for a limited time and in a succession of counties indicates a purpose behind such appointments. As sheriff, such an official could not only

[6] Cam, *Hundred*, p. 135.

[7] *Liber Memorandorum Ecclesie de Bernewelle*, ed. J. W. Clark (Cambridge, 1907), p. 238.

[8] See D. A. Carpenter, "The Decline of the Curial Sheriff in England, 1194-1258," *EHR* 91 (1976):1-32 (although his concern is solely financial) and also, for some indicative statistics, Table 2.1, below. The most prominent of the itinerant sheriffs who were also royal ministers were William Brewer (sheriff of Devon [Mich. '79-Mich. '89], Berks [Mich. '90-Mich. '93 ('94)], Oxon [Mich. '90-East. '94], Notts/Derbs [East. '94-East. '00], Hants [East. '99-Mich. '99], Devon [East. '00-Mich. '00], Cornub [East. '00-Mich. '00], Hants [East. '00-East. '01], Berks [East. '01-20 May '02], Oxon [East. '01-21 Mar. '02], Cornub [East. '02-5 Apr. '04], Notts/Derbs [Mich. '03-18 Oct. '04], Devon [East. '02-Mich. '09], Som/Dorset [3 Dec. '07-Xmas '09], Wilts [Mich. '07-Xmas '09], Sussex [17 June '08-Xmas '09]); Hugh Bardolf (sheriff of Cornub [East. '84-Mich. '87], Wilts [East. '87-Mich. '89], Som/Dorset [Mich. '88-Mich. '89], Staffs [East. '90-Mich. '90], War/Leics [Mich. '90-Mich. '91], Ebor [Mich. '91-East. '94], Westm [Mich. '92-Mich. '99], N'hbld [Mich. '98-East. '99], Cornub [East. '99-East. '00], Cumbld [East. '99-Mich. '00], Devon [East. '99-Mich. '00], Devon [East. '99-East. '00], Notts/Derbs [East. '00-Mich. '03]); Geoffrey fitz Peter (sheriff of N'hants [Mich. '84-Mich. '89], Essex/Herts [Mich. '90-Mich. '93], N'hants [Mich. '91-East. '94], Staffs [Mich. '98-Mich. '04], Ebor [Mich. '98-Mich. '00], Westm [Mich. '99-East. '00], Beds/Bucks [Mich. '99-Mich. '04], Hants [East. '01-May '04], Shrops [East. '01-Mich. '04], Ebor [Mich. '02-1 Dec. '04]); and Hubert de Burgh (sheriff of Heref [Mich. '00-Mich. '04], Som/Dorset [Mich. '00-18 Oct. '04], Cornub [24 Feb. '02-East. '02], Berks [20 May '02-Mich. '04], Lincs [28 May '08-Mich. '13], Surrey /Sussex [25 Jan. '15-22 Apr. '16], Kent [25 June '15-Mich. '27], Westm [1 Feb. '28-Mich. '34]).

inquire thoroughly into the king's rights and the wrongs of previous officials, he could also instruct the judges of the counties. The distortions that would have been introduced into the trying of real actions by the provision of the petty assizes and the grand assize must have been substantial; the provision of the viscontiel writs would have further altered traditional county process. Instruction and persuasion by a prestigious royal agent, knowledgeable in the law and occupying an office of real local power, was vital to the rapid implementation of judicial innovations and the avoidance of legal chaos. Such royal justices who were appointed as sheriffs, of course, could not have been continuously present in their counties. Periodic visitations would have been equally effective; moreover, even an absentee sheriff remained personally responsible for the appointment and conduct of the person who discharged the duties of sheriff in his name. These appointments were evidently successful both in increasing royal revenues and in unifying county custom. Somerset and Dorset, in particular, felt so aggrieved by having William Brewer as sheriff that they made fine with the king so that they could elect their own sheriff from the men of the county.[9] The appointment of trusted persons in central government to successive positions of real local power increased royal revenue, provided royal influence in the determination of important disputes in the countryside, and unified the procedure of the courts with regard to the recent legal innovations.

During the thirteenth century, however, the importance of the lower courts—including the county courts—in the determination of major disputes declined; the coordination between the central government and local courts could no longer be profitably maintained by the appointment of such high-ranking sheriffs. After the climactic accumulation of sheriffdoms by Peter de Rivaux in 1232, there was no significant overlap between the body of central officials and those who were appointed sheriffs until the fifteenth century. Even by the end of the thirteenth century, however, sheriffs were still not distinctively men of their own county. It remained just as common to serve a second term as sheriff in a different county as it was to serve

[9] For the original grant and other similar agreements, see W. A. Morris, *The Medieval English Sheriff to 1300* (Manchester, 1927), p. 145. That grant was confirmed in 18 Henry III (C. 60/33, m. 7). Before that, in 1225, the counties of Somerset and Dorset had to make fine with the king for 200 marks to have Roger de la Ford as sheriff instead of Peter de Mauley (C. 60/16, m. 9). Roger de la Ford, however, was Mauley's man and favored Mauley's men in county process: *Somersetshire Pleas*, ed. Charles Chadwick-Healey, 2 vols., Somerset Record Society, vols. 11, 36 (London, 1897, 1923), 1:61-63.

a second term in the same county. The importance of the sheriff in local affairs did decline, and the people appointed were both less experienced—usually not experienced at all—in central government and tended to spend less time as sheriff.

In the fourteenth century sheriffs became clearly associated with their own county. It was unusual for any individual ever to be appointed successively to different counties, while it became normal for a relatively small number of county residents to serve as sheriff in informal rotation. Almost half of the sheriffs in the 1330s thus served more than one term in a given county. Furthermore, the average length of total time accumulated as a sheriff declined even further, so that two-thirds of sheriffs in the 1330s served less than a total of three years. In the fourteenth century, then, sheriffs tended to be men who were more local in outlook and less experienced in their duties. A single lengthy term as sheriff was no longer regarded by the Exchequer as a profitable appointment, and the ministerial sheriff who held office in many different counties and perhaps also in the central govenment was no longer necessary. Both the shorter terms and the degree of local identification indicate a decline in the overall importance of the sheriff and his court after 1300.

The sheriff was the convening and presiding officer in the county and hundred courts.[10] As such he was normally the dominant personality in the court. He could temporarily alter the date and, in some counties at least, the place at which the county met. He determined the order in which cases would come before the court and could therefore postpone a case until later in the day if he saw fit. He was also responsible for preserving order in the court. Thus Theobald de Hautein and Hugh de Humby were brought into the king's court in 1226, because they had prevented the sheriff of Lincolnshire and his bailiffs from holding the county, trithing, and wapentake courts.[11] In

[10] Cam, *Hundred* p. 157, citing one reference to a liberty bailiff and an uncertain reference from Bedfordshire, concluded that royal hundred bailiffs also heard the pleas in royal hundreds, even though she noted that lists of the duties of bailiffs in royal hundreds never include presiding over pleas. I find her assertion unconvincing. Liberty bailiffs were decidedly different from bailiffs of royal hundreds. Much evidence can be found for the former presiding over pleas; none for the latter. In Lincolnshire at least the undersheriff presided over hundred courts, and the schedules of courts (Appendix VIII) make it probable that there was normally a circuit. Moreover, amercements of hundred bailiffs for failing to execute orders of the hundred courts would have been improbable if hundred bailiffs had presided. Normally, then, bailiffs of royal hundreds did not preside over the sessions of the hundred courts.

[11] *CRR*, 12:434-35, 461. Although the inclusion of the wapentake courts in this description may be merely form, it is possible that the wapentake courts were still functioning at this time.

TABLE 2.1
Sheriffs' Terms and Experience

	1180-1190	1245-1255	1290-1300	1330-1340
Sheriffs considered*	69	95	82	122
Total Experience†				
1 yr or less	6%	12%	11%	20%
1 yr-3 yrs	22	33	39	43
3 yrs-5 yrs	17	20	23	17
5 yrs or more	55	35	27	20
5 yrs in a single term	20	29	18	9
Repetition in Office‡				
Service in more than one county	20%	11%	15%	2%
Service more than once in one county	12	10	15	44
Service more than once in one county and in more than one county	9	1	5	2

* Sheriffs of Rutland, Cornwall, Durham, Cheshire, Worcestershire, and London and Middlesex are consistently excluded from consideration.

† Experience is calculated not only in the period specified but also from the experience prior to and succeeding the relevant period. Identity of name is taken to mean identity of persons.

‡ Twinned counties are treated as only one county for these purposes.

1284 Hugh le Pruz, a knight of Devon, prohibited Thomas de Pyn, sheriff of Devon, from holding the county session after the meal on the second day of the session. Pyn reasonably saw this as an attempt to prevent him from fulfilling his duties as sheriff and thus "in manifest contempt of the king and in obstruction of royal power." He raised the hue and cry on Hugh and arrested him as a disturber of the king's peace. Since Hugh had not done anything violent, however, the legality of his prohibition, when he was brought before the barons of the Exchequer, depended on the reason for his actions.[12] There were occasions on which people went further. In 1236 twenty-five men of the county of Devon simply walked out of court, claiming that they would not hold pleas under that sheriff.[13] That, likewise, was wrong, as was the refusal to accept a sheriff because he was not sufficiently established in the county.[14] Such a refusal to acknowledge a sheriff's right to preside in county was in theory punishable by law, although in fact such disputes were normally compromised to

[12] Above, chapter 1, n. 78.
[13] CRR, 15:510-11.
[14] CRR, 3:129.

preserve the cooperation between the presiding officer and the judges upon which the good functioning of the county depended. During the session, the sheriff controlled pleading in a manner similar to the control exercised by the justices at Westminster. Although the sheriff could not render judgments, he could direct pleading and reject arguments unless and until a judgment was requested.[15] Finally, he had a limited control of the pleaders in the county court. While he could not permanently prevent a pleader from fulfilling his duties, he could put out of court temporarily any pleader who was performing unsatisfactorily.[16] The sheriff, therefore, was responsible for the orderly and proper functioning of the county court.

The sheriff's control over the county was nevertheless limited. When the sheriff of Devon had arrested Hugh le Pruz, it was still possible that the barons of the Exchequer would find that Hugh had been correct.[17] When Roger de Ford, sheriff of Somerset, so pressured the county court to rule in favor of one party, most of the judges withdrew from court. Withdrawal seems to have been lawful in such extreme circumstances.[18] The worst example of such perversion was Gilbert de Clifton, sheriff of Lancashire in 1284-85. It was alleged—but not proved—that Clifton had wrongfully sustained and maintained the plaintiff in *Osbaldeston v Punchardon*, a plaint of trespass in the county court. Clifton had so distrained the defendant that he was forced to put himself on a jury instead of waging his law; the sheriff had then seen to it that the jury was composed of the plaintiff's relatives. Clifton refused then to acknowledge the defendant's challenges concerning the jurors, so that the defendant felt it best to absent himself from court, leaving his pleader behind to protect his interests as well as he might. When the jury predictably ruled for the plaintiff, the pleader requested that a taxation of the damages be made by the defendant's peers, but Clifton threatened to imprison the pleader. None of the pleaders then dared to interfere any further in the case. Clifton proceeded to adjudge outrageous damages, seized the defendant's goods and valued them below their true value, and furthermore delivered half of the defendant's lands and tenements in Milton and Billington to the plaintiff until the damages of 100 marks had been raised.[19] At every stage Clifton was alleged to have misused

---

[15] Below, chapter 7, at n. 35 ff.

[16] Below, chapter 4, at n. 11.

[17] Above, at n. 12.

[18] *Somersetshire Pleas*, 11:61-63. See also *CRR*, 10:344-46.

[19] JUST. 1/408, m. 99d: "Et juratores inquisicionis eiusdem pronunciaverunt veredictum suum contra predictum Ricardum unde serviens ipsius Ricardi peciit taxaci-

the power he wielded as sheriff. That power was such that miscarriages of justice were possible. Seemingly, however, they were not a common occurrence; and the sheriff, at any rate, was open to prosecution for damages resulting from his actions, particularly after the end of his term.

Despite his powerful position in the county court, the sheriff had no authority to render judgments; he was not a judge. *Britton*, indeed, might seem to have given the county courts a dual nature, such that the judges gave judgments in cases initiated by plaint, but that in cases initiated by writ the sheriff as a royal justice rendered the judgments.[20] That interpretation, however, is almost surely wrong.[21] It is true, as the various cases already cited and even the *Summa Magna* demonstrate,[22] that the sheriff could and at times did usurp the function of rendering judgments. That usurpation, however, would not have been limited to cases brought by writ. In some cases, perhaps, the usurpation was not very clear, since the sheriff may have been simultaneously both the presiding officer and one of the judges. No law forbade the appointment of one of the judges as sheriff, and such appointments may have been relatively frequent. The form of the *justicies* writs themselves has created a mistaken but understandable impression that the sheriffs functioned as justices.[23] Despite the interpretation of *Britton* and the *justicies* writs and despite the confusion which might arise from an overly assertive sheriff or from a sheriff who was also a judge, it must be maintained that in the county courts the presiding officer by virtue of his office was neither judge nor justice.

There were instances, however, in which the sheriff seemed to act judicially. The writ of redisseisin, for instance, was provided as a remedy against those who, having once disseised another and having been ejected by judgment, redisseised the person of the same tenements. Process in redisseisin was brief; the writ merely directed the sheriff to take the coroners and twelve men to the tenement concerned, to make an inquest there, and then to arrest the defendant if

---

onem dampnorum secundum legem et consuetudinem regni, idem Gilbertus ei in tantum minabatur quod comiteretur gaole nisi se teneret quod non ausus erat ulterius inde se intromittere nec aliquis alius de servientibus comitatus. Postea idem Gilbertus adiudicavit dampna predicti Ade de predicto placito sine brevi ad centum marcarum et amerciavit ipsum Ricardum ad centum solidorum et ad dimidiam marcam pro defalta comitatus pro ipso et eodem die de facto suo proprio et non per pares ipsius Ricardi."

[20] *Britton*, ed. F. M. Nichols, 2 vols. (Oxford, 1865), p. 135.

[21] Below, chapter 7, at n. 35 ff.

[22] *Radulphi de Hengham Summae*, ed. W. H. Dunham (Cambridge, 1932), pp. 13-14.

[23] Below, chapter 7, at n. 35 ff.

the verdict was that there had been a redisseisin.[24] A similar situation arose with the writ of hate and spite (*de odio et atya*), which ordered the sheriff and coroners to make an inquest in open county as to whether a certain person was being appealed of a felony merely from the hate and spite of the appellant.[25] Such duties seem to correspond more to executive investigation and remedy than to ordinary litigation. Similar duties can be cited, as in the taking of a jury verdict to determine whether a *causa* clause was true,[26] the recording of cases for removal to the king's court,[27] and the taking of jury verdicts for cases pleaded at Westminster prior to the institutionalization of *nisi prius* procedure.[28] While such activities had something of a judicial aspect to them, they are not sufficient warrant for any claim that the sheriff acted as a judge in the county court.

Although the sheriff was not a justice, he did profit from the litigation determined in the county court. Glanvill states, as a general rule, the principle that sheriffs received the amercements arising from all pleas tried and determined in the county courts.[29] An even clearer statement of the principle was made as a result of an interesting hanging in Devon in 1244. Three men had acknowledged themselves thieves in a lower court, but the lower court's jurisdiction did not extend to handling such serious cases. The lord, therefore, surrendered that case to the sheriff and the county court, and the thieves were then hanged by judgment of the county. The sheriff, before royal justices, claimed that he had the right to keep their chattels, since he received all the profits of pleas determined by judgment of the county court. The knights of the county verified this by saying that he ought to receive all such proceeds whether they were from free men or from villeins.[30] This was a marginal and exceptional instance and illustrates so much the better the normal situation. The

---

[24] *Early Registers of Writs*, ed. Elsa de Haas and G.D.G. Hall, Selden Society, vol. 87 (London, 1970), p. 84 (CC. 168); Donald W. Sutherland, *The Assize of Novel Disseisin* (Oxford, 1973), pp. 63-64.

[25] *Early Registers of Writs*, p. 66 (CC. 109).

[26] CP. 52 quindene Hilary, 17 Edward I (Beds.); quindene Hilary, 21 Edward I (Northants. [*bis*]).

[27] Below, n. 53; chapter 6, at n. 69.

[28] Below, chapter 9, at nn. 94, 95.

[29] *Tractatus de legibus et consuetudinibus regni Anglie qui Glanvilla vocatur* [hereafter: *Glanvill*], ed. G.D.G. Hall (London, 1965), p. 113.

[30] JUST. 1/175, m. 45d: "Venit Henricus de Tracy et dicit quod ipsi latrones capti sunt in curia sua set quia contencio fuit in curia sua predicta que non potuit loquelam illam terminare fecit loquelam illam simul cum rettatis venire in comitatum. Et concessit curiam suam vicecomiti de eis illa vice ut fieret de eis quod ius dictaret. Et super hoc venit vicecomes et dicit idem. Et quesitum est quo devenerunt catalla eorum. Dicit quod ipse habet catalla eorum et debet habere omnes fructus [et profectus?] loquelarum

only sheriffs who did not profit from county litigation were those who had taken the office on the agreement that they would render account for all profits, receiving only a salary for their services. Normally, however, the sheriff had a vested interest in making the county court operate efficiently and justly.

The sheriff had other reasons for performing his duties efficiently. He took an oath upon becoming sheriff,[31] and he was liable at law for unjust or inefficient conduct. At least one sheriff was prosecuted specifically for violating that oath by accepting and executing writs that should have been issued under the great seal, whereas they were sealed only by the privy seal.[32] Sheriffs were also prosecuted for many other misdeeds, usually by the individuals who had been wronged, usually also for actions not specifically related to the county court. Geoffrey fitz Lawrence thus sued the heirs of Gilbert de Cheyles, a sheriff of Lincolnshire in the 1250s. In the king's court at that time Geoffrey had been amerced for a wrong he had committed; he paid the sheriff the ten marks he owed for delivery to the Exchequer and received from the sheriff a tally. Cheyles, however, had not delivered the money to the Exchequer; and Geoffrey was still able to bring his suit early in the reign of Edward I.[33] The heir of William de Boyville was similarly burdened with his ancestor's debts. Boyville had been allowed to collect 12d from every holder of a carucate of land in Leicestershire to build a prison in Leicester. In the Exchequer his heir was sued, because, it was alleged, Boyville had appropriated those buildings to his own uses.[34] Henry de Wodecroft had a different kind of complaint. His cart and three of his horses had been taken to carry supplies north to Scotland in 1303 for the king. The cart and horses had been valued at 44s, and the Exchequer had allowed that sum to the sheriff, John de Dene, for Wodecroft's compensation. Dene, however, had not paid, so that Wodecroft sued him in the Exchequer.[35] Similarly Gerard de Braybrok had to sue Walter le Baud, sheriff of Hertfordshire, for the £10 which the sheriff had levied but not yet paid him in compensation for his expenses in 1307 for going to Par-

---

quas potest terminare in comitatu suo per iudicium comitatus. Et similiter omnes milites comitatus dicunt illud idem, videlicet, quod debet habere omnes profectus de loquelis quas terminare possunt . . . suis tam de liberis quam de villanis."

[31] *EHD*, 4:555: an elaborate fifteenth-century sheriff's oath.

[32] E. 13/32, mm. 27, 45d.

[33] E. 13/2, m. 10d.

[34] E. 13/17, m. 27d.

[35] E. 13/29, m. 60d.

liament as a knight of the shire.[36] Sheriffs were expected to be honest and efficient.

Sheriffs were often called upon to defend themselves concerning their conduct in the execution of properly legal orders. Richard de Howell, sheriff of Lincolnshire around 1300, distrained two individuals who had made themselves mainpernors for the farm of the sheriff's bailiff. They prosecuted him in the Exchequer for unjust distraint.[37] Thomas de Burnham, sheriff of Lincolnshire only a few years later, was sued for distraining William de Welleby after forbidden to do so by the barons of the Exchequer; he defended himself by showing that he had been acting pursuant to a royal writ.[38] Thomas de Gardinis, sheriff of Gloucestershire, defended himself against an allegation of unlawful imprisonment by showing how he had been executing his duties through an itinerant bailiff. The bailiff had been forceably resisted and the hue and cry had been raised. The sheriff thus thought that the person had been justly imprisoned.[39] Such matters as the continuation of a case in the county court after reception of an order for its removal[40] and the unlawful supporting of litigants were also occasions for litigation.[41] In general, at least by the reign of Edward I, the central courts were open to provide redress against the sheriff and his officials, if the victims felt sufficiently aggrieved to bring their complaints. Prior to that, the eyres had provided at least some redress against officials. If the level of complaints is any good indication of the situation during the reign of Edward I, however, the misuse of power was neither as frequent nor as oppressive as a first examination of the Hundred Rolls might seem to indicate.

The sheriff kept the only written record of proceedings on civil litigation in the county court. The roll for any particular session listed in brief form the cases that came before the county court and the action taken and ordered in court on each case. It was vital for the sheriff, who was responsible for executing these orders, to have an accurate reminder of the dozens—at times, hundreds—of summonses and distraints to be made in the few weeks before the next session. As each order was executed or found impossible to execute, a notation to that effect was made in the roll. The action would then be reported

[36] E. 13/32, m. 12.
[37] E. 13/24, m. 14d.
[38] E. 13/32, m. 32.
[39] E. 13/20, m. 5.
[40] E. 13/21, mm. 23d, 38d.
[41] Above, at n. 19.

to the county the next session—the roll itself serving as a docket—and appropriate action taken by the court.[42] Since the roll also recorded the forfeitures of pledges and the amercements that were due the sheriff, the county rolls also served as a financial record. Thus, when the executor of John de Balliol, sheriff of Nottinghamshire and Derbyshire in 1261-64, was called into the Exchequer to account for the profits of the county, care was taken that the rolls would be available for the accounting process.[43] The importance of the rolls as a financial document was probably the reason why they were considered largely the property of the sheriff and remained in his hands even after the expiration of his term. There were times when the rolls were ordered to be rendered to the incoming sheriff,[44] but such was probably the case only when the new sheriff was going to account for the whole period covered by the rolls. There was never any indication that the rolls belonged to the county court or that the county court as such kept its own record of the proceedings.

The county rolls, however, were not completely privately owned documents; by the early thirteenth century they had already attained the status of a public resource. The county court was very dependent on the rolls for keeping track of the dozens of pleas and the process and pleading in each. In 1212 this dependence was shown both in the care with which the sheriff's clerk in Gloucestershire entrusted the rolls to an assistant to be guarded in his absence and by the role a fraudulent interpolation in the county rolls played in obtaining an unjust judgment in the county court.[45] The roll itself, of course, was not incontrovertible; it was not record in the strict sense. The judges were free to disagree with it and make a record at variance with the rolls.[46] It is inconceivable, however, that in recording the exact words in which a demandant stated his claim, the tenant stated his denial, and both made the wager of battle,[47] spoken perhaps three or four

[42] *Rolls from the Office of the Sheriff of Beds. and Bucks., 1332-1334*, ed. G. H. Fowler, Beds. Historical Record Society, Quarto Series, vol. 3 (Bedford, 1929). The other surviving rolls from county courts (except those from the county court of Cheshire) will be printed by the Selden Society.

[43] E. 13/2, m. 7d.

[44] *Select Cases in the Court of King's Bench*, ed. G. O. Sayles, 7 vols., Selden Society, vols. 55, 57, 58, 74, 76, 82, 88 (London, 1936-1971), 3:xcvi, n. 1.

[45] *CRR*, 6:230.

[46] In general, see G. T. Lapsley, "The Court, Record and Roll of the County in the Thirteenth Century," *Law Quarterly Review* 51 (1935):299-326, although his emphasis on the primacy of the judges does tend to undervalue the rolls (see below, chapter 6.)

[47] *Glanvill*, p. 100.

months previously, the judges would have begun in any other way than in consulting the rolls. Later in the thirteenth century, at least, the judges of a county court protested that a case in which they were alleged to have made a false judgment had taken place so long before that they could not remember what had happened. They had to search out the previous sheriffs and get possession of the rolls to record the plea.[48] Sheriffs were obliged to make the rolls available in this way.[49] Even in situations in which the court was not responding to a royal order litigants relied upon the county rolls. In one case around 1303 a litigant requested that the undersheriff check for himself by consulting the rolls the order in which the defendant had put himself on a jury and waged his law in a previous session.[50] In an earlier case a defendant had offered to prove his defence by reference to the county rolls in coordination with the "record" of the judges.[51] Even in regard to crown pleas the sheriff's roll functioned as a counter-roll to the record that the coroners kept.[52] While the sheriff's roll, at times called the county roll, was made by the sheriff ostensibly for his own purposes as presiding and executive officer and was normally retained in his possession, it was undoubtedly to a certain extent a public document and played an important part in the efficient functioning of the county court.

The sheriff's responsibilities were thus both numerous and varied, and most of his duties were discharged by his staff, some of whom operated in and out of the sheriff's headquarters, some of whom were dispersed through the county. The central staff is loosely referred to

[48] CP. 40/129, m. 64: "Loquela illa iamdiu placitata fuit tempore Philippi de Paunton tunc vicecomitis qui penes se habet rotulos et breve regis etc., per quod sectatores eiusdem comitatus sine inspeccione eorundem rotulorum et brevis recordum facere non potuerunt etc." JUST. 4, Lincoln eyre, 1276: "Loquela in brevi nominata placitata fuit tempore quo Thomas de Bolton fuit vicecomes Lincoln' unde rotuli comitatus Lincoln' de tempore predicti Thome traditi fuerunt Ricardo de Harington quondam vicecomiti eiusdem comitatus ad recordum de loquela predicta faciendum. Et quia rotuli predicti sunt in custodia magistri Jocei de Raytheby, executoris testamenti predicti Ricardi, et aliorum executorum suorum sine quibus rotulis comitatus predictus interitus est recordum de loquela predicta facere."

[49] CP. 40/17, m. 132d: an order to distrain executors to deliver the rolls so that a case could be recorded; CP. 40/133, m. 177: a case in which the sheriff was party to a plea so that the coroners were ordered to have the plea recorded; they were allowed access to the county rolls by the sheriff, but he refused to hand over the viscontiel writ concerned.

[50] Brit. Lib. Add. 31826, f. 266v [S.S.]: de la Bere v Cantelupe.

[51] Below, chapter 5 at n. 60.

[52] 3 Edward I, c. 10; R. F. Hunnisett, *The Medieval Coroner* (Cambridge, 1961), pp. 194-96.

as the sheriff's office and seems to have consisted of six or seven officials, not including the servants for the care of horses, upkeep of buildings, and, in some cases, maintenance of the castle. The most important of these officials was the undersheriff. He could function as a substitute for the sheriff in every function except those in which the sheriff was instructed to perform a duty in person, as when he was ordered to make a record in a liberty or to admeasure land.[53] Most, but not all, sheriffs had an undersheriff,[54] and the sheriff even of twinned counties seems normally to have had but one under-sheriff.[55] The sole exception to this was Lincolnshire, which seems once to have had three undersheriffs, although even for such an extraordinarily bureaucratic county this seems to have been abnormal.[56] The undersheriff was the person who normally presided over sessions of the county and royal hundred courts and during the reign of Edward I, at least, was thus probably rather more knowledgeable in the law than the sheriff. Robert de Somercote, for instance, admitted that he had presided over the county and "hundred" courts

[53] See Cam, *Hundred*, pp. 133-34; JUST. 1/483, m. 9 (1272): William de Malberthorpe, the undersheriff of Lincolnshire, recorded a plea which the sheriff had been ordered to record *"in propria persona"*; the justices did not see fit to raise any objections to the method of recording. CP. 52 quindene Michaelmas, 19 Edward I (Notts.) indicates that the sheriff felt that he should have gone in person, but that the undersheriff would suffice if necessary: "Misi subvicecomitem meum loco meo ad curiam Edmundi honoris Lancastr' quia personaliter interesse non potui pro quibusdam negociis domini regis expediendis"; the suitors, however, refused to record the plea. CP. 40/138, m. 89d (1301) records the reply of a sheriff who had sent his undersheriff, for whom the suitors had refused to record the plea. The justices ordered the sheriff to go to the court in person instead of ordering—as they would have done if the sending of the undersheriff had been sufficient—that the suitors be distrained.

[54] CP. 52 quindene Hilary, 19 Edward I (Wilts.): a sheriff who maintained that he had no undersheriff.

[55] Richard de Merston was mentioned separately as undersheriff of both Bedfordshire and Buckinghamshire (CP. 52 three weeks Easter, 4 Edward II); Richard Foun was undersheriff of both Nottinghamshire and Derbyshire (CP. 52 octave Michaelmas, 26 Edward I; CP. 52 morrow of All Souls, 27 Edward I); John de Bridport was undersheriff of Somerset and Dorset (CP. 52 quindene John the Baptist, 7 & 8 Edward II; CP. 52 octave Hilary 8 Edward II); John de Norwych was undersheriff of Norfolk and Suffolk (CP. 52 quindene Easter, 4 Edward II); William de Brochole was undersheriff of Sussex and Surrey (CP. 52 octave Michaelmas, 27 Edward I; CP. 52 quindene Martinmas, 27 Edward I).

[56] CP. 52 quindene Easter, 29 Edward I: Henry de Fenton (writs dated 28 January, 9 February, and 6 March); Geoffrey de Sneyth (writ dated 27 January); and Robert de Lughteburgh (writ dated 28 January). There was some laxity in these matters, so that it is possible that Sneyth and Lughteburgh were clerks instead of undersheriffs; nevertheless, the references at least indicate that it is probable that three of the sheriff's staff were empowered at one time to preside over the regional and county courts.

at the request of Richard de Harington, sheriff of Lincolnshire in 1274-75, for one quarter of the year, but for no longer.[57] Likewise, the standard reason for removing pleas from the county courts was alleged bias on the part of the undersheriff, who—as the clause in the writs mechanically recites—frequently held the pleas of the court in the absence of the sheriff. That bias derived most often either from consanguinity between the undersheriff and one of the litigants or from an annuity that had been granted the undersheriff, presumably at a previous time, for his legal services as pleader or attorney.[58] The services of the undersheriff thus allowed the sheriff to fulfil his commitments in the lower courts at the same time that he was performing his duties as the county executive officer of the king's court.

The undersheriff was not of necessity one of the financial officials of the sheriff: the receivers of money. Robert de Somercote, for instance, while he admitted having presided over courts, denied ever having been a receiver of money.[59] Similarly, in another case it was conceded that Simon de Hedon had been the undersheriff of John de Balliol, sheriff of Nottinghamshire and Derbyshire in 1261-64, but it was strongly denied that he had been a receiver. Furthermore, a jury confirmed Hedon's defence.[60] Since that kind of specific denial was necessary, however, it seems probable that undersheriffs were normally also receivers, but that the position of undersheriff was not so clearly defined that an undersheriff was necessarily also a receiver of money due the sheriff.

People who were not strictly appointed as undersheriffs could also preside over the various royal courts in the county. The sheriff's clerk at times presided over the county court.[61] In at least one case a coroner

---

[57] E. 13/10, mm. 5, 6.

[58] Below, chapter 4 at nn. 16-20.

[59] E. 13/10, mm. 5, 6.

[60] E. 13/3, m. 11d.

[61] E. 13/14, m. 5: "Lincs. Rogerus de Ussynton optulit se quarto die versus Walterum de Luda clericum vicecomitis de placito ad respondendum eidem Rogero quare cum idem Rogerus nuper iuste distrinxisset Alexandrum de Tykemote tenentem suum pro arreragiis cuiusdam annui redditus ac idem Alexander dictum Rogerum implacitasset coram prefato Waltero tunc temporis tenente placita decem wappentaciorum de Anecastre pro districcione predicta, idem Walterus eundem Alexandrum in eodem placito manutenebat et iniuste defendebat nec permisit predicto Rogero in aliquo iusticiam exhibi ad grave dampnum suum et contra statuta nostra etc." CP. 52 octave Hilary, 21 Edward I (John le Lorimer, sheriff's clerk in Wiltshire); CP. 52 octave Trinity, 19 Edward I (Philip Quynton, chief clerk of the sheriff of Dorset); JUST. 4, Surrey eyre, 1294 (William Brochole, chief clerk of the sheriff of Surrey, elsewhere [above, n. 55] called undersheriff.

presided over a session of the county court.[62] The case of John de Crossholm, however, probably best illustrates the sheriff's powers of designating the presiding officer of the county court. In 1290 John de Crossholm was prosecuted by Nicholas de Warwick for the king. It was alleged that Crossholm, while undersheriff and receiver of John Dyne, had taken bribes to falsify certain inquests concerning distraint for knighthood, had favored the opposition in every case concerning the king which came before the county, and had refused to issue bills of receipt unless he was paid 40d or half a mark. Crossholm denied that he was an undersheriff or held the position of an undersheriff or receiver, although he readily admitted that at times he presided over the sheriff's courts when requested to do so. The jury cleared him of the suspicions at least of his contemporaries.[63] Although Crossholm was elsewhere referred to as an undersheriff by a litigant,[64] he was probably only the bailiff of the bishop of Lincoln in Well wapentake.[65] It seems that the sheriff of Lincolnshire used local lawyers in the employ of others to fulfil his duties in the county. Those duties so coincided with the duties of the undersheriff that to many people there was little difference.

In addition to the undersheriff the sheriff employed several clerks on his central staff. The chief clerk was not frequently mentioned. Since his duties coincided to such a degree with those of the undersheriff, it is possible that a sheriff kept one or the other, but not both. In addition to the chief clerk, there were usually four other clerks on the sheriff's staff. Thus Gervase de Clifton, sheriff of Yorkshire in 1285-91, was twice called into the Exchequer of pleas as a defendant,

[62] CP. 40/89, m. 144d: "Quia Ricardus de Preston coronator comitatus predicti qui frequenter in absencia vicecomitis comitatus eiusdem tenet placita comitatus illius pro eo quod predictus Rogerus implacitat ipsum coronatorem in comitatu Lancastr' per breve regis de debito viginti marcarum quod idem Rogerus a prefato coronatore exigit, idem coronator in odium ipsius Rogeri fovet predictam Matillidem in appello predicto ut dicitur." Since the case was an appeal, in which the coroners would have been more involved anyway, it is possible that the coroner did not preside over the pleas of the county generally.

[63] E. 13/18, m. 17.

[64] CP. 52 octave Hilary, 21 Edward I (presiding over the county court); CP. 52 morrow Purification, 21 Edward I (presiding over the court of Ancaster).

[65] CP. 52 octave Hilary, 21 Edward I: "Quia Johannes de Crosseholme ballivus predicti episcopi de Welle wapentake coram quo loquela predicta per returnum brevis nostri in curia predicta deducitur inplacitatur per predictum Johannem filium Johannis coram predictis justiciariis per breve nostrum quod dicitur quare impedit propter quod idem ballivus in odium ipsius Johannis filii Johannis fovet predictum Willelmum in loquela predicta."

and both times he mentioned that he had four clerks. In the second case, the four clerks were carefully distinguished from his ten bailiffs, who were not part of the sheriff's office.[66]

The clerk most concerned with the legal system was the keeper and returner of writs. He took into his custody all the writs sent to the sheriff; these writs fell into two classes. The first class was the viscontiel writs. These the clerk filed by running a thong through them, forming what is known as a writ file. Some were writs that would initiate cases directly in the county court; others, because the defendants in the case were resident in a liberty, had to be delegated to the court of that liberty. In the latter situation, the clerk would be responsible for making a precise copy of the writ and forwarding it to the proper court. The second class of writs was the returnable writ, which either initiated or continued process on a case in a branch of the king's court. These the clerk separated into geographical areas so that the appropriate member of the sheriff's staff dispersed throughout the county—normally a bailiff—could be ordered to take the appropriate action. The order from the sheriff to his bailiff would be written and would often recite the writ verbatim.[67] The bailiff was required to answer the mandate, and his reply was endorsed on the writ. The clerk was bound to a tight schedule with these writs, for his duties implied seeing to it that all the appropriate writs were acted upon and returned to Westminster on the proper return day, always indicated in the writ itself.

The keeper and returner of writs was responsible for several scribal tasks. The written orders to bailiffs and the endorsing of writs have already been mentioned. In addition, sheriffs kept a roll on which were entered the endorsements made for each returnable writ.[68] Furthermore, from 1285 sheriffs were obligated by statute to provide upon request bills of receipt when a writ was delivered to them. The bill constituted proof that the sheriff had indeed received the writ and

[66] E. 13/15, m. 11d; E. 13/18, m. 12. There had been a complete turnover in his staff in between the cases, as was demanded at frequent intervals by the later sheriff's oath (EHD, 4:555.)

[67] JUST. 1/466, m. 2d. The sheriff would append phrases to either end of the form of the writ: "Vicecomes ballivo salutem. Mandatum domini regis in hec verba recepi: . . . ; et ideo tibi mando quod mandatum istud plenarie exequeris."

[68] Rolls from the Office of the Sheriff of Beds. and Bucks.; E. 163/2/42. Most writs returned from Lincolnshire were endorsed, in a notation meant only for the sheriff's office, "in rotulo" (see CP. 52 octave Michaelmas, 26 Edward I). For Kent, see JUST. 4/1, Kent eyre, 1293: the writ concerning the plea between the bishop of Rochester and the master of the Knights Templar is endorsed "transcribitur" and several others are endorsed as were the Lincolnshire writs.

that he had received it on a specific day. Thereafter the bill could be used as proof if the sheriff denied having received the writ or alleged that he had received it too late for execution.[69] The proper exercise of the office of keeper and returner of writs demanded literacy, accuracy, efficiency, a fair knowledge of the law, and a detailed knowledge of both county geography and county jurisdictions.

The keeper and returner of writs was an important person in the execution of county business and was thus the subject of some concern. Illiterate or overly burdened sheriffs customarily relied too heavily on their keepers and returners of writs, and that confidence was at times abused. Gervase de Clifton, sheriff of Yorkshire, thus prosecuted his clerk in the Exchequer. Clifton explained that he had committed to John de Coppegrave the custody of all royal writs, to make execution and to return them faithfully to the king's court. A justice of *oyer* and *terminer*, however, had delivered to Coppegrave writs with the names of certain wrongdoers included in a panel, instructing him to attach them to be present at the court of king's bench on a certain day. Coppegrave accepted the writs, but broke the seal and proceeded to make up a different list of wrongdoers, excluding the names of five of his friends.[70] This particular deception was discovered. Such abuses and the generally heavy reliance placed upon that clerk by the sheriff resulted in the provision of 1298 that the clerk would be responsible before the Exchequer together with the sheriff for the returns he had made. The sheriff nevertheless remained liable for the damages occasioned by his clerk's false return if the clerk was unable to pay the damages.[71]

Two more clerks were usually specially designated as the sheriff's receivers of money. They were in charge of supervising the sheriff's

[69] 13 Edward I, c. 39. See also E. 13/18, m. 17 (issuance of bill refused unless paid for); E. 13/18, m. 27d (issuance of bill refused); KB. 27/300, m. 59 (issuance of bill refused by sheriff, so that the coroners made the bill; if this allegation was found true by a jury the litigant was to receive damages from the sheriff for the delay); E. 13/21, m. 38d (issuance of bill by the undersheriff); E. 13/23, m. 33d (issue joined on whether the bill was forged, because the sheriff maintained that the writ had been received on a later day); CP. 40/133, m. 13d: "Et vicecomes modo mandat quod breve adeo tarde venit etc. Et quia attornatus predicti Rogeri profert quandam billetam sigillis Walteri de Ponte coronatoris eiusdem comitatus, Rogeri de Stoke, et Radulphi de Musselawe signatam que testatur quod predictus Rogerus in eorum presencia die martis proxima post festum sancti Valentini hoc anno predictum breve predicto vicecomiti liberavit, preceptum est coronatoribus comitatus predicti quod venire faciant hic a die sancti Johannis Baptiste in xv dies predictum vicecomitem, scilicet, Johannem de Novo Burgo, ad respondendum etc."

[70] E. 13/14, m. 6d.

[71] 26 Edward I.

finances, paying out money liberated by royal writ, receiving moneys due the sheriff either from the hundredal farms or from the profits arising from litigation, and collecting both the moneys and the tallies which the sheriff would need for his account in the Exchequer. In some counties the clerks had established a whole financial bureau on the pattern of the king's Exchequer.[72] Something about these men may be surmised from two of the staff of Simon de Kyme, sheriff of Yorkshire in 1300-1304: Simon de Wakefield and John Lungespeye. Wakefield had apparently begun his career in Northumberland as an undersheriff,[73] but soon found employment in Yorkshire. When Simon de Kyme left the county to serve in Scotland, Wakefield was left in control of Yorkshire. Apparently he did not see fit to await Kyme's return, for he left the county in the custody of a clerk named William de Skipton, who thereafter kept the county rolls, held the county sessions, and rendered account to the sheriff.[74] Wakefield had abandoned county office to serve in the Exchequer as the clerk of Roger de Hegham, a baron of the Exchequer.[75] How long he stayed at the Exchequer is uncertain, but by 1315 he was once more undersheriff of Yorkshire, because Simon Warde was appointed sheriff then with the express order to remove Wakefield from his office of undersheriff and from any other office in the county. That order, however, was soon revoked, because Nicholas de Meynill, the sheriff under whom he had served, and many other influential people testified that he had not been convicted of any wrong while in the service of Edward I. A letter patent was therefore issued proclaiming that he could once again be retained for service.[76] Wakefield was thus a man of a great deal of experience and must be presumed to have been fairly competent. While he was Kyme's undersheriff, however, a dispute had erupted between himself and John Lungespeye, one of

[72] Mabel H. Mills, "The Medieval Shire House," in *Studies Presented to Sir Hilary Jenkinson*, ed. J. Conway Davies (London, 1957), p. 256.

[73] E. 13/29, m. 43d.

[74] E. 13/27, m. 12d. Kyme afterwards objected that he had not wanted Skipton as his undersheriff ("bene cognovit quod predictus Willelmus habuit rotulos comitatus et comitatum tenuit, sed non per ipsum Simonem nec per voluntatem suam"). It was apparently sufficient, however, that Kyme had assigned his next undersheriff to receive the account from William and that the account had been indeed received. Such retroactive approval made Kyme responsible also for a suspicious indenture made out by Skipton while he was clerk and undersheriff.

[75] E. 13/29, m. 43d.

[76] *CPR, 1313-1317*, m. 401. He was accused of threatening a woman with rape and other bodily injury while a clerk in Northumberland: *CIM*, 1:538.

Kyme's receivers. Wakefield had Lungespeye thrown into the Fleet gaol, but then ran into difficulties in the county. The Exchequer was demanding funds, and Lungespeye had to be brought back into the county immediately to serve as receiver, because "he is useful and necessary to raise the abovesaid debts, because he has a greater knowledge of the men of the said county than the other sheriff's clerks." The indispensable Lungespeye was therefore put by mainpernors so that he could return to Yorkshire until the crisis had passed.[77] It was not unusual for the receivers to have such special competence. Gilbert de Brunnolvesheved, undersheriff of Richard de Medburn in 1290-91, was called into the Exchequer to answer concerning several tallies. He maintained, as did most sheriffs, that he could not answer concerning the tallies without the help of the two receivers.[78] The receivers were financial experts, not merely clerks deputed to handle financial concerns which could equally well have been handled by any other clerk.

There was a fourth clerk, but his duties are not known precisely. He may well have been merely an assistant to the keeper and returner of writs, or he may have been delegated responsibility for the matters touching the lower courts. The county roll had to be made up, and the process during the month on each case had to be recorded as it was executed. Furthermore, throughout the month plaints were submitted to the sheriff's office; these had to be written up correctly, making sure sufficient information was included in the plaint. Perhaps also the fourth clerk accompanied the sheriff on those frequent occasions when the sheriff needed a scribe in the execution of his duties away from the office. At any rate, there was a fourth clerk, and it would have been difficult to believe that the keeper and returner of writs could have handled all the paper work necessary in the sheriff's office without substantial assistance.

The sheriff's office was likewise the base of at least one subordinate executive officer: the bailiff itinerant. Since the bailiff itinerant was not a person with financial responsibilities, he seldom appears in the records, but it seems that there was one in every county. Thus Richard de Nauton was the bailiff itinerant in Lincolnshire in 1301,[79] and

[77] E. 13/26, m. 73d: "utilis est et necessarius ad levandum predicta debita eo quod magis constat ei de noticia hominum dicti comitatus quam ceteris clericis dicti vicecomitis."
[78] E. 13/21, m. 58; Cam, *Hundred*, p. 135.
[79] E. 13/25, m. 61.

Robert de Danton was the bailiff itinerant in Hertfordshire in 1303-4.[80] Around 1293 John de Vernon held the office in Essex,[81] as did Hugh de Kingston twenty years later.[82] Robert de la Lee served William de Sutton, sheriff of Norfolk and Suffolk in 1298-1301, in that capacity at least in Norfolk.[83] Some years before that, William de Hagwe had been the bailiff itinerant in Gloucestershire.[84] In 1306 John Bekke, the bailiff itinerant in Berkshire, seized certain horses and carts for the carriage of food from Wantage to Windsor.[85] Thomas de Gardinis, sheriff of Gloucestershire in the mid-1290s, had to answer in the Exchequer for the actions of his bailiff itinerant. That bailiff had secured four oxen as a distraint against John de Stokwelle when the bailiff of the liberty had refused to execute the sheriff's mandate. The oxen had been placed in the lord's park within the liberty, as was proper, but Stokwelle had rescued them from the park. By judgment of the county court the bailiff itinerant had once again distrained Stokwelle, but the horse taken as distraint was once more rescued. The county court finally had ordered the bailiff to attach that recalcitrant by his body; when the man resisted, the bailiff itinerant had raised the hue and cry; and Stokwelle had thus been imprisoned.[86] Geoffrey de Bulecote, bailiff itinerant in fee, similarly executed a contested seizure in Derbyshire around 1290 and drove the animals across the county line to Nottingham to be valued and sold there.[87] In some counties the bailiff itinerant even had a subbailiff to assist him in his duties, as did Walter de Huntingfeld, bailiff itinerant of Suffolk.[88] The bailiff itinerant was thus concerned with the execution of any viscontiel duty which did not pertain to any single hundred or which pertained to an area such as a liberty in which the sheriff had no official responsible solely to himself. Each county needed such a bailiff; the burdens of business in most counties and the frequent difficulty in executing their duties would often require that he have at least one subbailiff to assist him.

The sheriff thus retained a sizeable staff in his office. The undersheriff was his alter ego and the most important of the central vis-

[80] E. 13/27, m. 38d.
[81] E. 13/20, m. 56.
[82] E. 13/38, m. 10.
[83] E. 13/24, m. 57.
[84] E. 13/16, m. 4d.
[85] E. 13/27, m. 61.
[86] E. 13/20, m. 5.
[87] E. 13/18, m. 25d.
[88] E. 13/19, m. 30d.

contiel officials. The four clerks were equally divided between financial supervision and the burdens of legal recording and the expediting of viscontiel duties. The bailiff itinerant was the sheriff's miscellaneous official, delegated to handle all duties which could not be taken care of by one of the dispersed staff. In addition to these officials, the sheriff would have had a castle constable and a gaoler—neither of whom necessarily belonged to the sheriff's office[89]—and several lesser servants who functioned as subbailiffs, grooms, and messengers. The success of an individual in his term as sheriff would have depended to a great extent on his ability to choose his assistants well. During his term he was probably more occupied in coordinating the work of these subordinates than in the direct and personal execution of royal orders.

The sheriff's dispersed staff consisted of bailiffs and subbailiffs. While the main lines of the system were administratively relatively simple, the final product of a viscontiel bureaucracy in a county like Lincolnshire was rather complex. If we put to one side the territories of the ancient demesne and of the baronial and borough liberties, Lincolnshire, from the sheriff's point of view, consisted of the three trithings and Kesteven and Holland. Each of these regions, of course, was further divided into wapentakes or hundreds, but the sheriff only had to concern himself with the five regions. Each region had its own bureaucratic staff headed by a bailiff. Thus William de Thivelby was the bailiff of the south trithing in 1306,[90] but Simon Secke of Louthe had succeeded him in that position by 1313.[91] In the last years of the thirteenth century Ralph Notebroun was the chief bailiff of the west trithing,[92] and in 1299 Simon de Croxton was the bailiff of the north trithing.[93] Roger de Leke had been bailiff of the region of Holland for a short time under Richard de Harington, but had rendered up his office to that sheriff at a great county session.[94] In 1292 Adam de Lontone was the chief bailiff of Kesteven.[95] Finally, Ralph de Arnhal, sheriff of Lincolnshire in 1281-82, was mentioned as having five bailiffs: Gilbert le Moyne, Ralph de la Ford, Roger de Leke, Walter

[89] Some castle constables served simultaneously as receivers of money, as did William de Thorp in Norwich for William Gerberge, sheriff in 1294-95. In this case Thorp as receiver even had his own clerk, Roger le Noreis: E. 13/20, m. 25d.

[90] E. 13/27, m. 17d.

[91] E. 13/29, m. 45d.

[92] E. 13/23, m. 41.

[93] E. 13/25, m. 18.

[94] E. 13/6.

[95] E. 13/17, m. 39d.

Deudamor, and Adam de Grymolby.[96] They undoubtedly were the chief bailiffs of the five regions of Lincolnshire.[97]

Each of those chief bailiffs held his region at farm, that is, he obtained his position by bidding and committing himself to pay a certain sum, called his farm, to the sheriff. If he collected more than that amount from the proceeds of his office, it was his profit; if less, his loss. Geoffrey de Ross in 1318 committed himself to pay £67.6.8 as the annual farm for Holland.[98] It was alleged that the farm for the west trithing to which John de Dighton had obliged himself in 1299 was 52 marks.[99] The farming of offices was not unique to Lincolnshire at this time. Ralph de Alegate, for instance, held the whole county of Middlesex at farm from the sheriffs of London, William le Mazerer and Robert de Basing, for £5, excepting only half of all things forfeited and promising to acquit them of all amercements during the term.[100] The exceptionally small farm in this instance is indicative of the decline in common litigation in the Middlesex county court. Richard de Whitacre, sheriff, sued William de Walmeford, his receiver from 29 September 1306 to 29 September 1307, for the moneys arising from Exchequer summonses, farms, profits, and writs while he was sheriff, amounting to £1,300 from Leicestershire and £400 from Warwickshire. The sums were undoubtedly inflated; but Walmeford, with the precision appropriate to his office, did acknowledge having received the tidy sum of £562.11.5 3/4 from the Exchequer summonses and the farms.[101] Farming of offices had been normal earlier but was unpopular, because it tempted officials to promise to exact more from the countryside. The fifteenth-century sheriff's oath commits the sheriff to avoid farming out his offices.[102]

Each of the five regions of Lincolnshire had a court, and each of these courts had jurisdiction even in actions initiated by viscontiel writ. These courts were thus rather important and determined actions of replevin, mesne, annuity, account, detinue of charters, et cetera, unlike the hundred courts of other counties. The situation was anom-

---

[96] E. 13/10, m. 13.

[97] There is one mention of a bailiff of Lindsey, the northern half of Lincolnshire composed of the three trithings: Henry de Walmeford in 1297 (E. 13/22, m. 56). Since that is the only mention of such an office and since the trithings elsewhere related directly to the sheriff, this must have been an exceptional situation.

[98] E. 13/43, m. 4.

[99] E. 13/24, m. 13.

[100] E. 13/13, m. 6.

[101] CP. 40/187, m. 240.

[102] *EHD*, 4:555.

alous, since it meant that the regional courts virtually had the franchise of return of writs, even though they were not and never had been courts of liberties.[103] The precise relationship of county to trithing was a matter of dispute early in the thirteenth century,[104] and still in 1274 the court of common pleas felt that a false judgment writ that specified a suit which had been in the county court was sufficiently good for a suit that had actually been in the south trithing.[105] Soon thereafter, however, the trithings were accorded decisively independent status, since, when *recordari* writs issued out of chancery for the regional courts, they were in the *accedas* form which was appropriate for a court of a liberty.[106] As befitted such courts, each maintained its own plea rolls. Thus in an action of false judgment in 1293 the sheriff declined to record the plea, because the writ did not concord with the rolls of the court of Kesteven.[107] In 1313 Robert de Godesfeld was delayed by the fraudulent entry of process in the rolls of the south trithing, whereas the case had been brought in the county court.[108]

While the chief bailiff was not responsible for presiding over the regional court, he was responsible for the rolls of the region and for the execution of the viscontiel duties pertaining to his region. In executing a royal writ, Thomas de Burneham had sent his written mandate to the bailiff of Holland,[109] who would in turn be responsible for ordering his subbailiff in the hundred to perform the action ordered. In Kesteven in 1299 Elias Hereward was mentioned as the

[103] Below, chapter 9 at nn. 63-71.

[104] *CRR*, 12:434-35, 461.

[105] CP. 40/5, m. 66: "Et vicecomes nichil inde fecit set mandavit quod predicta loquela non fuit in comitatu etc set in suthtriddingo. Et quia omnes loquele que sunt in suthdrggo [sic] pertinent ad ipsum vicecomitem eo quod triddingum illud est de corpore comitatus sicut prius preceptum est vicecomiti quod in pleno comitatu etc recordari faciat etc."

[106] CP. 40/60, m. 32 (south trithing); CP. 40/60, m. 81d (Kesteven); CP. 40/67, m. 5d (Holland).

[107] CP. 52 morrow of the Purification, 21 Edward I: "Et quia hoc breve in nullo concordat cum rotulis ubi placitaverunt, ideo de hoc brevi nichil actum est."

[108] *CPR, 1307-1313*, pp. 549-50.

[109] E. 13/32, m. 27: "Et unde dicti Hugo [de Quappelade] et Fulco [Julian de Quappelade] protulerunt coram baronibus quoddam preceptum quod dicunt predictum vicecomitem per quendam Philippum clericum suum fecisse de quodam brevi quod sic receperat sub parvo sigillo justiciariorum de banco regis et quod mandavit sub sigillo suo ballivo de Holand ad capiendum Henricum Pye de Quappelade, Galfridum de Giddyng et Simonem Bere ita quod eos haberet coram rege in octabis sancti Hillarii proximo preterito ad respondendum Rogero filio Johannis militi de placito transgressionis. . . . contra formam sacramenti quod dictus vicecomes prestitit tempore quo officium suum admisit."

51

regional keeper and returner of writs;[110] each of the regions probably needed a similar clerk, together with a financial clerk to supervise the collection of money for the farm and of the debts exacted by Exchequer summonses, for which the chief bailiff would have to account to the sheriff. Lincolnshire thus had a middle tier of bureaucracy, a regional office with its own clerical staff involved in relaying orders already sent from the king's court to the sheriff, from the sheriff to the region, and finally from the region on down to the lowly bailiffs. Reports on action taken would then have had to have been relayed back from the bailiff to the regional headquarters, from there to the sheriff, and from the sheriff to Westminster. Lincolnshire was unique in having this intermediate tier of bureaucrats, with the possible exception of Yorkshire.[111] It is not unlikely, however, that the bailiffs of other counties, directly accountable to the sheriff without the intervention of a regional office, were rather more sophisticated than has been thought.

The lowest level of county bureaucracy was the hundred bailiff and his assistants. In Lincolnshire they were answerable to the regional bailiff; elsewhere, directly to the sheriff. In 1303, for instance, Thomas Prestman of Thimbleby was bailiff of Walshcroft wapentake in the north trithing.[112] Adam Bename was bailiff of Kirton wapentake in 1300 and of Skirbeck wapentake from 1301 to 1303, both wapentakes in Holland.[113] Hugh Amory, Robert Walding, and Philip Breton were the subbailiffs of Calceworth wapentake around 1292 who placed William Air under attachment for a plea in the court of common pleas.[114] Geoffrey Totel and John Manneby were the subbailiffs of Loutheske wapentake around 1293.[115] These people, their underlings—the cacherels and bedels who almost never make an appearance in the Exchequer rolls[116]—and the itinerant bailiff and his helpers were the ones actually engaged in distraining animals and collecting the money which was eventually conveyed to the sheriff for his account in the Exchequer.

Hundred bailiffs, like the regional bailiffs, purchased their office, except for the few hereditary bailiffs.[117] The sheriff's insurance of

[110] E. 13/25, m. 18: "clericus et retornator brevium domini regis in wappentacium de Kesteven."

[111] Information concerning Yorkshire riding personnel is very sparse.

[112] E. 13/26, mm. 62, 62d.

[113] E. 13/26, m. 32.

[114] E. 13/18, m. 43d.

[115] E. 13/19, m. 85.

[116] Cam, *Hundred*, p. 156.

[117] Ibid., p. 145.

their diligence was the contract by which the office was sold, several of which have survived.[118] In 1299, for instance, William de Batheleye purchased the office of bailiff of Agbrigg wapentake in Yorkshire for the term from Michaelmas 1299 to Michaelmas 1300. He undertook to pay the sheriff seventeen marks, half at mid-Lent, half on the Feast of the Exaltation of the Holy Cross, each due date thus falling a few weeks prior to the sheriff's own accounting date in the Exchequer. Batheleye further undertook that if he was convicted of any response made falsely, negligently, mendaciously, fictitiously, faultily, or badly, or if he did not prove fully satisfactory in the execution of any royal order whatsoever, whether it might concern the levying of royal debts or the suitable preparation of royal writs from term to term, or if he did not give a good and faithful answer, then the sheriff was allowed to punish him. That punishment would consist of the bailiff's removal from office and his replacement by someone of the sheriff's choice. No allowance would be made Batheleye from his farm, but he would still owe the sheriff the whole 17 marks to which he had committed himself. Furthermore, if the sheriff was amerced because of anything the bailiff or the bailiff's subbailiffs had done, Batheleye, his heirs, and his executors were likewise bound to acquit the sheriff not only of the amercement but also of any damages. Before entering office, Batheleye even had to find mainpernors that he would fulfil his obligations; they, of course, would also be liable if Batheleye defaulted without sufficient assets.[119] If the sheriff was answerable in the king's court for the actions of his underlings, they were likewise answerable to him. It is difficult to imagine a more comprehensive liability than Batheleye had to assume. On the bailiff's part, one must presume a knowledge of the law sufficient to fulfil his duties competently so that he could avoid amercements and make a profit. For the sheriff, such a contract provided substantial control over the bailiff, making him accountable to the sheriff in all his deeds even though the office had been purchased.

The bailiff was expected to collect the money for his farm and enough over that to yield him a fair profit from the perquisites of his office. In a few instances there were customary payments made

118 Ibid., p. 146.

119 E. 13/24, m. 48: "concedens quod si convictus fuerim de aliquo responso falso negligenter, mendacie, ficte, stulte, vel male facto, vel quocumque execucione seu mandato domini regis sive fuerit de debitis domini regis levandis seu de brevibus eiusdem arayandis de termino in terminum tempestive non plenarie satisfecerim, vel bonum et fidelem responsum non dederim, licebit tunc eidem domino Roberto me de ballia mea removere et alium pro libito suo constituere et quod nichil allocetur michi de firma predicte ballie sed quod ego et heredes mei et executores . . ."

to the bailiff from individuals or certain lands; in other cases, there were privileges to be exercised within the bailiwick. In most hundreds, however, the bailiffs received some form of payment for the duties actually performed.[120] The fees which Michael Dalton in the seventeenth century thought legitimate ran from a few pence for every stage in a personal action to a few shillings for every stage in a mixed or real action, the execution of the judgment in a case usually being somewhat more expensive. In levying money, the proper fee was something like 5 percent of any levy up to £100, and 2½ percent of the levy exceeding that figure.[121] Those fees might be indicative of the fees charged by bailiffs in the thirteenth and fourteenth centuries. Then one bailiff was charging 4d for every distraint made in levying the king's debts, and it was also alleged that it was general practice for bailiffs to take from debtors three halfpence for every sixpence or eightpence collected by Exchequer summons.[122] The worth of the hundred to the bailiff would depend not only on the population of the hundred, but also on the litigiousness of its inhabitants.

The sheriff thus presided over a large and at times frequently changing bureaucracy of executive and clerical personnel resident both in the sheriff's office and throughout the county. The number of persons employed varied from county to county. At one time the sheriff of Cornwall was summoned to appear in the Exchequer with his sixteen subbailiffs—who probably functioned as his bailiffs[123]—whereas the sheriff of Yorkshire a little later seems to have had only ten bailiffs.[124] The size of the bureaucracy, however, would have depended much more on the number of people employed by each bailiff than on the number of bailiffs responsible directly to the sheriff. Some bailiffs had not only subbailiffs, but also a hundred clerk.[125] In Lincolnshire the sheriff had only five chief bailiffs directly subordinate to himself, but the total number of people involved in the execution of his duties probably approached one hundred. Each official was bound to the next higher tier in the bureaucracy by oath and was

[120] Cam, *Hundred*, pp. 150-53.

[121] Michael Dalton, *The Office and Authority of Sheriffs* (London, 1682), pp. 184-85.

[122] Cam, *Hundred*, p. 151.

[123] Since all Cornish bailiffs were bailiffs as of fee (ibid., p. 145) and since only the undersheriff and the subbailiffs were summoned, it seems that the bailiffs might not have actually functioned. E. 13/12, m. 18d.

[124] E. 13/18, m. 12.

[125] E. 13/26, m. 11d: in Yorkshire in 1303 John Lungespeye was undersheriff, Stephen de Homerton was bailiff of the wapentake of Staincliffe, and Stephen had both a subbailiff and a clerk. Cam, *Hundred*, p. 153.

liable at law not only for his own deeds but also for the deeds of his underlings. In theory, then, this was a very tight organization. In practice, it was capable of handling a large amount of litigation and innumerable executive orders, with a concomitantly voluminous amount of scribal work. Moreover, it does not seem to have been as corrupt as the occasional virulent protest might indicate, although no one would say that it was a faultless servant of the public interest. The sheriff himself stood at the peak of the organizational pyramid in the county. He was the one who chose the most important of the county functionaries and who thus controlled the way to positions in the county bureaucracy. By the reign of Edward I it is probably mistaken to describe the sheriff solely in terms of his judicial or financial duties. He was also an organizer and administrator, coordinating his central staff, delegating duties to his subordinates, looking after the various royal courts in the county, checking to make sure the king's money and bailiff's farms were being properly collected, and occasionally executing an order that called for his personal attention. Most litigation in the county and much of the strength of the royal purse relied—successfully, as it turned out—on the sheriff and the organization he put together.

3

Suit and

Judges

❧

MEDIEVAL legal theory, the words of common-law writs, and modern historians identify suitors as the judges of the county, hundred, and baronial courts. They had a specific tenurial obligation to attend the court and render judgments; that attendance would be at every session, at a specific number of sessions each year, or even only in particular circumstances. Distrained to secure their attendance and amerced for absence, they could further be forced to delay or render immediately their judgment at the behest of a royal writ. They were also inevitably heavily amerced by the king's court if, at the complaint of the losing party, the judgment they had rendered was found to be false. Since the obligation of suit was tenurial and not based on professional qualifications, the position of the suitors as the judges of the lower courts has made the county and hundred courts seem irrevocably amateur to the historian, even if allowance is occasionally made for the knowledge gradually accumulated by long-term residents and attendants of a particular county or for suitors who were particularly active. Moreover, it has been assumed that the doctrine, the actual obligation, and the consequences of suit of court continued through and well beyond the thirteenth century. This chapter first examines the constitution of the county court of Cheshire—the court around which, because of superior documentation, discussion of suit and judges must revolve—and then examines the growth, meaning, and decline of suit as a meaningful obligation.

Cheshire was abnormal in several vital ways. Like Durham, before the end of the twelfth century it had already established itself as a franchise court, belonging to a private person and not to the king. Sometime around the reign of Edward I it was recognized as a county palatine, but its peculiarities derive not from the title but rather from its ancient and continued freedom from royal jurisdiction.[1] Unlike the normal county court, Cheshire's jurisdiction resembled that of the king's court. It entertained litigation by writs of assize—writs that were issued by the chancery of the earl of Chester—and had complete jurisdiction in crown pleas as well as the normal royal jurisdiction in real and personal litigation. Furthermore, pleas were not removeable before judgment from the county court to the king's court; the residents of Cheshire, except in extreme circumstances, looked no higher than Chester in litigation.[2] Similarly, the presiding officer in Cheshire county court was not the sheriff, but rather the justice of the earl. Review of cases was undertaken by the earl and his council, so that, when the king became the earl of Chester, such cases thereby found their way into the court of king's bench and occasionally into Parliament.[3] The relationship between justiciar and sheriff in Cheshire was similar to that between the king's justice and the normal sheriff in the rest of England. This sheriff, however, presided only over the sessions of the Cheshire hundreds, which met every two, or sometimes three, weeks.[4]

Cheshire also preserved several odd institutions. The grith serjeants, local police officers kept by the sheriff in areas in which the frankpledge system had not developed, survived at least into the fourteenth century.[5] The earl could receive felons from other counties

[1] In general see Geoffrey Barraclough, "The Earldom and County Palatine of Chester," *Trans. Hist. Soc. Lancashire and Cheshire* 103 (1951):23-59; and James W. Alexander, "New Evidence of the Palantine of Chester," *EHR* 85 (1970):715-29.

[2] In general see *Calendar of County Court . . . Rolls of Chester*, ed. R. Stewart-Brown, Publications of the Chetham Society, n.s., vol. 84 (Aberdeen, 1925).

[3] *CR, 1247-1251*, p. 349; Chester 29/21, m. 3 (1308), a case brought to the king in Parliament by a writ under privy seal before judgment: "E facez dire a Johan Fiton qe sil cleyme nul dreit en les tenementz contenuz en mesme la petition dont il dit estre disseisiz quil viegne a moustrer ent son dreit devant nous et nostre conseill et a nostre prochein parlement qe serra a treis semeines procheines apres cest seint Michel sil veie quil face a faire a son profit."

[4] Chester 29/25, m. 3, Mascy v Fouleshurst: "ipse est vicecomes Cestris' ad voluntatem domini regis tenens hundreda comitatus Cestris' de quindena in quindenam." Chester 29/22, m. 22d, Tofte v Walshe: "idem Rogerus de Tofte est unus iudicatorum in hundredo domini regis de Norwyco et sectam debet ad quemlibet hundredum de tribus septimanis in tres septimanas ut iudicator." Chester 29/22, m. 25, Fitz Brown v Earl of Lincoln: "ipse (Henry de Whytelegh) est hundredarius et minister domini regis de feodo de hundredo de Haulton [actually a liberty, not a hundred] et racione libertatis eiusdem hundredi in curia illius hundredi tenta apud Haulton vel alibi pro voluntate sua in hundredo predicto tenendo de quindena in quindenam habet cognicionem placitorum tam de debitis, contractibus, transgressionibus, convencionibus quam de aliis placitis infra libertatem hundredi predicti emergentibus ad sectam quorumcumque conquerencium." See also Chester 29/33, m. 7.

[5] Chester 29/33, m. 3d: "ubi de iure esse non deberent nisi undecim servientes pacis

fleeing into his county and enlist them in his advowry. With certain restrictions, they were given a new start in life; and the earl was provided with a pool of men with whom he could expect to prevail against the Welsh.[6] In procedural matters, those socage tenants whose income was estimated at less than 40s served as summoners for writs of summons.[7] In the judges of its courts also, Cheshire has been held unique, since there was a clear distinction drawn between the two sets of people obliged to attend the county court: the judges (*iudices, iudicatores*) and the suitors (*sectatores*). That distinction, foreign to almost every other region of England, causes obvious terminological difficulties when comparing Cheshire judges to the judges of the other county courts, who were often called suitors. Finally, Cheshire county court is undeniably unique as a lower court in having a set of extant plea rolls from the end of the thirteenth century to nearly modern times which provides accurate documentation of the court's consti-

---

et quatuor garcones tantum in comitatu Cestr' modo sunt viginti servientes pacis et duo magistri cum duobus equis et octo garconibus ad onerandum patriam de putura sua minus iuste." See R. Stewart-Brown, *The Serjeants of the Peace in Medieval England and Wales* (Manchester, 1936), pp. 1-32.

[6] In response to a petition by the men of the earl's advowry, a jury described the institution in Chester 29/30, m. 37: "quidam Ranulphus de Davenham senescallus domini Ranulphi quondam comitis Cestr' in comitatu isto, ipso domino Ranulpho in partibus Jerosolom agente, primo ordinavit et introduxit advocariam domini comitis in comitatu isto sub hac forma, quod quicumque nativi, felones, fugitivi, extranei, et adventitii de forinsecis comitatibus infra comitatum Cestr' moram facere volentes in eodem comitatu morari non permitterentur nisi eidem Ranulpho de Davenham pro licencia commorandi in comitatu isto redditum annuum prestassent ita quod idem Ranulphus de Davenham omnes adventicios, nativos, fugitivos, felones aliunde in comitatu isto venientes advocarie sue admisit per sic quod iidem homines annuum redditum, videlicet quidam eorum sex denarios quidam plus et quidam minus veluti arcus, sagittas, barbatas, et huiusmodi, pro licencia ab ipso optinenda ad commorandum in patria solverent. Idemque Ranulphus de Davenham post mortem eorundem hominum advocarie ex consuetudine similiter preter redditum illum percepit meliorem armatum quem habuerunt die obitus sui tantum." The jury continued on to say that the custom had been continued to their day, but that the men of the advowry were now being called upon to put in a twice-yearly appearance. The twice-yearly appearances were therefore abandoned. Some other cases concerning the earl's advowry: Chester 29/29, mm. 3, 21d; Chester 29/18, m. 14d (the rolls of the advowry mentioned); Chester 29/20, m. 19 (two men arrested during the county session for causing an affray in the garden outside the county hall claimed the liberty of the advowry and were delivered to the guard of the advowry of the constable of Chester).

[7] Chester 29/32, m. 20, Hendebody v Ratheboun: "tanquam ballivus vicecomitis Cestri' in hundredo de Broxton . . . dicit quod talis est consuetudo in comitatu Cestr' quod omnes illi qui tenent terras et tenementa in eodem comitatu in socagium que non attingunt valorem quadraginta solidorum per annum et non per servicium militare debent facere summoniciones assisarum, juratorum, et brevium quociens per prefatum vicecomitem seu bedellos suos super hoc ex parte domini comitis Cestr' super hoc fuerunt onerati." This custom was not disputed by the opposition, who only alleged that his land was worth more than 40s. See also mm. 8d, 17d.

tution. This documentation, except for the first few rolls which were long ago calendared, as yet have been scarcely touched by historians.[8]

The constitution of Cheshire's courts can be examined thoroughly only in the late thirteenth and fourteenth centuries. It is hazardous to assume from a few late thirteenth-century examples that Cheshire judges had some direct connection with the judges mentioned in various Danelaw territories in the Domesday Book or with the Danish lawmen,[9] or even with the judges who appear in the pipe roll of 31 Henry I.[10] Nor can one assume that the judges had to be chosen from a specific set of people who passed the knowledge of Cheshire legal custom down from father to son[11] or that there were fewer judges than mere suitors.[12] All these assumptions seem wrong or, at least, unjustified by the evidence.

The hundred courts, the courts of liberties, and the county court of Cheshire distinguished between suit owed as a suitor and suit owed as a judge. The sheriff was obliged, for instance, at least by 1309, to insure that at least four people in every hundred owed suit as a judge. In that year Roger de Tofte had been exacted as a judge of Northwich hundred, had defaulted, and was amerced. When he was distrained, he brought his case before the county court and claimed that he performed suit as a suitor and not as a judge. The jury agreed with Tofte, and they were therefore required to name the fourth judge, since there had to be four judges in every hundred: *"in quolibet hundredo esse debent quatuor iudicatores ad minus."* They named the lord of Tatton.[13] A similar distraint was made by judgment of the judges and suitors of Eddisbury hundred in 1311.[14] Then, in 1312 Sheriff Richard de Fouleshurst executed a distraint by judgment of the suitors and judges of Bucklow hundred on one he believed to be

---

[8] The survival of the rolls is undoubtedly the result of the royal assumption of the earldom, partly the result of the higher nature of Cheshire county court and the greater authority in Cheshire of the rolls. The residents of both Cheshire and Durham had to petition Parliament to be allowed to aver the county against the rolls, an averment taken for granted in other counties: *Rotuli Parliamentorum*, 6 vols. (London, 1767), 2:171.

[9] G. T. Lapsley, "Buzones," *EHR* 47 (1932):557.

[10] Ibid., p. 558.

[11] *Calendar of County Court . . . Rolls of Chester*, ed. Stewart-Brown, pp. xxxii-xxxviii.

[12] *A Middlewich Chartulary*, ed. Joan Varley and James Tait, 2 vols., Chetham Society, vols. 105, 108 (Manchester, 1941-1944), 1:62.

[13] Chester 29/22, m. 22d, Tofte v Walshe: "dicit quod ipse nec antecessores sui numquam fuerunt iudicatores in eadem curia facientes sectam ad predictam curiam ut iudicator, set fecerunt sectam ad eandem curiam ut sectator et non ut iudicator."

[14] Chester 29/24, m. 15, Bundelegh v Fouleshurst.

a judge: Robert de Mascy of Tatton. Mascy denied in the county court that he owed such a suit, and the jury upheld his protest. Once again, they were required to name a fourth judge to complete the requisite number for the hundred.[15] Thomas Tuchet's court of Tattenhall in Broxton hundred had both judges and suitors,[16] as did the court of the earl of Lincoln in Haughton.[17] The borough courts of Chester,[18] Middlewich,[19] Northwich,[20] and Macclesfield[21] all had at least judges, as did the court of the liberty of Caldy in the Wirral peninsula,[22] the king's court of Willaston,[23] and the court of Weaverham, which belonged to the abbey of Vale Royal.[24] There can be no doubt that the distinction between judges and suitors was normal in Cheshire courts and not merely an oddity of a few areas in Cheshire.

[15] Chester 29/25, m. 3, Mascy v Fouleshurst: (the jury answered that) "predictus Robertus tamquam iudicator nullam sectam debet ad hundredum de Buckelowe nec ipse nec antecessores sui nec tenentes manerii de Tatton aliquam sectam tamquam iudicator uncquam facere consueverunt nec de iure facere debuerunt, quia predictum manerium nuncquam fuit inde oneratum. Et quia in quolibet hundredo esse debent quatuor iudicatores ad minus et iidem iuratores predictum Robertum calumpniatum per vicecomitem pro quarto iudicatore etc, inde acquietaverunt, iniunctum est eisdem iuratoribus quod dicant quis sectam illam tamquam iudicator facere debeat et quod tenementum inde onerari. Et predicti iuratores dicunt quod Plumlegh ab antiquo inde oneratus fuit et quicumque fuerunt inde tenentes tamquam iudicator sectam illam de iure facere debent."

[16] Chester 29/26, m. 25d, Pate v Tuchet: "ipse et antecessores sui habuerunt quandam curiam de quindena in quindenam et quod ipse et omnes domini maneriorum in comitatu Cestrie tentorum per baroniam secundum consuetudinem Cestris' hactenus optentam habent cognicionem placitorum parvarum transgressionum in curiis suis de omnibus tenentibus infra feodum et dominium suum . . . [and because of a trespass committed by Pate, he was summoned to court but did not come, wherefore] per iudices et sectatores eiusdem curie consideratum fuit quod idem Willelmus attachiaretur essendi ad curiam proximo sequentem, videlicet, a dicto die in xv dies etc."

[17] Chester 29/10, m. 7d, Dutton v Court of Haughton.

[18] *Chartulary or Register of the Abbey of Saint Werburgh, Chester*, ed. James Tait, 2 vols., Chetham Society, vols. 79, 82 (Manchester, 1920-1923), 2:341; *Selected Rolls of the Chester City Courts*, ed. A. Hopkins, Chetham Society, 3d series, vol. 2 (Manchester, 1950), pp. l-li.

[19] *Middlewich Chartulary*, 1:30.

[20] IPM, Edward I, 2:478. That borough also had a court for adjudicating matters between outsiders, which met two-weekly: Chester 29/29, m. 28.

[21] SC. 2/155/85 (1348).

[22] Chester 29/38, m. 6, Kirkeby v Merton. The court met three-weekly.

[23] IPM, Edward I, 2:161, called a hundred as was usual with liberties in Cheshire.

[24] *The Ledger Book of Vale Royal Abbey*, ed. John Brounbill, The Record Society, vol. 68 (Edinburgh, 1914), p. 110. Six of these judges were lords of manors; three additional individuals were required also to find a judge. W. O. Ault, *Private Jurisdictions in England* (New Haven, 1923), pp. 252-56, states without amplification that nine judges were owed. Lapsley, "*Buzones*," p. 560 follows him without comment. It seems nevertheless that the three individuals found one judge, so that there were only seven judges in all.

The earliest clear reference to that distinction is in 1216 in the Cheshire Magna Carta, for that county, because of the power of the earl of Chester there, merited its own charter granted by the earl. It stipulated that, should the judges or suitors of county and hundred make a default, the judges would be amerced only 2s and the suitors would only be amerced 12d.[25] The phrase "judges and suitors" appears frequently enough in the county plea rolls to establish that there was a definite distinction drawn between them there. Furthermore, a list of the known judges of the county shows that there were at least two from each of six Cheshire hundreds and at least five from Eddisbury hundred.[26] The seventh Cheshire hundred, Macclesfield, was a liberty and thus would not have had judges proper in the county court.

Judgments in the county court of Cheshire were described as issuing from the judges or from the judges and suitors. The difference between the two formulae must be in part conjectural. In *fitz Richard v Bulkyleigh*, for instance, the dispute concerned a claim of escheat for land which had belonged to a self-confessed thief who had been captured by the hue and cry and beheaded by the grith serjeants. The legal point at issue was whether a writ that specified that the death had occurred by hanging—and it was maintained that such a writ would have been good elsewhere in England for odd executions—was suitable in such a case in Cheshire. The justice enjoined the judges and suitors to proceed to judgment at the session after the pleading had occurred, the arguments were recited before the judges, and the plaintiff was nonsuited because the judges found that his pleading had varied from the information given in his writ.[27] The judges, by this form of recital, seem to have rendered the judgment, even though the suitors were somehow considered in the process. A record from

---

[25] *Chartulary . . . of Saint Werburgh*, 2:104; confirmed later in Chester 29/22, m. 45. See Chester 29/33, m. 7, Verdun v Spenser: a default of suit owed two-weekly for which Verdun "tendit eisdem Thome et Johanni duodecim denarios pro defalta predicta prout decet uni sectatori secundum consuetudinem comitatus Cestris'."

[26] Unless otherwise noted, the source is Chester 29/50, m. 14, fitz Thomas v Fyton: Wirral Hundred: Neston (*IPM*, Edward I, 2:161), Blacon; Broxton Hundred: Pulford, Coddington, Cholmondeley (Chester 34/1, m. 7; the suit for Cholmondeley was not owed after the early thirteenth century); Eddisbury Hundred: Clotton, Tiverton, Haughton, Alpraham, Wettenhall; Bucklow Hundred: Hale, Mere, Plumley; Northwich Hundred: Leftwich, Moulton (See also Chester 29/82, m. 1), Twemlow; Nantwich Hundred: Crewe (*IPM*, Edward I, 4:179; perhaps not a judge), Hatherton, Buerton.

[27] Chester 29/30, m. 28: "Iniunctum est iudicatoribus et sectatoribus comitatus per iusticiarium ex parte domini comitis quod procedant ad iudicium faciendum si etc; per quod, recitatis racionibus predictis coram predictis iudicatoribus et plenius intellectis, videtur eisdem iudicatoribus quod cum predictus Ricardus deferat . . ." The case also appears in Chester 29/29, m. 26.

the earl of Lincoln's court of Haughton more specifically mentioned that in 1298 "the judges of that court with the assent of the suitors of that court decided" the judgment.[28]

Only in 1325, however, is there a precise description of court procedure for the Cheshire county court. In that year a memorandum on county procedure was entered in the rolls on 4 June.[29]

> Memorandum: that at this county session the justice asked the judges and suitors of the abovesaid county why, whereas the abovesaid county should be held by the justice, and the duty of justices elsewhere throughout all England is to give judgments and decisions by themselves in all pleas before them, they claim to take the place of the justice in making judgments and decisions, a claim which does not appear consonant to right. He also asked how and in what way they made judgments.
>
> They said that their ancestors, judges and suitors of the abovesaid county, from time immemorial to the present have rendered the judgments and decisions of the abovesaid county both in pleas of the crown and in all other pleas whatsoever, excepting this, that if any royal minister shall have transgressed in anything against the lord of the county or the king who shall be earl of Chester at the time, the justice at the time shall judge him as it seems proper to himself. And they say that they hold their lands and tenements by the abovesaid service.
>
> They also say that this is the way to proceed in rendering judgments. Should there be any dissent among them in rendering a judgment, they will have day for advisement until the next county and, if necessary, through three sessions at most. Then, if they do not accord, the judgment will be made according to the decision of the greater part of the abovesaid judges and suitors. And they say that the judges should first say what seems to them should be the judgment and the suitors should afterwards consent or contradict, and so finally judgment will be given according to the greater part of them as has been said.
>
> And they say that if they give any false judgment among them in any plea of the abovesaid county the lord king at his own suit or at the suit of some other party shall make the abovesaid record and process come before the king himself or his justices by his writ. They shall be allowed time to look over the abovesaid record and process through three county sessions after the arrival of the writ and to consult among themselves if anything should be emended, and they will emend it. And then they will send the record and process to the court, and not before. And if any error should be found in the abovesaid judgment by the

---

[28] Chester 29/10, m. 7d, Dutton v Court of Haughton: "Et iudicatores illius curie per assensum sectatorum prefate curie consideraverunt quod predicti Petrus et Robertus fuerunt indefensi."

[29] Appendix III.

abovesaid justices and it is revoked and annulled before them, they will give the lord king one hundred pounds for that false judgment, and this they will do as often as they give any false judgment in any plea as soon as anything of this kind is revoked and annulled.

And they say that they and their ancestors have always, up to the present, used and enjoyed this custom etc.

Regrettably, there are problems even in such an admirably clear document. The easiest interpretation would accord the suitors rough equality with the judges. The judges thus would merely have had precedence in the legal argument, but they could be overruled if the suitors opposed them, since the majority vote which determined the judgment would be taken from the combined body of judges and suitors. That interpretation cannot be substantiated from actual cases. Rather, the document seems to mean that the judges would first discuss, and the suitors would afterwards give their opinions. A vote was then taken in each group. The majority of the judges decided the judgment. If the majority of the suitors accorded with them, the suitors were joined with the judges in the record as rendering the judgment. If not, the judges alone were listed as having rendered the judgment. Only such an interpretation can explain cases such as *fitz Richard v Bulkyleigh*, mentioned above, in which both judges and suitors were enjoined to render judgment, but in which the judgment itself was enrolled as having been rendered by the judges, with no reference to the suitors.

The case which most clearly illustrates this view is *fitz Thomas v Fyton*, an action of attaint on an assize of novel disseisin. The assize had been held in county court also, and judgment had been in favor of the plaintiff, fitz Thomas. The attaint was pleaded on 27 April 1339, and then was adjourned twenty times in succession because of the difficulty in securing the presence of all the parties concerned. On 24 October 1341 the attaint jury reversed the decision of the original assize, but the case was adjourned six weeks for judgment. On that day Thomas Fyton asked that judgment be rendered in accordance with the verdict, but fitz Thomas objected on a technicality. He alleged that the county session should only last from the first hour of Tuesday until sunset the following Wednesday; any verdict given after that time was invalid and discontinued the case. Fyton, of course, defended the verdict, maintaining that the verdict had been given in the presence of the justice, judges, and suitors and had been delivered before the adjournment of the court and before the fixing of the next county day. Moreover, he pointed out that the verdict had been received by the justice, judges, and suitors and had been enrolled and the parties had been given their day for judgment. The point at issue was a nicety of county custom, and of the thirty-one judges in court, sixteen ruled in favor of fitz Thomas; fifteen in favor of Fyton. Fyton would therefore have had to begin his two-and-a-half year battle over again despite a verdict in his favor. The salient point, however, is that after the vote by the judges, the roll mentions that it was the custom of the county that, when the greater part of judges and suitors agreed to render a judgment, such a judgment should be given according to the assent of that greater part. Only judges, however, were mentioned as rendering the judgment. Furthermore, when the king's court reversed that judgment, the sixteen judges who had voted against Fyton were listed for the amercement. No suitors were mentioned. In such a close decision, it is reasonable to believe that the suitors had voted for Fyton and were therefore disassociated from the judgment. The judges, in short, had determined the case.[30] This case would thus strongly indicate that the formula "the judges and suitors considered" would be used only when the suitors agreed with the judges.

There are other indications of such an interpretation. The formula provided by the court of Haughton in 1298 was "the judges rendered judgment with the assent of the suitors," thereby suggesting a supportive and not a determining role for the suitors.[31] The role of the judges was always emphasized. In 1402 a judgment was prefaced by the following formula: "it was decided by the judges of the abovesaid county, to whom pertain all judgments of pleas both by writs and by bills in whatsoever county sessions of Cheshire held at Chester."[32] In 1403 the judges were asked to render judgment. They needed further advisement and retired into a room within the hall of pleas. They returned almost immediately, however, and rendered judgment. The suitors were not mentioned in this process, and it is difficult to see how they could have contributed significantly to a judgment made in this way.[33] Even as late as 1500, however, the phrase "judges and

---

[30] Chester 29/50, mm. 13-14: "Et quia consuetudo eiusdem comitatus talis est quod ubi maior pars iudicatorum et sectatorum eiusdem comitatus consentit alicui iudicio reddendo, procedendum est ad iudicium secundum assensum eiusdem maioris partis etc., videtur curie hic quod predictus processus discontinuatur etc.

[31] Below, chapter 9, at nn. 94, 95.

[32] Chester 29/106, m. 17d: "consideratum est per iudicatores comitatus predicti ad quos omnia iudicia placitorum tam per brevia quam per billas in quibuscumque comitatibus Cestrie tentis apud Cestre pertinent . . .''

[33] Chester 29/107, m. 8d, Grey v Donne: "Et super hoc iidem iudicatores per pre-

suitors" continues to appear in the rolls.[34] The suitors in all probability were never in a position to determine judgments against the decision of the judges; the most they could aspire to would have been argument and persuasion.[35]

The process for reversing judgments which the memorandum described can be verified from the rolls. In 1292 the county court had already claimed that it enjoyed the privilege both of having three sessions delay between the reception of the writ and the sending of the record to the king's court and also of emending the record before sending it if they found any error. That claim specified that when the writ came, the barons, seneschals, and judges were to be summoned to hear, examine, and—if need be—emend the record.[36] Such cases, however, were rare before the reign of Edward III. In *Lasceles v Prior of Birkenhead* around 1330 the judges examined the record of the previous case, found that they had erred, reversed their decision, and continued with the case.[37] Two decades later in *Leycester v Cha-*

dictum iusticiarium ad iudicium predictum reddendum onerati in quandam cameram infra aulam placitorum hic ad capiendum avisamentum de iudicio suo predicto reddendo inierunt et instanter postmodum in aulam predictam coram prefato iusticiario revenerunt et iidem iudicatores per predictum iusticiarium quesiti si ipsi de iudicio suo predicto reddendo avisati sint etc., qui dicunt quod sic."

[34] *Middlewich Chartulary*, 1:62.

[35] Something here must be said of Wormelow Hundred in Herefordshire. A *sicut pluries* writ of false judgment (Abbot of Lyra v de la More) on a writ of right heard there specified that the sheriff should distrain "omnes sectatores curie nostre de Wormelawe et eciam omnes homines ad quos pertinent omnia iudicia facere in eadem curia." A panel appended to that writ lists both groups. Forty-eight suitors are listed, almost all of whom seem to have been Welsh. Only nineteen of the suitors were able to be distrained. The separate group to whom it pertained to make judgments were the master of the Knights Templar in England (distrained by 100s), Richard le Brut (40s), Richard de Baskervill (40s), John le Rous (40d), William de Tryllek (20d), Roger fitz Wronoc (20d), Yenan ap Gurgenon (20d), Philip ap Eynon (40d), Griffin ap Yenan (nil), and the prior of the Hospital of St. John of Jerusalem in England (who had a prohibition against distraint for suit in return for a payment of 40s/yr). Brut and Baskervill each held the lands of two of the judges, so that originally and still in theory there were twelve judges of Wormelow Hundred. There might be a temptation to compare this hundred with Cheshire, but that would be wrong. Wormelow was both a hundred and a manor court, and that can explain the lower order of suitors there. Cheshire county court was not also a manor court, nor do the suitors seem a necessarily lesser kind of people—at least in the degree exhibited at Wormelow. (Cp. 52 octave Michaelmas, 30 Edward I [loose in Box AD]; see also CP. 52 month Michaelmas, 29 Edward I [loose in Box AC]; the case is likewise well recorded in the plea rolls.)

[36] *Select Cases in the Court of King's Bench*, ed. G. O. Sayles, 7 vols., Selden Society, vols. 55, 57, 58, 74, 76, 82, 88 (London, 1936-1971), 2:112.

[37] Chester 29/42, m. 8: "per quod predicti iudicatores habito inde avisamento trium comitatuum post adventum brevis predicti ad corrigendum errorem si quis foret secundum consuetudinem comitatus Cestrie ad comitatum hic die martis proxima post festum sancte Trinitatis proximo sequens consideraverunt quod loquela predicta in

terton the judges had the record read aloud and then required the plaintiff to specify the error he found in it. He replied that the grand assize which had given verdict against him had been composed of fifteen jurors, whereas there should have been only twelve. The judges agreed that such procedure was erroneous, revoked and annulled their earlier judgment; and the parties were summoned for the next session to continue their case, presumably to place the issue once again before a grand assize.[38] Finally, in the one case found in which the king's court examined the record and found the judgment false, the amercement placed on the court was the £100 that the memorandum specified. That amercement, however, fell only on those who had supported the false judgment; those who had dissented were not amerced.[39]

The memorandum states that the judges and suitors held their lands and tenements by the service of rendering judgments. While this was surely an adequate explanation for them, it is necessary to define more precisely the nature of suit, who or what owed suit, and how the obligation was performed. Suit was owed both by judges and by suitors and was owed by both tenants-in-chief and rere-vassals. Hugh de Pulford, for instance, was found to have owed suit for the manors and tenements he held from Simon, son of Ralph de Ormesby.[40] Thomas Danyers, around 1355, was found to have held two acres of land from the earl by baronial service in proportion to his tenement, but it was for the manor of Hale which Danyers held from Hamo de Mascy that he owed the service of attending the county court every six weeks and rendering judgments in all pleas and plaints there before the earl and his justice. That service was explicitly men-

---

eodem statu quo prius ante iudicium redditum fuerat et quod partes predicte premunite essent ad procedendum et defendendum in forma iuris etc." See also Chester 29/52, m. 15.

[38] Chester 29/67, m. 73.

[39] Chester 29/50, m. 14d, fitz Thomas v Fyton: the justice ordered the sheriff to reverse the previous judgment in accordance with the judgment in king's bench "et quod de terris et catallis iudicatorum de Hale, Plumlegh, Mere, Twemelowe, Lefoewych, Multon, Wetenhale, Teverton, Clotton, Halghton, Alperham, Pulford, Codynton, Blakene, Hatherton, et Buryrton qui predictum iudicium reddiderunt fieri faciat centum libras pro iudicio illo tamquam erroneo revocato et adnullato secundum consuetudinem in comitatu Cestrie hactenus usitatam etc." The record of the case is also contained in KB. 27/330, m. 129-129c. The justices there, having conferred with the chancellor "et aliis discretis de consilio domini regis cum magna et diligenti deliberacione" ruled that the judgment was erroneous, arguing that it had been properly continued according to the written record. The question remains, however, whether the verdict should have been enrolled in the first place. Once the verdict had been enrolled, however, it seems that there was no way to discontinue the plea by that kind of exception.

[40] *IPM*, Edward I, 2:478.

tioned as a great serjeanty.[41] It is clear from other sources that the suit was owed as a judge.[42] When Danyers died, his wife still held land from the earl, but it was for the three messuages and forty acres which she held from the lord of Dunham that she owed suit. That land was now described as a socage tenure.[43] About the same time, Richard de Wynynton was found to have been obliged to attend county sessions and render judgments as service for the manor of Winnington, which he held from three different lords.[44] The abbey of Vale Royal, however, held most of Twemlow directly from the king as earl, and it had to petition the king to be relieved of the burdens of the service of a judge. They showed how the tenements had been granted them in free alms with no secular service due, so that the king granted their petition.[45] Suit was therefore owed by both rere-vassals and tenants-in-chief and was not solely attached to knight's fees.

Suit was due primarily from a manor, and from a person only as the tenant of the manor. Robert de Mascy was distrained for the suit as a judge due from the manor of Tatton to Bucklow hundred; the jury returned that the manor of Plumley was anciently burdened with that suit.[46] Richard de Wynynton rendered judgments at county for his manor of Winnington.[47] Richard, son of Hugh de Chelmondelegh,

[41] Chester 3/3, 28 Edward III, no. 2: "idem Thomas tenuit coniunctim feoffatus cum uxore sua manerium de Hale de predicto Hamone de Mascy per servicium veniendi ad comitatum Cestr' de sex septimanis in sex septimanas et ibidem coram domino comite Cestr' et justiciario suo reddendi iudicia in omnibus placitis et querelis ibidem motis vel movendis, quod quidem servicium est magna seriantia."

[42] Above, n. 39.

[43] Chester 3/5, 38 Edward III, no. 5: "et fuit seisita et tenuit die quo obiit in dominico suo ut de feodo tria mesuagia et xl acras terre de domino de Dunham in socagio per servicium inveniendi unum iudicem in comitatu Cestrie." That land was valued at 46s 8d per annum; see above, at n. 7, for one significance of the 40s yearly value of land.

[44] Chester 3/3, 31 Edward III, no. 3: "Item dicunt quod predictus Ricardus de Wynynton debet esse in propria persona ad quemlibet comitatum Cestrie ad reddendum iudicia pro manerio de Wynynton."

[45] Chester 28/58, m. 14d: "Peticio: A conseil lour tres honourable seignour . . . counte de Cestre moustront les seous chapeleyns et moyns abbe et covent de Valereal qe par la ou ils sount enfeoffez par la chartre le roi Edward aiel . . . de les troys parties de la ville de Twemelowe a tenir en pure et perpetuel almoigne sanz nul seculer service ou charge a lui faire et par mesme la chartre graunta qe eux et lours successours fussent quite a touz jours des shires et des hundredes et de touz autres seutes . . . la veignount les ministres lour dite seignour et lour destreynount outraiousement de jour en autre de trover un iuggeour a counte de Cestre et aussint de contribution faire a la paiement de les deniers forfes par reson des ascuns iuggementz devant ces heures en le dite counte renduz et puis reverses encountre les ditz chartre et confermement, de quele duresce ils priont remedie . . ." See also The Ledger Book, p. 43.

[46] Above, n. 15.

[47] Above, n. 44.

answered for the suit due from his manor to hundred and county.[48] There are also, it must be admitted, several specific references to suit being owed from townships rather than manors. Thus Richard de Fouleshurst specified that many townships owed suit to the hundred courts, some as judges and some as suitors. As sheriff, he had distrained John le Cocker for the suit which Pickmere township owed to Bucklow hundred. Cocker denied owing the suit, so that the sheriff was ordered to distrain all the free tenants of the township to show who owed the suit or why they did not owe suit. The presumption, obviously, was that every township owed suit unless it could prove otherwise. The ones distrained, however, were simply Cocker's coparceners and fellow lords of the township.[49] That phrase, lord of the township (*dominus ville*), occurs again. In a different case Fouleshurst stated that the township of Haughton owed suit and that the earl had been seised of the suit from that township by the hands of the lord of the township.[50] Such terminology, strange to the historian who

---

[48] Chester 34/1 (1357): "Et Ricardus venit et quo ad quietum esse de sectis comitatus, hundredi de Dunstan, et de uno iudice inveniendo dicit quod quidam Ranulphus quondam comes Cestrie per cartam suam concessit Hugoni de Chelmondele antecessori predicti Ricardi cuius heres ipse est et heredibus suis quietanciam secte comitatus Cestrie et hundredi predicti et de uno iudice inveniendo etc. Et profert hic in curia cartam predictam que premissa testatur in hec verba: 'Omnibus presentibus et futuris has litteras visuris et audituris Ranulphus de Cestr' et Linc' salutem. Sciatis me hac presenti carta mea confirmasse Hugoni de Chelmundelegh et heredibus suis de me et heredibus meis quietanciam secte comitatus Cestrie et hundredi de Dunstan et de uno iudice quem nobis debuit de terra sua de Chelmundele, quod volumus et firmiter precipimus quod predictus Hugo et heredes sui quieti sint de predicta secta et de predicto iudice de me et heredibus meis.' " Notice particularly the separation of suit and the obligation of finding a judge.

[49] Chester 29/27, m. 6, Cocker v Fouleshurst: "Dicit enim quod ipse est vicecomes domini comitis Cestrie in comitatu Cestrie ad voluntatem domini comitis tenens hundreda per totum comitatum Cestrie excepto hundredo de Macclesfeld, ad que hundreda plures ville eorundem debent sectam, quedam ut sectatores et quedam ut iudicatores. Et quia villata de Pykemere debet sectam facere ad hundredum de Bokelowe ut sectator et sectam illam iam subtraxit, idem Ricardus tamquam ballivus domini comitis de hundredo predicto pro predicta secta subtracta de predicta villata predictum iumentum nomine districcionis cepit sicut ei bene licuit . . . Et preceptum est vicecomiti quod distringat omnes liberos tenentes eiusdem ville quod sint ad proximum comitatum ostensuri quis vel qui illorum onerari debent si domino comiti debeatur vel ad ipsos exhonerandos si non debeatur etc." At a later session, m. 11, the case was repleaded: "Et quia villata de Pykemere sectam debet ad hundredum de Buckelowe ut sectator prout per rotulos de sectis domino comiti debitis sibi liberatos invenit et secta illa per predictos Johannem, Johannem, et Hugonem filium Henrici dominos et parcenarios predicte ville iam subtracta extitit, idem Ricardus tamquam vicecomes etc." They replied that "ipsi nec eorum antecessores domini et parcenarii predicte ville nuncquam fecerunt aliquam sectam ad hundredum de Buckelowe ut sectator nec ut iudicator nec ipsi de iure aliquam sectam ibidem facere debent nec aliqua secta de predicta villata ad predictum hundredum uncquam debita fuit."

[50] Chester 29/24, m. 15, Bundelegh v Fouleshurst: "ad quem hundredum [Eddisbury]

---

would carefully distinguish between manors and townships and who would prefer to think that only manors could properly have lords, would have been common in a county like Cheshire in which manors and townships were largely coextensive. There is, moreover, one instance of three-quarters of a township owing a suit, but "township" should probably here be interpreted as "manor."[51] Finally, the earliest and most official source mentioning the matter, the Cheshire Magna Carta, grants the privilege that one could acquit all the suits due from manors held in demesne—townships are not mentioned—by the service of sending a seneschal.[52] The emphasis on lordship and the specific mentions of suits owed by manors is sufficient evidence that in Cheshire the manor was the basic unit that owed suit, not the township or a person.

The obligation imposed by suit could be fulfilled either in person or by a qualified person sent in one's place. Thus Richard de Wynynton had to appear in person,[53] as did Thomas Danyers.[54] When Danyers died, however, his wife was obliged to find a judge, presumably because a woman was presumed incapable of being a suitable judge.[55] Except for the instances of Wynynton and Danyers, however, the obligation was always stated in terms of finding a judge. Richard, son of Hugh de Chelmondelegh, claimed that he should be quit of finding a judge for his manor at county and hundred.[56] Roger de Montalt was to find a judge.[57] Hugh de Pulford was obliged to find

---

villata de Halghton de qua predictus Petrus est parcenarius dominii eiusdem villate debet unam sectam de hundredo in hundredum tanquam iudicator etc., de qua secta predictus dominus rex et antecessores sui hucusque seisiti fuerunt de dominis eiusdem ville etc., et quia ad hundredum tentum predicto die lune etc., villata de Halghton fecit defaltam consideratum fuit per sectatores et iudicatores eiusdem hundredi quod predicta villata distringatur. . . . Et predictus Petrus bene cognovit quod predicta villata de Halghton debet unam sectam ad quemlibet hundredum de Edesburi tanquam iudicator etc., set . . . dicit quod villata de Halghton ad hundredum de Edesburi tentum predicto die lune etc., nullam defaltam fecit, eo quod quidam Willelmus de Halghton unus parcenarius eiusdem villate . . . interfuit." The possibility of more than one suit being owed from Haughton—a possibility which would have been present only if suit was based on manors—was admitted, because a jury was taken on the point; it reported that "de villata de Halghton non debetur nisi unica secta ad hundredum de Edesburi tantum tanquam iudicator, quam quidem sectam Willelmus de Halghton ad quemlibet hundredum ibidem facit."

[51] Above, n. 45.
[52] The Chartulary of Saint Werburgh, 2:9.
[53] Above, n. 44.
[54] Above, n. 41.
[55] Above, n. 43.
[56] Above, n. 48.
[57] IPM, Edward I, 2:161.

a judge at each county.[58] The abbey of Vale Royal was dispensed from the obligation of finding a judge from Twemlow.[59] The lord of Tatton was said to be obliged to support a judge at hundred court.[60] Three individuals were obliged to find a judge at the court of Weaverham.[61] Finding a qualified person to attend in one's stead must be taken as the normal method of doing suit to Cheshire county court by the reign of Edward I.

The standards by which judges were measured were legal and not financial or aristocratic. The people who owed the suits were the ones who were assuredly wealthy and well-placed in Cheshire society. If they themselves were competent, of course, they could attend in person; the obligation normally stated that they were to find a judge, and that was undoubtedly what most people who owed suit did. The measure of the legal competence of the judges is the sophistication of the argument in the county court; that, in turn, can be inferred from those who were pleaders there. The names of pleaders began to be enrolled in the Cheshire rolls only at the beginning of the reign of Edward II, just as the names of pleaders in the Bench began to be enrolled in the plea rolls only around 1292. Just as in the Bench, however, pleaders must have been active in the county court of Cheshire well before that date. Some of the Cheshire pleaders were men of little national significance and indeterminable competence: men like Roger de Capinhurst, a pleader in Cheshire county court in 1326 and a merchant of Chester.[62] He was apparently succeeded as pleader by his son, John de Capinhurst.[63] There were also, however, pleaders

---

[58] Ibid., 2:478. Even without the county memorandum this reference refutes the idea that judges were like suitors for afforcement of court in other counties, suggested by Ault, *Private Jurisdictions*, p. 256, and followed by *Calendar of County Court . . . Rolls of Chester*, ed. Stewart-Brown, p. xxxvi.

[59] Above, n. 45.

[60] Chester 29/22, m. 22d, Tofte v Walshe: "Et predicti juratores quesiti pro rege ex quo idem Rogerus non est iudicator hundredi predicti et in hundredo predicto quatuor iudicatores ad minus esse debeat quis onus predicte secte ut iudicator de iure supportare debeat, dicunt quod dominus de Tatton onus predicte secte ut iudicator supportare debet de iure. Ideo preceptum est vicecomiti quod distringat predictum dominum de Tattone ad predictam sectam tamquam iudicator faciendam etc."

[61] Above, n. 24.

[62] Chester 29/38, m. 15 (1326); *CPR, 1327-1330*, p. 196.

[63] Chester 29/40, m. 3. Other pleaders: R. de Frodesham (Chester 29/28, m. 27; 29/30, m. 5d; 29/38, m. 9d [1315-1326]), Robert de Hampton (Chester 29/21, m. 14 [1309]), R. de Mere (Chester 29/50, m. 9 [1338]), Richard de la Pole (Chester 29/40, m. 18d, 20 [1328]), R. le Roter (Chester 29/29, m. 7; 29/38, mm. 5, 9d, 15 [1316-1326]), Adam de Swynesheved (Chester 29/39, m. 16 [1327]), T. de Thornton (Chester 29/28, m. 27 [1315]), R. de Westbury (Chester 29/25, m. 33d; 29/28, m. 27; 29/29, m. 23d; 29/30, m. 5d [1313-1316]), R. de Wonre (Chester 29/38, m. 15 [1326]). Such

who were very sophisticated in the law and who would have pleaded far more subtly than an amateur judge could have readily followed. William de Miggele was a pleader in Cheshire county court at least from 1307 to 1313,[64] and during that period he was also a pleader in the court of common pleas.[65] John de Lancaster was a prominent pleader in Cheshire from 1315 until 1330,[66] and during that period he served frequently on commissions of *oyer* and *terminer* and as keeper of the peace in the northern counties.[67] From 1316 to 1330 John de Horneby pleaded in Cheshire,[68] and this was during the time that he was also chirographer in the court of common pleas.[69] Both Horneby and Lancaster also pleaded in the eyre of Northamptonshire in 1329-30.[70] Henry de Hambury was a Cheshire pleader for over a decade in the reign of Edward II,[71] was eventually appointed to the Bench in Ireland,[72] and in 1329-30 was a justice in the court of king's bench in England.[73] Even William de Shareshull, chief justice of the court of king's bench from 1350 to 1361, pleaded in Cheshire county court in 1329.[74] That was five years after he had started pleading in the king's court and only four years before he was appointed justice in the court of common pleas.[75] The legal argument these men used must have been comparable in complexity and subtlety to the argument they used in the king's court. Because of the quality of pleading in the court, Cheshire judges had to be skilled in the law, not simply knowledgeable about Cheshire custom. Moreover, since they were subject ultimately to correction by the king's court, their standards of legal practice had to meet the high standards of the king's court.

---

entries do not provide even a nearly complete list of pleaders, only a list of those few who acted in the making of a chirograph.

[64] Chester 29/20, m. 5; 29/21, m. 1; 29/25, m. 8d.

[65] *Year Books of 4 Edward II*, ed. G. J. Turner, Selden Society, vol. 26 (London, 1911), p. ciii, and succeeding year book volumes.

[66] Chester 29/28, m. 27; 29/38, mm. 3, 5, 8; 29/39, m. 9; 29/40, m. 17; 29/41, m. 7.

[67] *CPR, 1313-1317*, pp. 124, 421, 699; *CPR, 1317-1321*, pp. 303, 305, 606, 610, etc.

[68] Chester 29/28, m. 27; 29/29, m. 23d; 29/38, mm. 3, 8, 11, 15; 29/39, m. 20; 29/40, mm. 3, 17; 29/41, m. 17.

[69] *CPR, 1313-1318*, pp. 38, 195, 464.

[70] Lincoln's Inn, Hale MSS, 137(1), fols. 1-47. I owe this reference to Professor D. W. Sutherland.

[71] Chester 29/20, m. 11; 29/27, m. 9; 29/29, mm. 23d, 27; 29/30, mm. 5d, 9d.

[72] *CCR, 1327-1330*, pp. 431, 511.

[73] *Select Cases in the Court of King's Bench*, 4:lxxxviii.

[74] Chester 29/40, m. 11.

[75] Bertha H. Putnam, *The Place in Legal History of Sir William Shareshull, Chief Justice of the King's Bench, 1350-1361* (Cambridge, 1950), pp. 21-22.

The judges of Cheshire's county court were probably the bailiffs or seneschals of those who owed suit and were obliged to find a judge. As the presiding officer of a local court, a seneschal or bailiff would have been familiar with the law; he would also have been familiar with the details of pleading, since pleaders operated also in the local courts of Cheshire.[76] Moreover, he would have already been retained by the lord for legal services and as a matter of course would have been present in the county court to defend the lord's interests by aiding his men and claiming those pleas pertinent to his lord's court. No other person would have been so knowledgeable about the current status of the lord's legal affairs and his lands and so responsive to his interests. The major landholders of Cheshire had a vested interest in maintaining a high level of excellence in the county court and in seeing to it that their interests were intelligently and forcefully presented. The seneschals and bailiffs were among the most skilled legal people working in the county, and they were the logical choice to be judges in the county court.

A few references were made specifically to seneschals in the county court of Cheshire. The best example of the seneschal functioning as a judge relates to Robert de Montalt. William Gerard alleged that Montalt's liberty of Hawarden was within the county and that the county court was seised of the pleas concerning lands and tenements within that liberty. The judges and suitors ruled that the manor of Hawarden was indeed in the body of the county and that Montalt held the manor from the king—the earl of Chester—by the service of seneschalcy (so that he himself was thus the seneschal of Cheshire) and also by the service of finding one seneschal to do suit for him at each county session.[77] This once standard form gave way to actual practice. The Cheshire Magna Carta also made it clear that this was

[76] Chester 29/10, m. 7d, Suthdeneheved v Dutton, an action of false judgment heard in the county court of Cheshire. The relevant part of the record of the lower court: "et predictus Ranulphus (de Suthdeneheved) petit si predicti Petrus et Robertus velint narratorem suum advocare de defensione predicta per predictum narratorem suum facta. Et predicti Petrus et Robertus, habito super hoc consilio, venerunt et advocaverunt defensionem predictam per narratorem suum factam."

[77] Chester 29/25, m. 28, Gerard v Montalt: "predictum manerium de Hawardyn est infra comitatum Cestr' et de corpore eiusdem comitatus et predictus Robertus tenet predictum manerium de domino rege comite Cestrie per seneschalciam et ad inveniendum unum senescallum ad sectam pro eo faciendam de comitatu in comitatum, de qua quidem secta dominus rex seisitus est. Ideo videtur curie quod predictus Robertus summoneri debet ad tenementa sua predicta in Hawardyn." (The attempt was made, but the bailiff was intercepted by some Welshmen hired by Montalt and was prevented from reaching Hawarden [at least now in Flint].)

the one acceptable and economical method of performing suit, since it allowed lords to acquit their demesne manors of suit by sending their seneschals.[78] As early as that, then, the manor was giving way to the larger unit of lordship, with the number of suits owed by the manors of a single lord reduced to one. Thus Hugh de Pulford held several manors, but he was obliged to find only one judge. The judge went for the manor of Pulford itself; and he was undoubtedly, as the Cheshire Magna Carta allowed, Hugh de Pulford's seneschal.[79] One explanation of a Cheshire custom, however, does stipulate that barons, seneschals, and judges were to be summoned; it is possible to interpret this as an implication that there were three sharply differentiated groups.[80] The better interpretation is that the groups were not completely identical, although they could overlap to a large extent. The meaning of the passage would then be that all concerned should be summoned. There would have been seneschals present who were not judges: the seneschals of those who did not owe suit. Thus, when the privileges of the borough of Macclesfield were questioned, the county court had to make use of special procedures. Since the borough was a liberty within the larger liberty of Macclesfield hundred, the testimony of the seneschals of that hundred was particularly vital, but none of them would have been judges. Thus, testimony was given "by the judges, seneschals, and suitors of the county"; that was the only instance in which that formula was used.[81]

The county court of Cheshire had three constitutive elements. The earl's justice was the presiding officer. He convoked the court and decided when a judgment was required, and then saw to it that the judgment was not only delivered but also—through his executive officer, the sheriff—executed. The court also had more than thirty judges. They were the ones who were primarily engaged in the court's deliberations and were chiefly responsible for the judgments of the county. They took the initiative in rendering the judgments, decided the judgments by a majority vote, and could not be overruled by the

---

[78] *Chartulary of Saint Werburgh*, 2:104.

[79] *IPM*, Edward I, 2:161.

[80] Lapsley, *"Buzones,"* pp. 557-58.

[81] Chester 29/21, m. 17, Fouleshurst v Pikard, in which the burgesses of Macclesfield claimed that they should not be impleaded outside their borough by reason of a charter granted by Edward I: "Et quia testatum est per iudices, seneschallos [this word interlined], et sectatores comitatus quod burgenses predicti burgi a tempore confeccionis predicte carte domini regis predicta libertate uti et gaudere consueverunt, ideo predicti burgenses modo habeant libertatem." The case was to come before the justice of Cheshire on his next eyre at Macclesfield.

suitors. The judges of the court were provided by tenurial arrangements. Those who held manors or groups of manors and not specifically exempted were obliged to attend at times in person as judges, but more often to send suitable people, usually their seneschals, to attend and function in their place as judges. The final constitutive element of the county court was the body of suitors, a body of uncertain numbers and origin, about whom little may be known. At least in the hundred courts the lord of a manor could be either a judge or a suitor, so that the differentiating criterion between judge and suitor was not that between one who held a manor and one who held less than a manor—although wealth of a more substantial character, that is, between the holder of one manor and the holder of many manors, cannot be ruled out as a possible criterion. Women who held substantial tenements could be obliged to find a judge, so that the criterion was not purely sexual. Nor does it seem that the suitors were people who merely attended themselves when they could have sent another in their place. The only criterion ever cited is that of ancient custom. Despite the peculiarities of Cheshire in so many things, the interaction of these three groups stands as a clear example of the way in which the duties of the presiding officer could be severed from the responsibilities of rendering judgments and of the way in which one county provided its judges and delivered its judgments. On the whole, in this Cheshire was not atypical.

Cheshire was unique among fourteenth-century county courts in using clear terminology to distinguish groups in those who attended the county court as the result of the tenurial service of suit; it was also probably unique in having a relatively passive body such as the suitors. Lancashire county court was the only other county court even to utilize the word "judge" in the fourteenth century. Some of the lower courts in Lancashire did distinguish between judges and suitors. The courts of Penwortham and Clitheroe in the 1320s are the conspicuous examples. In each case, the rolls of the court not only mention judges, but also list them as associated with a specific manor— such as the "judge of Euxton"—whereas suitors are mentioned by name.[82] Other Lancashire lower courts only make mention of judges. Thus ten people owed suit to the court of Manchester in 1322, and they were called "judges of the court of Manchester, by custom from

---

[82] *Some Court Rolls of the Lordships, Wapentakes, and Demesne Manors of Thomas, Earl of Lancaster*, ed. William Farrer, The Record Society, vol. 41 (n.p., 1901), pp. 40, 45, 48; Ault, *Private Jurisdictions*, pp. 267-93.

of old." Each was the lord of a manor.[83] Judges were mentioned also in Lonsdale,[84] Amounderness,[85] West Derby,[86] and Salford hundreds;[87] and in each the obligation of suit was attached to an individual manor or group of manors. Some local Lancashire courts thus had both judges and suitors, while others seem to have known only judges, as seems to have been the case in certain lower courts in Cheshire.

Lancashire county court in the thirteenth century expressed obligations of suit in a manner identical to that of contemporary Cheshire. Thus, at the beginning of the century there are references to people who owed suit to county and had to find a judge,[88] while by mid-century the obligation was expressed merely as having to find a judge at the county court.[89] Even in the county court there were references to judges, but by 1315 most of them were making an annual payment to be released from the burdens of suit.[90] There is no proof that there was in Lancashire county court a body of relatively passive suitors distinct from the judges.[91] Since Lancashire did have such people in some of its lower courts, however, it was natural for the county court to refer to those who owed suit as judges, rather than, as was the

[83] *Mamecestre*, ed. John Harland, 3 vols., Chetham Society, vols. 53, 56, 58 (Manchester, 1859-1863), 2:398.

[84] *Some Court Rolls*, pp. 108, 112, 134; *Lancashire Inquests, Extents, and Feudal Aids*, ed. William Farrer, 3 vols., The Record Society, vols. 48, 54, 70 (Liverpool, 1903-1915), 3:145-52.

[85] *Lancashire Inquests*, 3:112-16; *Some Court Rolls*, pp. 114, 117.

[86] *Lancashire Inquests*, 3:90-95.

[87] Ibid., 3:102-6; *Book of Fees*, prepared under the superintendence of the Deputy Keeper of the Records, 3 vols. (London, 1920-1931), 1:217-19; *Some Court Rolls*, pp. 150, 151, 154, 160, 161. Only four to six lords were named in each list; possibly that was the number of judges at any one time.

[88] Compare *Book of Fees*, 1:217-19, with the charter above, n. 48.

[89] *IPM*, Henry III, 1:63, 66. *Lancashire Inquests*, 1:213, has William de Clifton obligated to find a suitor to the county court. Because of the oddity of the phrase and the fact that Clifton later was mentioned as having a judge (*Some Court Rolls*, p. 114), no conclusions can be made on the basis of that reference with regard to suitors.

[90] DL. 29/1/3, m. 1; E. 370/5/40. The latter document, which must be dated 1324, has a list of judges in the form "De iudice de Tarleton de fine pro respectu secte sue hoc anno—2s." The other judges were from Coppull (2s), Eccleston (6s 8d), Adlington (2s), Barton (5s), Ince (3s 4d), Great Crosby (3s 4d), Little Crosby (3s 4d), Garston (4s), Allerton (5s), Astley (4s), Whiston (3s), Westleigh (3s 4d), Whittington (2s), Dalton (2s), Warton (5s), Thornton (2s), "Oldemmores" (3s 4d), Ashton (4s), Pilkington (6s 8d), Sefton (2s), Windle and "Burnhul" (13s 4d), Stretford (6s 8d), and Manchester and "Kynerdeley" (20s).

[91] Previously the emphasis has been placed on the judges, identifying them as the peculiarity of Cheshire, and perhaps of Lancashire also. This view was satisfactory as long as the numbers of the Cheshire judges were unknown and as long as it was not known that the judges also owed suit and could therefore, in some sense, also be called suitors. It seems better to realize that the relatively passive Cheshire suitors are the anomalous feature.

custom in all counties except Cheshire and Lancashire, as suitors.

The normal English county court did not make Cheshire's distinction between suit as a judge and suit as a suitor. Thus, in referring to counties other than Cheshire and Lancashire, "suitor" refers simply to one who owed suit, with no implication of any lesser role in rendering judgments, whereas "judge" may be used in the nontechnical sense denoting any person entitled to render judgments, but who was not so entitled because of his status as presiding officer. The terminological ambiguities raised by the Cheshire constitution are unavoidable; some comfort may be had in remembering that the lawyer in the thirteenth and fourteenth century would have been faced with the same difficulty.

The most basic fact about the suitor to the county court was that he came within the jurisdiction of the county court; he could be called upon to defend himself in that forum. Since suitors were, by and large, the important people of the county, the obligation to attend was an important supplement to mesne procedure. They were expected to be present at county court regularly—or at least predictably—and could not delay litigation as easily as would have been possible otherwise. Much of the reluctance of certain suitors to attend the county was probably related to the desire to avoid a dangerous suit pending in county court. The important landholders who were justiciable in some other lower court but not in the county court did not owe suit. Thus there were no suitors to the Oxfordshire county court due from Oxford itself or from the suburbs of Oxford within its liberty[92] or from the whole southern half of the county so dominated by the honor of Wallingford.[93] Cambridgeshire county court claimed no suits from its shire town or from the Isle of Ely.[94] Neither Blackburn hundred in Lancashire nor Macclesfield hundred in Cheshire had anyone who owed suit to the county court. While not everyone who was justiciable in county owed suit, still suit was first and foremost a statement about justiciability.

The suitors were also the judges in the county court; they thus rendered judgments, took responsibility for those judgments, and were responsible for the county's record. The *Summa Magna* thus warned the suitors not to let the sheriff usurp the power of giving judgments, because the suitors would still be held responsible.[95] When

[92] *RH*, pp. 724-875.
[93] Ibid.
[94] *Liber Memorandorum*, ed. J. W. Clark (Cambridge, 1907), pp. 238-63.
[95] *Radulphi de Hengham Summae*, ed. W. H. Dunham (Cambridge, 1932), p. 14.

the sheriff was ordered to record a plea and the judges refused to make the record, it was the suitors who were distrained to come to Westminster to make the record before the king's justices.[96] In one instance the king's justice specified the relationship between making the record and rendering the judgments. In the county court held at the beginning of the Lancashire eyre of 1292 the sheriff was ordered to record the proceedings on a writ of right between two brothers, Adam and Thomas. The sheriff replied that he could not record the plea because Gilbert de Clifton had been sheriff then, he had retained the county rolls in his possession, and, furthermore, the suitors were not present. The account in the eyre rolls then states that the suitors had to know about judgments they had rendered themselves, so the sheriff was ordered to distrain them to come into the eyre. All but eighteen of them came and recorded the plea. The older brother, Adam, was the tenant and had merely put himself on the mercy of the county, not defending even the words of court. He only explained the circumstances of his birth. Before he was born his father had pledged faith to his mother, but they had been married in church only after his birth. On that day, when the marriage was solemnized, his parents had lain under a maniple in the church, and he had been placed with them under the maniple, apparently symbolizing the church's acceptance of him as their legitimate child. The suitors of the county, however, had rightly ruled that he was undefended and awarded seisin of the land to the second son, Thomas.[97] Had the

[96] CP. 40/36, m. 136 is the only recorded instance of distraints actually made on county suitors for this purpose, although it was commonplace for suitors in other courts and at times distraints were ordered for county suitors. CP. 40/41, m. 33 shows that the county suitors were not finally compelled, even in that case, to come to Westminster, since both parties granted that the record could be made in open county court.

[97] JUST. 1/408, m. 42: "ita quod vicecomes alias testabatur quod ad comitatum tentum die lune in principio itineris predicta loquela recordari non potuit quia placitatum fuit tempore Gilberti de Clifton quondam vicecomitis etc., qui rotulos habuit de tempore illo etc., ita quod ob defectum sectatorum, qui ignorare non debent iudicia per ipsos reddita, preceptum fuit vicecomiti quod distringat omnes sectatores comitatus." They came and recorded the plea, particularly Adam's plea: "Et Adam presens fuit et non defendit verba curie nec aliud dixit nisi tantum quod peciit pacem dei et domini regis de terris et tenementis suis et quod pater suus antequam ipse natus fuit affidavit matrem ipsius Ade. Et postea die desponsalium quando pater et mater eius iacuerunt sub panno in ecclesia ipse Adam appositus fuit cum eis sub eodem panno etc. Et predictus Adam licet sepius quesitus nichil aliud voluit dicere, per quod sectatores comitatus consideraverunt ipsum esse indefensum et quod predictus Thomas recuperasset versus eum seisinam de predictis tenementis." For this ceremony, see F. Pollock and F. W. Maitland, The History of English Law before the Time of Edward I, 2 vols., 2nd ed. (Cambridge, 1968), 2:397-98.

judgment been found false, the amercement of the county would have been levied from all the suitors. Even though it was normally stated that the community of the county was amerced, those in the liberties of the county did not contribute, because, of course, they did not owe suit.[98] The suitors were thus considered the ultimate source of record in the county court and were also responsible for rendering the judgments.

As in Cheshire, the obligation of suit to county court was determined tenurially according to relations of lordship, that is, suit was owed from the manor or from aggregates of manors. Specific manors from Cumberland to Wiltshire, from Cambridgeshire to Gloucestershire were said specifically to owe suit.[99] Suit in Lancashire was definitely owed by manors. If the manor had been divided, as with the manor of Thornton in Amounderness hundred, both lords owed suit for their part of the manor.[100] At times the lord of many manors owed but one suit for his whole fee; thus the heir of Adam de Freckelton held four manors and owed but one suit.[101] The aggregation of manors that owed but a single suit had been allowed at least by the time of the *Leges Henrici* in the early twelfth century. That treatise stated as a rule—well before the more restrictive rule allowed by the Cheshire Magna Carta a century later—that a baron or his seneschal could acquit the suit due not only from his lands but also from the tenants of the lands within his lordship.[102] The ordinary lord of the

---

[98] C. 60/29, m. 6 (14 Henry III): "Mandavit vicecomiti Devon' quod demanda quam facit W. Exon' episcopo et hominibus suis de comitatu suo occasione contencionis orte inter ipsum episcopum et homines suos et ceteros homines de comitatu suo dicentes predictum episcopum et homines suos debere participes esse . . . in misericordiis acquietandis quotiens totus comitatus incidit in misericordiam pro falso iudicio vel alio delicto et ex contrario asserente se et homines suos quietos esse debere . . . de misericordiis quidem predictis se et homines suos participes esse non debere eo quod sectam ad comitatum non faciunt neque ad hundredum ponat in respectum usque in xv dies a die sancte Trinitatis . . ." CP. 40/181, mm. 104d, 100d; "Lincs'. Preceptum fuit vicecomiti quod de terris et catallis omnium sectatorum comitatus sui exceptis libertatibus eiusdem comitatus in ballia sua fieri faceret viginti marcas et illas haberet hic ad hunc diem ad reddendum Philippo de Lyndesey que ei in curia hic per consideracionem eiusdem curie regis adiudicate fuerunt pro dampnis suis que habuit occasione cuiusdam falsi iudicii in eodem comitatu reddendi etc."

[99] E. 370/5/32; E. 370/6/10; *Liber Memorandorum*, pp. 240, 253, 262-63; *RH*, 2:57-58, 81-82, 232; *Cartularium Prioratus de Gyseburne Ebor' Dioeceseos*, ed. W. Brown, 2 vols., Surtees Society, vols. 86, 88 (Durham, 1889-1891), 1:320; *Lancashire Inquests*, 2:78-79; *Red Book of Worcester*, ed. Marjory Hollings, Worcestershire Historical Society (London, 1934-1937), p. 127; *Cartularium Monasterii de Rameseia*, ed. W. H. Hart and Ponsonby Lyons, 3 vols., Rerum Brittanicarum medii aevi scriptores, vol. 79 (London, 1884-1893), 2:27.

[100] *Lancashire Inquests*, 2:111.

[101] Ibid., 2:109.

[102] *Leges Henrici Primi*, ed. L. J. Downer (Oxford, 1972), p. 130.

manor might thus himself be specially exempt from suit by royal grant or not obliged to perform his suit in person because of the attendance of his baron. The barons of a county, however, were presumed to owe suit unless they could prove otherwise;[103] they surely held at least one manor in the county and probably had several manors within their lordship. Surveys would not take this principle of substitution into account, of course, because the suit was still owed by the manor. The typical suitor thus remained the lord of the manor.

Occasionally, however, a suitor was a person of much less stature than the lord of a whole manor. The burdens of suit could be transferred to one's tenant as well as to one's lord. The *Leges Henrici* mentioned this principle also, by stating that the reeve, priest, and four men of the township could go in place of the lord.[104] This seems to have been a very old practice. Cranfield, Bedfordshire, is an excellent early example. In 1135 it was said to "defend" its suit by four virgates, that is, by sending the tenants of those four virgates. Two of the virgates were held by substantial men who each held half a hide. The third man held only his virgate, and the fourth virgate was held by the priest of the village, who went to county as the fourth of the four men.[105] Even by 1135 Ramsey Abbey had so abrogated its responsibilities toward Cranfield that their attendance was customary and the suit was already appendant to the four virgates. This transformation of substitution into custom and tenurial duties will account for many of the lesser men who owed suit.

Both principles of substitution illustrate one of the major early functions of suit: the preservation of the peace of the county. Naomi Hurnard long ago pointed out that such substitution was only reasonable if the reeve, priest, and four men went to the county to provide information, that is, to make presentments concerning crimes suspected by the manorial courts. She thought that the four men must have been villeins,[106] but the men of Cranfield seem rather like free tenants; the manorial court, of course, did not exclude free men from its functions. The manorial court in the early twelfth century would often not have been very distinct from the lord's court anyway. Furthermore, the principle of baronial substitution implies that information would be provided also about the baron's free tenants. Lords were to some extent responsible for the men over whom they

---

[103] *PQW*, p. 4.

[104] *Leges Henrici Primi*, p. 100.

[105] *Cartularium Monasterii de Rameseia*, 3:301.

[106] Naomi D. Hurnard, "The Jury of Presentment and the Assize of Clarendon," *EHR* 56 (1941):383-84.

held sway; they protected them in county court, but they would also be expected to deliver them up or provide information about them when they had committed crimes. When the lesser men did perform suit, however, their functions did not extend as far as their lord's. The *Leges Henrici* expressly excludes the poorer portion of the county from rendering judgments;[107] even without the testimony of that treatise, it would have been extremely difficult to imagine a county court of the twelfth century so democratic that a villein could pass judgment on a baron. The attendance of these lesser men to provide information was thus a minimal fulfillment of the obligations of suit, and perhaps that is why some suits were said only to be "defended," although the usage of the thirteenth century in this regard is not consistent.[108]

The total number of suits due a thirteenth-century county court was seldom extremely large, and the number of suitors likely to be present at any given session continued to decline during the thirteenth century as it had in the twelfth century. Between 1236 and 1238 the county court of Cambridgeshire could claim 162 suits.[109] By 1279, however, at least twenty and probably about sixty of these suits had been subtracted from the county court, many presumably transferred to the courts of liberties.[110] Moreover, of the suits that remained, only eight were clearly suits due every month.[111] Again, between 1236 and 1238 the county court of Huntingdonshire could claim only forty-nine suitors.[112] One of the four Huntingdonshire hundreds at that time, however, listed no suitors at all, because they were then the subject of litigation; but forty years later that same hundred listed only six suitors to the county court.[113] It would be surprising if the total number of suitors to Huntingdonshire county court exceeded sixty in 1238 or thirty in 1279. Furthermore, in 1279 only three suits were supposed to require attendance at county every month.[114] In

---

[107] *Leges Henrici Primi*, p. 131.

[108] Chester 30/5, m. 11 is a thought-provoking instance from Wales, in which the burgesses of Rhuddlan "clamant quod uxores sue in eorum absencia defendere possunt sectas domino regi debitas in curia predicta."

[109] Helen Cam, *The Hundred and the Hundred Rolls* (London, 1930), p. 110.

[110] *RH*, 2:407-590.

[111] Ibid., 2:467, 472, 477, 478, 497, 499, 536, 598.

[112] *Liber Memorandorum*, pp. 262-72. Fowler's disregard for the Huntingdonshire list (*Rolls from . . . Beds. and Bucks.*, ed. G. H. Fowler, Beds. Historical Record Society, Quarto Series, vol. 3 [Bedford, 1929], p. 49), apparently followed also by Helen Cam, is based only on the notion that there could not have been so few suitors.

[113] *RH*, 2:601-82.

[114] Ibid., 2:629, 682. Since two of these were probably specified because the obligation had been divided, it cannot be certain that they were the only ones owed monthly.

1255 the Shropshire county court could claim 102 suits, but the survey listed several more that had been subtracted and made it clear that 102 suitors were not expected to be present every session.[115] In 1279 something over sixty suits were owed to the Oxfordshire county court and required the attendance of the suitor only twice a year at the great county sessions. Only four to eight suitors—the precise number is difficult to determine—were obliged to attend every session.[116] Finally, in 1280 it seems that there were sixty-two suitors to the county court of Essex. That list did not specify the frequency of attendance of the suitors, but it is reasonable to assume that almost all were due only twice yearly.[117] In the early thirteenth century, then, the county courts might lay claim to anything between sixty to a couple hundred suits; toward the end of the century it is likely that the number had been at least halved. Since almost all of those suits were due but twice a year, it is likely that a sheriff could enforce the attendance of no more than one or two dozen suitors at the normal county session.

Along with the status of the county courts themselves, the importance of the obligation of suit to county court declined near the beginning of the reign of Edward I. Up until about 1270 the obligations of suit were actually enforced. Thus, Henry III continued to grant exemptions from suit to county court. In 1266 he granted that the Hospital of St. Johns outside the East Gate of Oxford and its men would be quit of suit to county courts.[118] In the same year he reconsidered a grant which had first been made to Hugh Giffard and his heirs acquitting them of suits to county and hundred; in the reconsideration he first extended and then annulled an additional privilege which would have included in the acquittance also their men, tenements, and fees as a favor to Hugh's heir: Walter, bishop of Bath and Wells.[119] Again in 1266 Henry granted his son Edmund, earl of Leicester, and his heirs that they would hold all their lands and fees quit of suits to county and hundred.[120] There are numerous other examples. Furthermore, sheriffs enforced the obligations of suit by distraint. Sheriffs' accounts prior to the reign of Edward I commonly

---

Nevertheless, the figure is believable when compared to other counties.

[115] *RH*, 2:52-84.

[116] *RH*, 2:732, 740, 824, 831, 838, 859.

[117] CP. 40/36, m. 136.

[118] *Calendar of Charter Rolls*, prepared under the superintendence of the Deputy Keeper of the Records, 6 vols. (London, 1903-1927), 2:309.

[119] Ibid., 2:67.

[120] Ibid., 2:67.

record amercements of suitors for default of court.[121] Individuals even sought freedom from the sheriff's distraint to perform suit while they were in tenure of some office.[122] All these things are sound indications that the duty of suit was still of some importance and was still enforced prior to about 1270.

After about 1270 the situation changed. When a grant of exemption from suit to county court was made, it was made as only one of a long list of exemptions and was not requested specially. No temporary exemptions can be found in the Patent or Close Rolls. From that time also the sheriffs' accounts—even though few survive from the reign of Edward I—cease to mention distraint for suit of county. The one fourteenth-century account that mentions such a distraint is from Worcestershire.[123] Since the earl of Warwick was hereditary sheriff of that county, however, such entries cannot be held indicative of any general practice. *The Court Baron,* written about 1308, states that the defaults of suitors in county courts were not enrolled and that this differed from the practice of other lower courts.[124] Maitland concluded from that comment alone that suit to county was no longer being enforced.[125]

There are a few records of distraints for suit to county court in the reign of Edward I. In 1276 a sworn inquest was taken in Lancashire in open county; it testified that Gilbert de Clifton did not permit the sheriff's bailiffs to distrain in Rochdale for a suit owed to the county court and to the wapentake court from the fee of the earl of Lincoln. Clifton went so far as to notify the sheriff that he would meet posse with posse: *poneret posse contra posse.*[126] Many suits in Lancashire,

---

[121] E. 370/5/32, E. 101/505/10 (Gloucestershire, 1230s); E. 370/6/10 (Staffordshire, 1236); E. 370/6/11, E. 370/5/71 (Norfolk & Suffolk, 1259, 1267); E. 370/5/30, printed in W. A. Morris, *The Early English County Court,* University of California Publications in History, vol. 14, no. 2 (Berkeley, 1926), pp. 201, 204-5 (Essex & Hertfordshire, 1259); E. 370/5/3 (Oxfordshire, 1258-59); E. 370/6/22, E. 370/6/25 (Yorkshire, 1259, 1263). Other accounts in this time period have amercements that may have been for default of suit at county court but are ambiguous.

[122] *CPR, 1247-1258,* p. 558; *CPR, 1258-1266,* pp. 132, 127; *CPR, 1266-1272,* p. 421; *CCR, 1259-1261,* pp. 44, 100, 248; and many others.

[123] E. 370/9/26.

[124] *The Court Baron,* ed. F. W. Maitland, Selden Society, vol. 4 (London, 1890), pp. 80-81.

[125] Pollock and Maitland, *History of English Law,* 1:544.

[126] KB. 29/21, m. 8: "Gilbertus de Clifton non permisit ballivos vicecomitis facere districciones pro duabus sectis debitis ad comitatum Lanc' et eciam pro duabus sectis debitis ad wapentakium infra comitatum pro feodo comitis Lincoln' in Rachedale, set mandavit dicto vicecomiti quod non faceret huiusmodi districciones et si faceret poneret posse contra posse et quod dicti ballivi vicecomitis non fecerunt dictas districciones propria sua voluntate immo fecerunt dictas districciones auctoritate regia et de mandato

however, had been commuted into annual payments, and the dispute may thus have more concerned a perquisite of office rather than an obligation of attendance.[127] Also in 1276 Gerard de Insula sued Edmund, earl of Cornwall, and Peter de Wakerley for distraining him, in contravention of a royal prohibition, to do monthly suit to the county court of Rutland for his manor of Burley. They came to issue on the seisin of the suit, but no verdict was recorded. Nevertheless, the last person alleged to have been in seisin of the suit was Richard of Alemane, so that that suit had not been performed for at least four years.[128] Later on, John de Eure prosecuted Gerard de Salveyn, because Salveyn would not collect the arrears due Eure from his term as sheriff of Yorkshire (1310-1311), even though Eure had presented him with a royal writ ordering the collection. Among the particulars listed were at least five amercements of individuals for not having come to the great county.[129] These undoubtedly relate to suit, but in Yorkshire as in Lancashire many suits had been commuted into monetary payments which were made annually in person at the Michaelmas great county session.[130] Not even such a reference is sufficient to prove that suit was still enforced as an obligation to attend county court and render judgments.

The obligation of suit to county also arose a couple of times in relation to the obligations of mesne tenants. The first of these once

---

dicti vicecomitis domini regis et per iudicium tocius comitatus in wapentakio. Item dicunt quod mandavit litteras suas predictas domino Henrico de Lee tanquam vicecomiti domini regis et non tanquam ballivo domini Eadmundi et quod bene patet quod fuit in contemptu domini regis." On m. 26 Clifton challenged the impartiality of such an inquest taken before Lee. The text mentions two suits, but this clearly means the same as the Oxfordshire survey when it mentions *duos adventus*: two appearances each year.

[127] Above, at n. 90.

[128] CP. 40/15, m. 33d: "Et unde queritur quod cum ipse die martis proxima post festum sancti Dunstani anno regni regis nunc tercio detulisset ei regiam prohibicionem ne distringat predictos Gerardum et Aliciam ad predictam sectam faciendam, iidem Edmundus et Petrus spreta prohibicione predicta distringunt ipsos ad faciendam sectam ad predictum comitatum de mense in mensem occasione predicti manerii contra prohibicionem predictam . . . Quidam Johannes de Armenters avunculus predicte Alicie cuius heres ipsa est dum idem manerium fuit in manu sua fecit predictam sectam ad predictum comitatum tempore regis Henrici filii regis Johannis predicti dum idem comitatus fuit in manu sua et similiter tempore Ricardi regis Alemanie comitis Cornubie qui comitatum illum postea tenuit, ita quod tam predicti reges Johannes et Henricus quam predictus Ricardus comes fuerunt in seisina de predicta secta toto tempore suo quousque predicti Gerardus et Alicia se de predicta secta facienda subtraxerunt."

[129] E. 13/35, m. 14.

[130] E. 370/6/27, a list from the fifteenth century of "fines magni comitatus Ebor' et trithingorum de Craykhowe, Yarletre, et Wyndegates" listing approximately sixty people and the fines they paid; PQW, p. 199.

again involved a Yorkshire suit. Arnold de Percy had agreed by final concord to acquit Master William de Pykering of all the services from certain lands in Norton and Sutton near Malton. The services included doing suit to the county court, the east trithing (sic), and Buckrose wapentake once a year.[131] Once again this seems to have involved the annual payments to the sheriff and not the obligation of attending to render judgments. The other instance was in 1297 and is rather more complicated: *Redeswell v Gelham*. In 1260 a final concord had been made putting the lands in question in fee tail on Redeswell's ancestor with three remainders, so that Gelham, as the heir of the grantor, was obliged to acquit Redeswell, the son and heir of the second remainderman, of the rent of 3s and the suit owed to the Essex county court and the hundred of Hinckford. Gelham admitted the final concord and acknowledged himself obliged to pay the rent, so that the dispute properly concerned only the suit. He maintained that he should not be obliged as mesne to acquit Redeswell of the suit. That kind of suit, he thought, was owed not only by reason of a tenement but also by reason of the person who was tenant, so that a mesne could not be obliged to acquit the proper tenant of the suit.[132] This was an interesting defense, but no judgment was given on the demurrer. Since the suit in question was clearly due only twice a year and the obligation of the mesne tenant had been embodied in a final concord, it is likely that the suit to county court had to be mentioned to litigate concerning the suit to hundred court. In that way the case would have been a dispute over suit to the sheriff's tourn. There is thus no clear evidence from common litigation concerning suits that suit to county court was still in the reign of Edward I an obligation that required personal attendance at the county court to render judgments.

The actual role of the suitors themselves was exaggerated by the

---

[131] CP. 40/135, m. 101. The suit was described as "ad comitatum Ebor' et ad trithingum regis et esttrithingum et eciam ad wapentakium regis de Bukros semel per annum."

[132] CP. 40/121, m. 173. The suit was described as "duas sectas ad comitatum Essex per annum et alias duas sectas ad hundredum ipsius regis de Hengford per annum." This should be interpreted as going to the county court and hundred court twice in the year, since the only suits known to have been owed to the Essex county court were due only at the great county sessions (Morris, *Early English County Court*, p. 201). The defense was "et idem Johannes bene cognovit predictum finem et quicquid in eo continetur, set dicit quod de predictis sectis ea racione predictum Simonem versus dominum regem aquietare non debet etc., quia dicit quod huiusmodi secte non solum debentur racione tenementi tantum immo tam racione persone tenentis quam racione tenementi et per consequens medius intervenire non potest in hoc casu ad huiusmodi sectas faciendas cum persona personam aquietare non possit in hac parte etc. Et super hoc petit iudicium etc."

king's court. The occasions on which a judgment of the county court was said to have been rendered by the suitors are very rare. Moreover, when clerks in the king's court transcribed sheriffs' responses and county records, they often made the enrollments coincide with the accepted legal formulae. This corrective urge is shown best in *Prat v Prat*. During the process in that case the sheriff made a return that the suitors and seneschals could not make the record.[133] When the enrollment was made in the plea rolls, however, it was made in abridged form: that the suitors could not make the record. The clerk omitted the very interesting reference to the seneschals.[134] Curial theory thus provided a strong motivation to "correct" the records of lower courts.

Early sources and the county courts themselves seldom mentioned suitors as such participating in judgments. Counties usually mentioned that a judgment was made, not specifying who had rendered the judgment. When people who functioned as judges were mentioned, they were listed either by name or called something such as "the knights and other free men of the county."[135] In 1236, when the men were listed who had prevented the sheriff from holding the county court merely by absenting themselves—clearly, then, the judges of the court—the word "suitors" was not mentioned at all.[136] Not even the writ of false judgment mentioned the suitors. That writ was only concerned with the law-worthy knights who were supposed to have been present at the making of the record and who were to bear the record to the king's court.[137] Some lawyers maintained that the four knights had to be suitors, and in 1293 the justices of the court

[133] CP. 52 octave Trinity, 27 Edward I: "In pleno comitatu Notingham ex parte domini regis precepi et iniunxi sectatoribus et seneschalis eiusdem comitatus qui iudicia placitorum et querelarum reddere debent et solent quod michi fecissent recordum loquele que fuit in eodem comitatu per breve domini regis inter partes in hoc brevi nominatas, qui michi responderunt quod loquela illa placitata fuit iam est diu tempore Philippi de Paunton de comitatu Lyncoln' dudum vicecomitis Notingham' qui penes se habet illud breve domini regis una cum rotulis placiti eiusdem querele, sine quo brevi et inspeccione rotulorum predictorum dicunt quod nesciunt nec possunt recordum loquele predicte michi facere, eo quod non currit eis in memoria qualiter loquela illa erat placitata, set dicto Philippo vicecomiti cum omni festinacione qua possunt appropinquabunt pro brevi illo et inspeccione rotulorum illorum habendis."

[134] CP. 40/129, m. 64: "Et vicecomes nichil inde fecit set mandavit quod loquela illa iam diu placitata fuit tempore Philippi de Paunton tunc vicecomitis et qui penes se habet rotulos et breve regis etc., per quod sectatores eiusdem comitatus sine inspeccione eorundem rotulorum et brevis recordum facere non potuerunt etc."

[135] CP. 52 three weeks Easter, 15 Edward I [S.S.]; three weeks Easter, 21 Edward I [S.S.]; octave John the Baptist, 21 Edward I; etc.

[136] *CRR*, 15:510-11.

[137] *Early Registers of Writs*, ed. Elsa de Haas and G.D.G. Hall, Selden Society, vol. 87 (London, 1970), p. 114 (R. 29).

of common pleas came close to affirming that opinion. In that year they summoned the sheriff of Cambridgeshire to answer why he had sent four knights to testify to the record of the county "who were not suitors of the same county and who were not present at the making of the record."[138] In dealing with borough courts, however, the justices were satisfied merely with the attendance of the men at the making of the record; and objections that they were not suitors were disregarded.[139] One report even points out expressly that the writ demanded knights who were present at the making of the record and not suitors.[140] There is good reason to think that the opinion that the knights had to be suitors was a new concern, derived from the succeeding process in litigation concerning a false judgment; that process could entail both the distraint and the amercement of the suitors.[141]

Suitors, by and large, played little or no role in normal county procedure by around 1300, even though their liability and their role according to legal theory remained unchanged. In Kent, for instance, the suitors apparently came only when specifically summoned. Thus in 1290 the new sheriff of Kent endorsed a writ with the explanation that he had held only one county session and the suitors had not come, so that he was unable to record the plea on time.[142] Eight months earlier the former sheriff of Kent had similarly endorsed a writ explaining that he could not record a plea for lack of suitors.[143] It is unlikely that suitors were in fact completely absent; some would certainly have been present to litigate in the county court. The sheriff, however, was probably unable to utilize them as suitors (i.e., to render

---

[138] CP. 40/102, m. 252. See also CP. 40/5, m. 35: "Et vicecomes nichil inde fecit set mandavit quod sectatores comitatus absentaverunt se ad faciendum recordum illud. Et ideo preceptum est vicecomiti quod venire faciat hic a die sancti Martini in xv dies xij de legalioribus et probioribus militibus [et?] sectatoribus predicti comitatus ad faciendum recordum illud."

[139] Lincoln's Inn, Hale MSS 188, fol. 41r: "*Berr[eford]*. Fet nous donkes autres qe ceo record. *Les iiij.* Ceo ne devoms fere, car nous ne sumes de la curt. E dautrepart il ne furent a judgment rendu. *Ber'*. Futez present a cel record fere en la curt en presence de vicont? *Lez iiij.* Oyl. *Berr'*. Est ceo meme le record? *Les iiij.* Oyl. *Berr'*. De pus qe vous avez conu que vous futez present a cel record fere e que ceo est meyme le record, nous tenoms meyme le record avoue. E vous que portez cest bref, pledez."

[140] Brit. Lib., Add. 31826, fol. 411r: "dicitur in brevi 'ex illis qui recordo interfuerint' et non 'ex sectatoribus.' "

[141] CP. 40/36, m. 136.

[142] JUST. 4, Kent Eyre 1293, Payseryr v Tregoz: "Vicecomes qui nunc est non tenuit nisi unicum comitatum postquam istud breve sibi liberatum fuit, ad quem comitatum sectatores comitatus non venerunt, per quod recordum fieri non potuit."

[143] Ibid., Grey v Keu: "Adeo tarde michi fuit liberatum quod predicta loquela non potuit recordari pro defectu sectatorum comitatus infra terminum in brevi contentum."

judgments) unless they were summoned. In such a situation, it can be doubted whether the role of the suitors even when present amounted to more than mere formality. Furthermore, some counties had no suitors. Warwickshire county court had had suitors earlier in the thirteenth century.[144] Around 1303, however, lawyers familiar with the workings of the county courts of Warwickshire and Leicestershire stated clearly several times that those counties had no suitors.[145] Once that fact was used to refute the opinion that the four knights in the writ of false judgment had to be suitors. That report even compared Leicestershire county court to a portmansmote, which likewise had no suitors.[146] Nevertheless, forms had to be maintained. When the king's court required information concerning an appeal in Warwickshire county court, it ordered the sheriff to secure the testimony of the coroners, the suitors, and a special jury. The sheriff had to send, therefore, three responses. His reply first reported that the coroners testified that there had been no such appeal. Then he included a purely formal response said to be from the suitors—*quod predicti sectatores testantur*—and concluded with some additional information provided by the jury.[147] Had the sheriff not included some kind of answer from suitors—even though there were none—he would have been amerced. Curial formalism did much to give the suitors a life after death.

The obligation of suit, therefore, was predicated upon lordship and based primarily on the manor. At times the performance of the suit or the obligation of the suit itself was either passed upwards to a lord's baron or down to a lord's tenant according to the ancient principles of substitution. Suit itself implied inclusion in the jurisdiction of the county court and carried with it responsibility for the judgments rendered in the court. Suit carried with it also the obligation of attending the court to render those judgments, but in Cheshire the person who owed the suit was often expected to send a competent person in his place. Likewise, in the other English counties there is

[144] *RH*, 2:226; *CR*, 1253-1254, p. 72.

[145] *Casus Placitorum*, ed. W. H. Dunham, Selden Society, vol. 69 (London, 1950), p. lxxxvii: "Per Sutham in pleno comitatu: In isto comitatu Warr' quant ad comitatum nulli sunt sectatores." For Sutham, see below, chapter 4, at notes 47-61. It is possible that this note later in the eyre of London sparked the comment "Il isunt ascun contez ou nul suyter ne est, e si tenunt pleez." (*The Eyre of London, 14 Edward II* [A.D. 1321], ed. Helen M. Cam, 2 vols., Selden Society, vols. 85, 86 [London, 1968-1969], 2:253.)

[146] Brit. Lib., Add. 31826, fol. 240r: "Si breve de falso iudicio debeat portari, oportet esse iiij sectatores curie propter verba brevis. Contra: ad comitatum Leyc' nulli sunt sectatores; item ad portmannesmot in nundinis nulli sectatores etc."

[147] E. 13/20, m. 50.

little proof that the suitors were themselves actually involved in rendering the judgments required in the normal county session, even though they remained liable for them. Attendance of suitors was generally required only twice a year, and even this obligation was allowed in some counties to lapse by the end of the thirteenth century. Even before the reign of Edward I, however, when the obligations of suit were still enforced, the county court was not a democratic assembly of the knights of the county, the group who typically comprised the majority of the suitors. The actual functioning of the county court was dominated by the barons of the county through their legal experts, the seneschals and bailiffs. As in Cheshire, these individuals were the ones who actually performed the obligations of suit, even if they were not the ones who owed suit. It is, thus, the role of the early lawyers in the lower courts that must be examined in the next chapter.

4

Professional

Lawyers

PROFESSIONAL[1] LAWYERS were an integral part of English lower courts; they were the people who functioned as pleaders, attorneys, seignorial bailiffs, and seneschals, as well as occasionally filling royal positions such as undersheriff, sheriff, and county clerk. Just as the pleaders in the court of common pleas customarily functioned also as justices commissioned to take assizes or to deliver gaols, these lawyers not uncommonly served also in many legal capacities concurrently. It was this multiplicity of function that made them so influential in the county and so important in the legal system. A pleader, for instance, was not usually simply a pleader; he was also the agent of a powerful lord—an earl or a baron, an abbot or a bishop—and spoke with his lord's authority and was known to have been commissioned to dispose of his lord's affairs. His power was based on the wealth of the aristocrats he served as well as on his knowledge of the intricate world of legal technicality. Nor was he restricted to acting in one court alone, but was rather necessarily intimately involved with the proceedings in numerous lower courts and often also in the king's court, unintentionally creating strong bonds of common legal thought between the various courts of the country. It was these people, the

[1] I consider a person involved in legal activities a professional lawyer when, for a period of years, that person appears to be spending the major part of his time in legal functions and deriving the greater part of his income from those activities or, at least, from the investments made from that income, and when that person possesses a specialized knowledge differentiating him from laymen. I do not believe one needed a formal education—such as in the later Inns of Court—in the thirteenth century to become a professional. The skill was acquired equally well either by apprenticeship or by long observation, private study, and gradually increasing involvement. Nor do I think it needs to be shown that such a person offered his services to all comers. Some early lawyers would have been as closely attached to a noble as some modern lawyers are to large corporations. The lawyers I studied so obviously meet these qualifications that I feel it unnecessary to belabor that point.

professional lawyers, who were in fact the judges of the county court, not the suitors—the country squires and knights—of traditional theory.

Pleading was the focal point of litigation in the secular courts of medieval England. According to very strict standards the plaintiff or demandant was required to explain his case, setting forth all the necessary details in a formal speech known as the count or declaration. The defendant or tenant was then required to make two defenses, one very short and formal, the other meeting some part or all of the count with a direct denial or an allegation of justifying circumstances to which the plaintiff in turn would be required to respond. It was possible, however, for the defendant first to dispute formalities, such as a defect in the process by which he had been brought into court or in the words used in the count. Furthermore, either side could demur, that is, question whether the facts as set forth by the opposition were sufficient in law to constitute—depending on the party producing the demurrer—a case against him or an adequate defense. The whole point of pleading was for the court to force the parties through a series of accusations, justifications, and denials to rest the resolution of the dispute on an issue of law or fact. If the parties agreed to demur, it was for the court to resolve the whole case by deciding that legal point. If the parties settled on a question of fact, the truth of the matter was determined by putting that issue to trial either by compurgation or by a sworn verdict. In certain kinds of cases, the question arrived at by pleading would not be narrow at all, but would encompass a broad range of considerations—such as, "does x or y have the greater right to hold that tenement"—and would be tried by battle or taken into the king's court and tried by the grand assize. In any case, the trial itself was an afterthought, as it were, to the pleading. Both in the county courts and in the courts of liberties as well as in the king's court, jurors were not present during the pleading and were summoned only after the issue had been arrived at to fulfil what was considered the relatively simple function of telling the truth about a factual issue.[2] The presentation of evidence to the

[2] The form for joinder in issue and summoning a jury in Prat v Prat in the county court of Nottinghamshire (CP. 52 morrow All Souls, 27 Edward I [S.S.]) is common and demonstrates that the jury was not present: "Et predictus Thomas Prat venit et defendit vim et iniuriam quando etc., et dicit quod nec predictus Adam nec predicti Johannes, Walterus, et Willelmus executores testamenti predicti predictam pecunie summam sibi tradiderunt nec illam de eis recepit et hoc petit quod inquiratur. Et predicta Isabella dicit quod sic et petit similiter quod inquiratur. Et preceptum est ballivo quod venire faciat ad proximum comitatum xij etc. qui nec etc."

sworn jurors can be seen only occasionally in the king's court during the thirteenth century and assumed an important place in legal thought only much later.[3] Pleading was the activity that demanded the legal expertise and knowledge in medieval England which today is so concentrated on the trial.

The formalism of the courts demanded that statements made by the parties themselves be irrevocable. The legal function—not the original reason for his presence—of the pleader was to circumvent that formalism. The pleader was legally a person absolutely distinct from his client, very unlike the attorney, who was legally identical with his client in most respects. The pleader, therefore, could state the plaintiff's count without binding him. Only if, on reflection and perhaps after consultation, the client considered that the count had been made accurately, completely, and according to the proper form, would he avow the pleader. Avowing the pleader bound the client to the words spoken by him, so that thereafter it was considered that the client himself had spoken. If, on the other hand, he discovered some error in what had been said, he could disavow the pleader and count over again. The formalism was thus balanced by a legal device for reconsideration and reflection: the pleader.

Avowing a pleader, like many other actions in court, was a ritual and not merely an oral statement. Admittedly, the year book reports of cases in the court of common pleas only note that this or that litigant was asked if he avowed his pleader and that the litigant responded affirmatively. Nevertheless, there is evidence that the answer was given ceremonially, not orally. In the related matter of appointing an attorney in the king's court, clients were often mystified, if only because of the strangeness of the place and of court procedure. In one instance, two attorneys of a litigant wanted to have themselves appointed also for the man's wife, a measure that would probably have been to her disadvantage. The entry in the rolls, like the reports in the year books, stated that the justice involved had asked if the wife was present and she had answered affirmatively. The ceremony was only explained because the justice felt something was wrong and

---

[3] See, in general, S.F.C. Milsom, *Historical Foundations of the Common Law* (London, 1969), pp. 25-50 and Donald W. Sutherland, *The Assize of Novel Disseisin* (Oxford, 1963), pp. 69-73. Two cases that indicate the earliest separation so far observed between pleading to the assize and evidence presented to the assize are apparently from the 1290s: Brit. Lib. Add. 31826, fols. 60r, 321r. The latter case indicates that when an assize is taken even by the defendant's default a pleader can put in evidence for him before the assize. The evidence, in that case, was a rendition of the words exchanged between the parties in a render of land.

went on to interrogate the woman. She then told him that she was not the wife at all and had no idea of what was happening. She was there to appoint an attorney in her own case, and the two attorneys had merely raised her hand. That had been the affirmative response.[4] This ritual, the raising of a hand in combination with the attorney's, was a visible association of the client with the attorney. Another case, this time from the county court of Staffordshire in 1285, makes it clear that a pleader was avowed in a very similar manner. The pleader held up his hand, as if swearing, toward the opponent; and the client came and placed his hand on the pleader's.[5] Such a visible sign of association was much safer than a mere oral affirmation, which could have been readily denied afterwards.

Pleaders, however, were engaged in legal argument as much as they were involved in the formal statement of count and defense. There could be complicated arguments concerning whether the viscontiel writ was sufficient or whether the dispute had to be prosecuted by two different writs,[6] concerning the ability of a party to remove a case from county court into the court of common pleas after it had been only partially determined,[7] concerning whether all the defendants in particular circumstances had to enter separate defenses,[8] concerning the precise words in the writ and their possible implications on land tenure.[9] In short, any defense or response could be the result of lengthy legal argument involving several pleaders and the presiding officer. A pleader tested his opinions about the law in a particular instance both against the arguments that other pleaders could bring to bear and against the influential opinions of the presiding officer. Eventually, he would settle on the optimal response for his client, by which the client would have the greatest advantage or, at least, face the least damage. The enrollment which finally appeared on the county rolls was a formalized, abbreviated, and rationalized version of the complicated and taxing argument that had taken place in court.[10]

By 1293—and probably long before that—pleaders in the lower

[4] CP. 40/180, m. 18d. They were banned from functioning further in the king's court.

[5] Robert C. Palmer, "County Year Book Reports," *EHR* 91 (1976):800–801.

[6] Brit. Lib. Add. 31826, fol. 266r [S.S.].

[7] Ibid., fol. 266v [S.S.].

[8] Ibid. [S.S.].

[9] Ibid., fol. 268r [S.S.].

[10] Derived from a comparison of county year book reports and the writ file records, both of which will be included in the future Selden Society volume *The Medieval County Courts*.

courts were fully professional, occupying an acknowledged and fairly independent office in the court and thinking explicitly of those for whom they pleaded as clients. Thus Peter, son of William de Trebingham, prosecuted Theobald de Nevill, the undersheriff in Cornwall for Edmund, earl of Cornwall, in the Exchequer of pleas. Peter alleged that the undersheriff had refused to allow him to plead in any court before him, that is, at least in the county court and probably also in the hundred and stannary courts and the court of the borough of Lostwithiel. The undersheriff's defense was that Peter had been pleading for a client—*pro quodam cliente*—and had been disavowed three or four times. He had therefore suspended Peter from his office as pleader—*ab officio narrandi suspendebat*—for that day only.[11] The pleader was clearly a professional, and the pleading of this case indicates that the undersheriff would have acted illegally had he suspended him for no reason or for longer than the one day. Litigants, not the presiding officer, were the ultimate arbiters of who would plead for them.

At times pleaders were hired for an individual case. William de Bolton and three associates were paid 10s by the bakers at the fair of St. Ives in 1275 for their counsel and for refraining from harassing the bakers when the bailiffs tested their bread for proper weight.[12] Bolton alone was promised 4s by John Goldsmith to defend Simon Blake. Blake had admitted using a false rod for measuring and had alleged that he had received the rod from one Thomas de Toraux. Bolton accepted the case only on condition that Blake would not settle the dispute on his own. For some reason Goldsmith then refused to pay Bolton's fee and induced Blake to withdraw from his case. The court of the fair was prepared to allow Bolton to sue not only for his

[11] E. 13/19, m. 68: "Cornub'. Petrus filius Willelmi de Trebingham venit coram baronibus et queritur quod Theobaldus de Nevill vicecomes [sic] Cornubie non permittit predictum Petrum placitare coram eodem vicecomite in aliqua curia nec aliqua negocia prosequi coram eo, eo quod cepit de eodem Petro et capere fecit die jovis proxima ante festum sancti Georgii anno regis Edwardi xxj unum equum suum precii viginti solidorum et illum hucusque detinuit et adhuc detinet nullam causam assignando quare huiusmodi districcionem ei fecit ad dampnum suum xx m. Et hoc offert etc.

Et predictus Theobaldus venit et defendit vim iniuriam et quicquid etc., et dicit quod predictus Petrus quadam vice placitavit coram eo pro quodam cliente ipsius Petri et post narracionem suam pro eodem cliente idem Petrus ter vel quater fuit disadvocatus per eundem clientem suum propter quod predictus Theobaldus eundem Petrum eo die et quo ad illum diem ab officio narrandi suspendebat. Et quo ad predictum equum dicit quod nullum equum cepit de predicto Petro nec capere fecit. Et hoc petit quod inquiratur. Et predictus Petrus similiter." See *CRR* 6:173 (1211).

[12] *Select Pleas in Manorial and Other Seignorial Courts*, ed. F. W. Maitland, Selden Society, vol. 2 (London, 1888), p. 159.

original fee but also for the money he had hoped to force from Toraux.[13] Morgan de Dichton, a pleader in the county court of York-shire a few years earlier, had been more careful than Bolton. When he had accepted Ranulf fitz Robert of Newsholme as his client and had agreed to prosecute a case of wardship for Ranulf in the county court, he had covenanted with Ranulf that if peace was made without Dichton's assent, Ranulf would pay him £30. Ranulf nevertheless concorded with the defendant within a fortnight. His only defense was that the litigation had failed for lack of any action by Dichton and that the money he had received from the defendant had been given him freely by the defendant's attorney only later for the sake of charity. Dichton finally settled for a payment of 40s, and that was 10s more than Ranulf had received from the defendant, although far less than their covenant had first stipulated.[14] Not all contracts were so complicated. Simon Wyberd in 1272 had received 4 marks from Nicholas le Thogh to counsel and aid him against his adversaries in the hundred court of Middleton. Nicholas was displeased with the results, since he afterwards sued Wyberd, charging him with im-prisonment, extortion of the 4 marks, and the making of false ac-cusations that Nicholas had murdered his wife.[15] That fee had simply been paid in advance.

More frequently pleaders were retained with annuities. Just as one retained a knight by conferring on him the right to receive a specified

---

[13] Ibid., p. 155.

[14] JUST. 1/1050, m. 38 (52 Henry III): "Et unde predictus Morganus queritur quod, cum convenisset inter eos quod predictus Morganus sequeretur quoddam placitum in comitatu Ebor' motum inter predictum Ranulphum et quendam Robertum filium Wil-lelmi de Stutevile de quadam custodia terre et heredis Roberti de Neusum que pertinebat ad ipsum Ranulphum ita videlicet quod si predictus Ranulphus pacem fecerit cum predicto Roberto de eodem placito sine assensu et voluntate ipsius Morgani quod idem Ranulphus teneretur eidem Morgano in triginta libris eidem solvendis, infra quindenam post concordiam factam idem Ranulphus postea sine voluntate et assensu ipsius Mor-gani et ipso irrequisito pacem fecit cum predicto Roberto pro centum libris quas ab eo recepit. Et dicit quod idem Ranulphus semper postea ei detinuit predictas triginta libras et reddere contradicit, unde dicit quod deterioratus est et dampnum habet ad valenciam xl librarum et inde producit sectam.

Et Ranulphus venit et defendit vim et iniuriam quando etc. Et bene concedit quod convenit inter eos de prosequicione [sic] predicti placiti sicut predictum est, set dicit quod racione predicte prosequicionis non potest petere ab ipso aliquem denarium, quia dicit quod predictus Morganus reliquit prosequicionem predicti placiti in comitatu predicto per quod loquela illa periit in eodem comitatu. Et dicit quod Robertus de Stutevill de Clivelaund attornatus predicti Roberti filii Willelmi gratis et caritatis intuitu et postquam predicta loquela perierat in comitatu dedit ei triginta solidos.

Et Morganus dicit quod ipse viriliter prosequebatur predictum placitum in comitatu quousque predictus Ranulphus invito et irrequisito pacem fecit cum predicto Roberto per quod ipse prosequi non potuit pro ipso Ranulpho ponit se super patriam."

[15] JUST. 1/367, m. 53.

payment every year for life, a pleader would be hired by granting him an annuity, so that the lawyer's fee (payment) was still a fee (conditional grant for life). Such a grant even carried with it the ethics associated with the grant for knight service, particularly in respect to escheat for nonfulfillment or traitorous activities. Thus, when Robert de Duffhus attempted to regain the arrears on seven years of his annuity from William le Deneys, Deneys objected that Duffhus had not only refused to aid and counsel him in the hundred of Bosmere in a case concerning one robe, but had even aided the opposition. He maintained—and it was the law—that such a failure would have prevented Duffhus from prosecuting for his arrears; the feudal felony—if we may use a term already archaic at that time—absolved the lord/client from any obligation to his man/lawyer. Duffhus, however, was able to prove by the jury that he had been faithful to Deneys and thus recovered his arrears.[16] He did not, however, have to demonstrate that he had done anything during those seven years except aid his client in those cases where his default was alleged. In 1281 Elyas de Staunton Horald had retained William Pakeman with an annuity of one mark to be paid *de camera* (as seemed to be uniform practice for those annuities made to lawyers claimed in the court of common pleas) in twice-yearly installments. The grant was made "in return for William's homage, service, and counsel." Thereafter, in 1297, Pakeman sued Elyas to obtain ten years' arrears of that annuity. Elyas alleged that in 1285 he had gone to William and asked his aid and counsel against John de Asgarthorp, who had brought a suit of trespass against him in the county court of Leicestershire. Pakeman, however, had abandoned Elyas and had pleaded against him in that plea. Pakeman's only answer was that he had not counselled Elyas' opponent in that plea.[17] Similar charges were levelled against Stephen Angot by the prior of Bromehill concerning a plea in the court of

[16] CP. 40/90, m. 107; see Robert C. Palmer, "The Origins of the Legal Profession in England," *Irish Jurist* 11 (1976):129.

[17] CP. 40/121, m. 146: "Et Elyas . . . bene cognovit predictum scriptum esse factum suum set dicit quod predictus Willelmus per scriptum illud nichil de predicto redditu nec de arreragiis eiusdem exigere potest, quia dicit quod quidam Johannes de Asgarthorp implacitavit ipsum Elyam in comitatu predicto de placito transgressionis anno regni domini regis nunc terciodecimo ita quod idem Elyas adivit predictum Willelmum et requisivit ipsum ut asisteret eidem Elye in auxilio et consilio in placito predicto. Et dicit quod idem Willelmus elongavit se a consilio ipsius Elye et adhesit parti predicti Johannis et placitavit cum ipso Johanne contra ipsum Elyam in eodem placito in comitatu predicto etc., unde cum in predicto scripto contineatur quod idem Elyas concessit predicto Willelmo predictum annuum redditum pro servicio suo habendo ac idem Willelmus in predicto placito a consilio ipsius Elye se subtraxit et contra ipsum sicut predictum est placitavit, petit iudicium etc."

Clare.[18] Likewise, in 1302 John de la Chapele, suing for his arrears, was met by the same defense from the abbot of Heppe (?). In his count John only mentioned the faithful counsel and aid rendered and to be rendered, the phrases that counts for such annuities often mentioned. This once, however, the terms of the actual deed found their way into the plea roll. The deed specified that the grant was made for his aid and counsel in business touching the abbot and the monastery, for services already rendered and services to be rendered in the future at the abbey's expense whenever he was reasonably requested to do so. Furthermore, if John happened to suffer the loss of his horse while on abbey business outside the diocese of Carlisle, the abbot and monastery would provide him with another or, at least, the value of the horse in money. Finally, John could reside at the monastery when he wanted, would be admitted to an adequate and decent place in the house, and would be treated honestly with regard to food and drink. He was allowed to bring with him two servants with horses; and they would also be looked after; indeed, the servants and horses were to be treated as if they belonged to the cellarer himself. In addition to all this, John's annuity was supposed to be 2 marks, received from the abbot's treasury. That annuity was not paid, and the abbot alleged that John had defaulted in his obligations toward the abbot in a case in the county court of Westmorland.[19] In 1304 Simon, vicar of Finchingfield, had granted an annuity of 40s to John de Finchingfeld, who was described as a pleader in hundred courts and other courts in Essex. When John attempted to regain 100s of that annuity, the vicar defended himself by alleging that John had pleaded against him in two cases of debt in the hundred court of Hinckford in 1307.[20] In every case, then, the legal ethics touching

[18] CP. 40/129, m. 120: "Quia dicit quod predictus Stephanus per formam predicti scripti obligatur eidem priori et eiusdem loci conventui ad homagium et servicium eis facienda etc. Et dicit quod predictus Stephanus in curia comitis Gloucestrie de Clare in qua idem prior fuit inplacitatus per quemdam Walterum de Brethenham de placito detencionis averiorum fuit de consilio predicti Walteri contra ipsum priorem et stetit cum ipso Waltero in eodem placito anno regni regis nunc vicesimo."

[19] CP. 40/143, m. 113: "in negociis suis et domum suam tangentibus prestito et prestando in posterum sumptibus suis cum ab eis racionabiliter fuerit requisitus et si occasione servicii sui facti extra Karl' diocesem dictus Johannes equum amittat, dicti abbas et conventus eidem Johanni equum equivalentem vel saltem precium restaurabunt. Concesserunt eciam eidem Johanni quod quandocumque in domum eorundem moram trahere voluerit, quod honesto loco competenti admittatur et tractabitur in cibo et potu prout decet honeste cum duobus garconibus suis et duobus equis suis ut garconibus et equis celararii sui."

[20] CP. 40/179, m. 549: "Et dicit quod predictus Johannes narrator est in hundredis et aliis curiis in comitatu predicto per quod racione servicii sui sibi prestandi in agendis ipsius Simonis in predictis hundredis et curiis et alibi etc., obligavit se eidem in annuo redditu predicto etc., ac idem Simon postmodum . . . habuisset quoddam placitum

lawyers in the lower courts centered on the annuity. The lawyer's right to his annuity was determined by the ancient principles that governed the knight's right to his fee.

The careers of the lawyers who functioned in Warwickshire county court around 1303 show the kind of person who would have been hired to plead in county courts and the way in which these lawyers continued to function in county administration after they had completed their period of properly legal activity. The county year book reports from Warwickshire name fourteen—or, perhaps, fifteen—lawyers who functioned in that court.[21] One of these was the undersheriff; the rest, pleaders. Their careers reveal two major characteristics: aristocratic allegiances and high professional ability.

The undersheriff of the reports, of course, functioned as the presiding officer and was a competent lawyer. He is mentioned in the reports only as "Warwick"; he was almost certainly Robert de Warwick, occasionally also called Robert le Belleyetere.[22] Before he had been appointed undersheriff, he had been an attorney in the court of common pleas. He first appeared in that function in 1294, but his work there was infrequent until 1300. From 1300 to 1304 clients appointed him their attorney 168 times. He appeared occasionally during the next three years and then ceased to function as an attorney in the king's court.[23] He seems first to have served as undersheriff

debiti etc., placitandum in hundredo de Heyngford in comitatu predicto versus Walterum Colbeyn et eciam . . . habuisset quoddam aliud placitum debiti etc., in eodem hundredo placitandum versus magistrum Philippum Walerand et ipsum Johannem in eodem hundredo diebus et annis supradictis inventum requisisset ut servicium suum circa eadem placita impenderet ut tenebatur per scriptum predictum, dictus Johannes ei assistere noluit etc., immo contra ipsum stetit in predictis placitis."

[21] The total number of cases in which each person mentioned appeared in county year book reports are as follows: Sheriff, 3; Warwick, 6; Crompe, 20; Sutham, 13; John Heyford, Eyford, 9; Boydin, 4; Adam des Okes, Hokes, 4; Hoke(le?), 1; Payn, 4; Wolleward, 1; Alne, 1; R. Attemere, 1; H. de Hurst, 1; Scherem(an?), 1; Stamp', 1; Stoke, 1. For a further breakdown in these figures, see Palmer, "County Year Book Reports," p. 780.

[22] Nicholas de Warwick, despite his interests in Warwickshire, would have been an unlikely person to have been undersheriff, since he was heavily burdened by his duties as king's serjeant:

[23] Robert le Belleyetere's position in the county court in 1308 and his later appointment as undersheriff in Worcestershire make him almost surely the person who appears in the reports. It is unclear if he is the same person as Robert le Seynter of Warwick. Seynter did appear regularly in Beauchamp charters (Brit. Lib. Add. 28024, fols. 69r, 69v, 70, 77, 77v) and functioned occasionally as an attorney in the court of common pleas (CP. 40/131, m. 374 [bis], CP. 40/133, m. 206 [bis]). There are some coincidences which would indicate they were the same person: both had a father named William, a wife named Matilda, and lands in Claverdon (CPR, 1307-1313, p. 325; CPR, 1313-1317, pp. 247, 256; CP. 52 quindene John the Baptist, 28 Edward I, Gloucestershire). They were at least related. JUST. 1/1023, m. 25 (1275) records a voucher to warranty of Henry le Belleyetere, whose ancestor was named Simon le Seynter. It is more

TABLE 4.1
County Pleaders as King's Court Attorneys

Year	Number of Appointments as Attorney in the Bench for:					
	Sutham	Heyford	Boydin	Crompe	Warwick	Stoke
1288	3	1				
1289	4					
1290	2		2	2		
1291	19		15	5		
1292	7		4	2		
1293	6		5			
1294	8	1	7		4	
1295	5	5	2	1		
1296	9	10	2	8	1	
1297	14	12	4	3		
1298	15	14	7	2		
1299	29	29	12	11	2	
1300	41	15	15		17	
1301	23	28	6		34	
1302	43	29	10		40	1
1303	14	2	20	1	41	2
1304	26	15	17		26	
1305	10	3	7		4	3
1306	1	1	6		1	
1307			1		2	
1308			2			

SOURCE: CP. 40/65 to CP. 40/178.

in Warwickshire for John de Dene, sheriff in 1302-1304, but was
almost certainly once again undersheriff for Dene in 1308.[24] Then,
in 1310, Guy Beauchamp, earl of Warwick and hereditary sheriff of
Worcestershire, made Warwick the undersheriff of Worcestershire.
He presided over that county with the normal responsibilities of a
sheriff.[25] After the earl's death in 1315, Warwick was subjected to

possible that they were the same person, because, even though Robert le Belleyetere's
father had been called Belleyetere, the name was still not firmly attached to the family;
E. 13/37, m. 34d refers to Warwick as "Robertus de Warewyk dictus Belleyetere."

[24] For the undersheriffs of Warwickshire and Leicestershire around 1303, see Palmer,
"County Year Book Reports," p. 779. Warwick's position in 1308 is indicated in CP.
40/173, m. 444d, Warwick v Reymund: "Et vicecomes nichil inde fecit set mandavit
quod causa non est vera etc. Et quia non pertinet ad ipsum causam illam iudicare, ideo
sicut prius . . ." The content of a *causa* clause very seldom appears in the plea rolls,
but the substantive rule that illuminates that entry appears in Brit. Lib. Add. 31826,
fol. 415v: "En prise de avers ou bref vent a vicont fesant mencion de cause de re-
muement qe touche ly ou ses clers si ne peut il pas memes trier sa cause, sed si breve
dicat quia distrinxit in feodo suo, tunc bene potest quia est causa aliena."

[25] *List of Sheriffs for England and Wales* (1898; reprint/ed. New York, 1963), p.
157.

two commissions on his conduct while in office.[26] All along, his career seems to have been dependent on the earl. Twice he had been appointed attorney by the executor of William Beauchamp, the previous earl of Warwick.[27] It was only after Guy became earl, moreover, that Warwick had begun his period of intensive activity in the court of common pleas. Finally, John de Dene, the sheriff who made Warwick undersheriff in Warwickshire and Leicestershire, was an associate of the earl, since he was made Beauchamp's general attorney in 1304.[28] The earl's power in Warwickshire and his position in the Exchequer gave him control over the appointment of the sheriff in that county, and his sheriff would employ men loyal to the earl.

After the earl's death in 1315, Warwick resumed his activity in Warwickshire. In 1318 he acted on a commission of *oyer* and *terminer*,[29] and around that time he was also a coroner.[30] He had used his lands in Warwickshire and Worcestershire as security for loans in 1313 and 1317,[31] and conceivably it was this indebtedness which caused him to be removed from his office as coroner. The reason specified for his removal—the lack of qualifications—frequently referred to the insufficiency of the person's real property holdings.[32] Even thereafter, however, he was active in county affairs. In 1323, for instance, he made fine with the king for allegedly corrupt dealings in the assessment and collection of a lay subsidy.[33] Warwick's problems were at least partly related to his political affiliations. His association with the earl of Warwick would have initially put him in opposition to Edward II. Still in 1317 he was associated with Peter de Lymesy, who had needed a pardon for the death of Piers Gaveston and who would need a pardon a few years later for hostile actions taken toward the Despensers.[34] In 1322, after the exile of the Despensers, a writ was issued for Warwick's arrest.[35] His position seems to have remained hazardous for the rest of the reign, because in 1327, soon after Roger Mortimer came to power, Warwick was one of the many who were granted a general pardon.[36] His position, however,

---

[26] *CPR, 1313-1317*, pp. 244, 427.

[27] CP. 40/133, m. 213; CP. 40/138, m. 191.

[28] CP. 40/151, m. 254d.

[29] *CPR, 1317-1321*, p. 272.

[30] *CCR, 1318-1323*, p. 264.

[31] *CCR, 1313-1318*, pp. 76, 471.

[32] R. F. Hunnisett, *The Medieval Coroner* (Cambridge, 1961), pp. 174-75.

[33] *Lay Subsidy Roll for Warwickshire, 6 Edward III*, ed. W. F. Carter, Dugdale Society, vol. 6 (London, 1926), p. 98.

[34] *CPR, 1313-1317*, p. 21; *CPR, 1321-1324*, p. 17.

[35] *CPR, 1321-1324*, p. 71.

[36] *CPR, 1327-1330*, p. 47.

required special attention, since his pardon reappears alone in the Patent Rolls in 1328.[37] He was obviously respectable while Mortimer was in power, and in 1329-30 he sat in Parliament for the borough of Warwick with John Sotemay, and then in 1330 he and Sotemay were the representatives elected to Parliament for Warwickshire.[38] Soon after Mortimer fell, Warwick was himself hanged for felony.[39] Neither the date nor the reason for his hanging can be ascertained. In 1332, however, his son William had already died in prison, having turned approver against his companions in diverse felonies committed in Staffordshire, Nottinghamshire, and Lincolnshire. The one misdeed actually mentioned was that William, William de Burton, and Richard de Burton had despoiled Richard Willoughby, a royal justice, of 100 marks in Lincolnshire sometime around December 1331. William was said to have retained only 50s of the loot.[40] His case was undoubtedly related to his father's death, although whether Robert himself was found guilty of receiving a felon—his son—or William attacked the justice only after his father was hanged is not known. In any event, it is probable that Warwick's persistent opposition to Edward II led finally to his death.

Warwick's real possessions and their treatment after his death allow some definition of his sources of revenue, for grants of land could be used to hire a lawyer as well as grants of an annuity. After the king had taken his customary year, day, and waste of the felon's lands, the lands escheated back to Warwick's various lords. From the earl of Warwick, his main patron, he had held a messuage, a carucate of land, and sixteen acres of meadow in Claverdon, Warwickshire.[41] He had also held some land in Newark from the bishop of Lincoln.[42] The bishop of Coventry and Lichfield likewise laid claim to some houses which Warwick and his sons had held in Warwick itself,[43] but he later surrendered his claim to the bishop of Worcester.[44] Also in Warwick, he had held one toft and one-fourth of a messuage from the College

[37] Ibid., p. 256.

[38] *Members of Parliament*, 3 vols. (London, 1878-1891), 1:90, 93.

[39] *CIM*, 2:324; *CCR, 1333-1337*, p. 548. Both of these would place his death around 1331; other writs would date his death in 1332.

[40] KB. 27/290, m. 12d. (c.p.)

[41] *CIM*, 2:330; *CCR, 1333-1337*, p. 53. Warwick had entered most of this land—one messuage and a half a virgate—through one Joan, daughter of Christine de Shireborne: JUST. 1/968, m. 14.

[42] *CPR, 1340-1343*, p. 302. Warwick's father, William ye Belleyeter, was familiar with Newark also, since he was accused in 1285 of having raped Sibyl, daughter of Hugh de Newark, in Lincoln: KB. 27/94, m. 14.

[43] *CFR, 1327-1337*, p. 326.

[44] *CCR, 1333-1337*, p. 548.

of St. Mary. The college, receiving back this land, put it once again to a similar use, furthering its interests with the important legal personnel of the county by regranting the lands to John Sotemay, William de Sutton, and John Sparry.[45] What would not appear in such posthumous dealings were the many annuities Warwick must have accumulated. Of these only one is known: he received an annuity of 6s 8d from Nicholas de Pyrye. That annuity had been sufficient reason for a litigant to remove a case from the county court of Worcestershire in 1315 for fear that Warwick would favor Pyrye, who was the plaintiff in the action.[46] Despite his troubles, Warwick had still been fairly comfortably provided for at the time of his death. Good lawyers seldom starve.

Thomas de Sutham did not rise as high as Warwick, but he was preeminently a professional lawyer. By the number of his appearances in the county year book reports, he was one of the most prominent of the pleaders in the Warwickshire county court.[47] As early as 1285 he had also acted as attorney in the eyre of Warwickshire.[48] In 1288 he began to practice as an attorney in the court of common pleas, and by the end of 1306 he had been appointed attorney 289 times. His busiest years in that court were from 1299 to 1304, when he averaged almost thirty appointments each year.[49] He appeared early in 1307 as a pleader before a justice of assize[50] and died in 1308.[51] He had acted frequently in the settlement of lands during his career, serving as attorney five times in final concords between 1292 and 1305.[52] He had also appeared twice as an attorney in the Exchequer

[45] CIM, 2:324. A different writ, a memorandum of the livery by Roger le Mercer— Hokkele's clerk during his term as sheriff—and the three deeds are in E. 164/22, fols. 52v-53v. Sutton received the toft for a rent of 12d annually. He was a coroner (JUST. 3/123, m. 15; Select Cases Concerning the Law Merchant, ed. H. Hall, 3 vols., Selden Society, vols. 23, 46, 49 [London, 1908-1932], 3:44). See also below, n. 91. Sotemay received most of the fourth of the messuage for a rent of 4d annually. He was at least a sometime attorney (CP. 40/138, m. 308 [ter]), sat in Parliament (above, n. 38), and was at this time the undersheriff of Worcestershire for earl Thomas de Beauchamp (List of Sheriffs, p. 157.) Sparry received only a plot from the fourth of a messuage at a rent of 2d annually. He later presided over the presentations concerning the Statute of Laborers in 1357 (JUST. 1/975). That particular piece of land appears again in CPR, 1338-1340, pp. 7-8, in a grant of an adjoining plot which was witnessed by Heyford, Sutton, Sotemay, Roger le Mercer, and others.

[46] CP. 52 octave Hilary, 8 Edward II.

[47] Above, n. 21.

[48] JUST. 1/956, m. 32d.

[49] Above, Table 4.1.

[50] JUST. 1/965, m. 22.

[51] CP. 40/174, m. 183 (the appearance of his executors).

[52] Warwickshire Feet of Fines, ed. Ethel Stokes and Lucy Drucker, Dugdale Society, vol. 15 (London, 1939), nos. 1091, 1153, 1195, 1209, 1210.

of pleas around 1300[53] and had appeared occasionally as an attorney before justices of assize.[54] His career as a lawyer was long and busy; he had served as pleader in the county court and in the king's court and had had long years of experience in the king's court as an attorney.

Like Warwick, Sutham also had a strong association with the aristocracy. His principal client was the prior of Coventry. As early as 1288 he handled a case for Thomas de Pavy, prior of Coventry.[55] His affiliation with the priory was confirmed under the succeeding prior, and in all Sutham handled thirty cases for the priory, spread evenly over his career and continuing up to 1305.[56] In 1299 he was appointed general attorney for the archdeacon of Coventry;[57] in 1301, for the prior of Coventry.[58] He appeared seven times as a witness to charters preserved in the Coventry chartulary, all seemingly previous to 1305.[59] Even though the priory was his principal client and therefore probably also his chief patron, he maintained close ties with several other people. He represented the abbot of Combe eight times[60] and John de Broughton four times as an attorney in the court of common pleas.[61] His twelve appearances in the county show him acting as pleader for other individuals. His reliance on the priory thus did not preclude his being employed by others.

John de Heyford was another of the principal pleaders in Warwickshire.[62] Like Sutham, Heyford was not restricted to functioning in the county court. Between 1288 and 1306 he was appointed attorney 165 times in the court of common pleas,[63] and he also appeared in the Exchequer of pleas as an attorney ten times.[64] He served as an attorney in five Warwickshire final concords from 1296 to 1302 and also in several final concords concerning lands in Gloucestershire and

[53] E. 13/21, m. 32; E. 13/22, m. 42d.

[54] JUST. 1/965, m. 5; JUST. 1/968, m. 25d.

[55] CP. 40/75, m. 202d.

[56] CP. 40/93, m. 165 [bis]; CP. 40/91, m. 335; CP. 40/106, m. 325 [bis]; CP. 40/113, m. 161; CP. 40/116, m. 145; CP. 40/119, m. 155d; CP. 40/121, m. 318d [ter]; CP. 40/122, m. 213 [bis]; CP. 40/124, m. 92d [bis]; CP. 40/127, m. 186; CP. 40/130, m. 379d [ter]; CP. 40/142, m. 215 [bis]; CP. 40/144, m. 365 [ter]; CP. 40/145, m. 427d; CP. 40/147, m. 223d; CP. 40/155, m. 252d; CP. 40/153, m. 527d [bis].

[57] CPR, 1292-1301, p. 400.

[58] Ibid., p. 562.

[59] E. 164/21, fols. 84v, 91r [bis], 92v, 93r, 94r, 95r. Only the second last reference is dated: 1303.

[60] CP. 40/106, m. 325d [bis]; CP. 40/107, m. 159d [bis]; CP. 40/142, m. 221 [ter]; CP. 40/146, m. 233.

[61] CP. 40/134, mm. 213, 214d; CP. 40/138, m. 195d; CP. 40/135, m. 409.

[62] Above, n. 21.

[63] Above, Table 4.1.

[64] E. 13/20, m. 52d; E. 13/21, mm. 6, 6d [bis]; E. 13/22, mm. 44d, 58; E. 13/25, m. 22; E. 13/26, mm. 1d, 26, 42d.

Oxfordshire.[65] He functioned regularly as essoiner and pledge before justices of assize in Warwickshire.[66] After he discontinued his work in the court of common pleas, he remained active in the county. He assisted, for instance, in the collection of lay subsidies.[67] In 1332 he was appointed one of the keepers of the peace in Warwickshire.[68] In 1334 he served as one of the keepers of the temporalities of the see of Worcester.[69] Before his disappearance from royal records in 1338, he had served on seven commissions of *oyer* and *terminer* in Warwickshire.[70] As with Warwick, Heyford's extensive legal business in the first few decades of adulthood had prepared him to assume key positions in the governance of the county.

Heyford's sources of patronage can also be traced. His earliest case—a solitary one in the court of common pleas in 1288—was for the abbot of Stoneleigh; he handled another eight cases for the abbot before 1304.[71] He also appeared for the abbot five times in the Exchequer of pleas,[72] so that he seems to have been principally affiliated to that abbey. He also acted frequently for John Pecche, serving as his attorney ten times after 1296,[73] and for John de Broughton, for whom he was an attorney seven times.[74] At times Heyford and Sutham were appointed together on a case, since it was the custom at that time for litigants to appoint two attorneys, either of whom could act in the plea.

Thomas Boydin of Stretton was the third of the four most active pleaders in the Warwickshire county court,[75] and his career was sim-

---

[65] *Warwickshire Feet of Fines*, nos. 1119, 1139, 1142, 1174, 1181; CP. 25 (1)75/38, no. 222 (Glouc.); CP. 25 (1)188/12, nos. 71, 75 (Oxon.).

[66] JUST. 1/964, mm. 9, 14; JUST. 1/965, m. 22; JUST. 1/1327, m. 10.

[67] *Lay Subsidy Roll for Warwickshire*, pp. 24, 98.

[68] *CPR, 1330-1334*, pp. 294, 296.

[69] Ibid., p. 526. In *CPR, 1338-1340*, p. 8, he appears as a witness of a charter for the bishop. This diocese, of course, included much of Warwickshire.

[70] *CPR, 1330-1334*, pp. 286, 447, 505, 578; *CPR, 1338-1340*, p. 147. In *CPR, 1334-1338*, p. 296, he was appointed to a special commission to investigate the shipping of silver from England; p. 326, he was ordered, along with others, to supervise the taking of an inquest. *CPR, 1324-1327*, p. 265, a commission of gaol delivery in Worcestershire.

[71] CP. 40/75, m. 196; CP. 40/104, m. 169; CP. 40/107, m. 156d; CP. 40/108, m. 158d; CP. 40/129, m. 186 [bis]; CP. 40/134, m. 213d; CP. 40/144, m. 387; CP. 40/151, m. 240.

[72] E. 13/21, m. 6d [bis]; E. 13/22, m. 58; E. 13/26, mm. 26, 42d.

[73] CP. 40/111, m. 173; CP. 40/123, m. 180d [bis]; CP. 40/126, mm. 208, 208d; CP. 40/127, m. 178 (with Sutham); CP. 40/136, mm. 207d, 211; CP. 40/139, m. 221; CP. 40/135, m. 233.

[74] CP. 40/127, m. 186; CP. 40/130, mm. 367, 377; CP. 40/134, m. 314d (with Sutham); CP. 40/139, m. 221d; CP. 40/135, m. 401; CP. 40/144, m. 373; CP. 40/151, m. 238d.

[75] Above, n. 21.

ilar to Heyford's. He too acted as an attorney in the court of common pleas. His first case there was in 1290, when he represented his father, William Boydin, in an action of false judgment on a case of debt.[76] From 1290 to 1308 Boydin was appointed attorney 144 times. His most active period there was between 1299 and 1304, when he averaged over thirteen appointments a year.[77] He was also an attorney four times in the Exchequer of pleas[78] and handled four Warwickshire final concords.[79] Furthermore, Boydin acted more often as a general attorney than the other pleaders. After four appearances as attorney for Edward de Sumervill in the court of common pleas between 1301 and 1304, Boydin was made his general attorney in 1305 while Sumervill accompanied Walter Langton.[80] In 1308 Boydin was appointed general attorney by the abbot of St. Mary, St-Pierre-sur-Dives, for a period of four years.[81] In 1304 the abbot of St. Nicholas, Angers, appointed him general attorney for three years along with William Purfrey.[82] His services then must have been satisfactory, for in 1322 the abbot reappointed him for a period of three years.[83]

There can be no doubt that Boydin's chief patron was John de Hastings. Between 1299 and 1308 he was appointed attorney by Hastings or his general attorney thirty-five times in the court of common pleas and twice in the Exchequer of pleas.[84] This was one-third of his total caseload for the period. In 1296 he had prosecuted William Reymund, bailiff of Knightlow hundred, acting something like a public prosecutor and charging Reymund with various corrupt practices. Reymund was found guilty, was obliged to pay triple damages to the individuals concerned, and was then sent to gaol.[85] Boydin's concern with Knightlow hundred may have come from his association with Hastings, since Hastings held that hundred at farm from the king.

[76] CP. 40/82, m. 123d.

[77] Above, Table 4.1.

[78] E. 13/21, m. 31d; E. 13/22, m. 42d; E. 13/24, m. 26; E. 13/27, m. 66. He was also a mainpernor: E. 13/26, m. 68d.

[79] Warwickshire Feet of Fines, nos. 1179, 1226, 1227, 1263.

[80] CP. 40/134, m. 215; CP. 40/136, m. 212; CP. 40/145, m. 442d; CP. 40/150, m. 267d; CPR, 1301-1307, p. 388.

[81] CPR, 1307-1313, p. 98.

[82] CFR, 1272-1307, p. 494.

[83] CPR, 1321-1324, p. 202.

[84] CP. 40/127, m. 188; CP. 40/133, m. 206d [decies]; CP. 40/134, m. 216d; CP. 40/145, m. 439d [quinquies]; CP. 40/146, m. 231d [septies]; CP. 40/150, m. 251; CP. 40/149, m. 419d [quinquies]; CP. 40/155, m. 251 [bis]; CP. 40/159, m. 277. The cases in CP. 40/145, 146, 150, and 149 were appointments made by Hastings's general attorney, Robert de Herle (appointment of Herle and Robert de Heyle: CP. 40/146, m. 225d). E. 13/22, m. 24; E. 13/24, m. 26.

[85] E. 13/20, m. 57.

The hundred was only rejoined to the body of the county in 1305.[86] Boydin remained with the Hastings family after his patron's death in 1313. In 1322 Boydin was made general attorney of John de Hastings, his former patron's son and heir.[87] In 1324 he, along with Robert de Heyle, was commissioned to receive the Hastings inheritance from Aymer de Valence, late earl of Pembroke, and to answer the claims for dower from the widow.[88] The following year, after his patron's death, Boydin was appointed keeper during pleasure of all the Hastings lands in Warwickshire and Leicestershire, since the heir was still a minor.[89] In 1327 he was appointed to a commission of *oyer* and *terminer* in Worcestershire[90] and was also commissioned to survey and report concerning the condition of Warwick castle.[91] He died only a few year later.[92] In twenty years he had worked his way from being a pleader and retained attorney to being a trusted administrator in the very highest ranks of the Hastings retinue.

Nicholas Crompe of Coventry was the pleader who appeared most frequently—twenty times—in the county year book reports.[93] He had acted as attorney also in the court of common pleas, but in only thirty-five cases in the years between 1290 and 1303.[94] In thirteen of these cases his client was Robert de Montalt,[95] and it was in the Montalt half of Coventry that Crompe was assessed 20s for the 1327 lay subsidy.[96] Even though he seldom appeared in the court of common pleas, his legal activity seems to have been fairly constant and also to have continued beyond 1303. In 1309, for instance, he was accused of champerty.[97] In 1315 he was the seneschal of the earl of Lancaster and held the view of frankpledge at Kenilworth.[98] He died sometime after his charitable donation to St. John's Hospital in Coventry in 1329[99] and before the lay subsidy assessment of 1332. The

[86] E. 368/75, m. 4.

[87] *CPR, 1321-1324*, p. 190.

[88] *CCR, 1323-1327*, p. 323.

[89] *CFR, 1319-1327*, p. 327.

[90] *CPR, 1324-1327*, p. 352.

[91] Ibid., with William de Sutton: above, n. 45.

[92] KB. 27/284, m. 20d (the appearance of his executors).

[93] Above, n. 21.

[94] Above, Table 4.1.

[95] CP. 40/111, m. 174; CP. 40/121, m. 323; CP. 40/126, m. 199d [quater]; CP. 40/129, m. 188 [septies].

[96] *PQW*, p. 395; *Feudal Aids*, prepared under the superintendence of the Deputy Keeper of the Records, 6 vols. (London, 1890-1920), 5:176; E. 179/192/4, m. 3d.

[97] CP. 40/178, m. 327; CP. 40/179, m. 37. The plaintiff withdrew from the suit.

[98] *The Stoneleigh Leger Book*, ed. R. H. Hilton, Dugdale Society, vol. 24 (Oxford, 1960); *Feudal Aids*, 5:177.

[99] *CPR, 1327-1330*, p. 395.

sparse record of activity in the court of common pleas is sufficient warning against presuming that it was only experience in the king's court that could make a lawyer competent.

If Crompe's activity was mostly local, that of Adam des Okes was completely so. He did not function as an attorney in the king's court at all; but, if one can judge from the frequency of his appearances in the county reports, he was as important a pleader in the county court as was Boydin.[100] His expertise allowed him to claim exceptionally large annuities for his services. The prior of Kenilworth had granted him an annuity of one robe and 6½ marks. In 1304 Okes claimed four years' arrears of that annuity from the prior.[101] A few years later he was also collecting an annuity of 40s and 1 mark for his robes each year from the Knights Templars' house of Balsall,[102] and he was still collecting that rent early in the reign of Edward III.[103] It seems, even, that he was the owner of British Library manuscript Lansdowne 564, because documents relating to his suit concerning his tenement in Whitleigh have been written into that book on folios that had been left blank.[104] That particular volume would have been very helpful to him, because it contains two registers of writs, one exceptionally fine in its detailing of writs that could be purchased to initiate litigation in the county courts. In 1295 he had been a bailiff of the prior of Coventry, and on the prior's behalf had appeared in successive sessions of the court of Knightlow hundred to claim a plea of debt for the prior's court.[105] Finally, he was used as a witness. When a defendant

[100] Above, n. 21.

[101] CP. 40/151, m. 34d.

[102] CCR, 1307-1313, p. 471.

[103] SC. 6/1040/21.

[104] Fols. 4r, 18v. I am particularly indebted to Dr. Paul Brand for pointing out this connection.

[105] CP. 40/113, m. 50: "Hundredum de Knyghth' tentum apud Wolfmerthston die jovis proxima ante festum sancti Barnabe anno supradicto [23 Edward I]. Johannes le Govere per attornatum suum optulit se versus Robertum de Shepeye in placito debiti. Et venit Adam des Okes ballivus predicti prioris de Coventr' et peciit curiam domini sui de predicto Roberto. Et similiter Robertus de Stoke ballivus Rogeri de Monte Alto ad curias suas petendas in comitatu Warr' in hundredo de Knygth' de hominibus ipsius Rogeri tenentibus per servicium militare et peciit curiam domini sui de predicto Roberti de Shepeye. Et predictus Adam ballivus predicti prioris dicit quod predictus Rogerus de Monte Alto curiam suam de predicto Roberto de Shepeye in predicto placito habere non debet; dicit enim quod ballivus Rogeri de Monte Alto ad curias suas petendas non venit ad proximum hundredum nec ad tria hundreda proximo sequencia ad curiam domini sui de predicto Roberto de Shepeye petendam. Dicit enim quod tenementum ubi predictus Robertus de Shepeye summonitus fuit non tenetur per servicium militare de predicto Rogero set tenetur in liberum burgagium prout tota villa de Coventr' tenetur, de quo burgagio predictus prior curiam suam habere debet."

in court Christian felt that the case in that court pertained rather to a secular jurisdiction, he could obtain a royal prohibition forbidding the ecclesiastical court to proceed any further with the case. That prohibition had to be delivered to the judges of the ecclesiastical court in the presence of witnesses. Gilbert le Harpur of Chesterton presented his prohibition concerning a case of debt which was before the prior of St. Radegund in the presence of Adam des Okes and several others in 1297 at the manor of the Knights Templars in the suburb of Warwick.[106] Okes was a prominent and competent professional lawyer.

One of the county reports details a comment made by a person named "Hoke."[107] This may, of course, have been a reference to Okes, but it also may have been a reference to Henry de Hokkele, who could be expected to have been in the county court. Hokkele appeared in the court of common pleas as an attorney over fifty times between 1304 and 1308,[108] and served twice as the general attorney for Robert de Napton.[109] He represented Theobald de Verdun, Sr., in the court of common pleas four times in 1307,[110] and thereafter represented him in the Exchequer of pleas in three cases, each involving a different former sheriff of Warwickshire.[111] The year after Robert de Warwick was hanged, a Henry de Hokkele became sheriff of Warwickshire.[112] Thus, whoever is designated by that ambiguous reference, he was a professional lawyer.

The person designated in the county reports as "Wolle" and "Wolleward" appeared only once in those reports and then again before the king's justices.[113] I have previously identified him as William de Wollewardinton, a Warwickshire attorney who first appeared in 1301 and thereafter was associated with Walter de Cantilupe, John de Cantilupe, and Nicholas de Warwick. The identification was reinforced by the fact that the only county report in which he is mentioned has him pleading on behalf of Eustace de Cantilupe.[114] It now seems that this identification was wrong; the pleader concerned was probably William de Wolleward, seemingly a different person. In 1297 in the

---

[106] CP. 40/129, m. 107.
[107] Above, n. 21.
[108] The number of cases per year: 1304, 1; 1305, 12; 1306, 17; 1307, 12; 1308, 14.
[109] CPR, 1301-1307, pp. 131, 209.
[110] CP. 40/164, m. 366.
[111] E. 13/34, m. 63.
[112] List of Sheriffs, p. 145.
[113] Brit. Lib. Add. 31826, fols. 261r; 266v.
[114] Palmer, "County Year Book Reports," pp. 790-91.

court of common pleas he was accused of taking and wrongfully detaining a horse that belonged to John Attecross. Wolleward explained that previously one Robert de Fynteford had prosecuted Attecross in the county court on a viscontiel writ of suit to mill. The parties had put themselves on a jury, and the jury had returned its verdict for Fynteford, who was therefore to recover the suit of Attecross to his mill and also ½ mark in damages. Wolleward, as the king's bailiff in that county, had taken the horse to execute that judgment by distraint. The horse had been taken in 1294.[115] Later, in 1299, Wolleward was prosecuted in the court of common pleas as a receiver of money of Robert de Hasele in an action of account.[116] In 1307 he pleaded before the justices of trailbaston in Warwick.[117] First as one of the sheriff's bailiffs, then, it seems, as the bailiff of Robert de Hasele, Wolleward had gained the legal experience and knowledge to appear even before royal justices as a pleader.

It is impossible to assign an identity to the person known in the county reports as "Payn." There were several attorneys by that name in the Midlands,[118] and there was even an influential Warwick family with that name.[119] Whoever he was, however, he was sufficiently competent to plead before the justices of assize in 1307 and 1308 in Warwickshire and Northamptonshire.[120] This kind of activity was not completely abnormal for county pleaders, for Crompe, Boydin, Heyford, and Sutham also appeared as pleaders before justices of assize.[121] Payn must have been as competent as the other prominent pleaders, even though his career cannot be adequately documented.

A further five of the pleaders in the Warwickshire county court have left but little documentary evidence for their activity. Robert de Alne was a clerk, and he at times functioned as a pledge in litigation in the court of common pleas.[122] He served also as one of the auditors for John de Plumton, a receiver of money for Philip de Geyton, sheriff of Warwickshire from 1300 to 1302; Plumton was found in arrears,

[115] CP. 40/116, m. 48.

[116] CP. 40/126, m. 72d.

[117] Brit. Lib. Add. 31826, fol. 261r (JUST. 1/967, m. 10).

[118] Nicholas Payn of Kenilworth (CP. 40/110, m. 274; CP. 40/111, m. 167d); Philip Payn (CP. 40/176, m. 174; CP. 40/149, mm. 429, 429d, 430), and John Payn (E. 13/29, m. 60d; CP. 40/149, mm. 428, 429d; CP. 40/161, m. 565).

[119] H. A. Cronne, *The Borough of Warwick in the Middle Ages*, Dugdale Occasional Papers, no. 10 (Oxford, 1954), p. 19.

[120] Brit. Lib. Add. 31826, fol. 261r (JUST. 1/967, m. 4), 262r (JUST. 1/1347, m. 4?), 269v, 270r.

[121] Ibid., fol. 262r.

[122] CP. 52 octave Trinity, 28 Edward I; quindene Easter, 27 Edward I; E. 13/26, m. 18.

imprisoned, and finally made to account.[123] He was also able to wield some influence with the justices of assize, since he caused an amercement to be remitted.[124] Very little is known about three other pleaders—Henry de la Hurst, Shereman, and "Stamp"—and what is known does not aid in evaluating their legal competence.[125] The fifth pleader, Richard Attemere of Whitacre, was probably the Richard de Whytacre who became sheriff of Warwickshire and Leicestershire on 1 October 1305.[126] He had at least been involved in some quasi-legal activities for a few years, since in 1299 he stood pledge for some litigants in the court of common pleas.[127] All five of these people, whose careers are much less open to investigation than the others, appeared only once in the reports; they were almost certainly not as influential in the county court as were people like Sutham, Crompe, Heyford, and Boydin.

The final person mentioned as a pleader in the county reports appeared but once also: Robert de Stoke.[128] As early as 1292 Stoke was probably bailiff of Roger de Montalt's court in Coventry. At any rate, he had successfully prosecuted a case of trespass against William de Bosco in such a way that Bosco subsequently brought an action of false judgment.[129] In 1295 he was definitely Montalt's bailiff and responsible for claiming pleas for the court of Coventry.[130] About that same time he functioned as a witness to the delivery to Robert fitz John of a prohibition forbidding him to distrain William fitz Geoffrey to do suit to the court of Barnacle.[131] He was appointed general attorney for the abbot of Thorney in 1293,[132] served a few times as an attorney in the court of common pleas,[133] and in 1317 was appointed general attorney for the prior of Bath.[134] He was still active in the county court of Warwickshire in 1311 and 1313.[135] By

---

[123] E. 13/26, m. 68d.

[124] JUST. 1/1322, m. 19.

[125] Palmer, "County Year Book Reports," p. 792.

[126] *List of Sheriffs*, p. 144.

[127] CP. 52 octave Michaelmas, 26 Edward I; quindene Easter, 27 Edward I.

[128] Above, n. 21.

[129] CP. 40/93, m. 91d. The enrollment makes it seem possible that Stoke was the presiding officer.

[130] Above, n. 105.

[131] CP. 40/114, m. 185.

[132] *CPR, 1292-1301*, p. 7.

[133] Above, Table 4.1.

[134] *CPR, 1317-1321*, p. 16.

[135] CP. 52 quindene Easter, 4 Edward II (as one of the four knights [the other three were Henry de Gothmundele, Thomas Boydin, and Henry le Bretun] who affixed his seal to a *recordari* record; the other three are demonstrably professional lawyers). C. 255/9/2, 2 (an inquest concerning the repair of the ruinous Warwick gaol taken in open county, apparently from men who were there for professional reasons; among

that time he was assuming an even more prominent role in the governance of Warwickshire. He was one of the chief assessors and collectors for five lay subsidies: those in 1308, 1309, 1316, and 1319.[136] He was commissioned six times to deliver individuals from the gaols of Leicester and Warwick between 1314 and 1323, and the appointment of 1314 singled him out as the one member of the commission who had to be present.[137] During the same period he was on fourteen commissions of *oyer* and *terminer* and carried out three special inquiries, such as the investigation into armed bands in the county.[138] Twice in 1314 and once again in 1318 he was commissioned to conduct investigations into the conduct of the sheriff, the sheriff's bailiffs, and other officials in the county.[139] Finally, he was appointed keeper of the peace twice in 1318 and again in 1320, all three times in Warwickshire.[140] Unlike Robert de Warwick, his loyalties lay with the king. He may have been suspect in 1321,[141] but in 1322 he was made keeper of the lands and castles held by the rebels in Warwickshire, Oxfordshire, Bedfordshire, and Buckinghamshire.[142] Stoke is precisely the kind of person whom historians, seeing only his activity after 1308 in administration, have labeled county squires; it is apparent from his early career that, if he was a squire in the 1310s, it was only because he had been a lawyer previously, and his legal skills were probably a prerequisite for his later functions.

Warwick, Sutham, Boydin, Heyford, Crompe, Stoke, and perhaps Payn could function not only in the county court, but also in the king's court. Their remuneration for services as attorney there was substantial, and their duties were at times demanding, as can be determined from examining the pay of other attorneys in the court of common pleas at about that time. In 1245 John de Scalariis committed his suit for five knights fees into the hands of Warin de Monte Caniso, promising him 50 marks in recompense for his trouble and

---

the jurors were Robert de Stoke, Thomas Boydin, Adam des Okes, Robert le Seynter, and Henry de Hokkele).

[136] *CPR, 1307-1313*, pp. 34, 185; *CPR, 1313-1317*, pp. 474, 530; *CPR, 1317-1321*, p. 348.

[137] *CPR, 1313-1317*, pp. 225, 493; *CPR, 1317-1321*, p. 537; *CPR, 1321-1324*, pp. 60, 257, 370.

[138] *CPR, 1313-1317*, pp. 325, 494, 581; *CPR, 1317-1321*, pp. 82, 97, 100, 294, 304 [bis], 369; *CPR, 1321-1324*, pp. 58, 161, 172, 216, 310, 316.

[139] *CPR, 1313-1317*, pp. 129, 243; *CPR, 1317-1321*, p. 299.

[140] *CPR, 1317-1321*, pp. 185, 289, 462.

[141] *CFR, 1319-1327*, p. 86.

[142] *CCR, 1318-1323*, pp. 441, 537, 540, 572, 577. In "County Year Book Reports," p. 794, I declined to classify Stoke as a professional lawyer; the additional information included here makes it necessary to reverse that opinion.

expenses.[143] In 1289 Henry de Coleville agreed to pay William de Overe 20s a year to be his attorney in the court of common pleas, and Overe eventually claimed 5 marks for his pay and his expenses in purchasing writs.[144] Isabel de Bernewell paid John le Vyneter 10s to prosecute her suit in the court of common pleas.[145] In 1292 Warin de Northampton was paid 16s to defend Hugh de Eynesbury in a plea of trespass in the king's court.[146] Richard de Whytacre, one of the people mentioned in the county reports, agreed in 1307 to pay Henry de Snypeston 2½ marks over and above his expenses—which amounted to ½ mark, undoubtedly for the purchase of a writ—to be his attorney in the court of common pleas in a case of trespass.[147] John fitz Thomas hired Richard de Duyland to help in the recovery of his land in a suit in the king's court and agreed to pay him 8 marks. Duyland considered it part of his duty to talk often with those in the neighborhood concerning John's right—sounding out the jury in advance—but then decided simply to purchase the land for himself. That left him open to prosecution for conspiracy.[148] In 1294 Master Nicholas de Huntingdon hired William de Tykesore as his attorney in the court of common pleas, and Tykesore even pleaded the case for him, waging law for Nicholas.[149] Furthermore, it was the attorney who would have

---

[143] JUST. 1/233, m. 7.

[144] CP. 40/98, m. 123d. [145] CP. 40/95, m. 61d.

[146] CP. 40/102, m. 93d. [147] CP. 40/187, m. 234.

[148] CP. 40/112, m. 17d: "ipse pluries cum vicinis suis super iure predicti Johannis de predicta terra tractavit, qui asserebant omnino ipsum Johannem nullum ius habere in predictis tenementis et de hoc sepius predictum Johannem premunivit per quod ipsum iuvare non potuit."

[149] CP. 40/108, m. 70d: "Lond'; Midd'. Magister Nicholaus de Hunt' queritur de Willelmo de Tykesore quod cum in crastino sancti Johannis Baptiste anno regis nunc vicesimo secundo apud London in quadam taberna prope Wolfchthagh convenisset inter ipsos Nicholaum et Willelmum quod idem Willelmus foret attornatus ipsius Nicholai in quadam loquela inter quendam Willelmum Pryde de sancto Edmundo querentem et ipsum Nicholaum in curia hic pendente de placito prohibicionis etc., ac idem Nicholaus secundum convencionem predictam fecisset predictum Willelmum in curia hic attornatum suum in loquela predicta etc., ita quod idem Willelmus attornatus etc., in termino sancte Trinitatis hic eodem anno placitavit pro predicto Nicholao cum predicto Willelmo Pryde et vadiavit ei inde legem etc., pro predicto Nicholao etc. Et inde datus fuisset eis dies in crastino animarum proximo sequente, ita quod idem Nicholaus ad diem illum veniret cum lege sua in propria persona etc., predictus Willelmus attornatus etc., ad prefatum crastinum animarum ipsum Nicholaum non fecit essoniari prout potuit et debuit etc., nec ipsum Nicholaum premunivit ante diem illum quod vadiavit legem in forma predicta etc., per quod idem Nicholaus tamquam indefensus etc. ad prefatum crastinum animarum in curia hic condempnatus fuit versus predictum Willelmum Pryde in decem libris et preter penam quam versus dominum regem in hac parte reportaturus est etc., unde dicit quod deterioratus est et dampnum habet ad valenciam decem librarum, et inde producit sectam etc.

Et Willelmus de Tykesovere venit et bene cognovit quod fuit attornatus predicti Nicholai ad unum diem tantum in loquela predicta, scilicet in octabis sancti Trinitatis anno regis nunc vicesimo secundo et quod pro prefato Nicholao ad prefatum terminum

had to hire the pleader if the case was likely to be difficult, to inform the pleader of the details of the case and the likely exceptions that could be made, and to decide during pleading whether to avow the pleader. The attorney's function, therefore, went far beyond merely purchasing writs and seeing to the continuation of the plea; he had to be conversant with the courts and the arguments which could be useful to the pleaders.

The pleaders in the county courts were thus fully professional lawyers. The county courts in the reign of Edward I still disposed of very important litigation, and the legal technicality and strategy in the county courts were much the same as in the king's court. It is no surprise that professionals were required. For most purposes, the pleaders formed a relatively small group, with four or five individuals doing most of the pleading, a dozen or so more occasionally contributing to the legal argument. Frequently they had had long experience in legal matters in the king's court and could look forward to several decades of exercise of authority on commissions within their county. The functions they performed as lawyers were varied; they were pleaders and attorneys, pledges and bailiffs. They were, in their many capacities, seen as specialists, people with an uncommon skill, and were paid accordingly. As a pleader, one might expect to receive several dozen annuities from individuals to secure one's counsel and aid in litigation, with each annuity running between 6s 8d and 20s. As an attorney in the king's court, a pleader would be hired either for the individual case or for cases in general by an annuity. If hired for an individual case, his pay could range from 10s plus costs to much more, depending on the importance of the case. It was possible to take on more than forty cases a year as an attorney in the court of common pleas. Finally, most lawyers seemed attached to an aristocrat, and the remuneration from that source would be expected to exceed any normal annuity. Local lawyers were thus paid well, but not extravagantly; such might be expected for a skilled but extensive profession. They made the county court a professional and legally respectable institution, rather than the amateur court presented by modern historians.

---

sancte Trinitatis vadiavit legem etc., pro predicto Nicholao etc., set dicit quod ante finem eiusdem termini venit predictus Nicholaus in aula hic et idem Willelmus de Tikesovere premunivit predictum Nicholaum quod esset hic in predicto crastino animarum ad faciendum legem suam in propria persona etc; et quod ipse non fuit attornatus ipsius Nicholai nisi ad unum diem tantum, scilicet in predictis octabis sancte Trinitatis etc et quod postquam placitavit pro ipso Nicholao sicut predictum est etc., premunivit predictum Nicholaum quod esset hic ad predictum crastinum animarum ad faciendum legem suam etc.; et de hoc ponit se super patriam."

5

Seneschals and Bailiffs

҂

THE PLEADERS of the county courts were not professional pleaders; they were professional lawyers who performed a variety of functions, including pleading and acting as attorneys. They were also the seignorial seneschals and bailiffs and, therefore, judges of the county courts. The emphasis traditionally given the suitors in this regard has made the county courts seem both amateur and democratic. The functions of the seneschals and bailiffs, however, demonstrate not only the sophistication of the county courts but also the degree to which the county courts embodied the ties between lord and man.

The *Leges Henrici* in 1114 stated the principle that the attendance at the county court of the baron or his seneschal would acquit the obligations of suit owed by the tenants of all the manors within the baron's lordship.[1] This firmly stated principle was not completely unrelated to the other method of substitution already mentioned: the sending of the priest, reeve, and four men of the township.[2] The transition between the two methods can be seen with the lands of Burton Abbey. A survey of the abbey's tenants in 1114 listed several individuals who were obligated to attend the county court.[3] Edric the Old, however, was a reeve. It was said that he went to pleas, the county, and the hundreds for the abbot's land; no obligation was mentioned.[4] Edric went, apparently, as a recognized representative of his lord. From such representation, it would be a short—albeit significant—step to representation by seneschal. There are no recorded

---

[1] *Leges Henrici Primi*, ed. L. J. Downer (Oxford, 1972), p. 130.
[2] Ibid., p. 100 (above, chapter 3 at n. 104).
[3] C.G.O. Bridgeman, "The Burton Abbey Twelfth-Century Surveys," In *Collections for a History of Staffordshire*, William Salt Arch. Soc., n.s., vol. 9 (London, 1918), pp. 216, 242, 245.
[4] Ibid., p. 231.

instances of seneschals actually acquitting a baron's men of their obligation to attend the county court in the twelfth century, but there can be little doubt that such was common practice, both because of the strong position in society of the barons and because of the clarity of the principle in the *Leges Henrici*.

In the thirteenth century, indeed, seneschals often performed the suits due from barons and their tenants. In 1226 the seneschal of John Marschal attended the court of Kesteven for him and attempted to give a judgment.[5] In 1227 the duty of a seneschal was described clearly in a final concord between William de Lancaster and Robert de Vipont, hereditary sheriff of Westmorland. William granted that he and his heirs would do suit to the county court by seneschal or other bailiff if they could not act in person. That seneschal both claimed the pleas that pertained to William's baronial court and performed the suit due from William, his knights, and the other men of his lands. That kind of attendance was to be insufficient in only two instances. The first was when one or other of those men was actually involved as a litigant in the county court, one more indication that suit was partially concerned with securing the attendance of litigants in court. The other instance concerned afforcement of court. When the county court was faced with having to render a difficult judgment, the seneschal was to bring with him the knights and the discreet and wise men of Kendal—the word "suitor" is not used—to perform the judgment along with the other men of the county.[6] In

[5] *CRR*, 12:435.

[6] JUST. 1/982, m. 22: "Hec est finalis concordia facta in curia domini regis apud Appelby a die sancti Hillarii in xv dies anno regni regis Henrici filii regis Johannis undecimo coram Martino de Pateshull, Johanne de Ayvill, Willelmo de Insula, et Ricardo Duket justiciariis itinerantibus et aliis domini regis fidelibus tunc ibi presentibus inter Willelmum de Lancastr' filium Gilberti filii Rogeri filii Reynfridi ex una parte et Robertum de Veteri Ponte ex altera parte de secta facienda ad comitatum Westmorl' de terris ipsius Willelmi in Kendale et in Westmorl' unde idem Willelmus questus fuit quod predictus Robertus iniuste exigebat ab eo predictam sectam et unde placitum fuit inter eos in eadem curia, scilicet quod predictus Willelmus concessit pro se et heredibus suis quod ipse et heredes sui decetero facient sectam ad predictum comitatum pro predictis terris per senescallos ipsorum de senescallo in senescallum vel per alium ballivum idoneum ad hoc attornatum si ipse vel heredes sui in propria persona venire non potuerunt vel noluerunt. Et si talia placita attachiata fuerunt vel summonita de hominibus manentibus in predictis terris ipsius Willelmi vel heredum suorum unde barones curiam suam habere debeant secundum consuetudinem regni Anglie senescalli ipsius Willelmi vel heredum suorum curiam domini sui inde exigent et illam sine contradiccione habebunt. Et si contencio fuerit inter vicecomitem et senescallum de curia habenda, per consideracionem comitatus terminetur utrum illam habere debeat nec ne. Vicecomes autem Westmorl' habebit in terra ipsius Willelmi et heredum suorum de Kendale duos servientes ad equum et duos ad pedem cum opus fuerit pro negociis domini regis et vicecomitis faciendis et pro pace assecuranda et conservanda,

a similar vein the earl of Albemarle had read in the county court of Cumberland at Carlisle in 1231 an undertaking making himself, his bailiffs, and his seneschal liable for the services and exactions which had been expected from the township of Appleton.[7]

Not all lords would want to acquit their men of suit; there were financial considerations to be taken into account. Many tenants owed suit to county, hundred, and the lord's court. When suit was still enforced, some of these lords had the right to collect the fines and amercements levied on their tenants, and this included the amercements for default of suit. Both the bishop of Ely and the bishop of Norwich claimed such liberties.[8] The bishop of Ely, indeed, claimed the amercements levied from all men within the hundreds of Mitford, Wicklow, Thredling, and Winston, whether the men were of his own fee or not.[9] Such a financial right would take at least some of the motivation out of relieving tenants of the performance of suit.

Sending the seneschal in place of his tenants, while it meant assuming a burden, was likewise a method of exercising power and solidifying baronial control over his tenants. It represented the barony

---

qui servientes in pleno comitatu super sacrosancta jurabunt quod nullum hominem de predictis terris occasionabunt vel iniuste gravabunt vel contra regni consuetudinem tractabunt vel garbas in autumpno colligent nec agnos exigent nec alicui eorum aliquam malam toltam facient et ubi hospicium suum capient moderate se habebunt et sine gravamine hospitis sui de honesto hospicio pacatos se tenebunt nec aliquem denarium pro hospicio remittendo capient. Et servientes vicecomitis itinerabunt in terris ipsius Willelmi et heredum suorum in Westmorl' extra Kendale sicut itinerare solent. Omnes eciam homines manentes in predictis terris fideliter adiuvabunt ipsos servientes cum opus fuerit ad pacem domini regis observandam et ad negocia sua et vicecomitis facienda. Concessit eciam predictus Robertus pro se et heredibus suis quod si summoniciones fieri debeant per homines de Kendale, ipse illas facient de loquelis motis in terra de Kendale et quod pro summonicionibus vel aliis levibus causis non trahentur ad remotas partes Westmorl' per quod possint gravari. Et sciendum quod senescallus vel ballivus ipsius Willelmi vel heredum suorum facient predictam sectam pro militibus et aliis hominibus de terris ipsius Willelmi et heredum suorum nisi forte trahantur in placitis vel aforciamentis alicuius iudicii. Et tunc dicatur senescallo vel ballivo attornato quod ad proximum comitatum adducat secum de militibus et aliis discretis et sapientibus de predicta terra de Kendale ad iudicium illud simul cum illis faciendum. Et pro hac concessione, fine, et concordia predictus Robertus remisit et quietum clamavit de se et heredibus suis ipsi Willelmo et heredibus suis omnia dampna que dicebat se habere occasione predicte contencionis que fuit inter eos de predicta secta usque ad diem quo hec concordia facta fuit. Omnia autem predicta concessa sunt a predicto Willelmo et Roberto quantum ad eos et heredes ipsorum pertinet." Partially paraphrased without reference in *Some Court Rolls*, ed. William Farrer, The Record Society, vol. 41 (n.p., 1901), p. xi.

[7] *Cartularium Prioratus de Gyseburne*, ed. W. Brown, 2 vols., Surtees Society, vols. 86, 88 (Durham, 1889-1891), 1:320.

[8] *CRR*, 10:165-66; *CRR*, 13:550-51.

[9] C. 60/32, m. 4.

as a unit and was therefore widely used. In 1255 John fitz Alan performed the six suits he owed to the county court of Shropshire, one of which was for the whole hundred of Purslow, by seneschal.[10] That seneschal was in a position to acquit also the fifteen suits owed by fitz Alan's tenants.[11] Ralph le Butiler, lord of Wem, owed two suits and performed them by seneschal, and it is clearly noted that the seneschal customarily acquitted his tenants of four other suits.[12] Sir Odo de Hodenet's function had been encrusted in tenurial services. He was the hereditary seneschal of the fee of Montgomery, and the only one of that fee burdened with the obligation of suit to county court; the representation had apparently been made tenurial along with the granting of the office in fee.[13] Hodenet was not restricted, however, to acting solely for the fee of Montgomery. He also performed the suit due from Ragdon for the abbot of Buildwas[14] and owed suit for Hope Bowdler held of William de Cantilupe and also for two hides in "Welbur" held of the fee of Caus.[15] Hodenet did have at least some legal interests, if only from his duties to various courts and from commissions he received from the king.[16] He was in a position to acquit several fees of the obligations of suit; and the fee of Caus alone had fourteen tenants who owed suit. There were in all 102 suits due the county court of Shropshire in 1255; the activities of seneschals could easily have made a fully attended session a meeting of only six or eight judges.

In the pleas of *quo warranto* during the reign of Edward I seneschals were occasionally mentioned in connection with the county courts. In 1289 Gilbert de Thornton alleged that Ralph Beauchamp, as a baron, by the common law owed suit to the county court of Bedfordshire either in person or by seneschal. Thornton was concerned lest the pleas of the county fail for lack of suitors, once again illustrating the custom among royal justices of equating suitors and

[10] *RH*, 2:56 [bis], 71 [bis], 76, 77. The suit from Purslow hundred was said to be done by bailiff "quasi pro hundredo" but it may be suspected that only one person, seneschal or bailiff, went for fitz Alan.

[11] *RH*, 2:56-58, 62, 70, 75-77, 82.

[12] *RH*, 2:58. Two other suits owed by the fee of Wem were not performed by the seneschal but rather were listed as having been subtracted.

[13] *RH*, 2:58.

[14] *RH*, 2:70.

[15] *RH*, 2:62, 66, 70.

[16] *CPR, 1247-1258*, pp. 47, 521; *CPR, 1258-1266*, p. 491; *CPR, 1266-1272*, p. 129; *CPR, 1272-1281*, pp. 47, 48, 122, 338; *CPR, 1281-1292*, p. 65; *Close Rolls: Henry III, 1251-1253*, prepared under the superintendence of the Deputy Keeper of Records, 14 vols. (London, 1902-1938), pp. 85, 87.

seneschals.[17] Norman Darcy, in a similar inquiry in Lincolnshire, was asked whether he or his ancestors had ever done suit in person or held his tenements by the service of finding a seneschal in the county court like the other barons of Lincolnshire.[18] The expression used here is reminiscent of the expressions used for judges in the Cheshire county court. The case of Baldwin Wake is even more interesting. Wake was himself a baron and held various lands in Yorkshire which were thought to owe suit. The manor of Ayton he held of Nicholas Meynill and paid him 3s yearly for fine of county. Meynill held further of Peter de Mortimer and paid him the same fine. Mortimer was the tenant-in-chief and did suit by his seneschal, so that Wake was acquitted of the suit from that tenement. The "fine of county" was apparently the financial incentive—hardened into tenurial services—for the lord to acquit the suit by sending his seneschal; such fines are ubiquitous in Yorkshire. Wake also held Hemlington of Robert de Nevill, who held further of Robert de Bruce. Thus the tenement was part of the honor of Chester, which owed no suit to the county court. Wake also held a third tenement, Tunstall, and did suit to the county court for that tenement at the session after Michaelmas. Finally, Wake did suit by his seneschal to the county court for the lands of his own barony. His tenements and his suits clearly demonstrate the link between lordship and suit, since he did not acquit the lands he held in other baronies by sending his own seneschal.[19]

The final concord between Lancaster and Vipont mentioned earlier,[20] specified that the seneschal's duties went beyond acquitting suit: he was there also to claim the pleas of the baronial court. Even when a lord and his men were exempt from suit, the lord had to have a representative present at county to claim pleas. This presence was not an obligation owed to the king or the sheriff; it was, rather, the maintenance of the baron's jurisdiction and the exercise of his rightful power over men. An excellent example of claiming pleas in the twelfth century comes from a relation of events in a special joint session of the counties of Norfolk and Suffolk at Norwich sometime between 1148 and 1153. Hervy de Glanvill, father of Ranulf de Glanvill, testified during that session that he had attended county court for fifty years. During that time, whenever anyone from the eight-and-a-half hundreds of the abbey of Bury St. Edmunds had been impleaded in

[17] *PQW*, p. 4.
[18] Ibid., p. 414.
[19] Ibid., p. 199.
[20] Above, n. 6.

the county court, that plea had been claimed by the abbot, his seneschal, or some other of the abbot's ministers. Furthermore, the claim had always been allowed except in cases of treasure trove and murder.[21] Glanvill's statement not only confirms the antiquity of the function of claiming pleas, it also indicates that persons less than the seneschal could be used for that purpose.

Such lesser ministers were often used to coordinate the various jurisdictions, and, while it was generally said that they were obligated to attend the county court, that obligation was an obligation to their lord, not, as in the case of suit, an obligation to the king. Adam de Scotriva in 1182 thus held some land in Warwickshire from the bishop of Worcester for the service of following county and hundred, carrying the bishop's money both inside and outside the county, and summoning the bishop whenever necessary to county court. If Adam's service was in any way defective and caused the bishop's land to suffer, he was to pay the damages.[22] Adam was obviously not a simple peasant, and the penalty clause might well describe the liability assumed by an official or perhaps an apprentice lawyer. At about the same time Osbert fitz Solomon held some land from the bishop of Worcester in Gloucestershire for which he was obliged to follow the county and to coordinate the bishop's activities—presumably the activities of the bishop's court—with the king's.[23] The bishop also had seven tenants in Gloucestershire who acquitted his demesne lands of suit. Five of them went in turns, two by two, and two went every session, so that there were always the four required to be present at each county session. An eighth person, however, one Ainulf, was obliged to the bishop, not to the king, to attend the county sessions to make sure that the bishop's demesne lost nothing by any default of those obliged to attend the county.[24] Such functionaries would have been common because of the jurisdictional overlaps between the county court and the lower courts.

These people continued to be necessary in the thirteenth century. In 1252 Nicholas Nugun held some land from the abbot of Ramsey for the service of following the county court and there exacting the abbot's liberties.[25] The bishop of Worcester in 1299 had a multiplicity

---

[21] Helen Cam, "An East Anglian Shire-Moot of Stephen's Reign, 1148-1153," *EHR* 39 (1924):569-71.

[22] *Red Book of Worcester*, ed. Marjory Hollings, Worcestershire Hist. Soc. (London, 1934-1937), p. 260.

[23] Ibid., p. 350.

[24] Ibid., pp. 429-30.

[25] *Cartularium Monasterii de Rameseia*, ed. W. H. Hart and Ponsonby Lyons, 3 vols., Rerum Brittanicarum medii aevi scriptores, vol. 79 (London, 1884-1893), 1:405.

of such people. In Gloucestershire the prior of Studley held lands from the bishop for the service of attending the county court to exact and testify concerning the liberty of the manor of Withington. He also made forinsec summonses of the hundred and executed distraints; the prior—or, rather, the prior's own deputy—thus functioned as a bailiff.[26] John de Marisco held land in Bibury for the service of following the county court of Gloucestershire to exact and testify concerning the liberty of that manor. He was also obliged to procure supplies for the bishop and carry the writs of the bishop and seneschal throughout the bishopric of Worcester and even elsewhere.[27] He, also, seems like a bailiff. In 1299 Thomas Boumond held land in Hampton Lucy for the service of following the county court of Warwickshire to exact and testify to those things that pertained to the liberty of the bishop. He also owed suit to the bishop's court of Hampton Lucy and to the bishop's hundred of Pathlow.[28] He would thus have been well acquainted with the courts concerning which he was to testify and probably functioned in an administrative capacity within those courts. In all these instances the suit was owed to the lord, not to the king. The lord would have consistently appointed a skilled person to this task. Claiming a court was not a simple matter; it involved jurisdictional issues, always a contentious and complicated subject. Even in the reign of Edward I the adjudication in a claim of court could easily result in an action of false judgment.[29] Claiming court demanded considerable knowledge of men, tenures, and pleas, together with the ability to state one's case lucidly and persuasively. On that knowledge and ability depended the maintenance of the lord's jurisdiction, precious not only for its financial perquisites but also because it embodied the lord's power over his men and his right to mediate their quarrels.

It was clearly the seneschals and bailiffs who dominated the county courts, at least when the bishops, abbots, earls, and barons were not present. Two general statements in the reign of Edward I lead to this conclusion. The first is chapter 33 of the Statute of Westminster I. That statute prohibited any seneschal—or anyone else not appointed attorney by his lord to do suit—from giving or pronouncing judgments in the county courts unless they were specifically requested to

[26] *Red Book of Worcester*, p. 356.
[27] Ibid., p. 369.
[28] Ibid., p. 265.
[29] CP. 40/3, m. 18d, Scache v Wytman; CP. 40/17, m. 141d, Prior of Deerhurst v Countess of Gloucester and Hereford; CP. 40/27, m. 81d, Hamelton v Court of Rotherham; above, chapter 4, n. 105.

do this by the suitors or their attorneys.[30] The wording of the statute correctly treats the seneschals as different from both the suitors and suitors' attorneys. It assumes, however, that seneschals and others who were not suitors had been rendering judgments. There is no indication that the statute changed county procedure in the least—unless, perhaps, more seneschals were appointed as attorneys to do suit. There is no known litigation based on the statute. The second general statement is from *Fleta*, the legal tract written a little over a decade after Westminster I. The author of that treatise was still concerned with seneschals. He stated that they

> often influence the judgment of the court, like a bell-wether, and they try to put obstacles in the way of the distrainee and to render false judgments, since they can do so without risk of corporal punishment or monetary penalty, because they are not suitors of the court. And even if the county court should be amerced for a false judgment, this would not be to their prejudice.[31]

It is doubtful, of course, that the seneschals were all that corrupt, but the author of *Fleta* confirms that seneschals were clearly different from suitors, that they were not held responsible for the judgments they rendered, and that they were the dominating power within the county courts.

In Warwickshire county court by the end of the reign of Edward I there were no suitors and the judgments were rendered by a body known as the four benches. That group was casually described as "the coroners, the seneschals, and the others of the county court."[32] Coroners have been known to perform a great variety of functions in the county as a whole. They received the confessions and abjurations of the realm made by felons and held inquests concerning dead bodies, and in that capacity could put people on oath without the warrant of a royal writ. In the sheriff's tourns they recorded indictments. On the king's orders they could carry out almost any duty the sheriff normally performed but in which, in a particular case, he was thought biased. In the county court they kept record of the pleas of the crown and were therefore particularly involved in appeals and outlawry.[33]

---

[30] Westminster I, c. 33.

[31] *Fleta: Commentarius Juris Anglicani*, ed. H. G. Richardson and G. O. Sayles, 2 vols., Selden Society, vols. 72, 89 (London, 1953-1972), 2:225.

[32] Brit. Lib., Add. 31826, fol. 266v: "Warr' in quodam placito fit fere iiij banks. Coroners, a vous est primes a dire vostre avis, qe vous estis les iures le rey; e pus voloums saver des autre banks. *Boydin*. Que syuters nunt il point. E pur coe les coroners e les seneschals e les autres del conte si deivent doner les jugemens."

[33] R. F. Hunnisett, *The Medieval Coroner* (Cambridge, 1961), pp. 1, 55-70, 75-86.

As part of the four benches, they were apparently also judges of the county court. This should not be terribly surprising, since they were not only royal officials but also prominent landlords in the county, although not of the first rank.

It is unlikely that the coroners were more important than the seneschals. The coroners in Warwickshire county in the first decade of the fourteenth century, as far as I have been able to determine, were Robert Wandard, Richard de Peyto, Simon de Blaggrove,[34] Thomas de Woleny,[35] William Corbyzun,[36] John de Upton,[37] and William de Whytington.[38] The coroner for the honor of Leicester was Lawrence le Seler,[39] and the coroner for Coventry was John Lewyn.[40] None of them were mentioned in the county year book reports. That index of their influence may, of course, be faulty. They must have gained invaluable knowledge of local jurisdictions and of the law in their constant attendance of county sessions. Moreover, their legal expertise should not be dismissed without investigation. Robert de Warwick, an experienced lawyer and undersheriff, became a coroner of Warwickshire for a time.[41] Such a person would have undoubtedly been a valued judge. Nevertheless, their position must seem subordinate until there is some confirmation of their role as judges outside matters touching the crown.

The people shown by the county reports to have rendered the judgments of Warwickshire county court were the pleaders. In one case a judgment was required from the open county court in a case of trespass; it was Thomas Boydin who answered that the defendant could not be arrested because the viscontiel writ did not contain the crucial words *contra pacem*.[42] In another case, John de Heyford spoke out and contradicted the sheriff, maintaining that he could not amerce the litigants in the case, because the case fell outside the jurisdiction of the county court.[43] In a third case, it seems that Crompe was the one who rendered the judgment that the party was undefended because he had not defended an allegation in a case of replevin in the manner that would have been required in the mise of a grand assize.[44]

[34] E. 372/147, m. 5d (circa 1302).
[35] Ibid.; JUST. 1/966, mm. 4, 5, 5d; JUST. 3/100, m. 13. (1301-1305)
[36] JUST. 1/966, mm. 2d, 4, 10; JUST. 3/101, m. 12. (1298-1305)
[37] JUST. 3/100, m. 13; JUST. 1/966, m. 7. (1301-1306)
[38] JUST. 3/101, m. 12; JUST. 1/966, m. 10. (1301-1307)
[39] JUST. 3/100, m. 7.
[40] JUST. 1/966, m. 2; E. 164/21, fols. 93r, 96v.
[41] CCR, 1318-1323, p. 264.
[42] Brit. Lib., Add. 31826, fol. 267r [S.S.].
[43] Ibid., fol. 263v [S.S.].
[44] Ibid., fol. 264v [S.S.].

The pleaders, in rendering such judgments, were functioning not as pleaders, but rather as seignorial bailiffs. Crompe, Wolward, Okes, and Stoke have all been shown to have been bailiffs or seneschals at about this time.[45] Boydin was once mentioned as the bailiff of John de Hastings.[46] The close relationship of Boydin, Sutham, and Heyford to particular clients makes it seem very likely that that relationship was formalized as the relationship between lord and bailiff. That kind of relationship would not have taken the form of a contract with a pleader, but rather the form in which Simon Senevill, lord of Lockington in Leicestershire, hired Simon Pakeman. The contract granted Pakeman an annuity of one robe worth 20s and also 20s in money each year for holding the court of Lockington and attending to Senevill's business wherever it might be, as long as Pakeman could reasonably be there.[47] The annuity was larger than that by which one hired a pleader; it was smaller than what would have been expected from John de Hastings or the Knights Templar. The business that Pakeman would see to would undoubtedly have included Senevill's business at county court, including both his personal litigation and the claiming of his pleas. It was thus lawyers, operating as bailiffs and seneschals for their lords—and concurrently as pleaders for others—who rendered the judgments in the county court of Warwickshire.

It might be possible to maintain that these people were functioning as attorneys to do suit. It had been possible since 1234 to appoint an attorney to perform one's suit.[48] Such would not have been strange

[45] Above, chapter 4, nn. 98, 105, 115, 130.

[46] CP. 40/138, m. 81d, an assize of novel disseisin.

[47] CP. 40/183, m. 61: "A touz ceus qe cest present esont verront ou orrount, Simon de Senevill seigneur de Lokynton saluz en dieu. Sachez moi aver graunte et done a Simon Pakemon de Worthynton une robe pris de xx s et xx s de sterling par an a tute sa vie a resceyvre la robe a la nativite nostre seignour annowel et les xx s as treis termes del an [specified], pur ce qe lavantdit Simon deit tenir mes courtz de Lokynton et estre entendaunt a tute mes busoignes la ou ie ai a fere et la ou lavantdit Simon pust estre. Et si il aveigne qe lavauntdit robe ou les avantdiz xx s seyent arere, ie voil et graunt pur moi et pur mes heyrs qe lavantdit Simon Pakeman puysse destreyndre par my mon manor de Lokynton dekes atant qil soit plenerement parpaie. Done a Lokynton le lundy procheyn apres Lassumpcion nostre dame lan du regne le roi Edward fiz au roi Henri trente tierz." CP. 40/173, m. 145 concerns a contract made in 1290 by which John Lythfot was granted 100s yearly as seneschal of the decan and chapter of St. Ethelbert in Hereford; he was seneschal for eighteen years.

[48] Below, chapter 9, n. 101. It should be noted that the attorney to perform suit was not simply a peasant who attended in one's stead. As shown in the reference and in the entry in the hundred rolls concerning Richard de la Leye and Simon fitz Stephen—Richard's attorney to perform suit in 1279—the attorney was expected to function also in the prosecution of pleas inside and outside the county boundaries (RH, 2:235).

procedure, since attorneys functioned commonly in county court litigation as early as the reign of Henry II.[49] A good attorney would certainly have made a competent judge, even if he lacked the prestige of his lord. Westminster I, chapter 33, would tend to indicate that conclusion also,[50] and the pleaders certainly functioned often enough as general attorneys. Still, to any lawyer the presence of attorneys to do suit would have been identical to the presence of the suitors themselves, and Thomas Sutham very clearly stated that Warwickshire county court had no suitors.[51] Moreover, coroners and seneschals were mentioned as part of the four benches, and since seignorial bailiffs stood in relationship to their seneschals as did the undersheriff to the sheriff, it must be maintained that the lawyers who functioned as pleaders functioned also as judges because they were seneschals and bailiffs, not because they were attorneys to do suit.

The phrase "the four benches" was already in the reign of Edward I antiquated. It first appeared in the twelfth century[52] and was not restricted to any one region of the country. In *Swarbraund v de la Haye*, a case in the court of the abbot of Wellow in Lincolnshire in 1276, Swarbraund omitted any mention of two ancestors in the descent of the right to the tenements in question, so that the four benches of that court ruled that the parties should appear the following session to hear their judgment, which went against the demandants.[53] In 1289 John, son of John de Stanerne, presented two people who had been members of the four benches of the ancient demesne court of Brigstock, Northamptonshire, when a certain judgment, allegedly false, was made.[54] John de Asseley in similarly challenging a record

[49] *Glanvill*, pp. 132-34; Robert C. Palmer, "The Origins of the Legal Profession in England," *Irish Jurist* 11 (1976):140.

[50] Above, at n. 30.

[51] Above, chapter 3, n. 145.

[52] See the *Revised Medieval Latin Word-List*, prep. R. E. Latham (London, 1965), p. 43. Earlier I tried to ascribe an identity to each of the benches, but this seems futile working from the sources I have. One simply cannot go beyond coroners and seneschals without merely guessing.

[53] CP. 40/30, m. 10d: "et per narratorem suum pecierunt iudicium super hoc quod predicti Gilbertus et Matillidis uxor eius obliti fuerunt in sua narracione duas sorores primogenitas ad quas jus debuit descendere adeo bene sicuti predictis Matillidi et Alicie, unde consideratum est per quatuor bancos dicte curie quod propter oblivionem dictarum sororum venirent partes ad proximam curiam ad audiendum iudicium tam de principali placito quam super excepcionem prepositam."

[54] CP. 40/86, m. 155: "Et quod talis fuit processus predicti placiti et non talis qualis predicti sectatores recordantur parati sunt verificare per quendam Ricardum de Gayton audientem et Simonem de Walkote intelligentem qui nunc sunt presentes et qui presentes fuerunt infra quatuor bancos curie predicte diebus et anno quibus predicti sectatores falsum iudicando premissa consideraverunt."

sent to the court of common pleas in 1277 by the hundred court of the city of Bath produced two individuals who had been "within the four benches" when that judgment was made.[55] This was precisely the procedure and terminology used in another case concerning a judgment made in the county court of Northumberland during the 1260s.[56] In 1283, however, Thomas de la Haye brought an action of replevin against Richard Delisle in the county court of Northumberland, and Delisle denied detaining the animals, so he was put to his law. He then proceeded to avow the taking for the farm and services due him. Since Thomas would neither affirm nor deny owing these services, Delisle asked for a judgment from the court. It was the seneschals who ruled that Delisle's statement would be taken to have been admitted, and they then respited the judgment until the next session.[57] Thus, even though Northumberland county court had a group known as the four benches, there, as in Warwickshire, it was the seneschals who actually rendered the judgments.

In Nottinghamshire county court, as in Warwickshire and Northumberland, the seneschals were the judges. In 1291 a case of false judgment came before the court of common pleas concerning *Gloucestre v Charrun*, an action that had been in that county court. Since the justices had ordered the sheriff to have the suitors record the plea and he had answered that they were unwilling to do so, the court issued the normal mandate to distrain all the suitors of the county court to come into the court of common pleas to record the plea before the justices. To this mandate the sheriff responded that the writ had come too late for him to inquire who the suitors of the county court were—a strange reply from a sheriff who had been in office over a year already if suitors were regularly functioning in court—and that he knew of only four. These four were the archbishop of York, Edmund Deyncurt, William le Graunt, and Hugh Bardolf. Deyncurt and William le Graunt appeared in the court of common pleas by

[55] CP. 40/18, m. 31: "quendam Henricum audientem et quendam Ricardum intelligentem qui predictis die et anno infra quatuor bancos predicte curie fuerunt." See *Casus Placitorum*, ed. W. H. Dunham, Selden Society, vol. 69 (London, 1950), p. 99 (there undated).

[56] *Three Early Assize Rolls for the County of Northumberland*, ed. William Page, Surtees Society, vol. 88 (Durham, 1891), p. 196.

[57] CP. 40/63, m. 24d: "Et bene advocat capcionem iustam pro firma sua et servicio sibi debito videlicet xxiiij^{or} marcis et relevio que aretro sunt de libero tenemento suo quod de eo tenet ad feodi firmam in villa predicta. Et hoc non contradixit nec verificavit quin ita fuit prout videbatur senescallis comitatus unde predictus Robertus super hoc petit iudicium etc. Et senescalli posuerunt iudicium in respectum de predicto comitatu usque comitatum die jovis proxima ante festum sancti Martini anno regis nunc terciodecimo."

sending William's seneschal; the other two did not appear, so that the sheriff was ordered to distrain all the suitors once again.[58] The sheriff improved on his previous performance the next term. He had distrained six people: the same four he had first distrained and Henry de Wodeburgh and Richard de Byngham. Byngham and William le Graunt appeared in person, but the archbishop and Deyncurt each sent only his seneschal. The plaintiff was disappointed by the lack of pressure such distraints would put on the county as a whole and complained that there were many suitors to the county court and that they all should have been distrained. It is clear that the sheriff considered that only those who actually rendered the judgments—the seneschals of the great men of the county—would have been necessary to make the record in the court of common pleas.[59]

This conclusion concerning the power of the seneschals in Nottinghamshire from the process in *Gloucestre v Charrun* is confirmed by another case: *Prat v Prat*. The original litigation was a case of debt for 20s brought in the county court of Nottinghamshire by a viscontiel writ issued 28 September 1293. Isabel Prat alleged that her grandfather, Adam Prat, had assigned that sum to her in 1269 and had given the money to his executors, of whom Thomas Prat, the defendant, was one. The other three executors had allegedly entrusted the 20s to Thomas for the use of Isabel. When Isabel came of age, however, and asked for the money, Thomas refused, denying that either Adam or the other executors had ever given him the money. They came to issue on this point in the county court, and a jury was summoned. The jury reached its verdict in favor of Thomas.

Isabel waited a little more than a year, until there was a new sheriff

---

[58] CP. 40/91, m. 1d: "Et vicecomes nichil fecit set mandavit quod breve adeo tarde venit quod non potuit inquirere qui sunt sectatores eiusdem comitatus nisi de Johanne archiepiscopo Ebor', Edmundo de Eyncurt, Willelmo le Graunt, et Hugone Bardolf quos testatur sectatores etc. Et qui quidem Edmundus et Willelmus le Graunt per senescallum ipsius Willelmi veniunt, et de archiepiscopo et Hugone testatur quod districti sunt etc., nec est pena eis infligenda eo quod nullum recordum facere possunt sine predictis Edmundo et Willelmo et aliis sectatoribus eiusdem comitatus de quorum nominibus vicecomes non certificat etc."

[59] CP. 40/92, m. 13: "Et vicecomes modo mandavit quod distrinxit omnes sectatores predicti comitatus quorum Johannes archiepiscopus Ebor' per senescallum, Edmundus de Eyncurt per senescallum suum, Ricardus de Byngham, et Willelmus le Graunt modo veniunt. Et Hugo Bardolf et Henricus de Wodeburgh sectatores non veniunt. Et predictus Hugo districtus fuit per catalla ad valenciam viginti solidorum. . . . Et quia testatum est quod plures sunt sectatores predicti comitatus, preceptum est vicecomiti sicut prius quod distringat omnes sectatores comitatus sui per omnes terras etc." *RH,* 2:27, records a complaint that William Peverel had been accustomed to find a seneschal in the county court of Nottinghamshire but had ceased doing so for some time. Apparently, the situation had not changed, since Peverel received no mention here.

in Nottinghamshire. She then purchased an identical writ on 7 February 1295 and made the same allegations against Thomas. Thomas reasonably objected that the same action had been in the county court before and that he had gone quit by judgment of the county. They came to issue on this, and the proof that was requested showed that the seneschals rendered the judgments in that county. Thomas put himself on the county rolls and on the record of the seneschals; Isabel put herself on the county rolls and the record of the county. Had the record of the county been a different form of record than the record of the seneschals, pleading could not have terminated there. The county rolls, however, were duly inspected, and the entries there agreed with the record of the seneschals of the county that Thomas had been acquitted previously. Isabel had once again lost her case.[60]

Isabel Prat, however, was a stubborn lady. That judgment had been given on 12 March 1296; by 20 April she had purchased a writ of false judgment. Process proceeded, as usual, very slowly and uninterestingly until late in 1299.[61] The writ issued then, returnable in Trinity term, has survived. It was a *sicut pluries* false judgment writ which also notified the sheriff that he had been heavily amerced for not obeying the previous writ. The sheriff's endorsement was that he had ordered and enjoined "the suitors and the seneschals of the county court, who should and were accustomed to render judgments of pleas and plaints," to record the case. They had answered him that the suit had been pleaded so long previously that they were unable to make the record without first inspecting the writ and the county rolls, which were still in the possession of previous sheriffs. They

[60] CP. 52 morrow All Souls, 27 Edward I [S.S.]: "Et predictus Thomas Prat venit et defendit vim et iniuriam etc., et dicit quod non tenetur respondere narracioni sue nec accioni, quia dicit quod alias coram vicecomiti in eodem comitatu isto videlicet anno regni regis Edwardi xxij protulit consimile breve versus eundem Thomam de eadem accione et per iudicium comitatus ab eadem accione recessit quietus et petit iudicium si modo de eadem accione de qua recessit quietus debeat respondere, et quod ita sit vocat rotulos ad warrantum una cum recordo seneschallorum. Et predicta Isabella dicit quod non recessit quietus de eadem accione seu narracione inter easdem personas, et quod ita sit petit recordum comitatus et rotulorum. Et datus est dies usque proximum comitatum. . . . Et compertum est per inspeccionem rotulorum placitorum comitatus de anno vicesimo secundo et per recordum seneschallorum eiusdem comitatus quod predicta Isabella tulit consimile breve versus eundem Thomam de debito predicto per eandem accionem quam nunc et capta super illa accione inquisicione recessit predictus Thomas inde quietus per finale iudicium et predicta Isabella in misericordia, per quod consideratum est ut prius quod predicta Isabella nichil capiat per breve suum set sit in misericordia pro falso clamore et predictus Thomas inde quietus."

[61] CP. 52 quindene Trinity, 24 Edward I; octave Trinity, 27 Edward I; CP. 40/125, m. 151d; CP. 40/129, m. 64; CP. 40/130, m. 236d.

said that they would hasten to these sheriffs to inspect the rolls.[62] On 30 June 1299 another writ issued out of the court of common pleas, and the records of both cases were finally made, sent, and filed in the writ files, but the case itself never came before the justices for judgment.[63] Nottinghamshire county court was obviously dominated by the seneschals.

In Lincolnshire also seneschals were a vital part of the county court. The *quo warranto* inquiries include the investigation into whether Norman Darcy or his ancestors had ever been obliged to find a seneschal in the county court.[64] In the court of Holland in 1291 the seneschals taxed the damages in one case and probably also rendered the judgment.[65] *Prior of Torksey v Talebot*, a case from 1279, is one of the rare instances in which the clerk of the court of common pleas was willing to let the sheriff's endorsement stand without correction. The sheriff had endorsed the writ that he had ordered the seneschals of the county court to record the plea, but that they had refused to do anything in the absence of the other seneschals and companions.[66]

Long ago F. W. Maitland noted that the county court of Yorkshire seemed to have been composed of the seneschals of the major lords of the county. He ascribed this phenomenon to the unusual size of Yorkshire and thought that constitution peculiar to Yorkshire, a special privilege because of the amount of travelling that the suitors

[62] CP. 52 octave Trinity, 27 Edward I: "In pleno comitatu Notingham ex parte domini regis precepi et iniunxi sectatoribus et senescallis eiusdem comitatus qui iudicia placitorum et querelarum reddere debent et solent quod michi fecissent recordum loquele que fuit in eodem comitatu per breve domini regis inter partes in hoc brevi nominatas, qui michi responderunt quod loquela illa placitata fuit iam est diu tempore Philippi de Paunton de comitatu Lyncoln' dudum vicecomitis Notingham' qui penes se habet illud breve domini regis una cum rotulis placiti eiusdem querele sine quo brevi et inspeccione rotulorum predictorum dicunt quod nesciunt nec possunt recordum loquele predicte michi facere eo quod non currit eis in memoria qualiter loquela illa erat placitata set dicto Philippo vicecomiti cum omni festinacione qua possunt appropinquabunt pro brevi illo et inspeccione rotulorum illorum habendis."

[63] CP. 52 morrow All Saints, 27 Edward I.

[64] *PQW*, p. 414.

[65] CP. 40/93, m. 49, Cobeldik v Pecche: "Et quia ipsa Lucia per attornatum suum recessit a predicta curia domini regis antequam plegios invenit de predicta lege facienda secundum consuetudinem Anglie consideratum fuit in eadem curia scilicet in predictis tribus wapentakiis domini regis quod predictus Rogerus recuperasset predictos quadraginta solidos et dampna sua que statim taxata fuerunt per senescallos illorum trium wapentakiorum ad dimidiam marcam et quod ipsa esset in misericordia pro iniusta detencione."

[66] CP. 40/31, m. 20: "Et de predicto recordo mandavit vicecomes quod preceperat senescallos predicti comitatus quod recordari facerent predictam loquelam, qui in absencia aliorum senescallorum ac scociorum nichil inde fecerunt."

would have to have done to attend.[67] It seems, rather, that Yorkshire in this was merely a normal county. The situation of Baldwin Wake, already examined, is a good indication of the importance of seneschals in that county court.[68] Another early mention of Yorkshire seneschals was made in 1276, when the sheriff of Yorkshire was ordered to have made before himself and the coroners a record of an outlawry proclaimed because of a felony committed by John Morel. Traditional theory would have it that if the sheriff went beyond the coroners for that kind of record, he would have gone to the judges of the court, that is, to the suitors. The sheriff, however, answered that he had ordered the coroners and the seneschals of the county to make the record, but they were unable to do so because of the time that had passed since the outlawry.[69] Once again, the judges of the county court were in fact the seneschals.

Seneschals were occasionally mentioned in other county courts. One would naturally expect Leicestershire to have been exactly like Warwickshire, both because they were twinned counties and because neither had suitors. In 1284 that expectation was confirmed: it was the knights and seneschals of the county who were called upon to testify concerning a long-standing dispute.[70] In 1281 the knights and seneschals of the county court of Derbyshire testified that the township of Bakewell was not a borough and that it did not have the liberties that pertained to a borough, so that the writ of mort dancestor could be used for litigation concerning tenements there.[71] As early

[67] F. Pollock and F. W. Maitland, *The History of English Law before the Time of Edward I*, 2 vols. 2nd ed. (Cambridge, 1968), 1:543.

[68] Above, at n. 19.

[69] CP. 40/14, m. 2: "Et vicecomes nichil inde fecit set mandavit quod senescalli et coronatores eiusdem comitatus nesciverunt facere recordum illud de tam longinquo tempore. Ideo sicut prius preceptum est vicecomiti quod coram eo etc., in pleno comitatu recordari faciat . . . et si noluerunt facere predictum recordum tunc distringat coronatores et omnes sectatores predicti comitatus per omnes terras etc., et quod de exitibus etc., et quod habeat corpora eorum hic ad prefatum terminum ad faciendum recordum illud." The coroners are not included here because they were part of the four benches, but rather because they were responsible for recording outlawries; the sheriff's enrollment of outlawry procedure in the county rolls only served as a counter-roll to the coroners' record.

[70] JUST. 1/457, m. 29: "convocare fecerunt omnes milites et seneschallos istius comitatus qui de rei veritate super hoc dicenda."

[71] JUST. 1/148, m. 3d: "et super hoc venit quidam Radulphus de Wyne ballivus regine de Baukeswell et dicit quod predicta villa de Blakewell est liber burgus et quod tenementa in eodem burgo possunt legari, per quod nullum tale breve iacit in eadem villa et petit quod istud breve hic non procedat. Et quia milites et senescalli comitatus precise testantur quod predicta villa non est burgus nec habet libertates que ad burgum pertinent, processum est ad capcionem predicte assise."

as 1269 the seneschals had an acknowledged position in the county court of Devon. The sheriff there was ordered to make a record of an action of right, but answered only that the writ had come too late for the seneschals and knights to record the plea.[72] If those knights the sheriff referred to were also suitors, they soon disappeared. In 1291 the sheriff of Devon testified that in Devon no knights owed suit to the county court. When he was required to have knights present to witness the making of a record, he seemingly used whoever happened to be present for other reasons.[73]

There can then be little doubt that seneschals were normally the judges in county courts during the reign of Edward, despite the insistence in writs that suitors were responsible for county judgments and record. This situation, however, was not novel. The author of the *Leges Henrici* in the early twelfth century boldly stated that the judges of the county court were the barons of the county.[74] Given the nature of twelfth-century England and the importance of the county courts then, that statement is not improbable. If it is true, however, it would mean that most often the county court judges would have been, in fact, the seneschals of the barons, earls, priors, abbots, and bishops of the county. Moreover, when the obligation of suit was systematized, it was normally due only at the great county sessions, so that the suitors could have been involved in the county court only on an irregular basis. Finally, there is little reason to suppose that the ordinary suitors had somehow between 1114 and 1272 democratized the county courts, appropriating to themselves the power of rendering judgments in county on important disputes concerning land titles, physical injuries, debts, and damage to property— the very things that a baron would have needed to influence if he was to fulfil his obligations to his men and retain their loyalty. Everything, then, would seem to argue against the presently accepted theory that lesser independent squires dominated the workings of the county courts.

[72] KB. 26/188, an added membrane: "adeo tarde venit ad comitatum quod senescalli et milites [et aliorum comitatus?] plene congregati ad faciendum recordum." The membrane is badly deteriorated.

[73] CP. 52 quindene St. John the Baptist, 19 Edward I, Molis v Trelosk: "Recordum loquele inter partes nominatas in hoc brevi non potuit pro defectu militum, quia milites nullam sectam debent ad comitatum nec fuerunt ibi aliqui milites ad testificandum recordum." Trelosk, it should be noted, was thereafter undersheriff of Devon (CP. 52 octave Hilary, 28 Edward I). See above, chapter 1, n. 78 for a specific reference to knights and suitors in the county court of Devon.

[74] *Leges Henrici Primi*, p. 130.

The opinion of historians concerning the importance of such suitors for rendering judgments rests ultimately, if we concern ourselves solely with historical argument, on the interpretation of two cases in the early thirteenth century. The first of these cases is the famous false judgment action of 1212 which concerned the *buzones*. Gloucestershire county was, in this case, accused and convicted of having made a false judgment; furthermore, that false judgment had been facilitated by tampering with the county rolls. At the termination of the case in the court of common pleas, it was not the county that was amerced; rather, five individuals and the litigant who had been successful in the county court were ordered to be arrested. Those five were called the *buzones* of judgments, and the circumstances of the case clearly indicate that they were the ones who in fact decided the judgments of the county court.[75] The case has been much written about, and G. T. Lapsley was the last to investigate the matter. After sketching the biographies of the men involved, he termed them voluntarily active, particularly business-loving suitors, men who were part of the lesser squirearchy of the county.[76] It should be noted immediately that he was unable to adduce any proof that any one of the five was actually a suitor, although at such an early date that kind of reference would have been purely fortuitous. Lapsley's biographical treatment of the problem nevertheless deserves more attention than was given it by Richardson and Sayles, who disregarded Lapsley's evidence showing that these particular *buzones* were not in themselves the major landholders and barons of Gloucestershire and went on to declare that the *buzones* were the barons of the shire.[77] In short, if Lapsley's assessment was sound, one must continue to maintain that the ordinary suitor was a major force in determining judgments in county at least during the reign of King John.

The character of the *buzones* is thus a clearly important matter. The only other references to individuals in county courts known as

[75] *CRR*, 6:208, 228-31.

[76] G. T. Lapsley, "Buzones," *EHR* 47 (1932):177-93, 545-67; also in idem, *Crown, Community and Parliament in the Later Middle Ages*, ed. Helen M. Cam and Geoffrey Barraclough (Oxford, 1951), pp. 63-110.

[77] H. G. Richardson and G. O. Sayles, *The Governance of Mediaeval England from the Conquest to the Magna Carta* (Edinburgh, 1963), p. 94: "Such divisions as we can perceive are between large landowners and small landowners, between the *barones comitatus* and the lesser freemen. These barons of the shire are the men whom Bracton will call buzones, the leading men who in the thirteenth, as in the twelfth, century determined what the judgment of the court should be." The thrust of their argument—in favor of a society dominated by the aristocracy—is undoubtedly correct.

buzones occur in Bracton.[78] Lapsley interpreted Bracton's remark as the placing of special administrative burdens on the *buzones* by the justices in eyre.[79] For him this interpretation had great constitutional import. He had elsewhere maintained that the members of Parliament in the early fourteenth century were essentially the kind of people he now considered the *buzones*. Those knights of the shire he saw as administratively inclined lesser squires, because of their involvement on royal commissions and in county offices; no serious consideration was given to any possibility of legal training or practice.[80] If he could show that such individuals were the dominant force in county courts in the early thirteenth century, then he would have established a major force in the origins of Parliament: those squires would have exercised so much power in local government that the king required some kind of formal consultation with them. The passage in Bracton, however, indicates no delegation of administrative burdens; Bracton only says that the justices should take the *buzones* aside, converse with them, and instruct them in regard to proper procedure concerning police duties incumbent on the whole population. It should be considered a briefing in the law; Maitland called it merely a colloquy.[81] It would not have been surprising if the justices held such a meeting with the seneschals, the presiding officers of the lower courts and the judges of the county court, for immediately afterwards the justices were to instruct the hundred bailiffs and sergeants concerning the selection of presentment juries. There is even a similarity between Bracton's description of the *buzones*—those upon whose nod depended the votes of the others of the county court—and Fleta's description of the seneschals as the bell-wethers of the flock.[82] Such considerations, taken together with what is already known about the county courts, establishes a presumption in favor of a theory that would make the *buzones* seneschals instead of particularly active but nonlawyerly suitors.

Biographical treatment of such lesser individuals in the early thirteenth century is much more hazardous than in the late thirteenth and early fourteenth century. For the pleaders in Warwickshire county

---

[78] Henry of Bracton, *De Legibus et Consuetudinibus Angliae*, ed. G. E. Woodbine, trans. Samuel Thorne, 4 vols. to date (Cambridge, Mass. and London, 1968-), 2:327-28.

[79] Lapsley, *"Buzones,"* p. 178.

[80] Lapsley, *Crown, Community and Parliament*, pp. 111-52.

[81] Pollock and Maitland, *History of English Law*, 1:553.

[82] Bracton, *De Legibus*, 2:327; *Fleta*, 2:225 (above at n. 31).

court around 1300 numerous resources were available, and the primary problem of research there was endurance, not paucity of sources. In the early thirteenth century, however, the king's court was not the scene of so much litigation, and there are fewer auxiliary records. Even so, for two of the individuals sufficient facts may be adduced to make them more like lawyers and seneschals than squires; for that early date two out of five is a high rate of proof and will serve to establish the probable composition of the group as a whole, given the presumption from Bracton and *Fleta*.

Lapsley described Walter de Aure, one of the *buzones*, as a "person of condition and some property in the county of Gloucester." The property ascribed to him was the manor of Awre, which came to Walter in 1204. That manor, however, was soon to be called ancient demesne land, and Walter only held it at farm, rendering his farm to the king.[83] After Walter's death, the farm was rendered by his son—who had the same name as his father—to the earl of Salisbury by a royal grant of 1218.[84] Walter's position in Awre was certainly not that of lord of the manor; he held only two virgates and six acres there.[85] He was, more likely, a royal bailiff. In several deeds from around 1200 Walter was mentioned as the bailiff of the hundred of Newnham, which was at least close to Awre.[86] Walter de Aure, junior, functioned seemingly as a bailiff to the inhabitants of Awre also, since they were ordered to obey him.[87] Lapsley felt, furthermore, that Walter's position as a squire was further indicated by his activities in the administration of other counties. Whether that would have been so or not, there is no proof that he actually was involved in other counties. It was asserted that he was an assessor of an aid in Oxfordshire in 1207, but the Patent Roll entry is ambiguous about the county concerned, and the other men of the commission seem to have been also from Gloucestershire.[88] The aid itself was probably to have been raised not in Oxfordshire at all, but rather in Gloucester-

---

[83] Lapsley, "*Buzones*," p. 187. It should be noted that his treatment of William de Eston is wholly irrelevant to the argument.

[84] Ibid., n. 4.

[85] *PR, 6 John*, p. 147. Perhaps this decreased after 1211: *PR, 14 John*, p. 142. Seventy years later Robert de Aure, perhaps his descendant, was sued for six acres in the ancient demesne manor court; the case finally came into the court of common pleas on an allegation of false judgment: CP. 40/60, m. 87.

[86] *Cartulary and Historical Notes of the Cistercian Abbey of Flaxley*, ed. A. W. Crawley-Boevey (Exeter, 1887), pp. 136, 143. *Rotuli Litterarum Clausarum, 1204-1224*, ed. Thomas D. Hardy, 2 vols., Record Commission (London, 1833-1844), 1:365b.

[87] Lapsley, "*Buzones*," p. 187, n. 4.

[88] Ibid., p. 188.

shire. It is much easier to conclude that Walter de Aure was a bailiff and lawyer, rather than a business-loving squire.

Philip de Beaumont was also labeled a member of the Gloucester-shire squirearchy, with lands in Gloucestershire, Somerset, and Dor-set, and with reversionary interests in lands in Oxfordshire. Fur-thermore, he was supposed to have been the hereditary farmer of the hundred of Shirwell in Devon.[89] Beaumont's interests in the Ox-fordshire lands and in the hundred of Shirwell may be immediately dismissed, since they rest on a confusion between two men named Philip de Beaumont. The Philip de Beaumont who was a *buzo* in Gloucestershire died seven years before the other Philip de Beaumont became involved in litigation concerning those rights.[90] Moreover, that later Philip de Beaumont was still underage in 1211, when the false judgment was made in the Gloucestershire county court.[91] Beau-mont's alleged holdings in Somerset and Dorset were derived from the fact that he was proffered as a champion for lands in those counties in 1201 and 1207.[92] While this probably was the *buzo* Philip de Beaumont, and while it is true that a champion was supposed to be the tenant of the one offering him as proof, there was no require-ment that the champion had to hold land in the same county as the land in dispute. It is unsure even how rigorously the rule concerning the champion's tenancy was enforced. At any rate, the duties of a champion at this time were more likely to have been undertaken by a lawyer than by a self-respecting squire.[93]

Philip de Beaumont cannot therefore be assumed to have held lands outside Gloucestershire, and even the origins of the tenements he held in Gloucestershire were other than Lapsley supposed. His hold-ings amounted to seven virgates and four acres of land in Dorsington and one hide in Marston, certainly sufficient holdings to place him, at the end of his life, among the respectable people of Gloucestershire. All that land, however, had been acquired during his lifetime; none of it was inherited. Moreover, he held one further tenement, a virgate in Marston held in villeinage.[94] It is conceivable—but certainly not open to proof—that the virgate in question was his original tenement

[89] Ibid.

[90] *CRR*, 7:316.

[91] *CRR*, 6:139.

[92] *CRR*, 2:29, 5:46.

[93] Palmer, "The Origins of the Legal Profession," pp. 141-45.

[94] *CRR*, 7:316; 9:140-41; *Rolls of the Justices in Eyre for Gloucestershire, War-wickshire, and Staffordshire, 1221, 1222*, ed. D. M. Stenton, Selden Society, vol. 59 (London, 1940), pp. 113-14.

and functioned as a life grant held at the will of his lord much in the way an annuity, revocable at refusal of service, served to retain a lawyer at the end of the thirteenth century. As a lawyer, his fees would have been high, particularly when he functioned as a champion;[95] he could easily have acquired the lands in Marston and Dorsington later with the proceeds from his legal services. There is, in short, no reason to believe that Philip de Beaumont was a voluntarily active, business-loving squire instead of a lawyer and seneschal or bailiff at the time he was mentioned as one of the *buzones*.

For the other three individuals called *buzones* there is not so much evidence, but neither is there evidence for calling them squires and suitors. They were, it is true, called knights of the shire in certain procedural contexts along with many other Gloucestershire residents. That should not, however, be taken to mean that they were knights "girt with a sword." Moreover, as bailiffs or seneschals they would not have been responsible for paying the amercement had the justices levied the customary amercement for false judgment on the county court. Only this can explain the extraordinary procedure followed by the justices in having them arrested. Since the county rolls had been tampered with, it was clearly a case of conspiracy and foul play. The culprits in this situation could only be punished by putting them in gaol until they agreed to make fine with the king for a sum of money. Had they been suitors, their punishment could have been inflicted in more ordinary ways. In all, the procedure, the biographies, the evidence concerning the activity of seneschals in county courts, and the passages in Bracton all lead to the conclusion that the *buzones* were the kind of people included generally in the vague category of lawyers: seneschals, bailiffs, pleaders, attorneys. Moreover, if that is so, Bracton's statements become even more intelligible. It is generally conceded that his statements imply that such a group of *buzones* would be found in every county visited by the justices in eyre; that would have been a perfectly understandable assumption if the *buzones* were seneschals and bailiffs. For such a group, similar in character but with diverse legal functions, the word "buzones" might readily be coined. Richardson and Sayles translate that word roughly as "big shots."[96] It is unlikely that such a slang expression would have been used for earls and barons who were by nature important; it is much more likely that it would be used for people who were exceeding their

[95] Palmer, "The Origins of the Legal Profession," p. 142 and n. 89.
[96] Richardson and Sayles, *Governance*, p. 94.

"natural" position, as a bailiff would have done in exercising the authority of his lord.

The second classic case always used to illustrate the activity of suitors in the county courts is the Lincolnshire case which arose after the 1225 issue of the Magna Carta. Theobald Hautein in this case was able to gain the support of the county judges and prevent the sheriff from holding the county court for a second day and also, later on, to prevent him from holding county pleas in the regional court of Kesteven. As usual, the record does not mention suitors explicitly. In the county court the sheriff was said to have addressed the knights and seneschals; in Kesteven he was said to have addressed the knights, even though one of the judges, with whom Hautein had some harsh words, was specifically mentioned as a seneschal.[97] It cannot be maintained that Hautein was simply an ordinary suitor; he was a professional lawyer. Unlike a century later, the king's court in 1225 did not entertain a sufficient volume of litigation to support a body of lawyers who functioned there and nowhere else. There were a great many people, however, who did work as attorneys in the king's court at that time, and a substantial number of them appeared often enough to dispel any notion that they were amateurs.[98] They were rather like the Warwickshire pleaders later on, functioning in both the king's court and the lower courts, but because the lower courts determined so much more important litigation in the early thirteenth century, their legal duties were focused much more intensively in those lower courts. Only rarely would a lawyer then have occasion to practice in the king's court. Theobald Hautein was this kind of person, appearing infrequently but repeatedly as an attorney in the king's court.[99] Furthermore, it was not unusual at that time for a seneschal to undertake attorney's duties. Whatever Theobald Hautein could claim as his warrant for speaking up in Lincolnshire county court, he was certainly not merely an ordinary suitor.

Suitors were certainly present in county courts in the early thir-

---

[97] CRR, 12:434-35, 461.

[98] Pleas Before the King or His Justices, 1198-1212, ed. Doris M. Stenton, 4 vols., Selden Society, vols. 67, 68, 83, 84 (London, 1948-1967), 3:ccxcv-cccxix.

[99] CRR, 1:229, 275; 3:57, 62; 4:5-6; 6:103; 7:168, 201, 282, 331; 9:64, 127, 174, 196, 380; 10:20, 170; Earliest Lincolnshire Assize Rolls, 1202-1209, ed. Doris M. Stenton, Lincolnshire Record Society, vol. 22 (Lincoln, 1926), nos. 924a, 1065, 1336; Rolls of the Justices in Eyre for Lincolnshire, 1218-9, and Worcestershire, 1221, ed. Doris M. Stenton, Selden Society, vol. 53 (London, 1934), no. 534; originally noticed by Lorna E. M. Walker, "Some Aspects of Local Jurisdictions in the 12th and 13th Centuries" (Master's thesis, University of London, 1958), p. 190.

teenth century. During the great county sessions their attendance was required. Some few suitors were obliged to attend every session. Many suitors would have been present at any given session if only because they were actually involved in litigation there. At times of great turmoil in the country as a whole or in the county, they could be expected to speak vehemently in the county courts. Nevertheless, no evidence has been adduced to indicate that the knightly squirearchy were an ongoing force in the administration of England in the thirteenth century, nor that they dominated the county courts and normally adjudicated disputes. The county courts were, rather, dominated by the aristocracy through their chosen and changeable delegates, their seneschals and bailiffs, by the sheriffs and undersheriffs, and by the coroners, who often were themselves men of a legal background. When, in the reign of Edward I, the obligation of suit was allowed to lapse—barring the occasional distraint or the care taken to secure the fines for which certain suits had been commuted—the rendering of judgments and recording of pleas remained with the seneschals and bailiffs. There was no startling alteration in county constitution; the county had been controlled and continued to be controlled by the legally skilled people of the county, by the presiding officers of the courts of the county. It is inaccurate, but there is still a comparison to be made between Cheshire suitors and the suitors of the other English counties. It is hard to imagine that the suitors of most counties had more authority in normal county affairs in comparison to the seneschals than the Cheshire suitors had in comparison to the judges.

The combination of legal functions for English lawyers set forth here and in the last chapter—county court judge, county pleader, seignorial bailiff or seneschal, attorney in the court of common pleas—resulted from the very nature of the origins of the legal profession. It has long been assumed that the legal profession was only beginning around 1200, taking its birth in the king's court; it was also assumed that professional lawyers could not have operated in the lower courts. The latter assumption has been proved abysmally untrue, and thus the way is open for a reinterpretation of the origins of the legal profession. It seems, from the structure of the profession around 1300 and the evidence of continuity in the activities of seneschals and bailiffs back through the twelfth century, that those seneschals and bailiffs were the first secular lawyers in England and that the lower courts were more important than the king's court in the genesis of the profession. Even the *Leges Henrici* held that a lord was obliged to defend his men in court as well as in battle.[100] Since the county courts were at this time more important than the king's court in terms of litigation actually handled and since very often hotly disputed real actions would have been removed from the lord's court into the county court by the process of tolt,[101] the lord had to maintain a strong presence in the county court. He could not, however, expect to be present in person at the numerous courts in which his men would be involved, nor could he expect to know the situation and the particulars of any given case as well as his seneschal or bailiff would.

The bailiffs and seneschals were the people who presided over the lower courts and were intimately involved in legal formalities. They were the people who would have been knowledgeable about the tenures of the lord's men in his jurisdiction and about the personalities involved, and would, furthermore, have been familiar with both the personnel and the customs of the county court. The seneschal or bailiff would most often have been the person who appeared with the litigant, speaking to the court, backed by the authority of his lord, and explaining the litigant's case.[102] The function of "speaking for" must have been so common in a society so formed around ties of lordship that it was quickly incorporated into legal structures and formalities. In the twelfth century they were seen only as seneschals or bailiffs performing their normal duties, as much for their lord and his men as, undoubtedly, for others, when working for others did not conflict with their lord's interests. Their skill, however, was uncommon; even in the early twelfth century many seneschals and bailiffs would have been sufficiently skilled and specialized for us to call them professional lawyers.

Thus, when it became possible in the course of the twelfth century also to appoint an attorney, the attorney was only a replacement for the litigant. The pleader, the person who "spoke for" the litigant, continued to be seen as a legally separate person. Such would have been the normal mode of operation of any court—king's court, county court, baronial court—that was not concerned only with the lowest levels of society. In the king's court, as the ties of lordship became weaker and as the king's court became the forum for a larger amount of litigation, the system begins to seem anomalous. Nevertheless, the legal stringency made acceptable by the existence of the pleader—the

---

[100] *Leges Henrici Primi*, p. 211.

[101] Below, chapter 6 at n. 7 ff.

[102] For bailiffs defending their lord's tenants, see Helen Cam, *The Hundred and the Hundred Rolls* (London, 1930), p. 168.

absolute, irrevocable acceptance of anything considered to have been said by the litigant himself—and the utility of having a relatively small and highly skilled group of lawyers in the king's court available for royal use, preserved the bifurcation of the legal profession into pleaders and attorneys—serjeants and solicitors—into the present day.[103] That system, however, was part and parcel of the constitution of the county courts as early as the twelfth century.

[103] Palmer, "The Origins of the Legal Profession in England," is a fuller exposition of this argument and a treatment of the development of both pleaders and attorneys.

PART II

Jurisdiction

6

Record,
Removal, and
Supervision

ONE OF THE most basic principles—albeit one seldom expressed—
which informed English legal procedures was the principle that a
litigant should receive a fair hearing and be accorded the benefits of
customary process. The principle was adhered to despite social and
constitutional factors that dictated that all lower courts—feudal, liberty, hundred, and county—could be expected at times to be irremediably biased. The typical English solution was the provision of
procedures that either removed the suit into a higher court before
damage had been done or allowed the aggrieved litigant to prosecute
the relevant court for allowing itself to become the worker of injustice.
Both procedures rested on the generally reliable assumption that higher
courts could be trusted to render more impartial justice. Such a legal
notion demanded methods for conveying court records, for removing
pleas, and for generally supervising the lower courts. The processes—
tolt, the writ *pone*, the procedure for the grand assize, the writ of
false judgment, the writ *recordari*—were all developed in the twelfth
century and were all important in integrating the varied English courts
into a legal system and in effecting de facto alterations of jurisdictional
boundaries.

In general the most important suits of normal inter-party litigation
involved real property, and county court jurisdiction clearly included
real matters, even if originally in something of a supervisory manner.
Anglo-Saxon laws state that a litigant should first summon his opponent three times in the hundred court. If the opponent did not then
come to respond, the litigant could proceed to the county court, which

141

would fix a day for the plea.[1] This specially fixed day was a special session of the county court, meeting on the land in question. These were the eleventh-century sessions that were additional to the regular twice-yearly sessions and that must have been concerned only with intractable problems.[2] Only when the demandant could not proceed with his plea in the hundred court—and, probably, only when the matter could not be resolved before that in the locality by the mediation of the local thane—did he enter the county.

By the early twelfth century private or seignorial courts had assumed a formalized place alongside the hundred courts. They exercised primary jurisdiction over many of the disputes concerning real property. In those courts the lord or his seneschal oversaw the adjudication of disputes concerning the lord's relationships with his tenants and concerning the tenures dependant on that relationship. Judgments were rendered by the tenants themselves, by the lord's men; those men had a vested interest in maintaining both the customs of the court that defined their own status and the rights of the lord upon whom they relied for the maintenance of their tenures against outsiders.

To a certain extent the seignorial court was closed to and implacably hostile toward the outside world. A dispute, for instance, concerning boundaries or encroachments in which the litigants were tenants of the same lord could be expected to be heard impartially in the lord's court. There would be no diminution of the lord's wealth; only the parties themselves could gain or lose by the suit. If an outsider claimed, however, he would face substantial vested interests. If he claimed the right to hold from the lord a tenement already held by another, it was the lord himself whose wealth would be diminished by successful prosecution. He had already accepted the current tenant as his man and was therefore obliged to warrant him that grant, even, if necessary, by making good the current tenant's loss through a further equivalent grant. If the outsider was merely complaining concerning a boundary, the lord would still have a vested interest. While it would be the tenant who would suffer the immediate loss, the lord would be deprived of the perquisites of lordship over that land, including the right to the escheat and the right to hold that piece of land during

---

[1] *Laws of the Kings of England from Edmund to Henry I*, ed. A. J. Robertson (Cambridge, 1925), pp. 182-83.

[2] Special sessions are not easy to identify, but in *Anglo-Saxon Charters*, ed. A. J. Robertson (Cambridge, 1956), p. 87, the meeting at Erith in Kent would certainly seem to have been one.

the minority of the current tenant's son. Both the lord and the tenant would thus have been hostile to outsiders attempting to litigate in their court.[3]

The solution to the latter problem, that of the boundary dispute between tenants of different lords, appears in the royal writ issued by Henry I between 1109 and 1111. The relevant portion of the writ is remarkable in that it specifies very precisely the kind of dispute concerned: pleas concerning the partition of lands or concerning encroachments. The writ does not speak in general terms concerning all pleas of land. Such pleas, if they arose between two of the king's barons, were to come before the king's court. If they arose between two vassals of a baron of the king's honor, the case would be heard in the baron's court. If, however, they arose between vassals of different barons—the precise instance in which feudal courts could be expected to be irremediably partial—the case was to be referred to the county court.[4] Considering the constitution of the county courts, this was an appropriate apportionment. Both barons would have been influential in the county court; and, if the case was sufficiently important, they could have assembled there their legal experts to plead the case down to trial by battle before the lords and seneschals of the county court. That rule, even in cases more important than those concerning boundaries and encroachments, was still applied in *Glanvill*: a dispute between parties who claimed to hold a given plot of land from different lords was a matter for the county court.[5]

The problem of the outsider who claimed a better right than the current tenant to hold a given tenement from the same lord was more difficult. The lord had a prima facie right to oversee the litigation, because both litigants claimed the benefit of a relationship with him. Moreover, the other tenants would not have been completely unsympathetic, because they could easily imagine such an outsider's position for their children. Nevertheless, since the lord was irrevocably committed to the current tenant, he would be hesitant even to allow the case into court. The impasse was broken by a royal writ that ordered the lord to do full right to the demandant, a writ properly harsh in tone because directed to an implacably prejudiced lord. This

[3] S.F.C. Milsom, *The Legal Framework of English Feudalism* (Cambridge, 1976), pp. 36-64; Robert C. Palmer, "The Feudal Framework of English Law," *Michigan Law Review* 79 (1981):1130-1164.

[4] Felix Lieberman, ed., *Die Gesetze der Angelsachsen*, 3 vols. (Halle an der Saale, 1898-1916), 1:524.

[5] *Glanvill*, p. 140

royal intervention was an important element in limiting the independence of the feudal court. The provision of the royal writ to force the introduction of the case into the feudal courts was an obvious necessity; no demandant could be sure of compelling a tenant to defend himself—and the lord's interests—in the lord's own court without outside intervention. By the end of the reign of Henry II, with more formalized rules concerning disseisins, that practical statement concerning seignorial bias had become institutionalized in the well-known rule that no tenant could be made to answer for his free tenement unless the demandant had a writ.[6]

The mere enforced introduction of a case was insufficient to insure impartial justice. The Charwelton case (ca. 1107-1111) is the earliest indication of the solution devised for that problem. Robert de Staverton was the outsider who claimed the land; the abbot of Thorney was both the lord of the court and the current tenant of the land. Staverton understandably had to obtain royal writs to succeed even in bringing the case before the court when the abbot refused to seise him of the land. The writ compelled the abbot to allow the case before his court, and the court then fixed a day when Staverton was to produce his evidences and witnesses. It seems, however, that his case was not altogether impregnable, and he still feared the prejudice of the court. He therefore obtained a further royal writ which instructed the sheriff to send wise and prudent men with him to the court on that day to see that he was treated justly. When the court met, however, Staverton produced neither witnesses nor charters, and the court therefore ruled against him.[7]

The writ for the sending of men must have been an optional part of the process of tolt, by which real actions were removed from a feudal court into the county court, although it is still possible that before the *nisi feceris* clause was included in writs of right tolt was always initiated by royal writ. However that may be, such a removal deprived the lord of his normal powers in his court and was only justified when it was proved that the court was doing an injustice. Tolt was therefore a process available only to the demandant; there was certainly no general presumption of prejudice toward the tenant which would have warranted such intervention on his behalf. The full process, as described in *Glanvill*, was fairly simple. Any demandant in a feudal court who felt that an injustice was being done him

---

[6] S.F.C. Milsom, *Legal Framework*, pp. 58-59.

[7] Doris M. Stenton, *English Justice between the Norman Conquest and the Great Charter* (London, 1965), pp. 138-39.

made his complaint to the sheriff. The sheriff would then send his bailiff and four knights of the county to that court, and the demandant would there prove by oath—his own and that of two men who had heard and understood—that the court was proceeding unjustly. If his proof was good, the case was thereby removed—"lifted"—into the county court.[8]

A royal writ may have been used to obtain the presence of the four men in the Charwelton case only because no wrong had yet been done or, perhaps, because the sheriff himself was prejudiced in the case and would not have been expected to act without being pressured by a royal order. At least in some instances the sheriff could act on his own. In 1220 an instance of tolt procedure was described during a case in the king's court. The demandant had attempted to prove to the sheriff that the court of Berkhamstead was not providing him justice, but the constable of the court tried to convince the sheriff that Berkhamstead had such a liberty that tolt procedure could not be used. The constable suggested that four knights be sent to the court to witness that justice was being done. The knights were sent, and the demandant—apparently by the witness of the knights—eventually had his case removed into the county court.[9] Even though the Charwelton case did not actually result in the removal of the case, it does demonstrate, by showing the sheriff's responsibility for the litigation in the lower courts, that tolt was already part of legal procedure early in the twelfth century.[10] It remained available, although infrequently used, to the end of the thirteenth century.[11]

Tolt served several different situations. The first was the situation mentioned above, in which the lord's court was purposely denying justice to the demandant. A second was a similar but more procedural situation. The writ of right patent had to be addressed to the lord

[8] *Glanvill*, p. 139.

[9] *CRR*, 9:80-81.

[10] Doris M. Stenton, *English Justice*, pp. 57, n. 13; 138-39. Considering the administrative structure analyzed by C. Warren Hollister and John Baldwin, "The Rise of Adminsitrative Kingship: Henry I and Philip Augustus," *AHR* 83 (1978):867-905, esp. pp. 882-87, the use of tolt would not be surprising. It would be hard to say, however, that tolt was used continually or beneficially throughout the reign of Stephen.

[11] Brit. Lib., Add. 31826, fol. 410v has a year book note from ca. 1300 that specifies tolt procedure, noting that the oath was to be taken by the demandant while standing halfway inside of the doorway of the court hall or—if there was no court—of the lord's home. *Brevia Placitata*, ed. G. J. Turner, Selden Society, vol. 66 (London, 1947), pp. 227-30 has a good example from 1300; *Cartulary of Tutbury Priory*, ed. Avrom Saltman, Staffordshire Record Soc., 4th ser., vol. 4 (Kendal, 1962), p. 261 has an example from 1456-57. The use of tolt, however, necessarily declined as the use of the writ of right patent declined.

from whom one claimed to hold the land; it could not be addressed to the sheriff. There was, in fact, no way a writ of right could initiate a plea directly in county. If the current tenant claimed to hold of a different lord, the demandant's lord could do nothing. If he did anything, it would seem a distraint out of fee or a disseisin. The demandant's lord would therefore default in providing justice, and the allegation of tolt would not be contested at all; it was the only method for bringing the case into litigation. A third situation for tolt would have been unusual. A distant heir, a stranger to the area, who found it hard to determine from whom he claimed the land but knew only that his ancestor had held it might well buy his writ of right patent addressed to the presumed lord. If that lord did not claim lordship over the land, tolt would take the case into the county. There the person who did claim lordship over the land would have to claim the case for his court. If he did not, he would be in danger of losing his lordship; the county could proceed to adjudicate the claim. The tenant would of course vouch his lord. The demandant, if he won, would receive the land, and homage would presumably accrue to the named lord. The real lord would have to provide the former tenant with *escambium*, but would have no claim over the new tenant. Such cases were undoubtedly infrequent.[12]

In tolt the witnesses would at times have had to judge whether justice was done, and the proper standards could only have been the customary usage of the court. It is unlikely, however, that the witnesses ever had great difficulty, since there were not innumerably different legal procedures in England. Immemorial custom was a powerful force, but the term is deceptive. A court's custom, unless written down, would change to conform to new situations and to the notions of justice and right process held by the individual members of the court. Most courts had suitors who went to county court at least occasionally, and the lord and the seneschal were bound to be familiar with process at county court and to be able to argue within the framework of the county's customs. The substantial original jurisdiction of the county court in some real matters and its supervisory role in others meant that the procedure practiced in the lower courts was constantly brought before the best legal minds in the county and, if unjustly aberrant, criticized and perhaps even ignored in county process. Some few courts were admittedly isolated and preserved their

[12] Examples of cases claimed by other lords after removal by tolt into a county court: *CRR*, 3:79 (1203); *CRR*, 4:264 (1206).

own customs. For most counties, however, customs undoubtedly tended to become uniform throughout the county and, to the extent that tenants and lords held land in nearby counties, even in regions. Only hardy counties, like Kent, Durham, and Cheshire, could resist the ever-present pressures toward uniformity in substantive issues regarding real property. Glanvill, of course, still complained about the diversity of practice in the lower courts, but he did not specify the way in which they differed.[13] As early as 1170 the king was able to establish uniform rules concerning essoins to be practiced in both the king's court and the county courts, and set down the variation of practice that was to prevail in feudal courts.[14] The local variations in legal procedure that survived through to the end of the reign of Henry II must have been in things even less important than essoins.

The county courts, while probably more impartial than the feudal courts, were still open to illicit pressure. One early thirteenth-century story, for instance, has the sheriff so pressuring the judges of the county for a judgment favorable to his own lord that most of the judges simply left court. The county, at the behest of the sheriff, even then proceeded to judgment with the few judges who remained.[15] Such situations, albeit often less dramatic, had to be expected. The same principle that lay behind the process of tolt might seem to dictate that a similar process be available to avoid the partiality of the county court. In the reign of Henry II that process was developed in the form of the writ *pone*.

The writ *pone* removed litigation from the county court into the king's court, and to that extent it was analogous to the process of tolt, which removed litigation from feudal courts into the county court. Tolt, however, was restricted exclusively to real actions and had even become an institutionalized threat in the writ of right patent: "if you do not do [full right to the demandant], the sheriff will." The *pone*, while in this chapter to be discussed mostly in connection with real actions, was available for a broad range of cases and soon

---

[13] *Glanvill*, p. 139. It should be noted, of course, that Glanvill here is only concerned with feudal courts. On p. 172 the varying customs of the county courts are mentioned, but concerning thefts and other things belonging to the sheriff; p. 113, in a comment on the writ for customs and services, makes it clear that county customs varied in some respects on real matters. The difference in tone between his comments on feudal court customs and on county court customs might indicate that the latter were not so diverse, at least in respect of real litigation.

[14] *Pleas Before the King or His Justices*, ed. D. M. Stenton, 4 vols., Selden Society, vols. 67, 68, 83, 84 (London, 1948-1967), 1:153-54.

[15] *Somersetshire Pleas*, ed. Charles Chadwyck-Healey, 2 vols., Somerset Record Society, vols. 11, 36 (London, 1897, 1923), 1:61-63.

could be used to remove almost any case which had been begun by writ from the county courts. The terms of the writ itself were admirably clear:

> The king to the sheriff, greeting. At the request of the demandant, put [*pone*] the plea which is in your county court by our writ between A. and B. concerning so much land before our justices at Westminster on such a day. And summon by good summoners the abovesaid B. that he be there to answer the aforesaid A. thereof. And have there the summoners and this writ. Witnessed by etc.[16]

The procedure involved was fairly simple. The sheriff merely summoned the tenant to appear at Westminster on the day assigned, returned the writ—and the writ that had served to initiate the case, if the case had not been begun by a writ of right patent—to the king's court, and terminated all process in the case upcoming in his county court. It was a peculiarity of the writ of right patent that the demandant retained the original writ in his possession, only surrendering it to obtain a final judgment.

The process connected with the writ *pone* was not as ancient as that involved in tolt. Glanvill already knew the *pone*, and in his time it was available for the removal of many writs.[17] It is possible but not probable that the *pone* was available before the 1180s, but good evidence is lacking.[18] Glanvill mentioned the *pone* only in his discussion of the writ of right of dower, but not with the writ of right patent for land. It is possible that in so doing he was considering the

---

[16] *Early Registers of Writs,* ed. Elsa de Haas and G.D.G. Hall, Selden Society, vol. 87 (London, 1970), p. 16 (Hib. 53) and p. 19 (CA 4) are early examples. CA 4 comes near the beginning of the writs, right after the writs of right.

[17] *Glanvill*, p. 61.

[18] The date for the origins of the writ *pone* would be a very important piece of information, but I have been unable to come to any firm conclusions. The first surviving writs *pone* are from 1199 (*Pleas before the King or His Justices*, 1: nos. 3477, 3500, 3519), but Glanvill in 1187-1189 was already very familiar with them. The entries in the pipe rolls are too ambiguous. Consider *PR, 31 Henry II*, p. 148: "Radulfus de Weleford debet ij m. pro habendo loquela sua in curia regis, que erat in comitatu versus priorem de Derherst." Such a payment was probably for a *pone*, but could have been for a *recordari*. The hazards can even be seen earlier with *PR, 18 Henry II*, p. 139: "Nicholaus debet v m. ut placitum quod fuit inter ipsum et sororem uxoris sue quod fuit in curia archiepiscopatus [archbishopric being vacant], sit in curia regis." Anyone familiar with the legal system a century later could easily see in this not only the use of a *pone* but also the existence of the administrative structure required for the franchise of return of writs. That entry could just as easily be evidence for a *recordari*, and I am not yet willing to rule out the possibility that it indicates the purchase of a *precipe* for a case that had foundered without final judgment in the lower court, that is, not an indication of a real removal of a case at all.

pone in its most proper position—perhaps in its original use[19]—but it cannot be concluded that the *pone* was not by then available also for the writ of right patent for land. Glanvill's attention may have been overly absorbed in his involved discussion of the procedures surrounding the grand assize. Similarly, he omitted mentioning the use of the *recordari* with the writ of right patent, even though he was clearly aware of that possibility: his example of the writ *recordari* was made to be used with the writ of right patent for land.[20] There is thus no pressing reason to think that the availability of the *pone* was different in Glanvill's time than later practice would indicate.

The *pone*, unlike tolt, initiated a procedure that was available to either demandant or tenant. The demandant was allowed the use of the *pone* with no restrictions. The tenant, however, was justifiably placed in a somewhat more restricted position. It was clearly in the tenant's interest to delay the plea, and removal by *pone* could thus have become merely a tactic for delaying justice. Still, the tenant needed the writ at times. In the feudal court, there was no reason to presume bias against him. In the county court, however, bias was not so predictable; the tenant could be the victim as easily as the demandant. Therefore, if the tenant was able to assign a sufficient cause, he too was allowed to remove the case by *pone*. The tenant's use was clear even in the time of Glanvill;[21] the reasons for its allowance are so obvious that the tenant's use of the *pone* is probably as old as the demandant's.

The basic assumption behind both tolt and the writ *pone* was that each higher level of court was less susceptible to bias; that presumption resulted in rules that *required* the removal of certain pleas. Glanvill made much of the impartiality of the king's court:

> His Highness's court is so impartial that no judge there is so shameless
> or audacious as to presume to turn aside at all from the path of justice

[19] The original use of the *pone*, if one must judge from the earliest mentions, concerns right to land. One would like to believe that the *pone* was not available for the writ of right patent in 1179, however, because a good modified *pone* with an explicit *causa* clause would seem to have been a better procedure than that instituted for the grand assize in that year. The writ of right of dower may have presented problems, given that the demandant was a woman and that there was a close relationship between demandant and tenant that made removal necessary. It is perhaps just as likely that the *pone* was introduced to supplement the standardized viscontiel writs, since it is possible that the early examples of the writ *pone* all concern right to land only as a result of that kind of coincidence that comes from a minority phenomenon embracing the more lucrative subject matter.

[20] *Glanvill*, p. 102.

[21] Ibid., p. 62.

or to digress in any respect from the way of truth. For there, indeed, a poor man is not oppressed by the power of his adversary, nor does favour or partiality drive any man away from the threshold of judgment.[22]

It was the impartiality of the king's court that probably lay behind the reason why the so-called petty assizes were a monopoly of the king's court. So also, when Henry II instituted the grand assize in 1179 as an alternative to the trial by battle, it was specified that the grand assize could be taken only in the king's court.

To discourage frivolous litigation, only the tenant could opt to have the suit determined by the grand assize; the demandant had always to be prepared to settle for the use of trial by battle. The tenant made his decision in whatever court the case was pending, whether in feudal, county, or king's court. That court then had to rule on whether that method of trial was appropriate and whether the mise of the grand assize—the formal statement by which the tenant asked for the grand assize—had been made correctly.[23] If the case was then pending in a lower court, the tenant was thereafter required to stop court process by bringing a writ of peace. That writ forced the demandant to take the initiative by purchasing a writ of summons, by which four knights were ordered to be summoned to the king's court to elect the twelve knights who would form the panel of the grand assize. The grand assize would then assemble in the king's court, and judgment would be given there in accordance with its sworn verdict. This procedure effected a removal of the case which did not depend upon tolt or the writ *pone*, for the mise could be made in any lower court that was then holding the plea. To the extent that the grand assize replaced trial by battle, the actual power of the lower courts to determine real litigation was diminished. It should be noted, however, that many cases would have been removed by tolt and *pone* anyway, and in the early thirteenth century the writs of entry reduced the number of cases that were brought by the writ of right patent.

Tolt, the writ *pone*, and the process of the grand assize had one fundamental rule in common: they could not be utilized in cases after final judgment had been rendered. Once a plea had been determined

[22] Ibid., p. 2.
[23] JUST. 1/996, m. 1d (1238-1239); *CRR*, 6:173 (1211; the adjudication of the grand assize postponed because too few knights were present); *Somersetshire Pleas*, 1:61-63 (tenant, having relied on a chirograph, not allowed to make his mise); *Civil Pleas of the Wiltshire Eyre, 1249*, ed. M. T. Clanchy, Wiltshire Record Society, vol. 26 (Devizes, 1970), p. 36 (the county court wrongly adjudged that a grand assize lay).

in a feudal court, tolt could no longer be assigned to have the case removed into the county court. Likewise, no plea that had been determined in the county court by judgment could be removed into the king's court by *pone*; the sheriff in such a case would merely endorse the writ with the answer that there was no such plea in his county court. Finally, once a plea had been determined by battle—and even after the parties had waged battle—the tenant could not renew his suit by bringing a writ of peace or by making the mise of the grand assize. All three processes were designed to avoid injustice or hardship before it had occurred, not to punish an offending court after it had done wrong.

That more complex problem arose when a litigant felt that a court had rendered a manifestly bad judgment. The appropriate remedy once again was a resort to a higher court. This had not always been so. Early court procedure allowed a judgment to be "falsed" immediately in the court in which it was made.[24] By the time of the *Leges Henrici*, however, false judgment was a case reserved for the king's court.[25] The writ that initiated the action of false judgment, at least from the end of the twelfth century, was called the *recordari facias loquelam*, but to avoid confusion with the *recordari*—and at the risk of implying a strict separation between the two writs which was perhaps not complete before 1275—I will refer to it as the writ of false judgment. The terms of the writ specify a procedure more complicated than that dictated by the *pone*:

> The king to the sheriff, greeting. We order you to cause to be recorded in your open county court the plea which was in the same county court by our writ between A. and B. concerning 2 messuages and 25 acres of land in Broadmore which A. claims as his right against B. and whereof B. complains a false judgment was made her in the same county court.

[24] F. Pollock and F. W. Maitland, *The History of English Law before the Time of Edward I*, 2 vols. 2nd ed. (Cambridge, 1968), 2:666. It is suggestive that *Rolls of the King's Court in the Reign of King Richard the First*, Pipe Roll Society, vol. 14 (London, 1891), p. 36, has one demandant falsing her lord's court in county court with her suit. Falsing of the doom may thus have something in common with the procedure of tolt as well as with false judgment.

[25] *Leges Henrici Primi*, ed. L. J. Downer (Oxford, 1972), p. 109. This, at least, is the traditional interpretation of that passage (Pollock and Maitland, *History of English Law*, 2:666), and it seems correct. Some hesitation, however, is justified. The passage does not actually specify the forum in which the cases will be heard, and the kinds of cases reserved for the king include, along with false judgment, failure of justice (*defectus iustitie*)—which sounds much like what is proved in tolt—and outlawry, which was a county court procedure, at least in more documentable times. Appeal in the county court would also seem to have been available for premeditated assault and rape. There must, then, remain some problems of interpretation.

Have that record before our justices at Westminster on the octaves of the holy Trinity under your seal and by four law-worthy knights of the same county from those who were present to make that record. And summon by good summoners the abovesaid A. that he should be before our aforementioned justices at Westminster at the aforementioned term to hear that record. And have there the names of the four knights, the summoners, and this writ. Witnessed by etc.[26]

The problems that must be considered with this writ, unlike with the *pone*, are numerous, but the issues concerning the recording of pleas are even more important because that process was later vital in effecting substantial jurisdictional alterations.

The writ of false judgment does not specify whether the case had already been determined. In the ordinary instance, of course, the losing party would not bring the writ until the suit had been lost by final judgment. Nevertheless, two early examples indicate that the county could be charged with a false judgment even before it had rendered final judgment on a case. In 1201 the prior of Coventry alleged that the county court of Leicestershire had made a false judgment in not allowing him the view of the land that was in dispute and had thereby forced him to wage (that is, promise and pledge) battle. He brought his writ of false judgment, then, after battle was waged but before it was made.[27] In a similar manner Ranulf fitz Henry brought a writ of false judgment against the county court of Yorkshire in 1228 concerning its adjudication of the trial by battle, again brought after battle was waged and before it was made.[28] Even as late as the reign of Edward I a county court could be charged with a false judgment concerning jurisdictional matters that arose in litigation. Thus, if a lord claimed jurisdiction over a case in the county court and his claim was not allowed, he could bring a writ of false judgment against the county court.[29] That judgment, of course, was in a sense final for him, since it would have excluded him from any further interest in the plea. Nevertheless, most cases of false judgment concern pleas in which the complainant had already lost his case, in some instances only because he had been so dissatisfied with a preliminary judgment that he had refused to plead further and was therefore ruled undefended.

The process prescribed in the writ was extremely cautious; this was

[26] See the exemplars in *Early Register of Writs*, pp. 45 (CC. 35), 114 (R. 29).
[27] *CRR*, 1:445.
[28] *CRR*, 13:113.
[29] Above, chapter 5, n. 29.

no ordinary piece of litigation, and no one was to be trusted. If the judgment was found to have been false—wrong—the county court would be heavily amerced, on the assumption that a wrong judgment could only result from malice. Therefore, the record of the case was to be made in the open county court to prevent the irregularities attendant upon secrecy. Furthermore, it was to be made in the presence of the sheriff, who was not responsible for the judgment and would not be amerced unless he had unlawfully coerced the judges. If the county court refused to record the plea, all the suitors could be distrained to go to Westminster to make the record there before the royal justices.[30] If the sheriff was lax in having the record made, the justices could even amerce him heavily until he complied with the writ's instructions.[31] There were thus sufficient sanctions to insure that the case would be recorded and the record sent to Westminster.

The record that was sent was not merely an oral record, even though the four law-worthy knights mentioned in the writ were intimately involved in the process. Sheriffs kept county rolls, it seems, by the beginning of the thirteenth century and probably earlier.[32] These rolls were used in the recording of the plea. Only in such a way could the judges remember the complex process in a real action which might have been determined some months previous to the arrival of the writ of false judgment. Moreover, some written documents had also to be conveyed; in 1212 the county court of Gloucestershire was amerced because it had not sent the writ of right by which it had had jurisdiction in the plea.[33] Nor, after consulting the rolls and the original writ, was it likely that the county would entrust the record to the memories of four knights. The record must have been written, probably by the sheriff's clerk from the county rolls. The record would then have been read in county court and examined and corrected by the judges. Only then would the record have been sent by the four knights. In such a way the judges could expect to receive a correct judgment in the king's court. The king's court itself would probably

[30] CP. 40/36, m. 136; such action was taken more frequently when the false judgment was alleged to have been made by a court lower than the county courts.

[31] CP. 52 octave Trinity, 27 Edward I: "Edwardus . . . vicecomiti Notingham, salutem. . . . Et scias quod graviter amerciatus es eo quod preceptum nostrum pluries inde tibi directum non es executus sicut tibi preceptum fuit. Et gravius amerciaberis nisi hoc preceptum nostrum plenius exequaris."

[32] *The Earliest Lincolnshire Assize Rolls*, ed. D. M. Stenton, Lincolnshire Record Society, vol. 22 (Lincoln, 1926), p. 45: "et vicecomes et totus comitatus testatur [quod] in pleno comitatu plus terre ei dederunt, unde divise notate sunt in rotulo vicecomitis."

[33] CRR, 6:231.

not have been altogether pleased with four knights trying to reach agreement among themselves concerning a past complex procedure which could not be mnemonically arranged. Otherwise, we must assume that they each memorized the record in part or in toto, reciting it nightly on their journey to Westminster. The original process was probably for the written record to be given to the four knights for them to convey to Westminster; the form of the writ Glanvill gives makes mention only of the four knights and not of the sheriff's seal.[34] By 1220, however, the record was said to be sent by the sheriff's letters and by four knights.[35] In that same year, one record arrived in the king's court even though the knights failed to appear; it was placed in the writ file for that term until the knights should appear.[36] At least one copy of the written record was then being sent separately by the sheriff, and the four knights were required to testify to its veracity and authenticity.

The four knights were sent to represent the county court. One of their functions was to bring the record or, at least, to testify concerning the record. Another, and equally important, function was to represent the county as defendant during the case. Thus, since it seemed wrong to pass judgment against a litigant in his absence, the four knights representing the county court had to be present when the king's court delivered its judgment in the action. One court deliberately delayed judgment for several terms by having one or other of the knights absent every session. Furthermore, when one of the knights died, another was ordered to be chosen in his place.[37] Finally, if they testified that the record was inadequate or wrong, they were presumed capable of making a better record without further consultation with the county court. They were representatives of the county, then, in a very full sense.

Such a function indicates that the four knights would have to have been closely connected with the county court. The writ, however, is ambiguous on that point. It merely states that the four were to have been among those present to record the plea, and such a gathering would always have included others, such as seneschals, bailiffs, and

---

[34] *Glanvill*, p. 102. The fact that that writ, in Glanvill's version, does not include the phrase *in pleno comitatu*, but only *in comitatu tuo*, would seem to make that a form already rather old in Glanvill's time.

[35] *CRR*, 9:93-94; *Early Registers of Writs*, p. 45 (CC. 35: "sub sigillo tuo et per iiii⁰ʳ legales milites," thus essentially through the letters of the sheriff, as the plea rolls state in the earlier reference).

[36] *CRR*, 9:289-90.

[37] CP. 40/80, m. 42.

attorneys, not just suitors. There was an opinion around 1300—an opinion that still has its followers—that the knights were required to be suitors. Perhaps this derived from the fact that if the county refused to make the record, it was the suitors who were to be distrained to make the record. A year book note from around 1300 makes mention of that opinion and refutes it by pointing both to the ambiguity of the writ and the fact that some counties had no suitors.[38] About that same time Bereford, J., was certainly not interested in whether the four representatives were suitors or not; he was only concerned with whether they had been present at the recording of the plea.[39] Likewise, in 1293, two of the four knights from Cambridgeshire county court acknowledged that they were suitors but denied that they had been at the making of the record, thus maintaining that they should have nothing to do with the case. The justices ordered that all the suitors should be distrained to come to Westminster to make the record.[40] It was knowledge of the process of recording rather than participation in the rendering of the judgment that was required, and there are instances from both early and late in the thirteenth century that some of the four had not been present when judgment was rendered.[41] The people sent to represent the county, even if they were not always suitors, were at least intimately involved with county litigation.

The record sent by the county court through the four knights was not an unchallengeable recounting of the proceedings. There were, it is true, other reasons for this, but in this context the county court was so involved in the case that the record could not be accepted uncritically. The complainant thus was allowed to amend the record if he could produce two witnesses to testify to the alteration. These witnesses were formally described as "one who had heard and one who had understood" the plea at that stage of process; the records occasionally specified that the two witnesses had been "within the

---

[38] Above, chapter 3, n. 146.

[39] Above, chapter 3, n. 139.

[40] CP. 40/102, m. 49d: "Et modo veniunt partes et similiter predicti quatuor milites etc. Et predicti Henricus de Lacy et Johannes de Caldecotes dicunt quod ipsi non sunt sectatores comitatus predicti nec interfuerunt predicto recordo etc. Et predicti Radulphus et Rogerus duo alii milites etc. bene cognoscunt quod ipsi sunt sectatores predicti comitatus set bene defendunt quod ipsi non debent predictum recordum advocare nec deadvocare etc. Ideo preceptum est vicecomiti quod venire faciat hic a die sancti Martini in xv dies omnes sectatores comitatus predicti ad faciendum recordum etc. Et vicecomes sit hic in propria persona ad prefatum terminum ad respondendum tam domino regi quam predicto Johanni de eo quod venire fecit hic milites ad faciendum recordum etc qui non sunt sectatores comitatus etc nec recordo etc interfuerunt."

[41] CRR, 6:230; above, chapter 3, n. 138.

four benches" at the time.[42] It is unlikely that the two men were necessarily judges of the court. Like the witnesses needed for the procedure of tolt and the witnesses presented in prohibition cases, they probably merely had to have been present. Nevertheless, the phrase "one who had understood" must indicate that some familiarity with legal matters was presumed on the part of at least one of the witnesses. With such witnesses, the complainant was allowed to correct the record. In this way, then, the king's court elaborated process to obtain a reliable report of county proceedings by which the justices could supervise the lower courts and reverse unjust judgments.

The disputability of the records sent by the county courts is one valuable index of their power to "bear record," to send an indisputable account of proceedings. The king's court, for instance, bore record in all things. No plea determined there could be tried again in any other court; no process or admission made in one case could later be denied. In Glanvill's time, the ability of the lower courts to bear record had recently been enlarged by an assize, the date and full content of which is unknown. Before that assize, county courts and lower courts in general were not considered courts of record. Thus, anyone could withdraw a statement by proving by compurgation that he had never made it, despite the recollection of the judges to the contrary. Likewise, before the assize, there was no regular process in which pleading and process in county litigation would be accepted and acted upon in the king's court. Before the reign of Henry II, of course, such an inability would have been insignificant, because little litigation went beyond the county courts. After that assize and because of the greater activity of the king's court in the reign of Henry II, the county courts were empowered to bear record in specific areas. Certain procedures demanded by the newly developed returnable writs—specifically mentioned were the taking of sureties and of pledges to prosecute—were thought best performed in county court. If they were indeed performed there, the county court bore record of them.[43] Another instance involved the removal of an action of right after battle waged. In such a situation the county court sent a record containing the demandant's claim, the tenant's denial, the terms in which battle had been awarded and waged, and—when necessary—the substitution of one champion for another. Of all that, the county court could bear record. Neither party could deny the substance or form contained in the record. It only remained for the king's court to supervise the

---

[42] Above, chapter 5, at nn. 52-56.
[43] *Glanvill*, pp. 18, 19, 103.

making of the battle.[44] The county court also had to bear record of the terms in which the mise of the grand assize was made. The tenant would have the terms of the mise in his writ of peace—and when he purchased that writ the mise would be enrolled in the plea rolls of the king's court—but that writ and enrollment were still subject to the record of the county.[45] In the false judgment process, however, Glanvill specified precisely the way in which the record sent by the county could be changed. He allowed the complainant two courses of action, both of which indicate that the record sent was not "record" in the strict sense. If there was an omission in the record, he could add to it by swearing, along with his two witnesses, to the truth of the addition. If he wished to contradict a point in the record, he had to deny the whole record. In such a case, the county court—if, indeed, Glanvill meant to include the county court in this part of the analysis[46]— could be made to do battle to uphold its judgment.[47] Glanvill specifically denied that the complainant could accept part of the record but deny specific points.[48] During the reign of Henry II, then, it had been found necessary to grant the county court some power of record, but only in specific areas necessary for the functioning of the king's court.

After Glanvill the rules regarding the treatment of county records became even more specific and were subject to certain alterations. By the 1220s it was standard for the complainant to accept most of the record and deny only specific points; it seems that the very possibility of denying the whole record was no longer admitted.[49] Although the county at times waged battle,[50] there is no recorded instance in which battle was actually made to uphold the judgment of a county court.

[44] *Glanvill*, p. 100; *CRR*, 7:75; *CRR*, 3:240 makes the statement that the county court did not bear record of the duel waged in Codeham v Polsted only because the duel had not been waged in the county court, but in a feudal court.

[45] *Glanvill*, pp. 29-30; Lincolns Inn, Misc. 87, fol. 11r, in a case in which the record had not been sent: "Howard . . . le bref de pees est le purchas le tenant e la summons le purchas le demandant; dounc le purchas le un asseez testmone le purchas lautre e cest asseez garrant de aler a la defaute apres etc. *Ber'*. Le bref de pees nest pas garrant, qe le demandant poet traverser ceo bref de pees a dedire la mise ou la forme del bref si ele seit disacordant a le record par pays, dounc, de pus qe nous navoms pas le record, nous agardoms un grant cape etc."

[46] *Glanvil*, p. 101, applies most readily to feudal courts, in that it mentions that the lord of the court would lose his court.

[47] Ibid.; examples of duel waged: *CRR*, 8:223 (but prevented by the king's council); *CRR*, 9:138 (not actually done); *CRR*, 13:16-17 (again waged but not done).

[48] *Glanvill*, p. 101; See *Rolls of the King's Court*, pp. 121, 124.

[49] *CRR*, 9:94-95, 132, 11:348, 12:220-21, 13:16-17, 15:377. *CRR*, 13:404-5: "Et quoniam predictus Johannes optulit defendere totum predictum recordum per unum intelligentem et unum videntem, quod non potuit facere nisi aliquod accidens vel demere vel apponere."

[50] Above, n. 47.

The record was changed either by the force of the oath of the complainant and his two witnesses, by the testimony of officials,[51] or by jury.[52] By the late thirteenth century the power of record of the county court was described by maxim—for a while not completely correct[53]—as limited to five instances: final judgments, wagers of battle, the mise of the grand assize, any outlawry, and law (compurgation) waged and failed.[54] With the decline in the utility and frequency of actions in the right during the thirteenth century and since the taking of pledges and securities pursuant to a returnable writ ceased to be regarded as a matter of county record, matters of outlawry, final judgments, and wager and failure of compurgation were the only matters which a fourteenth-century county court would normally have to record. Of these, outlawry was the only one that occurred with any frequency; the county's power of record in final judgments and failed compurgations, however, could be relied upon to bar repetitive proceedings.

By the end of the thirteenth century, however, Glanvill's treatment of the record of the lower courts must have seemed antiquated. He had started from the proposition that lower courts could not regularly bear record at all, making exceptions only in instances specifically ordained by assize or individually ordered by the king. By 1300, however, a year book reporter could blandly remark, in referring to county courts, that any court could bear record within itself.[55] That

[51] *CRR*, 6:228-31.

[52] CP. 40/86, m. 155.

[53] Below, at n. 86 ff.

[54] Brit. Lib., Add. MS 5925, fol. 59v: " . . . e demanda jugement de la defaut apres apparance en conte. . . . Le tenant luy demanda coment il voleit ceo averer, e le demandant dit par quant qe le court le roy lui agarderoit e le record du conte. E le tenant dit qe par agard de la court ne devereit etc., pur ceo qen le court nule defaute ne fit, ne par record du conte pur ceo qe conte ne porte mie record fors en v poinz, scilicet, en bataille gage, en mise de grant assize, en ley gage e failly, en utlagerie, en final jugement. Agarde fut qil avereit par record du conte. *Warr'*. Nous purrioms teu record par un oyant e un entendant dedire tel record, e demandoms voz agardz si par tel record puissont cel defaute averer. . . . *Bek'*. [J.] Responez a ceo qil tendent daverer par record du conte, pur ceo qe le conte porte record en teu cas . . . en ceo cas ne en nul autre cas fors en faux jugement puet hom dedire par un oyant etc., pur le inconvenience qe ensuereit." The maxim concerning the five points recurs repeatedly elsewhere, even though here it was denied.

[55] Brit. Lib., Add. 31826, fol. 236r: "De recordo. Il i ad une manere de record que vent hors de cunte e de curt de barun en banc pur error qe la partie suppose leintz e record qe vent hors du bank devant le rey simili de causa; dunt la manere de lun record nest pas semblable a lautre, qe banc port record en totes choses fet leintz. E quant record deit estre remue devant le rey, si serra cel record fet par eus memes sant presence de autre persone; mes cunte etc., ne port pas record si nun en cas e quant il deivent fere lur record par vertue de recordare, si ne le frunt il pas si nun en presence

writer did not specify the limits of such record. At least the county could bar a case from being tried twice before it.[56] Furthermore, it is unlikely that in the latter part of the thirteenth century statements made during a case could be denied against the record of the county judges; indeed, there is no documented instance of such procedure earlier in the century. The only significant difference concerning record around 1300 was felt to lie in the area of bearing record with regard to other courts. In the king's court, the justices could make such a record themselves and could bear record of pleading, process, and final judgment if the case was to be reviewed, say, in the king's bench. In county courts, however, record for use outside the county could be made only in the presence of the sheriff and at the order of the king and—at least after 1302[57]—could not concern pleading and process that had not been concluded by a final judgment. Pleading and process recorded by the county court could be denied by compurgation. The power of record of the county courts thus increased markedly from the accession of Henry II to the beginning of the fourteenth century. It became accepted that a county court could bear record within itself. Furthermore, it was provided that county courts could bear record to the king's court to the extent required for the efficient handling of litigation there. As actions in the right were routinely removed at an early stage to the king's court and as they declined in frequency, the actual instances in which the county court was called upon to bear record were increasingly reduced, with rare exceptions, to matters concerning outlawry.

Further interaction between the king's court and the county courts was dictated by the introduction of the petty assizes and the writs of entry, all of which had their venue in the king's court. With the acceptance of novel disseisin and mort dancestor as permanent forms of litigation, there was institutionalized in the English legal system a jurisdictional anomaly. Logically, the most definitive determination of a real dispute should have had its venue in the highest court, with preliminary determinations being made, if necessary, in the lower courts. Henry II, however, had no intention—and probably insufficient power—to rationalize the legal system so thoroughly or to

---

de vicont. Dautrepart, si peut lem en cas encuntre tels recors estre a le averement, ut in casu Johannis de Stanerne e Muriel sa femme tenentes ou seisine de terre fut agarde al demandant en lur absence. E checun court port record en ly memes. E tant cum lur record demert en curt si le peut il amender, mes nun pas apres."

[56] CP. 52 morrow All Souls, 27 Edward I, Notts: Prat v Prat [S.S.].

[57] Below, at n. 94.

undermine in such a way baronial power.[58] Litigation concerning the ultimate right to real property continued to begin and usually to be determined in the lower courts. The assizes, however, had their venue in the king's court and were restricted to determinations concerning questions of seisin or lawful possession. Thus it happened that defendants in novel disseisin would at times allege that the dispute had already been determined by judgment in a more definitive judicial process in a lower court.[59] The frequency of such defenses tended to diminish as litigants and lawyers became more familiar with the legal rules, and assizes were brought regularly, when applicable, before the right to the land was put in issue. Furthermore, many cases of right in lower courts were eventually removed into the king's court by tolt and *pone*, so that the king's court itself would have record of the prior case. Finally, as early as Glanvill's time, writs were available which challenged a particular point in a tenant's title.[60] Such writs were issued in various forms during John's reign,[61] and in the first few decades of the thirteenth century became formalized and began to occupy a position midway between the assizes and the writs of right. These writs of entry were concerned with title, and thus most disputes could be concluded in the king's court without continuing on with litigation by the writ of right patent in a feudal court. There was thus probably a declining need for a process to prove such allegations of previous litigation determined in the lower courts.

Such a defense, however infrequently made, should have been able to bar further litigation. In the assize of novel disseisin, the defense

---

[58] Milsom, *Legal Framework*, pp. 36-37.

[59] Donald W. Sutherland, *The Assize of Novel Disseisin* (Oxford, 1973), pp. 77-82.

[60] *Glanvill*, p. 125, 190-91.

[61] *Rotuli de Oblatis et Finibus in Turri Londinensi Asservati, Tempore Regis Johannis*, ed. Thomas Duffus Hardy (London, 1835) provides what seem to be the forms for some writs in John's reign, still indicating a great degree of variability and association with gages: p. 48 (the father "non habuit terram illam nisi in custodiam post obitum predicte Ysabelle uxoris sue, cuius heres ipsa est . . . et nisi fecerint"), p. 55 ("pro habendo brevi de recto de feodo dimidii militis cum pertinenciis in Winintorp vel escambium habeat ad valenciam, in quod feodum non habuit Jollanus ingressum nisi per ipsam Aliciam, ita quod illa loquela sit coram justiciariis apud Westm' a die Pasche in tres septimanas"), p. 199 ("cui terra illa fuit invadiata"), p. 334 ("precipe ut Radulphus de Clera juste et sine dilacione reddat Willelmo de Albern' terciam partem feodi . . . in quam non habet ingressum nisi per Hubertum . . . qui ipsum Willelmum injuste et sine iudicio dissaisivit dum idem Radulphus fuit in custodia ipsius archiepiscopi ut dicitur"), p. 340 ("in quam non habuit ingressum nisi per canonicos de Messenden qui in eam nullum habuerunt ingressum nisi per Willelmum filium Gaufridi qui eam habuit in custodia ut dicitur"). The first mention of "a writ of entry" I have seen in the fine rolls is in 1225: C. 60/23, m. 1: "Abbatissa Ebrulf' dat domino regi xx s pro habendo quodam precipe de ingressu coram justiciariis versus plures."

seems often to have been taken care of adequately by the normal questions put to the panel of the assize. They were assembled to answer concerning a disseisin made unjustly and without a judgment. Hugh de Chishampton was thus acquitted by an assize jury shortly before 1200 because he had not disseised the plaintiff unjustly and without a judgment, but rather by judgment of the county court.[62] Even prior to that, however, there is evidence that Roger de Hensteworth had been able to vouch the record of the county court of Hertfordshire to prove that he had recovered his land by judgment and had thus barred the assize even from answering the questions normally put to them.[63] In a like manner, Basilia Morel in 1203 and Halenald de Sifrewast in 1206 were each allowed to vouch their respective county court to warrant a previous judgment to prevent the issue going to a sworn panel and judgment again.[64] Such an option to bar the assize was obviously desirable to avoid the possibility that the assize jury would overlook the previous judgment.

When such a defense was made during a case in eyre, procedure should have been fairly simple. The county court was immediately available, and the sheriff was at the disposal of the justices in eyre. Around 1250, in the eyre of Norfolk, Robert de Hacun prosecuted Philip Burel in an action of entry, claiming that Hacun's mother, Sarra, had alienated the land to Burel, whereas she had only held the land as dower. Burel, however, defended himself by alleging a previous case in the county court. He had brought a writ of right against Sarra, and she had properly vouched her son to warrant her the land. Hacun had done so and then put himself on the grand assize against Burel, so that the county court ruled that Hacun should purchase his writ of peace and Burel should purchase his writ of summons. At the following session, however, seisin was awarded to Burel because it was found that Hacun had not yet obtained his writ of peace. Such a judgment should have barred further litigation by any writ of entry, so both parties put themselves upon the record of the county court and the rolls of the sheriff. They agreed in a very specific way that they would win or lose by this method of proof, obviating any possible objection that county courts were in some way deficient in record-bearing capability. Unfortunately, however, the record of the county

[62] CRR, 1:181.
[63] CRR, 1:72.
[64] Earliest Northamptonshire Assize Rolls, ed. D. M. Stenton, Northants. Record Soc., vol. 5 (Lincoln and London, 1930), p. 153; CRR, 4:158; Sutherland, The Assize of Novel Disseisin, p. 214, note A.

was not thereafter entered on the rolls, even though the margination to the entry indicates that the case was adjourned only one day to obtain the record.[65] The record should have been almost immediately available in such cases and was perhaps here hindered because the former plea may have taken place too long before. At least at the beginning of the thirteenth century, however, county courts were usually able to respond immediately to justices in eyre concerning events that had occurred in the county court.[66] It can be doubted whether in such situations any writ was required to obtain the record of the county.

In other instances, parties found it easier to obtain certification about previous litigation by altering the issue so that it could be put to a jury. In 1247, for instance, a defendant alleged prior litigation by writ of right in a county court, but then a jury was summoned to find whether the defendant had previously rendered the land to the plaintiff, thus making the case depend on a question of fact rather than an issue of record.[67] In 1294 the defendant in a case of debt in the court of common pleas alleged that the debt had already been recovered in the county court. Issue was taken, however, on whether or not the sheriff had executed the judgment, so that a jury was used instead of the county record.[68] Often a jury would seem a more satisfactory proof than record, particularly when the sheriff's rolls for that period seemed likely to be difficult to obtain. A jury, however, would never have been as certain as proof by record.

The need to provide county record as a method of proof for litigants in the court of common pleas (where the county court was not immediately available for consultation) was one of the varied functions

[65] JUST. 1/560, m. 11d: "et de hoc ponit se super recordo comitatus et rotulis vicecomitis etc. Et concessum est huc inde quod si compertum sit per recordum comitatus et per rotulos vicecomitis etc., quod summonitus esset ad warrantizandum predicte Sarre predictam terram et quod ei warrantizavit ita quod posuit se in mangnam assisam domini regis quod idem Philippus per defaltam suam recuperavit inde seisinam sicut predictum est quod predictus Robertus amitat inde clameum suum. Et si compertum sit per predictos rotulos quod predictus Robertus venit in comitatu et warantizavit predicte Sarre predictam terram et posuit se in mangnam assisam domini regis ita quod per defaltam quam fecit versus predictum Philippum recuperavit idem Philippus seisinam suam versus eum quod predictus Robertus recuperet inde seisinam suam."

[66] The most frequent examples concern matters of violence; as late as mid-century, however, in JUST. 1/560 (Norfolk eyre, 34 Henry III), the county court was vouched in a case of naifty and seemed to respond immediately that they had merely put the plea in respect and had not determined it by judgment.

[67] JUST. 1/4, m. 19.

[68] CP. 40/104, m. 62d.

of the writ *recordari*. That writ was exceptionally important; the *recordari* and the *pone* had an impact on the thirteenth century legal system perhaps even more important than that which tolt and the writ of false judgment—both of which were of decreasing importance after the middle of the thirteenth century—had had in the twelfth century. While, as proof of prior litigation, it would concern suits already determined, the form provided by Glanvill concerns a case still pending and demonstrates the versatility of the writ. In Glanvill's time, the terms of the writ were still very close to those for the writ of false judgment:

> The king to the sheriff, greeting. I order you that in your county court you should cause to be recorded the plea which is between such a one and such a one concerning so much land in that vill and have the record of that plea before me or my justices at that term through four law-worthy knights who were present to make that record. And summon by good summoners that one who claims the land that he should be there then with his plea and the other one who holds that land that he should be there to hear that record etc.[69]

The process prescribed by the writ indicates the limitations that restricted the use of the *recordari* until 1275. Until that date the four knights still had to travel to the king's court, as they did in the writ of false judgment and also in the process designed for the election of the knights of the grand assize. After 1275 the four knights were allowed merely to affix their seals to the record. That change in the form of the *recordari* and in process was made for very cogent reasons and redesigned the writ to fill a broader role, which will be treated later.[70] Prior to that time, however, the *recordari* had a somewhat limited function, serving as the mechanism by which the county court could bear record in special instances. Glanvill categorized these special instances in which the county record would be incontrovertible by the way in which process was *initiated*: by royal favor or by agreement of both parties.[71] It is better, if not so rigorous, to distinguish the various *uses* of the writ.

The writ *recordari* could be used as a proof of an exception alleged in the court of common pleas. *Hacun v Burel*, cited above, is a good example of the way in which both litigants could commit themselves to the proof by county as Glanvill suggested, even though there was

[69] *Glanvill*, p. 102.
[70] Below, at n. 86 ff.
[71] Ibid.

no need in that case for the *recordari*.[72] In 1225, however, the *recordari* was used in this way in *Vabadun v Hacun*. Both parties in that case put themselves on the record of the county court to prove the facts concerning an alleged disclaimer of a third party in the county court in previous litigation. The county court was therefore ordered to have the record at the king's court by four knights, that is, by the procedure ordered in the *recordari*.[73] Such uses were rare, since recourse to record happened most frequently in assizes and during eyres.

Another use of the *recordari* allowed lower courts the benefit of consultation with the king's court in difficult cases. The writ of false judgment would at first have seemed very harsh in those cases in which a lower court had come to a well-considered but different solution than the king's court if the lower court had to proceed to judgment without consultation. Glanvill, however, describes a process whereby any court—county, hundred, or liberty—confronted by a legal difficulty could adjourn itself into the king's court to receive there an authoritative decision. The procedure involved no penalty, and the case would be returned to the lord's court after the consultation so that the lord did not even lose the power to determine the case or to levy an amercement.[74] In such a case both parties had to be summoned to attend the king's court, and that is the directive in the form of the *recordari* given by Glanvill.[75] With such procedure lower courts should have proceeded to judgment only when sure of the law. The process thus balanced the stringency of the writ of false judgment and aided the king's court in unifying the law practiced in English courts.

Unfortunately, that process did not survive into the thirteenth century. It would have been easier, after the writ *pone* became commonly used, for the court merely to delay judgment so that the parties themselves could remove the case. The responsibility would thus have been permanently shifted to the shoulders of the king's justices. Such a replacement of the *recordari* by the *pone* might explain why Glanvill mentioned the *pone* only in connection with the writ of right of dower and not with the writ of right of land; the *recordari* might then have been the more frequently used writ in such cases.[76] In the normal

---

[72] Above, at n. 65.
[73] *CRR*, 12:239-40.
[74] *Glanvill*, pp. 102-3.
[75] *Glanvill*, p. 102. When one litigant initiated the removal, only the other party was summoned.
[76] *Glanvill*, p. 61.

instance, the writ of right patent for land would have been removed from the county court by the writs of peace and summons for the use of the grand assize or by the *recordari* if record was needed for the wager of battle[77] or if a difficult legal point arose. The use of the *pone* was exceptional. By the time of the first surviving plea rolls, however, the *pone* had already become commonly used with the writ of right patent and the *recordari* was used only occasionally. This is not to say that there was no consultation between the king's court and the county courts on difficult legal points, only that the consultation was not so formal that it required the removal of the case into the king's court by *recordari*.[78] The *pone*, then, probably superseded the *recordari* in this function, leaving the initiative totally to the parties themselves and divesting the county and lower courts of the responsibility for some of the more difficult legal problems.

One major early use of the *recordari* was, as Glanvill suggested, an example of royal favor. Very early, English kings had shown special favor to individuals and institutions by granting them a charter that prevented them from being impleaded elsewhere than before the king or his justices. This precluded them, at least in theory, from being prosecuted in feudal and county courts. In such cases, the demandant was apparently supposed to proceed against them by way of a writ of right *precipe*, which would bring the case immediately into the king's court without having first been in a lower court. When such favored individuals were nonetheless prosecuted by a writ of right patent or some other writ in lower courts, the *recordari* could be used to remove the plea into the king's court. This use of the *recordari* probably became somewhat more important after the Magna Carta and its restrictions on the use of the *precipe*.[79] The use of the *recordari* is difficult to determine in the plea rolls for such cases, and the best proof of the most frequent use of the *recordari* comes in the form of the writ provided in a register of writs from the 1260s. That writ was in the form necessary for removal of a plea by a defendant, specifying that the defendant had a charter by which he had been granted the liberty of not being impleaded except before the king or his justices.[80]

---

[77] *CRR*, 7:75.

[78] Relatively informal consultation was at least available later in the century for ecclesiastical courts presented with a prohibition: CP. 40/109, m. 27; CP. 40/110, m. 231.

[79] Magna Carta, c. 34. It may be that this was the use of the *precipe* that resulted in the clause.

[80] *Early Registers of Writs*, p. 46 (CC. 38), p. 115 (R. 33). CC. 38 is the first *recordari* in the printed registers of writs.

It is certainly not true that the charters could be relied upon simply to prevent a case from proceeding in a lower court. From later in the century, at least in plaints of replevin, county courts were not disposed to accept such charters without challenge. In at least three instances in the reign of Edward I—two involving the master of the Knights Templar;[81] the other, the prior of Sempringham[82]—the county courts of Bedfordshire, Leicestershire, and Lincolnshire chose to disregard the charter on the grounds that the county court had been seised of similar pleas in former times. That argument would have been just as applicable a century earlier. The charter guaranteed the right to purchase the *recordari*. That writ removed the suit into the king's court, where process would probably continue from the point it had reached in the lower court according to the record sent by the county court.

The *recordari* was also used to supervise the lower courts, at least after mid-century. In 1258 a plea came into the eyre of Suffolk by *recordari* for such a purpose. Robert Torymer had impleaded several people by a writ of right patent in the county court of Suffolk, but successive sheriffs had favored the tenants and delayed judgment for a long period of time. Torymer had thus purchased a writ *de recordo*, which ordered the sheriff to review the case in county court and to have the county proceed to judgment without delay. Not even then, however, did the sheriff see to it that judgment was given, so the county court was ordered to record the plea by virtue of the writ *recordari* returnable before the justices in eyre. The sheriff had the record drawn up, but the four knights then refused to put their seals to the record. Furthermore, the county court, then present in the eyre, refused to avow the record, so that the county itself was amerced. The plea was then adjourned from the eyre into the court of common pleas.[83] In such supervisory procedure the king's court was willing to accept the county court's record of pleading and the mise of the grand assize. The justices seem to have been ready to go to judgment merely on the basis of the record so that judgment would not be delayed.

Even during the reign of Edward I, when the *recordari* became almost exclusively associated with suits not begun by writ, this su-

---

[81] CP. 52 three weeks Easter, 21 Edward I [S.S.]; quindene Trinity, 21 Edward I [S.S.] (a subsequent recording of the first case for a case of false judgment); quindene Michaelmas, 19 Edward I [S.S.].

[82] CP. 52 quindene Easter, 13 Edward I [S.S.].

[83] JUST. 1/820, m. 14d.

pervisory use of the *recordari* continued, particularly to prevent fraudulent use of the *pone*. In 1275 a demandant had brought a case into the county court of Berkshire, presumably by tolt from a feudal court. The tenant had made use of essoins and had then asked for a formal view of the land to certify him precisely of the lands in dispute. The view was granted him, but then, at the following county session, he defaulted. Since by law no default was allowed after the view, the land was taken into the king's hand by judgment of the county court and the tenant was summoned to the following session to hear the judgment, which would certainly have been in the demandant's favor. Seeking to avoid the inevitable, the tenant purchased a *pone*, having given chancery an adequate but false reason for the removal of the case. On the appointed day the demandant appeared in the court of common pleas and explained the situation, showing how the tenant was using the *pone* to avoid the just judgment the county would have given. He concluded by asking that the court award him the land on the basis of the default made in the county court. Since this case had not reached the mise or the wager of battle in the lower court, it seems, no record had been sent with the *pone*. Thus, the record of the county would be needed to prove the alleged prior process. The pleaders for the tenant, who objected to such a use of the *recordari*, were Nicholas de Warwick and Gilbert de Thornton. Both were relatively young at the time, but the one would become king's attorney; the other, chief justice of the king's bench. They argued that the king's court could not do as the demandant asked. On the one hand, no default had occurred yet in the king's court. On the other hand, the ability of the county court to bear record was limited, in their view, to the five old uses. The justices ruled nevertheless that the county court could bear record in this case. Furthermore, in response to the pleaders' request that they be allowed to challenge the record in the traditional manner as in the action of false judgment, Beckingham, J., ruled that such challenges were available only in false judgment. The record was accordingly summoned up from the county court by the writ *recordari*, and the justices were apparently prepared to go to judgment on the basis of the record alone.[84]

The use of the *recordari* to prevent fraud perpetrated by means of the writ *pone* extended beyond litigation brought originally by the writ of right patent. In 1293 Walter de Mortlake purchased some

---

[84] Above, n. 54. The case is either Portes v Atton (CP. 40/13, m. 48) or else Todemers v Thedemers (CP. 40/11, m. 29). The *pone* is used in each for a similar purpose, but neither case is exactly the same as the report. The report is clearly no later than 1290.

timber from John de Lakinghith, agreeing to pay him 15 marks at a later date. On that date, early in 1294, Mortlake paid only a little more than half the money, so that Lakinghith brought a writ of debt for 7 marks 2s against him in the county court of Cambridgeshire. In court Mortlake asked if Lakinghith had anything to show the debt, and Lakinghith proffered the tally by which Mortlake had committed himself. Mortlake then denied that the tally was his, so that a jury was summoned to pass on the question of whether or not the tally was genuine. The jury rendered its verdict in favor of the plaintiff; but, before the county court could render its judgment, Mortlake withdrew from court. He was therefore summoned to hear the judgment at the following session. When he appeared, however, he brought with him the *pone* he had purchased, having given the chancery an adequate but false reason for removing the case: that the undersheriff was related to the plaintiff and was therefore favoring him in the plea. The case was accordingly removed into the court of common pleas, and, as usual with the *pone* when it was not used with the writ of right patent, no record was sent. There the fraud became apparent, and the plaintiff explained his predicament in detail. When Mortlake had refused to acknowledge the tally, it had been surrendered to the sheriff as the presiding officer of the court, as was the custom both in the king's court and in the other lower courts. When Mortlake had brought his *pone*, it had naturally not mentioned the tally. Thus, while the case was removed into the king's court, the tally remained in the custody of the sheriff. If the plaintiff was now required to plead again from the beginning, as would have been normal, he would surely have lost his suit, because the tally that showed the debt was no longer in his possession. At best he could have put the defendant to making his law; he could not have had a jury. The use of the *pone* had deprived the plaintiff of his reasonable showing of the debt, his *racionabilis monstracio*. Mettingham, C.J., took an interest in the case during an adjournment and discovered that the *causa* clause that Mortlake had used to obtain the *pone* was indeed false; this so supported the allegations of the plaintiff that the record of the case was called up by the writ *recordari* and the sheriff was required to forward the tally to the king's court. The justices, having discovered the truth of the plaintiff's case, thought it was unjust that he should be further delayed and so rendered judgment against Mortlake on the process and verdict previously obtained in the county court.[85]

[85] CP. 40/105, m. 37.

In 1275 the functions of the *recordari* were enormously expanded to include the removal of plaints from lower courts into the king's court;[86] that extension in function resulted also in a temporary extension of the record-bearing capability of the county courts. The process of the *recordari* was simplified for this new function, so that it no longer required the presence of the four knights at the king's court, but rather only the affixing of their seals to the written record of the case.[87] It was in 1287 that the first case appeared in which something of the status of that record can be determined: *Tilton v Diggeby*. The sheriff had sent the record to the justices, and the plaintiff had pleaded anew. The defendant, however, challenged the plaintiff's count in that his count specified a different day for the alleged wrong-doing than was contained in the record. That challenge was successful, and the plea was quashed.[88] The reasoning behind this case is fairly simple. Since the court had no original writ—the case having been brought in county court merely by plaint—the record, together with the *recordari*, acted in place of the original writ. Since the record specified one date and the plaintiff another, the court necessarily took the view that two different wrong-doings were being discussed, so that the justices had no warrant at all to hold the plea of which the plaintiff had counted.

There followed thereafter a series of cases in which the status of the county record was defined. In 1288 *Brynkelowe v Beler*, a case of replevin brought originally in the county court of Leicestershire and then removed by *recordari* into the court of common pleas, showed the willingness of the king's court to accept county pleading. The litigants had demurred in county court on a point of law. In the king's court the record sent by the sheriff was transcribed into the rolls of the court of common pleas, the plaintiff asked for his judgment, and

---

[86] Below, chapter 8 at n. 19.

[87] Ibid.

[88] CP. 40/69, m. 14: "Leyc'. Preceptum fuit vicecomiti quod in pleno comitatu suo recordari faceret loquelam que est in eodem comitatu . . . et quod partibus eundem diem prefigeret quod essent hic in loquela predicta prout iustum fuerit processure. Et Johannes de Diggeby venit et similiter Johannes de Tilton. Et unde Johannes de Tilton queritur quod predictus Johannes de Diggeby die veneris proxima post festum sancti Gothlaci anno regis nunc quarto decimo cepit duos equos ipsius Johannis de Tilton et eos detinuit contra vadium et plegios etc. Et Johannes de Diggeby dicit quod idem Johannes de Tilton in comitatu questus fuit quod predictus Johannes de Diggeby cepit predictos equos die veneris proxima ante festum sancti Botulphi anno predicto prout in predicto recordo continetur, unde petit iudicium de variacione illa. Et predictus Johannes de Tilton non potest hoc dedicere. Ideo predictus Johannes de Diggeby inde sine die, et Johannes de Tilton in misericordia. Et predictus Johannes de Diggeby habeat retornum averiorum etc."

the justices gave judgment on the basis of the record sent by the sheriff without further pleading.[89] It would not be far wrong to say that here the *recordari* had almost come full circle to serve Glanvill's purpose of having the king's court decide particularly difficult points. In 1289 the record of *Baudethun v Bacun*, another case of replevin brought originally by plaint in the county court of Norfolk, was likewise transcribed into the rolls of the court of common pleas, and a jury was ordered at least in part on the basis of that record.[90] Later that year, *Attehithe v Stokes*, originally brought in Clackclose hundred, Norfolk, had its pleading enrolled; and the litigants continued their pleading in the court of common pleas where the record left off, finally submitting an issue to a jury.[91] In Michaelmas term of 1289, *St. Licio v Seyton* gives the limit to which the court of common pleas was willing to accept *recordari* records. That case had been brought by plaint in the county court of Rutland and had been removed by *recordari*. The record, which was transcribed into the rolls of the court of common pleas, shows that the parties had pleaded to issue in county court on whether the land concerned in this plaint of replevin was common or several—a point touching real matters that should have been determined only by writ. The sheriff had summoned a jury anyway, and it had rendered its verdict that the land was common pasture. All this had been done in county court before the case had been removed. In the court of common pleas the litigants appeared and the plaintiff demanded his judgment from the verdict taken in the county court. The defendants left the court in contempt, and the justices went to judgment solely on the basis of the *recordari* record.[92] County pleading, process, and jury verdicts were not necessarily nullified by the king's court.

[89] CP. 40/73, m. 38d [S.S.]: ". . . Et predicti Johannes et Willelmus veniunt et predictus Johannes instanter petit iudicium suum. Et quia per predictum recordum quod vicecomes modo misit compertum est quod predictus Johannes assignatus fuit predicti Thome ad predictum redditum reddendum, consideratum est quod do cetero sit intendens predicto Thome de predicto redditu et non predicto Willelmo."

[90] CP. 40/78, m. 56 [S.S.]: "Et vicecomes modo misit recordum in hec verba: [There follows the pleading of the case, ending with] et dicit quod de capcione illa et detencione non est culpabilis; petit quod inquiratur. Et Willelmus similiter. Ideo preceptum est vicecomiti quod venire faciat hic a die sancti Johannis Baptiste in xv dies xij etc., per quos etc." It is difficult to know precisely where the county record terminates, but a plea of not guilty in a case of replevin makes it fairly certain that that issue was joined in county and not in the court of common pleas.

[91] CP. 40/79, m. 50d [S.S.].

[92] CP. 40/80, m. 159d [S.S.]: "Et Willelmus de Sancto Licio instanter petit recordum et iudicium suum. Et predicti Johannes, Adam, et Willelmus de Tykesovere postea recessit in contemptu curie. Et quia compertum est in predicta inquisicione quod predicta placia non est separalis pastura predicti Johannis immo communia pasture predicti

The *recordari* record was not so accepted, however, that it would necessarily bind both parties. In 1291 two cases illustrate this point, and the concluding passages to the entries are so similar that they seem to represent a conclusion of a general nature reached by the king's court. In both cases there had been extensive pleading and both parties had put themselves on a jury in the county court. In each case, when they arrived in the king's court, no verdict had yet been given. The record of the case sent by the sheriff was read aloud in court and was said to be understood and assented to by both parties. In both cases the defendant had removed the plea; in both cases the plaintiff did not want to replead the case, although the defendant did. The ruling of the court was not that the record was absolutely binding, but rather that since the plaintiff did not want to replead and the defendant had removed the plea, the plaintiff should not be put in the position of further damaging his case. Therefore, in both cases a *venire facias* issued to the sheriff to assemble a jury, just as would have been the case had the suit been completely pleaded in the court of common pleas.[93] Thus the king's court was willing to accept the record if the plaintiff had not been responsible for the removal and wanted the pleading that had been done in county court. The defendant was not allowed thus to delay justice. Such cases do not appear in the rolls after 1291, and it is probable that in similar instances the record was simply reformed by the scribes to look like a record of the king's court.

This enhanced power of the country court to bear some form of record was only temporary. In 1302 sheriffs stopped sending written

---

Willelmi de Sancto Licio consideratum est quod predicti Johannes, Adam, et Willelmus de Tykesovere iniuste ceperunt predicta averia et quod iidem Johannes, Adam, et Willelmus de Tykesovere pro iniusta capcione in misericordia. Et preceptum est vicecomiti quod inquirat de dampnis etc."

[93] CP. 40/83, m. 42, Abbot of Leicester v Abbot of Selby: "Et quia predictus abbas de Leyc' hic iterato noluit [placi]tare et predictus abbas de Seleby ad aliam responsionem dandam quam fecit in comitatu resilire non potest eo quod loquela illa ad impetraccionem [ipsius] abbatis hic ponita fuit et idem abbas de Seleby per sui ipsius impetraccionem aliquod commodum quod ad detrimentum ipsius abbatis Leyc' cedere [potest] in casu isto habere non debet, ideo datus est dies hic in crastino sancti Martini et preceptum est vicecomiti quod venire faciat . . ." CP. 40/83, m. 63d, De la Croyz v Gelham: "quia predictus Johannes de la Croyz noluit iterato hic placitare et predictus Edmundus ad aliam responsionem dandam quam prius fecerat in predicto hundredo resilire non potest eo quod loquela illa ad impetraccionem ipsius Edmundi hic posita fuit, et idem Edmundus per sui ipsius impetraccionem aliquid commodum quod ad detrimentum ipsius Johannis de la Croyz cedere possit habere non debet, datus est eis dies hic in crastino sancti Martini et preceptum est vicecomiti quod venire faciat. . . ."

records of pleading in response to *recordari* writs; the records sent thereafter were uniformly brief statements that recorded only the initial plaint and perhaps an essoin and the removal itself. This conclusion, however, is rather tentative; it is based solely on the fact that no more records of pleading summoned forth by *recordari* appear in the writ files.[94] It is conceivable that such records were thereafter handled in a different manner, but it is improbable that they would have so vanished without a trace. It is more probable that the arguments concerning the limits of county record began to make such procedure seem repugnant.[95] The change occurred, of course, right when such policies might easily be changed: at the death of one chief justice of the court of common pleas, John de Mettingham, and the appointment of another, Ralph de Hengham. From that time pleas that had reached pleading were no longer removeable by *recordari* or, at least, the pleading was voided simply by not being sent to the justices.

The writ *recordari* thus served as a means for proving exceptions, for the removal of cases in which a court found it was not competent to decide the issue (that is, in which the court either did not have the authority in law or was unable to decide what the law should be) or in which the king showed special favor to an individual, for supervision of the county courts and the processes that bound the county to the king's court, and, after the changes in 1275, for removal of plaints from the lower courts for a wide variety of reasons. From the late twelfth century and through the thirteenth century, the *recordari* played a vital role in coordinating the legal system.

A final tie between the county courts and the king's court was necessitated by the fact that a county court's jurisdiction was strictly limited to the geographical boundaries of the county itself. It seems that some such problem was behind *Normanvill v Alnatheby* in 1219. Normanvill was being impleaded for certain tenements by one Roger de Stapleton in the county court of Yorkshire. He had received the tenements originally from Alnatheby, so that Alnatheby was obliged by his charter to Normanvill to accept responsibility for the case. In normal procedure Normanvill would merely have vouched Alnatheby

---

[94] I have examined the writ files from 1302 to 1325, and they only contain the occasional record of a case summoned forth by a writ of false judgment. I have also looked at a few writ files from the reign of Richard II, and they seem to be devoid of even the simplest records. The writ files for the reign of Edward III are still not even sorted and are thus completely unavailable for examination.

[95] Above, n. 54. It is possible that the change was related to the death of Chief Justice Mettingham.

to warranty; Alnatheby would have been summoned by the court, would have appeared, and then would have taken over the defense of the case. Normanvill would then have become a relatively disinterested spectator, since if Alnatheby lost the case, he would be obliged to make a further grant equivalent in value to the lost lands and tenements to Normanvill. Alnatheby, however, was apparently resident outside the county, so that the county court could not make him appear. In such a case, the court might simply delay and induce one or other party to remove the case into the king's court by *pone*, where jurisdiction was not geographically restricted. Alternatively, however, and particularly when there was no special reason for removing the case, the tenant could bring a separate suit in the king's court to make the warrantor appear there. When he did and if he acknowledged that he was obliged to warrant the land, the king's court would order him then to appear in the county court. That was precisely the action of the king's court taken in regard to Alnatheby.[96] If there was some delay, the king's court could even order the county to postpone further process in the original case until the warrantor appeared.[97] In such ways, then, the king's court offset certain inherent limitations in the county courts' jurisdiction.

Tolt, the writs *pone* and *recordari*, the writ of false judgment, and the procedure to obtain the grand assize were all worked out during the twelfth century. The development of each can best be explained by adherence to very basic legal principles: the right to receive a fair hearing and to have a just judgment. Given the peculiar way in which political and social realities dictated that the courts had to function, these procedures offered a very reasonable measure of protection against frequent injustice. Furthermore, they were the institutionalized bonds between the courts which exerted constant pressure toward unifying and making common the varying customs in England. That pressure was first exerted by tolt on the county level, but the introduction of procedures that originated in the county but could terminate in the king's court and the standards forced on the lower courts by the writ of false judgment continued the process and welded the numerous English courts into a legal system.

[96] *CRR*, 8:146, 12:427.
[97] *CRR*, 14:272.

7

The
Viscontiel
Writs

I N   THE   CENTURY and a half following the accession of Henry II, English
law became a law of writs. Writs largely defined the character and
extent of the common law. The county courts were not unaffected
by the multiplication of writs, although never did writs initiate any-
where near most of the litigation in county courts. The writs that
did originate suits in county courts were called viscontiel writs, because they were addressed to the sheriff. The viscontiel writs, like
the other two great classes of original writs (returnable and seignorial
writs), were issued by chancery. Since they were issued by the same
body as the other original writs and were often removed from county
courts into the court of common pleas, viscontiel writs formed a part
of the legal knowledge of the people shaping the law. Thus these
writs were an integral part of the law; moreover, they left a lasting
imprint on the common law even after their own utility ended.

That viscontiel writs were available at all is an oddity that requires
explanation. Writs were troublesome to obtain and were purchased,
occasionally at great expense. Litigants were not so enthralled by
writs that they purchased them of a whim; chancery likewise did not
issue writs for no reason at all. They were issued because of some
legal necessity. Seignorial writs were purchased, at first, because pressure had to be applied to the lord of the court to which the jurisdiction
pertained. Returnable writs were purchased because the court of common pleas had no intrinsic jurisdiction, so that the jurisdiction over
each case had to be delegated specifically to the justices. The county
courts, however, were supposed to be omnicompetent, barring those
matters that involved the lord-tenant relationship and those matters

that increasingly the king specially mandated to the central courts exclusively. The fundamental problem with viscontiel writs, therefore, must be their very existence. That problem will be treated in this chapter and the next, although in format this chapter discusses the classes and origins of the viscontiel writs, both of which areas are logically prior to any analysis of the reasons for which viscontiel writs were provided.

The Classes of Viscontiel Writs

Viscontiel writs are best classified by form, particularly by the central operative verb, but also by the initial and concluding clauses; the explanation of these forms will provide an important method of determining the ideas embodied in the writs and the reasons for which they were provided. These classes, regrettably, are modern and not medieval; but they do correspond, albeit roughly, to substantive or procedural similarities in the writs. We shall designate in this way four classes by using the main verbs: *facias* (cause), *justicies* (justice), *audias* (hear), and *distringas* (distrain).

The Facias *Writs.* There were eight *facias* writs, each utilizing the command "cause" as the main directive of the writ. In their form there was little else that would put these writs into the same class. Even the word *"facias"* was not at all distinctive; it was the command most commonly used in directing the sheriff to take any action. The lack of further formal elements in common is indicative of the fact that the *facias* writs are generally the earliest viscontiel writs.

An examination of the *facias* writs illustrate this formal variety. The *facias* writ of replevin below has the various possible common clauses numbered and italicized to demonstrate the point.

> The king to the sheriff, greeting. (1) *We command you that, justly and without delay, you cause [facias] to be replevied to A. his beasts which* B. has taken and is holding unjustly, as he says; (2) *and afterwards, that you cause the said A. to be dealt with justly in the matter* (3) *that we may not further hear outcry thereof for want of justice.* Witness etc.

No other *facias* writ contained all three of the possible common clauses. The *facias* writ of repair of banks and ditches, indeed, contained none of the three; but that might be explained by the fact that it was provided late and was not long available to litigants. The other

175

seven *facias* writs appear in *Glanvill*. All contained the first clause, although in the two admeasurement writs the first clause was preceded by a further introduction. No other *facias* writ contained the second clause; only three other *facias* writs contained the third clause. This diversity, the general earliness of the *facias* writs, and the common use of the word *"facias"* in ad hoc writs argue that they might be seen more as those writs that for one reason or another were not put into a common form class.[1] Any common characteristic, therefore, could be seen as a procedural or substantive reason blocking the revision of their form into that of one of the other, later classes.

The Justicies *Writs.* The *justicies* writs were the largest class of viscontiel writs and were consistently in common form. In the following *justicies* writ of debt—a writ that will be discussed in several contexts in this and later chapters—the elements of the common form have been italicized.

> The king to the sheriff, greeting. *We command you to justice [*justicies*] B. that justly and without delay* he render to A. twenty shillings which he owes him, as he says, *as he shall reasonably be able to show [*sicut rationabiliter monstrare poterit*]* that he ought to render to him, *that we may not further hear outcry thereof for want of justice.* Witness etc.

There was absolutely no deviation from this common form from one *justicies* writ to another. As with all common form, however, the problem is to figure out what the words mean. The particular problems to be dealt with later in the chapter concern the meaning of the command to "justice" someone and the meaning of the clause specifying that the plaintiff shall have made reasonable proof.

The Audias *Writs.* The *audias* writs, like the *justicies* writs, were consistent in form. There were, basically, only two *audias* writs, the viscontiel writs of nuisance and of trespass. Each of these two writs, however, was available in a multiplicity of forms, for various kinds of nuisance and for a bewildering number of wrongs. The following

---

[1] The writ of replevin has clauses, 1, 2, and 3; naifty has only clause 1 and concludes with a penalty clause; the two admeasurement writs—that of dower and that of pasture—have clauses 1 and 3 but begin with a *questus est mihi* clause like the *audias* writs; rightful boundaries has clauses 1 and 3; rightful dower had only clause 1; rightful division has only clause 1 and concludes like a *justicies* writ, which it undoubtedly would have become had it survived (for the form, see *Glanvill*, p. 81). The writ for the repair of banks and ditches was completely irregular but was soon revised. The writ of aid, if one counts it as a *facias* writ, has only clause 1.

writ of trespass has the common form of the *audias* writs italicized; this writ will be discussed further in the next chapter.

> The king to the sheriff, greeting. *A. has complained to us* that B. took and carried away goods and chattels of the said A. to the value of so much found at N. etc. and inflicted other outrages upon him to the no small damage and loss of the said A. *And therefore we command you to hear that plea, and afterwards cause him to be justly dealt with therein, that we may hear no further complaint about this for want of justice.* Witness etc.

The command to the sheriff to hear the plea makes the *audias* writs, at least to the modern ear, the class of viscontiel writs that most clearly was intended to originate litigation.

Distringas *and Miscellaneous Writs.* The remaining viscontiel writs were much less important than the *facias, justicies,* or *audias* writs. The *distringas* writs were uniformly concerned with repair, whether of bridges, highways, or roads. They began with an explanatory clause and concluded with an order to distrain those who were justly obliged to make the specified repairs. They only appeared in the later thirteenth century and achieved a final form under Edward I. In addition to the *distringas* writs, there were also three miscellaneous writs. The *ne vexes* was addressed to the lord of the purchaser and not to the sheriff. Since, however, it was in the form of a prohibition, it could initiate a case in the county court if the prohibition—which concerned customs and services for which the tenant was being unjustly vexed—was ignored. A writ for easements appeared in *Glanvill* but not thereafter. Finally, there was also a writ for ordering the sheriff to distrain villeins to render their lord proper customs and services. The *distringas* and the miscellaneous writs, however, are relatively unimportant for our purposes and will not be discussed further.

Characteristics of the Classes

The classification of the writs by form into the three major classes of *facias, justicies,* and *audias* writs is justified by a further procedural or substantive similarity in the writs of the respective classes. It was not a matter of indifference in which form a writ was drawn. If that is so, then closer analysis of the common form can reasonably be expected to show why the writs were originally provided.

The Facias *Writs.* The unifying characteristic of the *facias* writs was a distinctively executive activity on the part of the sheriff which came as a prelude to the litigation or as an integral part of the suit. The writ of replevin is a particularly good example of this executive activity. The writ ordered the sheriff to intervene in what was essentially a standoff between the parties. In the original case, the lord had distrained his tenant to perform services which the tenant was reluctant to perform. The sheriff intervened to restore—replevy— the animals to their owner, the tenant, and to assure the lord that his claim for services would be placed immediately in litigation. The suit took the form of an action for animals taken and unjustly detained, and the focus of the case would be on the defendant/lord's reason for the distraint. The sheriff's executive activity in replevin was thus a prelude to the suit and a necessary precondition for putting the dispute into a litigious context.

A similarly executive role for the sheriff can be found in the two *facias* writs for admeasurement. The writ of admeasurement of dower was provided for the heir against the doweress who had been allocated too large a dower, perhaps by the lord and guardian while the heir was underage. The writ of admeasurement of pasture was provided against a user of common pasture who was pasturing more than his rightful share of animals. In each case, the determination of the suit involved normally a measurement of the land by a sworn panel to ascertain the proper division. That admeasurement took place on the land in question and not in the court. The writs of admeasurement thus also required particularly executive action by the sheriff.

The writ of rightful boundaries was similar in executive activity to the admeasurement writs. That writ was provided to determine the boundaries between townships, and the idea behind it was probably the determination of boundaries between two lordships. This writ was the closest thing English law knew to a viscontiel writ of right for land. Determination of the suit could be by the methods used in the writ of right, but it could also be settled in a manner similar to that used in the writs of admeasurement: a sworn panel that would demarcate the boundaries. That panel would be convoked by the sheriff, and it would be the sheriff who would preside over their demarcation made on the land outside the court.

The other *facias* writs likewise have an executive procedural element, although not as pronounced as in the above examples. Naifty was provided for the determination of a dispute between two lords concerning the ownership of a villein and—at least soon thereafter—

between a lord and the man he claimed as his villein. In either case the alleged villein was probably being held by a lord in safe custody and needed to be put into more neutral circumstances. The short-lived writ of rightful dower, provided at the death of a tenant-in-chief, required the sheriff to provide the widow with her dower and also to protect the deceased's chattels and pay his debts. Such a directive obviously required some executive activity on the land in question. The writ for repair of banks and ditches conceivably had an executive aspect, as did the short-lived writ for upholding a reasonable division of a deceased's chattels. In one degree or another, then, the *facias* writs envisaged procedures beyond ordinary mesne procedure which could not take place in court but rather involved a distinctively executive activity by the sheriff.

The Justicies *Writs.* Whereas *facias* writs were united by a procedural similarity, *justicies* writs were united by a substantive similarity. All *justicies* writs concerned the enforcement of rights and obligations. This large class of writs can be further subdivided into three groups.

The least frequently noticed group of *justicies* writs concerned the enforcement of one's rights to do something or have the use of something outside one's own free tenement. Thus there were *justicies* writs concerning the right to draw water, to water sheep, to mill free of multure, to have a right-of-way, to have common of fishery or free fishery, to have pasture or common of pasture, to run bulls and boars freely, to remove or have repaired a nuisance threatening one's free tenement, to have closed a customarily closed courtyard. These were clearly not suits for damages, but rather for the enforcement of a right outside one's own free tenement.

Another group of *justicies* writs concerned lord-tenant rights. Thus the writ of customs and services was provided for the lord to enforce performance of the customs and services due from his tenant, and the writ of acceptance of homage and relief allowed a tenant to force his prospective lord to acknowledge his tenancy. The writ of mesne allowed a tenant to force his lord to render the services due the lord's own lord for which the tenant was being distrained by his lord's default. The writs of wardship allowed lords to enforce their right of wardship over the lands and/or body of underage tenants, and similar writs were also provided for the proper guardians of socage tenants. Lords could also compel residents to perform suit to their hundred court or suit to their mill with *justicies* writs. This group of the *justicies* writs thus concerned the enforcement of rights over people.

The third and final group of *justicies* writs concerns the enforcement of obligations. *Justicies* writs were utilized to compel payment of debts, return of chattels detained, and return of deeds detained. The writ of covenant compelled the defendant to hold to an agreement. The *justicies* writ of annual rent compelled the payment of an annuity, and the writ of acquittance of pledges compelled one's pledge to fulfil his obligation to pay the plaintiff's creditor. The writ of account was used to make one's bailiff or partner render a formal account of one's goods, so that payment could then be made of what was owing. This substantial field of enforcement of obligations was probably the most important sphere of activity covered by *justicies* writs. All three groups of *justicies* writs, however, were thus concerned with the enforcement of rights and obligations.

The Audias *Writs.* The *audias* writs were not concerned with enforcing obligations, but rather with redressing wrongs. The writs of nuisance provided for the cessation of nuisances caused by houses, orchards, mills, sheepfolds, gates, watering-ponds, and ovens on another's free tenement which were having a deleterious affect on one's own free tenement. The writs of trespass were available to obtain damages for general personal injury, for injuries caused by a dog "incited" to bite, for chattels carried away, for chattels released in pledge and not returned, for damage caused by fishing in a free fishery, for damage caused by a broken dike, for grass mowed and carried away, for a sheepfold knocked down, for animals impounded and starved. The redress of wrongs seemed more appropriate for the *audias* form of viscontiel writ, just as the enforcement of rights and obligations fell regularly to the *justicies* form. And neither the *audias* nor the *justicies* demanded the executive activity required by the *facias* writs.

The Origins of the Viscontiel Writs

Viscontiel writs first became writs of course in the reign of Henry II. There had long been writs directing the sheriff to hold a certain plea;[2] those ad hoc writs, however, will not be a concern here. It is the standardized writs we are treating, because the standardization of

---

[2] See *Royal Writs in England*, ed. R. C. Van Caenegem, Selden Society, vol. 77 (London, 1959).

writs results in definable general legal effects. Therefore, the production of viscontiel writs of course must rank among the most important of the innovations of the reign of Henry II. The writs standardized during his reign were the *facias* writs and a few of the *justicies*
writs. The *audias* writs were not his creation. The *audias* writs of
nuisance, since they do not appear in viscontiel form in *Glanvill*,
probably originated sometime between 1189 and 1218.[3] The *audias*
writs of trespass date only from the reign of Edward I.[4] Likewise, the
distringas writs originated in the latter half of the thirteenth century.
It is with the early viscontiel writs that this chapter is concerned, so
that the *facias* and *justicies* writs will receive primary attention here.

The Writs in Glanvill. *Glanvill* contains both *facias* and *justicies*
writs. The *facias* writs, as already noted, were generally early; indeed,
seven of the eight *facias* writs were known to Glanvill, and the eighth
was late and short-lived. Both naifty and rightful boundaries had a
long history already, but naifty probably achieved its final and standardized form only around 1179,[5] while rightful boundaries, seemingly
standardized in *Glanvill*, did not reach its final form until later.[6]
Admeasurement of dower had achieved a final form already, but
admeasurement of pasture was in a form still to be modified.[7] Both
were probably already writs of course. Replevin was apparently standardized, but in 1189 it was still tied to disputes arising from distraints
made by lords for customs and services. It would come to be used by
neighbors for testing boundaries and for disputes as to whether land

[3] The precise date is difficult to determine. A reference to Janet Loengard's work on
nuisance in Donald W. Sutherland, *The Assize of Novel Disseisin* (Oxford, 1973), pp.
63, 216-17 (note D) might indicate that the writs of viscontiel nuisance originated late
in the reign of John. The earliest writ of viscontiel nuisance I have found is in the
Rotuli Litterarum Clausarum, ed. Thomas D. Hardy, 2 vols., Record Commission
(London, 1833, 1844), 1:376b (1218). A few months earlier, 1:364a, there was a writ
of viscontiel novel disseisin—no words of nuisance—concerning disseisin of the multure of a mill.

[4] Below, chapter 8, n. 53.

[5] *Royal Writs*, pp. 339-40; G.D.G. Hall, review of *Royal Writs*, ed. R. C. Van
Caenegem, *EHR* 76 (1961):319; Paul R. Hyams, "The Proof of Villein Status in the
Common Law," *EHR* 89 (1974):721-49. The reason for specifying the year 1179 is
the similarity between the process of naifty and *de libertate probanda* on the one hand
and the writ of right and the writs of summons and peace on the other.

[6] Compare *Glanvill*, p. 116 with *Early Registers of Writs*, ed. Elsa de Haas and
G.D.G. Hall, Selden Society, vol. 87 (London, 1970), p. 11 (Hib. 32). For the earlier
history see *Royal Writs*, no. 156; Felix Liebermann, *Die Gesetze der Angelsachsen*,
3 vols. (Halle an der Saale, 1898-1916), 1:524.

[7] Compare *Glanvill*, pp. 68-69, 137-38, with *Early Registers of Writs*, pp. 8, 12
(Hib. 19, 33).

was held in common or in severalty. These *facias* writs, then, were standardized very early, even if there were some modifications in form and use of the particular writ still to be made.

During the reign of Henry II there were only two standardized *justicies* writs—one for customs and services, the other for the restoration of chattels after an assize—and both were mentioned by Glanvill. These two writs were not of immense importance in the legal system, although both were very useful. The *justicies* writs were clearly of less importance in 1189 than the *facias* writs and almost certainly not as old. The *facias* writs were to retain their position of legal importance for a long time fairly unchanged; the *justicies* writs, however, were to increase dramatically both in number and in importance.

At least a beginning can now be made in explaining why viscontiel writs were even provided. For the *justicies* writs, there can be two different, but not necessarily incompatible, lines of explanation. The first would argue that a writ was required for Glanvill's two *justicies* situations because the county court was not the normal forum; some special delegation of jurisdiction was necessary. The customs and services situation, if one had only the writ, would have seemed appropriate for the lord's own court. Fortunately, Glanvill noted that that writ was provided specifically for those lords who were not sufficiently powerful to justice their own tenants.[8] The writ was needed because, since the case was seignorial in nature, it did not fall naturally into the jurisdiction of the county court. A similar explanation can be made for the writ of restoration of chattels after an assize of novel disseisin. One could argue that, since the assize had been an action of the king's court, measures taken pursuant to the assize would most naturally fall within the jurisdiction of the king's court, not within that of the county court. A writ would thus have been necessary to delegate the case to the county from the king's court. This line of reasoning presupposes some special need for the delegation of jurisdiction in the two early *justicies* writs.

Another mode of argument, however, is possible, since it cannot be proven that such situations required a writ. If those situations could be the base of litigation by plaint—and I think this the better explanation—the two writs were provided to give a better procedure. That better procedure will be determined later, but it would be understandable if the king wanted to give strong procedure for the

[8] *Glanvill*, p. 112.

restoration of chattels. The assize of novel disseisin was meant to proceed quickly; the intended consequences of the judgment should also follow quickly. The *justicies* writ here soon disappeared, because procedure was even more strongly fortified by awarding damages in the assize itself rather than ordering the chattels to be returned.[9] The reason why customs and services should have better than normal procedure will be treated later. Although one cannot dismiss jurisdictional elements in the provision of the *justicies* writs, however, it seems that procedural reasons were the more important.

The allocation of the *facias* writs to the county court and the reasons for their provision are likewise susceptible to explanation. Naifty and rightful boundaries were seen as disputes between lords. Neither of their courts was thus appropriate, and it would be improbable that they had a common lord except, perhaps, the king. Since both lands and villeins were normally things that pertained to a lord's court, however, a writ was necessary to bring the case before the county court; otherwise it would probably go to the court of the common lord: an honor court or the king's court. Moreover, at least in regard to rightful boundaries, a writ was becoming necessary solely because rights to realty were at stake. The writ of admeasurement of dower, like the writ of customs and services, was provided for the plaintiff/ lord. The doweress was here in possession and relied on the heir for the protection of her title. While the heir's court would have been the natural venue, it would have been unsavory in general and dangerous at law to allow the heir to preside over the lessening of the dower, seemingly against his warranty obligation. The writ allowed the county court to take the jurisdiction. Moreover, admeasurement could more easily be done by a lower court, although the king's court could certainly manage to order admeasurements. In replevin and admeasurement of pasture, the original situation seems to have been that of a lord proceeding without the use of his court; since the lord was unwilling to use his own court, the tenant, by means of the writ, was able to obtain a hearing in a more nearly neutral forum. The *facias* writs, then, were present to provide the county court with jurisdiction when by the ordinary rules of law the case belonged in a different court. They provided for the exceptions and served as supplements to normal procedure. For all of Glanvill's viscontiel writs, however, the uses expanded, so that the original rationale came soon to be insufficient to explain the variety of litigation the writs began.

[9] Sutherland, *The Assize of Novel Disseisin*, p. 52 (1198).

Dating the Origins of Viscontiel Debt. The determination of the rationale behind the *justicies* writs as a class is dependent on chronology. The writ of debt/detinue/acquittance of pledges is vital in this context, and it is obvious that an explanation for this writ which would be quite acceptable assuming that it was provided in 1185 or before might be unacceptable if it is shown that the writ was available only from around 1200. This problem will form the basis of a long discussion on the common form of the *facias, justicies,* and *audias* writs to determine why the *justicies* writs were provided. The problem of chronology arises because Glanvill does not list a viscontiel writ of debt. His omission of the *justicies* writ of debt is most easily taken to mean that it was not then available. Both Lady Stenton and R. C. Van Caenegem, however, have maintained that the *justicies* writs of debt and acquittance of pledges were nevertheless available at least from 1185.[10] If they are correct, Henry II did far more than Glanvill tells us, and the reason for the provision of the writs would be difficult to ascertain. Their argument thus requires careful consideration.

The point at issue is not whether debts were being recovered in county courts during the reign of Henry II (they certainly were)[11] but whether there were *justicies* writs for the purpose. Lady Stenton and R. C. Van Caenegem base their argument solely on five entries in the pipe rolls of 1185 and 1186. Both were familiar with the hazards of using the terse entries in the pipe rolls, so the texts themselves require some examination. The five entries are in the form of the following two:

> William de Georz owes 20s so that Hugh de Bere be justiced [*justicietur*] to acquit him of a pledge of 7 marks against the Jews of Leicester.[12]

> Deulebeie, Jew of Chichester, owes 1 mark of gold for having a writ concerning justicing [*justiciando*] Sauaricus concerning a debt he owes him.[13]

Since pipe rolls do seem to follow the wording of writs, it must be taken for granted that the word *"justicies"* appeared in the writs in these instances. To that extent, at least, one must say that there were *justicies* writs of debt and acquittance of pledges in the reign of Henry II.

---

[10] *Pleas before the King or His Justices,* ed. Doris M. Stenton, 4 vols., Selden Society, vols. 67, 68, 83, 84 (London, 1948-1967), 1:17; *Royal Writs,* p. 256.

[11] *PR, 31 Henry II,* p. 39.

[12] Ibid., p. 104. See *PR, 32 Henry II,* pp. 75, 94.

[13] *PR, 32 Henry II,* pp. 183, 79 (?).

The *justicies* writs of debt and acquittance of pledges at that time, however, were not viscontiel. Through the reign of John one can occasionally discover nonviscontiel *justicies* writs. The oblate roll for 1206, for instance, contains the following entry which must indicate a nonviscontiel *justicies* writ:

> Bona, who was the wife of Jacob, Jew of Lincoln, gives a fourth part of 40 marks which she claims in dower against Peitivin son of Jacob for having a writ concerning justicing [*justiciando*] the abovesaid Peitivin to render the abovesaid 40 marks as reasonably [she shall be able to show?] etc. She has a writ thereof directed to the justices of the Jews.[14]

Fortunately, there is a corresponding pipe roll entry for this case, and it comes very close in form to the pipe roll entries of 1185-86 in question:

> Bona, who was the wife of Jacob, Jew of Lincoln, owes 10 marks for justicing [*justiciando*] Peitivin that he render her 40 marks which he owes her, as she says.[15]

Since all five of the 1185-86 entries concerned Jews in one way or another, there is thus a strong reason for asserting that they evidence *justicies* writs directed to the justices of the Jews and not viscontiel *justicies* writs.

The vital entries might also, however, indicate unusual *justicies* writs directed to a central court. Surprisingly, there were occasional *justicies* writs addressed to royal justices. None of them concern the precise situations in the 1185-86 entries, but one at least relates to a suit for the money damages resulting from default of warranty.[16] Moreover, the king's court did handle cases of acquittance of pledges against creditor Jews,[17] and the king might well have been unwilling for such cases to be handled in a lower court. The 1185-86 entries in the pipe rolls cannot, therefore, be construed as evidence for viscontiel *justicies* writs. They must rather be taken to demonstrate the existence of unusual and short-lived forms of *justicies* writs for a central court, whether the court of the Jews or the king's court.

There is, in fact, no clear evidence of the viscontiel *justicies* writ

---

[14] *Rotuli de Oblatis et Finibus*, ed. Thomas Duffus Hardy (London, 1835), p. 350.
[15] *PR, 8 John*, p. 102.
[16] *Rotuli de Oblatis*, pp. 214, 358, 517. Ibid., p. 397, has a *justicies* of acquittance of pledges concerning a debt that was being exacted at the Exchequer of the Jews, but the venue of the case is unclear.
[17] *Rotuli Curiae Regis*, ed. Francis Palgrave, 2 vols., Record Commission (London, 1835), 2:108; *CRR*, 1:110, 3:298.

of debt/detinue until 1201. Van Caenegem thought that the 1185-86 entries signalled the beginning of a veritable flood of *justicies* writs.[18] The pipe rolls, however, merely repeated the 1185-86 entries, with no new similar entries until 1196.[19] In that year there is one entry for justicing a tenant to pay relief;[20] that entry could be interpreted either as a writ of customs and services or as a forerunner of debt.[21] In either interpretation, however, there is no indication of the venue. In 1197 there is another entry for a Jew prosecuting in debt.[22] In 1199 and 1200 there are several good candidates for *justicies* writs of debt, but most of them were clearly directed to the king's court.[23] Finally, in 1201, there is fairly good proof of a viscontiel *justicies* writ of debt. A widow was claiming 31 marks against Hugh English; chancery recorded that she received a writ to justice [*justiciando*] him to pay the debt and that the sheriff of Somerset "was ordered to justice the same Hugh."[24] In 1205, then, the form of one viscontiel *justicies* writ of debt was enrolled in the close rolls, so that at that point there can be no doubt:

> The king to the sheriff of Staffordshire, etc. We command you to justice the prior of Stanes that justly and without delay he render to Obec de Stanes 100s which he owes him, as he says, as he shall reasonably be able to show etc.[25]

[18] *Royal Writs*, p. 256.

[19] *PR, 32 Henry II*, p. 131; *33 Henry II*, pp. 71, 73, 87, 108, 117; *34 Henry II*, pp. 70, 71, 114, 187; . . . *2 Richard I*, pp. 38, 79, 128; *9 Richard I*, p. 219.

[20] *PR, 8 Richard I*, p. 177.

[21] Possible interpretations arise from *Glanvill*, p. 113 and *Rotuli Scaccarii Normanniae sub Regibus Anglie*, ed. Thomas Stapleton, 2 vols. (London, 1840), 2:476.

[22] *PR, 9 Richard I*, p. 113.

[23] *Rotuli de Oblatis*, pp. 10, 25, 51 (see *CRR*, 1:331; *PR, 2 John*, p. 234), 93 (see *PR, 3 John*, p. 290?), 115 (a writ of summons for 5 marks—apparently owed between parties—with the clause of reasonable proof). See also pp. 6 and 109, where the venue is not clear.

[24] *Rotuli de Oblatis*, p. 136. A comparison with *PR, 3 John*, p. 37, shows that this *justicies* writ was referred to as giving right concerning the debt, a phrase that has always been associated with returnable writs. This kind of entry greatly debilitates R. C. Van Caenegem's comparisons of the cost of *justicies* and *precipe* writs of debt. For this particular phenomenon see also *Rotuli de Oblatis*, pp. 129 (compare with *PR, 3 John*, p. 185), 304-5 (compare with *PR 7 John*, p. 179). Other relevant debt entries in the *Rotuli de Oblatis*: pp. 174 (bis), 213, 214, 215, 223, 236 (bis), 248-49, 253, 264 ("*brevi de debito . . . sicut racionabiliter etc.*"), 265, 269, 299, 304-5, 305, 309, 311, 312, 313, 322-23, 323, 327, 329 [all of these in 1205 or before; later examples not listed here]. Search for these cases in the *Curia Regis Rolls* has been fruitless.

[25] *Rotuli Litterarum Clausarum*, 1:23b; see also 1:29b (cancelled because it was entered—in not so informative a way—in the fine rolls); 1:24 (*justicies* acquittance of pledges against executors); 1:22b (which may not be original because it does not have the clause of reasonable proof; it might therefore be merely executive based on the king's knowledge of the debt).

The earliest example of the writ itself, then, is very close to the first firm evidence for the existence of the writ. Even at that early date, however, the viscontiel *justicies* writ of debt was in its final form.

The viscontiel *justicies* writ of debt was therefore provided between 1199 and 1201, and certainly no later than 1205. The finality of the form of the writ so early in its existence would argue that the development was purposeful and well considered. It may indeed have been modeled specifically on the *justicies* writs for the court of the Jews. This innovation had a lasting impact on the law of contracts, so that the rest of the chapter will be concerned with deciphering the common form of the *justicies* writ.

The "Manu-Militari" Theory for Justicies *Writs.* R. C. Van Caenegem has suggested, with a great deal of conviction, that the *justicies* writ of debt was not a writ that initiated litigation, but rather a writ that merely ordered execution. This hypothesis concerning the ideas behind the *justicies* writs is based on his view of the *precipe* writs of debt, which originated litigation in the king's court. He maintains that through the 1170s the *precipe* writ of debt did not originate litigation at all, but was executive in nature, merely envisaging collection of the debt. When the *precipe* writ of debt became "judicialized" in the 1180s, that is, when it came to originate litigation instead of execution, there remained a need for some device to collect debts. He argues that the *justicies* writ was developed at just that time as a *"manu-militari"* high-handed executive order merely to levy the debt.[26] A similar argument would then have to apply to other early *justicies* writs. The later origin of the *justicies* writ of debt, shown above, is certainly inconvenient for, but not disabling to, such an argument. If that argument can still stand, *justicies* writs, at least at first, had a great deal to do with sheriffs but nothing at all to do with the county courts. They would merely have been provided as executive orders.

Some color can be provided for the Van Caenegem argument by an analysis of the meaning of the word *"justicies."* The sheriff was ordered, not to give justice to the plaintiff, but rather to justice the defendant. G.D.G. Hall properly construed the word to mean "constrain."[27] The procedure envisaged by the word was probably distraint. In 1199 there is a writ of debt directed to the justiciar that is similar to a *justicies* writ, except that it used the word "distrain" for

[26] *Royal Writs*, pp. 254-56.
[27] See *Glanvill*, p. 113, but see his more cautious translation in *Early Registers of Writs*, p. 13 (Hib. 38).

"justice."[28] There are several other examples.[29] Likewise, there are writs that order the defendant to be justiced "by his lands and chattels" to render the debt. One such writ in 1205 makes one pause before asserting incautiously that *justicies* writs automatically implied litigation:

> The king to the sheriff of Hertfordshire. We command you to justice [*justicies*] Richard de Argenton by his lands and chattels that without delay he render to Hugh de Nevill 100 marks to our use for the forest.[30]

That writ seems clearly executive and not litigious in nature. There are significant differences, however, between that writ and the ordinary *justicies* writ. That writ omits the word "justly" (as in "that he justly and without delay render"), the "as he says" clause, the assertion of the indebtedness, and the clause of reasonable proof. Those omissions make the writ seem executive, but they are merely the result of a more important aspect of the writ: it does not involve the intervention of the king in a dispute between parties. Nevertheless, it must be granted that the word "*justicies*" does not always imply litigation.

The normal *justicies* writ, however, probably did imply litigation. When the king intervened between parties, the justicing was more likely to be by distraint to come to court. In an even milder vein, one writ from 1200 has the king justicing fourteen defendants by having them summoned before justices.[31] Moreover, the normal elements of the *justicies* writ—"justly," "as he says," and "as he shall reasonably be able to show"—add a distinctively litigious air to the writ. While those elements cannot be observed in the pipe rolls, their presence in the *Glanvill justicies* writs and the writs from around 1200 make it unlikely that *justicies* writs of debt ever were *manu militari* executive orders.

It would have been very unusual indeed for *justicies* writs to have been merely orders for levying moneys with no chance for a defense. In 1222 the writ of rightful boundaries was being treated in Ireland as an order simply to make a perambulation without giving the defendant a chance to defend. A writ close from the king expressed some surprise at this and noted that it was manifestly contrary to the custom of England, which custom was supposed to apply also to

---

[28] *Rotuli de Oblatis*, p. 25.
[29] Ibid., pp. 51, 214, 304-5, 359, 388, 390-91.
[30] *Rotuli Litterarum Clausarum*, 1:19b.
[31] *Rotuli de Oblatis*, p. 47.

Ireland.[32] Later, a further missive commanded that at least English custom concerning the writ of rightful boundaries should be applied in English areas where the Irish were excluded.[33] Although this concerned a *facias* writ, that kind of sentiment about the proper methods of settling disputes makes *manu-militari justicies* writs of debt highly improbable, except in those situations in which the king himself was party. It must be concluded, then, that *justicies* writs were original and not executive even at their origins.

The Viscontiel Justice Theory of Justicies *Writs.* A second theory concerning the reason the *justicies* writs were provided relates to the person who would render judgment. The theory suggests that when the suit was brought by writ the sheriff was established as a delegated royal justice in that case and would then render the judgment, whereas had the case been brought by plaint he would only have been the presiding officer and not a judgment-rendering justice.[34] That difference, indeed, would have prompted some individuals to buy such writs, particularly those who were allied to the current sheriff or who were fearful of some magnate who dominated most of the county but, in the circumstances, not the sheriff. Moreover, the theory is based on passages in *Glanvill*, *Bracton*, and *Fleta*. This theory, nonetheless, is incorrect.

The viscontiel justice theory is based on interpretations of certain passages in *Glanvill*, *Bracton*, and *Fleta*. The argument in favor of the theory will be put forth first using all three sources, and then alternative interpretations will be suggested. Glanvill was admirably concise:

> To put it generally, the pleas which are to be heard and determined by the sheriff are all those in which the sheriff has a writ from the lord king or his chief justice commanding him to constrain [*justiciando*] anyone, or as stated above, to do full right unless another does it.[35]

[32] *Rotuli Litterarum Clausarum*, 1:497b.

[33] Ibid., 1:532b. For further directions and information on the writ in Ireland, see *CR, 1234-1237*, pp. 157, 501.

[34] Hall, Review of *Royal Writs*, p. 319; S. E. Thorne, "Notes on Courts of Record in England," *West Virginia Law Quarterly* 40 (1934): 355: "But a distinction must be drawn between proceedings conducted by the county court and proceedings conducted by the sheriff in the county court. In the latter case the sheriff heard pleas not as sheriff but as *iustitiarius regis* by virtue of a delegation of authority from the king and as such had record." On pp. 356-357 he suggests that the sheriff lost this power as justice in the fifteenth century. See also Helen Cam, *The Hundred and the Hundred Rolls* (London, 1930), p. 117, asserting the same thesis but with neither argument nor proof.

[35] *Glanvill*, p. 141: "Et generaliter omnia illa unde breve habet domini regis vel

One must note specifically that Glanvill says the sheriff will hear and determine the cases. That wording certainly brings to mind a commission of *oyer* and *terminer* to justices which empowered them to dispose of a case completely. Glanvill was not quite that precise in this passage. He was, however, writing at a time when royal justices frequently doubled as sheriffs; that fact makes the theory very attractive. The *Glanvill* passage, if only analyzed to that extent, is thus a strong support for the viscontiel justice theory.

Bracton is less general in his statement about the sheriff acting as a justice. In writing about delegated justices, he does not mention the sheriff at all.[36] It is only in writing about replevin—a *facias*, not a *justicies* writ—that the sheriff is mentioned in this capacity:

> The sheriff is of necessity permitted to determine a plea of this kind, not by virtue of his office as sheriff, but as a justice of the lord king.[37]

Although this statement concerned the highly emotive situation involved in replevin, the statement would indeed seem to indicate that the sheriff could function as a royal justice when the case was brought by writ.

Fleta, like Bracton, deals only with replevin. This statement, however, is much more precise; it is the main support for the viscontiel justice theory, which is the traditional interpretation:

> In the county court there is a two-fold court. On the one hand the king has his court and his justice, namely the sheriff, whenever jurisdiction is delegated to him by writ, whereby he has the record, since it is he and not the suitors who is ordered '*quod iuste deduci faciat*' [that you cause (the said A.) to be dealt with justly (in this matter)]. On the other hand, the court is like that of a baron or the king held in any of their manors, and there the sheriff is no more than the king's bailiff and farmer, and judgments will be pronounced by the suitors and not by him and it is they who will be punished if they make a false judgment.[38]

---

capitalis iusticie ipse vicecomes de aliquo iusticiando, vel quod ipse rectum faciat nisi alius fecerit ut predictum est, ad ipsum vicecomitem pertinent audienda et terminanda."

[36] Henry of Bracton, *De Legibus et Consuetudinibus Angliae*, ed. G. E. Woodbine, trans. S. E. Thorne, 4 vols. to date (Cambridge, Mass. and London, 1968-), 2:307.

[37] Ibid., 2:439: "Sed quia placitum istud dilationem non capit, propter animalia muta et propter damnum quod evenire posset si diu detinerentur inclusa donec placitum de vetito namii terminaretur, ideo placitum de vetito namii vicecomiti conceditur terminandum, hac necessitate, quod quidem non habet ex officio vicecomitis, sed sicut iustitiarius ipsius domini regis."

[38] *Fleta*, ed. H. G. Richardson and G. O. Sayles, 2 vols., Selden Society, vols. 72, 89 (London, 1953-1972), 2:148: "In comitatu enim est curia duplex: habet enim rex curiam suam et iusticiam suam, videlicet vicecomitem, cum delegetur ei iurisdiccio per

This statement, like the others, seems to put the sheriff in a special position when the case is begun by writ. The viscontiel justice theory is therefore a theory with a much stronger prima facie foundation than the *manu-militari* theory.

None of the three passages cited, however, will actually bear the burden placed on it. In the second of the three passages, Bracton was not explaining who was to give judgment in cases of replevin. He was there concerned, rather, to explain why a plea touching the crown of the lord king should be held in a lower court. He resolved the problem by explaining the urgency of the matter and by stressing that the plea was held by delegated jurisdiction and not by virtue of the sheriff's own authority. Bracton was not, in short, concerned at that point with what happened when a case was determined before the sheriff. He did say that the sheriff was to determine the plea, but not in the context of any distinction between the powers of the sheriff and the powers of the suitors. Whereas the theory would try to expand the statement to show that the sheriff would render the judgment, it can just as easily be taken to mean that the sheriff would determine the case by having the judges of the county court render a judgment.

The third passage, the lengthy explanation by Fleta, is likewise open to a very different interpretation than the traditional one. The normal interpretation really demands an interpolation, since it sees here a distinction between procedure by writ and procedure by plaint. The interpolation necessary for this purpose would come immediately after the middle of the passage, so that it would read something like this: "On the other hand, *when the suit is begun merely by plaint*, the court is like that of a baron . . ." No one has ever even suggested that such an interpolation is justified; the distinction between writs and plaints has been read into the passage only because that distinction is so important to modern historians. Fleta was indeed trying to make a distinction, but it was not between cases begun by writ and cases begun by plaint. It concerned the different roles in county court when a case was brought by writ. On the one hand, he says, the sheriff has the jurisdiction. On the other hand, the suitors give the judgments. The county court thus has a dual nature when its jurisdiction derives from a writ. Far from being a proof that sheriffs rendered

---

breve, per quam recordum habet, cum sibi et non sectatoribus comitatus precipiatur quod iuste deduci faciat. Item eciam curia sapit naturam curie baronis vel regis, que habetur in aliquo suorum maneriorum, ubi vicecomes non est nisi ballivus et firmarius regis, ubi iudicia per sectatores erunt prolata qui sine vicecomite cum perperam iudicaverint puniantur." The translation used is in part my own.

judgments; this passage is a statement that the suitors (following general legal theory and not the de facto constitutional situation) rendered judgment in cases brought by writ.

In the first of the three passages cited, that from *Glanvill*, two kinds of writs are mentioned in which the sheriff would determine the case. In the first, the writ directed the sheriff to justice someone. In Glanvill's time, such a writ could only have been the writ of customs and services or the writ for restoration of chattels; the other *justicies* writs did not yet exist. The second kind of writ was, despite some confusion in the wording, the writs patent which were directed to a lord but ended with a clause specifying that the sheriff would do full right to the demandant if the lord did not. In neither case is the sheriff indicated to be in a stronger position than in the other. There has never been any suggestion, however, that the sheriff rendered judgments when the suit was removed into the county court by tolt; there are too many examples which show that the judgments were rendered by the county judges as usual. Moreover, it is well known that the amercement for a false judgment on a writ of right was levied from the suitors. But if this is so, then the same should be able to be maintained for the *justicies* writs Glanvill was concerned with; he grouped the two situations together. As for the Bracton passage, it must be understood that the sheriff determined the pleas not by his own judgment but by having the county judges render their judgment.

The parsing of text shows that the viscontiel justice theory need not be maintained because of the revered texts of Glanvill, Bracton and Fleta; the examination of particular cases brought by writ will show that the sheriff did not in fact render judgments. Since the viscontiel justice theory would apply equally well to all the classes of viscontiel writs, each class will be examined in turn.

The *facias* writs, although they did demand greater activity from the sheriff, did not transfer the duty of rendering judgments from the county judges to the sheriff. In regard to the *facias* writs of admeasurement, the crucial part of the suit took place on the land in question. The whole county did not meet there, although the sheriff at times summoned one or two hundreds to meet. In 1204 when the sheriff met the two hundreds on the site for an admeasurement, it was the two hundreds that gave him the judgment to proceed with the admeasurement in unusual circumstances; he did not make the decision himself.[39] Nor did the purchase of a writ of admeasurement

[39] *CRR*, 3:142-43.

mean necessarily that there would be an admeasurement. In 1235 in the king's court one Walter Walsh described the procedure in one case in the county court of Berkshire. He and his wife had been defendants, and the plaintiff had presented his writ to the sheriff in a session of the county court alleging that they had surcharged the pasture. The admeasurement did not take place at once. Rather, Walsh and his wife were able to contest the writ; they objected that the plaintiff only held her land in dower and that in such a situation she should not be able to obtain an admeasurement. The county court—wrongly, it seems—adjudged that there should be an admeasurement. The sheriff then executed the admeasurement on the pasture in question by judgment of the county court, with the result being returned into the county court. The county court then judged that there had indeed been a surcharge on the pasture and that Walsh and his wife should recompense the plaintiff 2 marks for damages.[40] There was obviously process before the county court; and the county court, not the sheriff, rendered judgments.

A case from the Warwickshire county court from around 1303 shows similarly that admeasurement cases did not assume mere execution on the land but rather a legal case before the county court. In this case there were several defendants; only one Richard and his wife—they claimed as her dower from her first husband—chose not to grant the admeasurement freely and immediately. The plaintiff therefore counted against the defendants severally. Richard challenged the count three times and the writ once. Two of the challenges to the count are worth noting. He objected that the plaintiff had not specified in the count the precise number of acres of pasture allegedly surcharged. Argument on this point involved comparisons of admeasurement of pasture with the assize of novel disseisin and the *quod permittat* for pasture. He also challenged the use of the words "common of pasture" in the count. His pleader thought the count should have concerned "common pasture"; the difference was not unimportant. Richard's best defense, however, was his challenge to the writ. He explained that that writ was not appropriate for use against them, because, whereas they held only as his wife's dower, the writ supposed them to have greater right in their tenement than they in fact had. The plaintiff's foresight paid off here, because of all the defendants it was probably only Richard and his wife whom he thought guilty of surcharging the pasture. Since there were other defendants who claimed to hold as of right and not as of dower, he

[40] CRR, 15:377.

was able to obtain the admeasurement of all the tenants and users. The other defendants were innocent and unworried, but they were necessarily joined to the action as defendants to gain redress against the doweress.[41] This case was clearly not an extrajudicial admeasurement. Moreover, as in the preceding case, the argument was done within the county court and not on the land, so that the likelihood of the sheriff acting as justice is lessened.

The writ of rightful boundaries also demanded the activity of the sheriff on the land in question, but it did not give the sheriff the power to render judgments. The 1222 instruction to Ireland indicated that in England the writ initiated litigation.[42] A case from 1230 shows the role of the county court. The case first proceeded by delays and essoins until both parties appeared in county court, when they were assigned a day to meet on the land in question. The sheriff, the local hundred court, and the parties then convened on the land; the plaintiff made his claim; and the defendant put himself on the grand assize. The sheriff, however, did not award the grand assize; rather, he adjourned the case back into the county court.[43] He was apparently incompetent on his own authority to rule that the mise was properly made. If the sheriff is to be considered here acting as a justice, he was doing so in no greater sense than did the justices who took juries at *nisi prius*, for they too merely presided and reported back to their court.

Justicies writs delegated no more authority to a sheriff than did the *facias* writs. *Prat v Prat*, a case brought by viscontiel writ of debt in the county court of Nottinghamshire, shows very clearly that the sheriff did not render the judgments. The case was brought by a woman against an executor of her grandfather's will. She claimed 20s from the assignation of her grandfather to which he had given her a right effective on the day and hour she came of full age.[44] When the judgment in the case was alleged to have been false, the sheriff, in an endorsement to one of the writs, noted that he had ordered the suitors and the seneschals of the county who ought and were accus-

[41] Brit. Lib., Add. 31826, f. 268r, v [S.S.], see also f. 235v.

[42] Above, at n. 32.

[43] *CRR*, 14:115-16.

[44] CP. 52 morrow All Souls, 27 Edward I: "quidam Adam Prat avus predicte Isabelle in festo Pentecostes anno regni regis Henrici . . . liij apud Retford assignasset eidem Isabelle predictos xx s et eos tradidisset quibusdam . . . executoribus testamenti sui solvendos predicte Isabelle quibuscumque die et hora plene etatis fuerit et eos petere voluerit ac predicti [executores] . . . eadem forma tradidissent denarios predictos ad opus predicti Isabelle."

tomed to render judgments of pleas and plaints to make the record.[45]
The sheriff there claimed no authority to render judgments by virtue
of a *justicies* writ, nor, despite what *Fleta* might be taken to indicate,
to bear record. Likewise, in 1300, *Cray v Cockfrydai* illustrates the
same locus of judgment. Juliana Cray claimed that she had lent each
of six defendants specific quantities of wheat of assigned value on 25
March 1297, which they were to pay her on the following 8 September
without any delay. By judgment of the county court of Dorset—the
sheriff was not mentioned—the defendants were found undefended;
Juliana received her £5.6s and also a half mark for damages.[46] In the
justicies writ of debt the judges and not the sheriff rendered judgment.

The same conclusion can almost certainly be made concerning all
other *justicies* writs, but for now proof can only be adduced for the
justicies writ of wardship. In 1287 Richard de Reskemer prosecuted
his case of wardship brought by *justicies* in the county court of Cornwall. He claimed the wardship of Joan Duraunt from Alice de Tinten
on the grounds that Joan's father had held his military tenement from
Richard's father. Alice denied having the custody of Joan in her own
name, but admitted that she had Joan's mother, Mabel. Richard nonetheless traced the sales whereby Joan had come into Alice's possession,
so that the county court adjudged that a jury should be taken. The
jury returned that Alice had possession of Joan and that Richard
should recover the wardship and a half mark in damages.[47] The sheriff
was not singled out as the one who rendered the judgment; it seems
rather that the ordinary county judges did.

While it is thus impossible to hold that *facias* or *justicies* writs in
general conveyed upon the sheriff the authority to render judgments,
Fleta might still lead some to believe that the phrase in the writ of
replevin—*"juste deduci facias"*—still conveyed that power on the
sheriff in that action alone. After all, *Fleta* put special emphasis on
those words, and neither the *justicies* writs nor the *facias* writs of

[45] Above, chapter 5, n. 62.
[46] Below, n. 62.
[47] CP. 52 three weeks Easter, 15 Edward I: ". . . predicta Alicia habuit et habet
custodiam et possessionem predicte Johanne filie et heredis predicti Johannis Duraunt
usque nunc et quod sit verum petit predictus Ricardus quod inquiratur, et predicta
Alicia petit similiter quod inquiratur. Et consideratum est per totum comitatum quod
inquisicio capiatur super premissis. Que quidem inquisicio jurata dicit quod predicta
Alicia habet possessionem et custodiam predicte Johanne et quod predictus Ricardus
habet jus habendi custodiam predicte Johanne, ideo consideratum est per totum comitatum quod predictus Ricardus recuperet custodiam predicte Johanne et dampna sua
que taxantur ad dimidiam marcam et quod predicta Alicia sit in misericordia pro iniusta
detencione predicte heredis" [S.S.].

rightful boundaries and admeasurement—the instances in which we have been able to cite cases—contain these words. Regrettably, proof here must be indirect. I have not seen any case of replevin brought by writ and determined in the county court that specifically mentioned judgments being made by the county court, but neither have I seen any in which the sheriff was specified as the one who gave the judgments. While the *juste deduci facias* was unique to replevin among the *facias* writs, however, it was an element of the common form of the *audias* writs. Therefore, if it conferred judgment-giving power on the sheriff in replevin, it must also have conferred that power on him in nuisance and trespass.

Formal or statutory arguments will not settle the problem. Even though writs of trespass and nuisance directed the sheriff to hear the case, that would not imply that the sheriff would not determine it by judgment of the county. A similar interpretation may be made of the Statute of Gloucester, which makes the curious statement that sheriffs should plead the pleas of trespass in county as they had been accustomed to do; one must interpret that as meaning that sheriffs should hear the pleas of trespass.[48] Nor was the sheriff judge in such cases because these were wrongs against the sheriff's peace. That argument would be as forceful in plaints as in writs, but in 1287 the county court of Derbyshire rendered judgment in *Wandesleye v Grey*, a plaint of trespass. The county court was also later amerced 40 marks because the judgment was false.[49] Such arguments will thus not determine the locus of judicial power in *audias* writs.

There are only two cases that cast light on the problem, and they would indicate that *juste deduci facias* did not commission the sheriff to render judgments. In one of the county year book reports, in a plea of viscontiel trespass—I take that to mean trespass brought by viscontiel writ—a judgment was asked "from the open county" and was apparently given by Boydin. That case was thus settled by the county judges.[50] Likewise, in a case of nuisance in the Notting-

[48] Statute of Gloucester, c. 8.

[49] CP. 40/73, m. 43: "Et judicium comitatus tale est, quod dictus Ranulphus sit in misericordia eo quod non separavit precium alnearum et fraxinum, desicut idem Ranulphus potuit recuperasse in apprecione fraxinum et quantum ad alneas amisisse, dicunt quod necesse esset quod unum appreciaretur per se et aliud per se. . . . Et predicti quatuor milites modo advocant predictum recordum, in quo reperitur falsum factum esse iudicium. Ideo consideratum est quod predictum iudicium sit falsum. Et totus comitatus in misericordia pro falso iudicio. Et amerciatur per justiciarios ad quadraginta marcas et vicecomes rehabere faciat predicto Ranulpho amerciamentum suum si quod ei solvit occasione predicti iudicii." See also below, chapter 8, n. 57.

[50] Brit. Lib., Add. 31826, fol. 267r [S.S.].

hamshire county court, the sheriff made the identical response concerning suitors and seneschals who were obliged to render judgments in pleas and plaints as he had made in the procedure on the *justicies* writ of debt *Prat v Prat*.[51] In short, there is no evidence that the *juste deduci facias* conferred any authority on the sheriff in *audias* writs other than presiding over the case and seeing to it that the case was determined. It must therefore be concluded that the same formula did nothing more than that in writs of replevin. Sheriffs in the thirteenth and fourteenth centuries thus had no mandate by viscontiel writs to render judgments in cases in the county courts.

A telling addendum to that conclusion comes from the fifteenth century. It has been argued that sheriff's powers declined in the fifteenth century, assuming that they were delegated justices in the thirteenth century and then gradually lost that position. On the contrary, the cases cited for that proposition are good statements not only of the law in the fifteenth century, but also of the law in the thirteenth century. The case in which Littleton explains the effect of *justicies* is a good example:

> *Danby*. In *justicies* the sheriff is judge, not the suitors, for the writ reads "that you justice T etc." and thus is a commission and command to the sheriff who holds the pleas as a justice, and well he may, for the plea is not in open county . . .
>
> *Littleton*. On the contrary, neither in *justicies* nor in any viscontiel action is the sheriff judge, but only the suitors, for he has no court except the county court and can hold no pleas except there—if he does it is *coram non judice*. And thus in replevin the command is *replegiari facias* yet is it held in the county court and the suitors are judges; in a writ of right to the lord *quod plenum rectum teneas etc.*, the suitors are judges; and so here, for the *justicies* has no other effect than to allow him to hold pleas involving more than 40s.[52]

Bracton, Fleta, and Glanvill would have agreed with Littleton. Viscontiel writs initiated county pleas, to be determined by the sheriff

[51] CP. 52 octave Trinity, 27 Edward I [S.S.].

[52] Translated by Thorne, "Notes on Courts of Record," p. 357 (Y.B., 39 Henry VI, Mich. 5); he also cites Y.B., 7 Edward IV, Hil. 27, such that when Moyle maintained that a writ of error would lie in a case brought by writ of right in a lesser court as it would, so he thought, for a *justicies*, Prisot denied it: "in neither case would a writ of error lie but only false judgment, for the suitors and not the bailiff are judges. *Moyle*. If the plea is held in the county by plaint then the suitors are judges, but if it is held by writ, as *justicies*, the sheriff is judge. *Quod fuit negatum*." It is completely possible, of course, that Danby and Moyle knew more of county procedure in their own day and that sheriffs actually were rendering judgments by that time, but on this we have no evidence.

by judgment of the county judges. Litigants, therefore, would not have purchased viscontiel writs nor would the king have provided viscontiel writs to make the sheriff judge in the case. Both the *manu-militari* and the viscontiel justice theory have thus been shown to be incorrect explanations for the provision of the *justicies* writs.

The Reasonable Proof Theory of Justicies *Writs.* The reason why *justicies* writs were originally provided was to make available in lower courts a better procedure than was available by custom. That better procedure is related to the clause of reasonable proof which is common form in the *justicies* writs: "as he shall reasonably be able to show" (*sicut racionabiliter monstrare poterit*). Investigation of the meaning of the clause must begin with the meaning to be given "*racionabilis*" and "*racionabiliter*" in the early years of the thirteenth century, then deal with the meaning of "*racionabilis monstracio*" and "*racionabiliter monstrare*," and finally determine the way in which that clause determined the procedure to be used in the *justicies* writs. I shall maintain that the *justicies* writ made available to the plaintiff a procedure that made written proof of an obligation or right the focal point of the suit.

One cannot argue that "*racionabilis*" and "*racionabiliter*" must be translated as "rational" and "rationally" with the implication that written documents were the sole means of "rational" proof. Even considering the forms of the writs, one must find that a weak argument. Writs referred to *racionabilis* dower, *racionabilis* portion of land, *racionabilis* boundary. In none of these writs was there a requirement of a deed. Likewise, phrases such as *racionabile* relief,[53] a *racionabile* exchange of land,[54] and *racionabiles* summonses and distraints[55] cannot be taken to mean rational relief, exchange, or summonses or even such things proved by written instruments. It is much better to think of reasonable or rightful dower, portions, boundaries, relief, exchange, or summonses. In the same way, when a lord tallaged his men *racionabiliter*,[56] or a sheriff delivered two virgates of land *racionabiliter*,[57] or a litigant removed the jurors whom he was able to remove *racionabiliter*,[58] one cannot think necessarily of written instruments or rationality, but rather of actions done rea-

[53] *CRR*, 1:86.
[54] *CRR*, 1:62, 81, 123, 298, 299.
[55] *CRR*, 1:58.
[56] *CRR*, 1:216.
[57] *CRR*, 1:329.
[58] *CRR*, 1:376.

sonably or rightfully. If the clause in the *justicies* writ indicates some procedure involving written documents, then, that relationship cannot be derived solely from a translation of *"racionabiliter."*

There was, however, a common usage of *"racionabiliter"* closely related to written documents that would make that relationship at least plausible. Moreover, once the word was removed from the writ transferring a case from the Bench into the court *coram rege*,[59] that usage was the most common. *"Racionabiliter"* here was used in the clause "as his deed *racionabiliter* attests," so that it was clearly associated with a written instrument.[60] In this context one must still speak of the deed reasonably or rightfully attesting. But nothing else but a deed or charter is said *testificare racionabiliter*. This does little to prove what *"racionabiliter monstrare"* meant, but it does lend color to the argument that follows.

The main interest of our inquiry is the meaning of the *"racionabiliter monstrare"* at the beginning of the thirteenth century, but the inquiry must begin rather in the late thirteenth century, when it meant proof by some written instrument or tally. The utility of a written instrument then—although not the meaning of the vital words—can best be seen by the typical procedure in *Blumvylle v Haghe*, a rather complicated case which came before the county court of Norfolk in 1292. Plaintiff claimed 10 marks from defendant as the result of an involved transaction. A vendor had sold 30 marks worth of oats to plaintiff's father, who had made a recognition of the resulting debt in chancery. That recognition purported to bind not only the original debtor, but also his heirs instead of his executors. Plaintiff, in repayment of his father's debt, had made one payment of 10 marks to the vendor's bailiff, who was the present defendant. Defendant had given plaintiff a letter patent acknowledging the payment, but thereafter had failed to deliver the money to his lord, the vendor, who soon died. The vendor's executors, therefore, acted on the recognition made in chancery, levying the 10 marks from plaintiff's goods and chattels by *scire facias*. Plaintiff was now trying to regain his 10 marks from defendant by bringing his *justicies* writ of debt in the county court. In court, Blumvylle, the plaintiff, meticulously explained the situation. Haghe's first step in his defense was, for us, the most important one: he asked if Blumvylle had any proof of the

---

[59] For the use of *racionabiliter* in that writ, see *CRR*, 1:443, 462; 2:15, 94. The first reference I have seen which would indicate the change is *CRR*, 5:79 (and 321).

[60] *CRR*, 4:156; 6:343; 7:72; 8:7; *Rotuli de Oblatis*, pp. 6, 13, 32, 42, 74, 146, 237, 238, 245, 317, 326, 335, 344, 360, 364, 386, 432, 437, 441, 442.

debt. Blumvylle produced the letter patent. Thereafter, according to standard rules applied both in county courts and in the king's court, Haghe could not simply wage his law—offer compurgation—as he could have done had Blumvylle only been able to produce suit, that is, two men who would attest the debt. Haghe therefore acknowledged the letter patent as his own—he could alternatively have tried to prove it was a forgery—but argued that the executors had not levied the money from Blumvylle because of his default, that he had indeed paid in the 10 marks to his lord. The question therefore went to a jury.[61] The primary point here was the presentation of the letter patent. A plaintiff in possession of such good prima facie proof was entitled to exact a more rigorous method of trial than compurgation. One would have liked to have seen the defendant obliged to counter the letter patent with a receipt from the bailiff's lord. Here, however, that more rigorous method of proof was the trial by jury. It is clear, therefore, that debts were claimed on the basis of written instruments in the county courts, at least at times by *justicies* writs, and that the procedure that ensued was advantageous to the plaintiff.

The words *"racionabiliter monstrare"* referred to the evidence that the plaintiff had as this kind of prima facie proof of the obligation or right. This is made clear in *Cray v Cockfrydai*, a case from Dorset county court in 1298 already mentioned briefly above. When Cray finished her count to recover the money promised for the loan of wheat to the defendants, they asked if she had anything of a reasonable showing—*"de racionabile demonstracione"*—to present concerning the debt. Cray said she only had good suit and offered to have it examined at her peril. The defendants objected to this offer in these words:

> The abovesaid Juliana sought against them the abovesaid debts by the writ of the lord king *'sicut racionabiliter monstrare poterit etc.'* [as in the *justicies* writ] and because the abovesaid Juliana has no writing nor other reasonable proof, they ask judgment if they ought to answer her simple suit.

The county court ruled that they should have accepted her offer and judged them undefended.[62] Their defense, however, had not been

---

[61] CP. 40/100, m. 31d. See *CCR, 1272-1279*, p. 342.

[62] CP. 52 octave Michaelmas, 26 Edward I: ". . . Et predicti Walterus et alii veniunt et defendunt vim etc., quando et petunt si quid de racionabili demonstracione habeat pro se quod eis ostendatur. Et predicta Juliana dicit quod habet sectam bonam quam periculo suo petit examinari. Et predicti Walterus et alii dicunt quod predicta Juliana petit versus eosdem debita predicta per breve domini regis 'sicut racionabiliter monstrare poterit' etc. Et quia predicta Juliana nullum habet scriptum nec aliquam raciona-

flippant; they were so confident of their stand that they sued out a writ of false judgment, initiating a case which unfortunately was never terminated by judgment.[63] Their defense was rejected because it had recently become outmoded law. The new 40s rule, treated later, had resulted in the demand that all claims of debt in such lower courts involving 40s or more be brought by writ, whether or not the plaintiff had written proof.[64] The defendants had taken a strong stand on good old law, only recently destroyed. The case clearly refers to a writing as a *racionabilis demonstracio*; the implication that other things could be similarly labelled must be interpreted in line with what we know concerning usage of the phrase, so that we might consider a sealed tally or court record as possibly included. In short, both the argument and the result is what would be expected if originally the clause of reasonable proof meant that the plaintiff had a written document, or at least something nearly equivalent.

Another case equating reasonable proof with proof better than suit is *Lakinghith v Mortlake*, already examined in some detail above. The case was brought in the county court of Cambridgeshire, and the defendant first challenged the tally presented by the plaintiff as a forgery so that a jury was summoned and the tally was put into the keeping of the sheriff. He then purchased a *pone*, removing the case into the king's court while leaving the tally in the possession of the sheriff. That, of course, stripped the plaintiff of the evidence by which he could force the defendant to put himself on a jury instead of compurgation. In the court of common pleas before Mettingham, C. J., Lakinghith explained the situation in detail, complaining that the *pone* had deprived him of his reasonable showing of the debt, his "*racionabilis monstracio*." The wrong, fortunately, was righted.[65] Once again, however, there had been an association between the *justicies* writ's clause of reasonable proof and the plaintiff's possession of proof higher than suit.

Merchant courts did not utilize writs for the prosecution of debts;

bilem demonstracionem petunt iudicium si ad simplicem sectam suam debet respondere. Et predicta Juliana dicit quod habet bonam sectam quam adhuc petit examinari, contra quam sectam se defendisse potuerunt per legem suam quam quidem legem facere recusaverunt; unde predicta Juliana de ipsis petit iudicium tanquam indefensis. Per quod consideratum fuit per comitatum quod predicti Walterus et alii sunt indefensi et quod predicta Juliana recuperet versus eos debita predicta una cum dampnis suis que taxantur ad dimidiam marcam. Et quod predicti Walterus et alii essent in misericordia pro iniusta detencione."

[63] Ibid.; CP. 40/125, m. 71d; CP. 40/126, m. 37d; CP. 40/130, m. 287; CP. 40/133, m. 33d; CP. 40/136, m. 105d; CP. 40/139, m. 16d.

[64] Below, chapter 8 at n. 91.

[65] Above, chapter 6 at n. 85.

but *Stavere v Scot*, in the court of King's Lynn, shows that that terminology was familiar outside the county courts. In 1293 Simon de Stavere claimed £10 with 20s damages from Adam Scot in that court by the law merchant. The debt had been incurred, apparently, by a simple loan. Scot immediately asked what Stavere had to hold him to the debt, and Stavere put forward a writing. Scot neither acknowledged nor denied the deed; rather he claimed that he should not be made to answer, because he was then prosecuting Stavere in Norfolk county court by a *justicies* writ for the detention of an obligatory deed for £10. Stavere rejected this move by claiming the merchants' right not to be prosecuted outside King's Lynn except for forinsec tenures; moreover, Scot would not assert positively that the deed Stavere had presented was the same deed for which Scot had brought his *justicies* writ of detinue of charters in county court. The court therefore ruled that, since Stavere according to the law merchant had reasonably shown—"*racionabiliter monstravit*"—by that deed that Scot owed him the money and since Scot refused to commit himself to a defense, Stavere should recover both the debt and his damages.[66] Once again, the plaintiff's presentation of written proof was equated with a reasonable showing, a *racionabilis monstracio*.

A fourth case also calls a deed a reasonable showing, and this time the words come from a justice. Alan de Sutton claimed seven quarters of wheat from a prior in the court of common pleas; it seems that it was a case brought by *justicies* in county upon which a *pone* had been purchased to remove it. After his count he proffered a deed, of which the prior had *oyer*. The deed specified that the wheat was owed for a loan that had been made, a point concerning which Alan's count had made no mention. The prior's pleader therefore demanded judgment because of the variance between the plaintiff's count and his "*renable demunstrance*." Bereford, J., went even beyond the defendant's request: "Even if his count were in accord with his *renable demunstrance*, he would have had no advantage, because his writing sounds in usury."[67] The plaintiff's reasonable proof was clearly the deed he proffered.

---

[66] CP. 40/105, m. 124d: "Et quia Simon secundum legem mercatoriam per illud scriptum racionabiliter monstravit quod predictus Adam tenetur ei in debito predicto per factum ipsius Ade quod predictus Adam non dedicit seu dedicere potuit nec ulterius voluit respondere, ideo consideratum est quod predictus Simon recuperet debitum suum predictum decem librarum et dampna sua predicta versus predictum Adam. Et predictus Adam in misericordia etc."

[67] Brit. Lib., Add. 31826, f. 102b: "*Hampton*. E demandom iugement de la variance entre sun cunte e sa renable demunstrance. *Bereford*. Tut ust sun cunte este acordant

Around 1290, at least, "*racionabilis monstracio*" had a fairly precise meaning. We have found those words used—except in the writs themselves—only four times, all four times in cases of debt. In three of the cases the phrase was explicitly used in reference to a written deed. The fourth time it was in reference to a tally, which, if written upon and sealed, would be the equivalent of a written deed. No other usage of the words has been found. That usage, at least in debt, broke down in the 1290s because of the aftereffects of the 40s rule, so that what these references show are the last few instances in which the usage was correct in debt/detinue. Since, however, debt/detinue was the most frequently used *justicies* writ, that development may have soon voided the original meaning of the phrase in general—although rules concerning the necessity of a writing in an individual action could well survive without being connected any longer to the phrase. What is at issue here, though, is the degree to which this usage in 1290 can be extended back to explain the reasons behind the original provision of the *justicies* writs.

Justicies debt in the 1290s provides the hypothesis that "*racionabilis monstracio*" indicated the plaintiff's ability to proffer written proof; *justicies* covenant is the action which will provide reasons for believing that that was the original meaning behind the clause of reasonable proof. Legal historians' main interest in covenant has stemmed from the fact that it was concerned only with agreements which could be proved by a deed under seal, so that the action of covenant never developed into a comprehensive action for dealing with contracts. The modern law of contracts grew up rather around the trespass-based action of *assumpsit*. The specialty rule has been ascribed either to a desire to limit the jurisdiction of the king's court or to a general principle that rights not provided by the common law had to be proved by specialty or, alternatively, that reliance on suit was to be discouraged. These explanations are all admittedly hypothetical. Furthermore, they rest on the assumption that the important events occurred in the reigns of Edward I and Edward II, while admitting that there had been some substantial feeling toward requiring specialty at an earlier time. No one has regarded the problem as possibly related to the form of the writ; A.W.B. Simpson, indeed, is little concerned with the thirteenth century in his treatment of the history of the law of contracts and devotes little effort to discovering why

---

a sa renable demunstrance il nust point eu avantage par ceo qe sun escrist soune en usure."

covenant was restricted to agreements supported by specialty.[68] The possible relation of the rule to the form of the writ, however, must be one of the first possibilities in any consideration of covenant; the part of the form particularly relevant here is the clause of reasonable proof. Investigation of that clause in covenant will eventually take us back into the early thirteenth century.

There were two forms of the writ of covenant. There was a returnable *precipe* form which initiated litigation in the king's court and a viscontiel *justicies* form which initiated litigation in the county courts. To illustrate the difference in form, the two writs are translated in parallel below:

Precipe Form	*Justicies* Form
The king to the sheriff, greeting. Command B. that justly and without delay he keep with A. the covenant made between them about one messuage with appurtenances in N. And if he does not and the said A. shall have given you security for prosecuting his claim, then summon by good summoners the aforesaid B. to be before our justices at Westminster on such a day to show why he does not. And have there the summoners and this writ. Witness etc.	The king to the sheriff, greeting. We command you that you justice B. that justly and without delay he keep a covenant made between them about one messuage with appurtenances in N., as he says, as he shall reasonably be able to show that he ought to keep with him, that we may not further hear outcry thereof for want of justice. Witness etc.

Both writs order the defendant to keep to his covenant. The only differences in the writs are those clearly pertaining to the different venue and the absence of the clause of reasonable proof in the *precipe* form. That absence will be shown to be important.

The very early history of covenant is difficult to discern. Glanvill does not have a writ of covenant, whether *justicies* or *precipe*. I do not know when the *precipe* writ of covenant took its final form. I do

---

[68] A.W.B. Simpson, *A History of the Common Law of Contract* (Oxford, 1975), pp. 10-13: a summary of various theories.

doubt, however, that there ever was a writ of covenant trespassory in nature, the existence of which has been inferred from entries which mention a plea concerning why B. does not hold to his covenant with A. Such pleas were begun by *precipe* in the standard form, the entry being only a reference to the final portion of the writ rather than to the central portion.[69] We shall not, therefore, have to worry about strange forms of covenant writs early in the thirteenth century.

It seems that there were standardized writs of covenant by around 1200. As early as the 1160s there was a viscontiel writ of covenant, but it was in *facias* form and probably not standardized.[70] The *precipe* writ of covenant was probably standardized by 1200, but this cannot be proven. The origins of the *justicies* writ of covenant proper may go back to 1202 with the mention of a payment so that a covenant made *racionabiliter* might be enforced according to the terms of the deed.[71] In 1207 there is a *justicies* writ of covenant in the close rolls, but without the clause of reasonable proof.[72] The first good form of the *justicies* writ of covenant comes in the Irish Register in the 1220s,[73] and that is rather earlier than one can manage for the *precipe* writ, at least for the moment. Despite the difficulty of determining the form of the writ from the sources, however, it is probably safe to assume that both writs were in final form very soon after 1200.

The necessity for specialty cannot be proven, but may be suspected for early covenant. Most of the entries that mention covenant are nothing more than procedure. A great many of those which get beyond procedure concern agreements for which the plaintiff could produce something more substantial than suit: a chirograph, a deed, or a recognition made before justices.[74] This would not be surprising. There seems to have been a close affinity between early covenant and the enforcement of fines. Moreover, early covenant often concerned leases of land, although even by the second decade of the thirteenth century covenant was going beyond such agreements. In matters concerning real property, however, a deed may well have been con-

[69] See *CRR*, 9:147 (compared with 8:316, 9:284, 292); 8:63, 268, 393; 9:149 (compared to 8:29, 9:11, 44, 129, 194).

[70] *Royal Writs*, p. 493 (no. 154).

[71] *PR, 4 John*, p. 126; *PR, 8 John*, p. 207.

[72] *Rotuli Litterarum Clausarum*, 1:83a: a sequel to the controversy concerning the marsh between Croyland and Spalding related in Doris M. Stenton, *English Justice between the Norman Conquest and the Great Charter* (London, 1965), pp. 148-211.

[73] *Early Registers of Writs*, p. 16.

[74] *Rotuli Curiae Regis*, 2:235; *CRR*, 1:104-5, 141, 147, 291; 2:24, 203. *CRR*, 2:24 suggests a relationship between covenant and warranty of charters.

sidered necessary. Nevertheless, that early period must remain a matter merely for hypothesis.

In the 1220s and thereafter it is occasionally possible to ascertain whether specialty was required in individual actions of covenant. In 1225 a defendant widow was able to rebut a covenant by compurgation; since no specialty was mentioned and the trial was by compurgation, it must be assumed that there was no deed.[75] There is nothing to indicate whether the writ that began that suit was a *justicies* writ—which would have had the clause of reasonable proof—or a *precipe* writ. In 1227 Hubert de Burgh in an action of covenant proffered the defendants' deeds; it was said that the deeds *racionabiliter* attested the covenant.[76] In 1234 the parties in a plea of covenant put themselves on the deed, which was supposedly in the custody of the chancellor. Although the plea failed because the deed was not in the custody of the chancellor, the case yields no solid information about the requirement of a deed, only that if a deed was alleged and taken issue upon, it had to be produced eventually.[77] In 1235 a plaintiff's action of covenant was ruled void because he did not have specialty, but perhaps also because the lack of specialty was here particularly serious since the defendant also alleged nontenure.[78] In 1236 the plaintiff in an action of covenant which was clearly begun by *justicies* proffered a chirograph which was very specific about the boundaries between his property and his neighbor's property; the dispute was about some of the land only: that portion which had been under water when the agreement was made.[79] It is important that such a dispute should have been begun by *justicies* in a lower court. Thus far, however, no proof has been able to be advanced concerning the precise stance of the court in regard to the relationship between specialty and the different forms of covenant. What evidence has been adduced, nevertheless, would not conflict with a theory that held specialty necessary in *justicies* but not in *precipe* covenant.

In the 1230s and 1240s specialty was required in the *justicies* writs, but not in the *precipe* writs of covenant; the reason for the differentiation was the clause of reasonable proof in the *justicies* writ. In 1238 the earlier custom of almost transcribing certain writs into the close rolls gave way at least for a brief time; in that year a paraphrase

---

[75] *CRR*, 12: no. 1865 (no. 495).
[76] *CRR*, 13: no. 59.
[77] *CRR*, 15: no. 1073.
[78] *CRR*, 15: no. 1365.
[79] *CRR*, 15: no. 1758.

of a *justicies* writ of covenant appears in the close rolls. The Latin illustrates clearly the degree to which it was a paraphrase:

Mandatum est [instead of *preceptum est*] vicecomiti Devon quod distringat [instead of *justicies*] Bernardum Bereng ad observandum [instead of *quod teneat*] conventionem inter ipsum et Henricum de Trublevill initam de manerio de Bradenech secundum quod in carta inter ipsos super hoc confecta plenius continetur [instead of *sicut racionabiliter monstrare poterit*], ut super hoc pro defectu tui decetero non audiamus querelam [instead of *ne amplius inde clamorem audiamus pro defectu iusticie*]. Teste rege [19 May]

(The sheriff of Devon was ordered to distrain Bernard Bereng to observe the agreement entered into between him and Henry de Trublevill concerning the manor of Bradninch according to that which is contained more fully in the deed made between them on this, so that we may not further hear complaint on this on account of your default.)[80]

This writ is a very strong indication that the clause of reasonable proof indicated that the plaintiff was to proffer a deed in support of his claim.

The same conclusion can be drawn from the different outcomes in two actions of covenant in the Berkshire Eyre of 1248. In both cases the plaintiff had no specialty. The first case had been initiated by a *justicies* writ of covenant and had then been removed into the eyre. That suit was quashed because the plaintiff had nothing to show the covenant except her simple word.[81] In the second case, the suit seems to have been initiated by *precipe*. Here the defendant denied the covenant and was allowed to wage his law; the plaintiff, therefore, had had no specialty.[82] The conclusion from the 1238 writ and the two cases in 1248 is not that judicial opinion was divided on the necessity for specialty in covenant, but that the form of the *justicies* writ demanded specialty, whereas the form of the *precipe* did not.

The requirement of specialty in *justicies* and not in *precipe* covenant is precisely the reverse of what the historian of contract law would have expected. The specialty requirement has been seen as a requirement instituted in the king's court for suits originating there. Its rationale was that it permitted the central court, which operated at a distance from the jury and the locality in which the covenant had

---

[80] *CR, 1237-1242*, p. 130; see also *PR, 10 John*, p. 155 (1208).
[81] *The Roll and Writ File of the Berkshire Eyre of 1248*, ed. M. T. Clanchy, Selden Society, vol. 90 (London, 1973), no. 272.
[82] Ibid., no. 444.

been made, to handle only those cases for which the plaintiff had good prima facie evidence. Merely verbal agreements were thought to have been left to the lower courts, which did indeed entertain litigation for a broad range of agreements. It seems clear, however, that in origin the specialty requirement—in the form of the clause of reasonable proof—pertained only to the *justicies* writ; the justices of the king's court seem not to have been terribly intimidated by the problem of proof presented by merely verbal agreements any more than they were by similar problems in debt.

For this conclusion to be plausible it first must be related to the later history of contracts, then we can return and evaluate its influence on deciphering the intention behind the *justicies* writs as a whole. In the decades around 1310 the specialty requirement was transferred to the *precipe* writ. What happened seems to have been based on the early predominance of the *justicies* writ in actual disputes in covenant. Before 1250 registers of writs did not contain a *precipe* writ of covenant, only a *justicies*. In the 1260s one can find a *precipe* in the register, but it is listed last after three *justicies* writs.[83] *Brevia Placitata*, written about mid-century, contains only the *justicies* writ; significantly, the model defense has the plaintiff forced to show his chirograph.[84] Up until about the reign of Edward I, then, it seems that the *justicies* must have been more prominent in legal thought than the *precipe*; because of the *pone*, of course, the *justicies* writ would have been commonly enough in the king's court. The extension of the requirement was made between 1290 and 1320.[85] The process by which it happened must be related to the concurrent problems with debt, which will be examined in the next chapter; those problems and their solutions destroyed the meaning of the clause of reasonable proof in the *justicies* writ of debt, weakening the relationship between the clause and specialty in legal thought. At the same time, the greater ease in removal of cases on the one hand brought *justicies* covenant even more frequently before the court and on the other hand diminished the reasons for distinguishing between viscontiel and returnable forms of actions. In the confusion, the formal origin of the specialty requirement was buried, while at the same time, since that was the

[83] *Early Registers of Writs*, p. 79.

[84] *Brevia Placitata*, ed. G. J. Turner, Selden Society, vol. 66 (London, 1947), pp. 21-22.

[85] J. H. Baker, *An Introduction to English Legal History* (London, 1979), p. 265, following the traditional interpretation, made 1290-1320 the crucial period, and I have no reason to think that that was not the crucial period in the king's court for the *precipe*.

most frequent situation before the justices, the requirement was preserved as a rule unrelated to the form of the writ. Justice Herle in the Waltham Hay case overtly used evidentiary reasons to strike down a bill of covenant brought without specialty: "A covenant is nothing but an agreement in words between parties, and it cannot be proved except by specialty."[86] Justices, then as now, will find a reason for what seems necessary. What Herle did here was to apply to covenant brought even without writ an old rule which relied on a specific writ form without realizing that it was something therefore quite new and unnecessary. The specialty rule in covenant was thus philosophically grounded in evidence, but historically rooted in a misconception.

The argument concerning the intent behind the provision of the *justicies* writs thus far can here be reviewed. The theory that would make those writs satisfy a need for high-handed debt collection has been dismissed as groundless. The traditional explanation of the writs as a commission to the sheriff which transferred the locus of responsibility for the judgment was shown likewise to be unsound. The explanation was therefore sought in the form of the writs themselves, particularly in the clause of reasonable proof which is part of the common form of the *justicies* writs. It was shown that around 1290 in actions of debt *racionabilis monstracio* was used to refer to specialty. Since earlier entries concerning actions of debt were insufficient to check earlier practice, the action of covenant was used to test the hypothetical relationship between the clause of reasonable proof and the requirement of specialty. It was found that in the 1230s and 1240s *justicies* covenant presupposed specialty, whereas specialty was not required in the *precipe* writ. Moreover, the evidence for covenant in even earlier decades is amenable to the same interpretation. Finally, it has been shown that such a history for covenant in the thirteenth century can be made to fit with the better-known history of covenant in the fourteenth century. Such an interpretation of the clause of reasonable proof would therefore seem possible. I will now proceed to test that interpretation against the best remaining interpretation—one which has not actually been made but which probably eventually would be made—then see if my interpretation is believable in the context of the chronological development of the *justicies* writs, and finally specify what that better procedure was which was thus related to specialty and newly provided by the *justicies* writs.

[86] *The Eyre of London, 14 Edward II (A.D. 1321)*, ed. Helen M. Cam, 2 vols., Selden Society, vols. 85, 86 (London, 1968-1969), 2:286.

The most probable alternative to the hypothesis that the clause of reasonable proof was related to a specialty rule would be that it was an oblique reference to local custom.[87] That argument would be hard to maintain because of all the above evidence, but even on its own terms it could not stand. Writs to sheriffs in the twelfth century were occasionally very precise about proof: the plaintiff was to prove by witnesses, by argument, or by lawful men of the county.[88] The ability of chancery to be precise did not disappear. One could, of course, argue that in changing to common form chancery failed to find a form that would correspond to every situation and so devised the clause of reasonable proof to encompass all such means as were considered appropriate by the lower court. But chancery was very able to refer precisely to customary law. Writs to Ireland often directed that justice be done "according to the law and custom of those parts."[89] Such writs were used also for high liberties in England; in 1206 a writ to the constable of Dover stated very precisely that the defendant was to be "justiced according to the custom of the Cinque Ports."[90] Chancery was thus prepared to refer to custom when it was relevant. Had the clause of reasonable proof been a reference to custom, problems would have arisen concerning the appropriate custom to be applied when the writ was removed into the king's court. No such dispute is reported. Such an interpretation, thus, would be mere assertion.

The specialty interpretation of the clause of reasonable proof is believable in the context of the chronological development of the *justicies* writs; the earliest *justicies* writs concern matters in which it

---

[87] The strongest support for such a suggestion is *Glanvill*, p. 113, where he states explicitly, after giving the form of the writ of customs and services containing the clause, that by that writ the plaintiff "will exact his services in reliefs or in other things according to the custom of the county." I make the following observations: (1) it may be that in Glanvill's time it was a reference to local custom, and the meaning of the phrase was changed around 1200 with the introduction of the new *justicies* writs; (2) the custom referred to may have pertained to other matters (i.e., how to prove the deed if it was challenged; additional procedures used); (3) "custom of the county" may have referred not at all to the procedure or to the deed here, but rather to the nature of the "other things" which could be claimed as service; (4) *Glanvill*, p. 83, might lead to a very much more trenchant conclusion in that it might be taken to indicate that reasonable proof would be by "law-worthy men of the neighborhood and by their oath." It is thus difficult to take *Glanvill*, p. 113, as a clear indication of the interpretation of the clause of reasonable proof.

[88] *Royal Writs*, no. 135, 149, 151.

[89] *Rotuli Litterarum Clausarum*, 1:219b; *Early Registers of Writs*, p. 17.

[90] *Rotuli de Oblatis*, p. 358. *CR, 1231-1234*, pp. 233 (Rutland), 239 (Wales), 278 (Ireland). *Rotuli Litterarum Clausarum*, 1:24a has a *justicies* that mentions specifically that acquittance of the debt is to be made "*secundum consuetudinem regni.*"

would have been reasonable to require written proof and which were unlikely to be left to local custom. The writ of customs and services was utilized originally for lords not sufficiently powerful to justice their tenants, most likely, then, for lords who did not have a court. A tenancy arrangement not protected by a local court stood the least chance of preserving customary rules; moreover, since there was no curial embodiment of the lord-man relationship, it was the situation in which specialty would most likely be required, particularly since Glanvill's form of the writ is only in the *debet*.[91] The writ for the restoration of chattels after an assize concerned a subject area closely regulated by the common law and not at all likely to be given over to customary settlement. The chattels were presumed to have been seised into the king's hand by the sheriff and so held, and the plaintiff was able to have his original judgment framed with an order to the sheriff to restore to him the chattels. If the sheriff did not do so, the writ for restoration of chattels was available. A copy of the judgment—or the writ ordering the sheriff to restore the plaintiff to his lands and chattels originally—was probably required as proof.[92] The third of Glanvill's writs to contain the clause was the *facias* writ for upholding a division made by a will. The clause of reasonable proof there demanded proof that the testator had made the will and that the will should stand. At the very least the plaintiff would need the will or a certified copy of it; preferably he would have the documents from the ecclesiastical court concerning probate. In Glanvill's time, therefore, no difficulty is produced by reading the clause of reasonable proof as an indication that the plaintiff could produce specialty.

Chronologically, the next group of writs to contain the clause consisted of the writs of debt/detinue, covenant, and wardship. These apparently developed in the first half of John's reign. The origins of debt/detinue and covenant have already been discussed. The *justicies* writ of wardship seems to have been provided at least by 1206.[93] By that time, however, there was probably also a *precipe* writ of wardship; there was certainly a *precipe* by 1214.[94] The first fully developed *justicies* writ of wardship I have found is a 1218 writ for wardship of the lands of a socage tenant.[95] For debt/detinue and covenant, the first two writs of this chronological group, it is not at all inconceivable

---

[91] *Glanvill*, p. 113.
[92] Ibid., p. 170.
[93] *Rotuli de Oblatis*, p. 359; *PR, 8 John*, p. 32.
[94] *Rotuli de Oblatis*, p. 536.
[95] *Rotuli Litterarum Clausarum*, 1:39.

that specialty could have been required. An origin prior to John's reign would have made such a requirement hard to believe, but by 1200 transactions involving real property or significant obligations were being made more frequently with written evidence, although it is possible that here we are confusing cause and effect. The writ of wardship might seem difficult to reconcile with a specialty requirement at first, but there is an analogy with customs and services on the one hand and, on the other hand, a real need for a subsidiary lord to establish claim to wardship over land in situations in which the lord-tenant relationship might not be strong. One could hypothesize an even more cogent reason by supposing the situation in which a lord had sold the wardship to another and then had not delivered over the ward. Such a situation would be analogous to covenant, and the plaintiff would stand in great need of further proof. As for the first group of writs, a specialty requirement would present no particular conceptual difficulty.

The next set of *justicies* writs probably also coexisted with *precipe* forms which did not appear in the early registers; it is with this set of writs that the first problem with the clause of reasonable proof appears. The group consists of mesne, detinue of charters, and account. A *precipe* (returnable) writ of mesne appears as early as 1205;[96] references to the *justicies* form, however, can only be found in 1225, 1229, and 1230,[97] but by then the form can already be discovered in the Irish Register of 1227.[98] The *precipe* for detinue of charters can be shown in 1214,[99] but the *justicies* form cannot be proven before 1226.[100] The writ of account is even more difficult to date. The *justicies*—or, at least, a viscontiel—form is referred to in 1225, 1227, and 1237.[101] A new writ of account ordering attachment was provided for the lower courts in 1260.[102] Then, in 1263, the close rolls contain a writ of account according to the law merchant, a *justicies* writ directed to the sheriff of Kent.[103] I cannot precisely date the *precipe*; but when account appears in the registers in the 1260s, it is the *precipe* and not the viscontiel *justicies* form which seems the more important. These three *justicies* writs can thus be dated no earlier than the mid-1220s.

[96] *Rotuli de Oblatis*, pp. 323, 327.
[97] *Rotuli Litterarum Clausarum*, 2:83b; *CR, 1227-1231*, pp. 278, 351.
[98] *Early Registers of Writs*, p. 15 (no. 47).
[99] *Rotuli de Oblatis*, pp. 536, 538.
[100] *Rotuli Litterarum Clausarum*, 2:149, 150.
[101] Ibid., 2:83b, 149; *CR, 1234-1237*, p. 517; see *Royal Writs*, p. 478.
[102] *CR, 1259-1261*, p. 162.
[103] *CR, 1261-1264*, pp. 306-7.

Any requirement of specialty in these writs would not be difficult to imagine for mesne or for account, but there would be some problem with detinue of charters. In the writ of account it might well be expected that the plaintiff would have some evidence that the defendant actually was his bailiff; otherwise, the plaintiff might simply have to resort to claiming a debt. In the writ of mesne, the plaintiff's possession of specialty was even more likely; indeed, in *Brevia Placitata* the typical defendant requires the plaintiff to produce his specialty.[104] It would seem odd, however, to require plaintiffs in detinue of charters to have some specialty. It was specialty for which they were suing. *Brevia Placitata* seems to presume that the plaintiff would not have specialty; the defendant there demands that the plaintiff's suit be examined.[105] It is possible, of course, that the *justicies* was first provided here for that very limited class of plaintiffs who could document their bailment of specialty, but that conclusion will be unlikely until it is shown that a substantial number of people did obtain written acknowledgement of such a bailment. A more suitable explanation is that detinue of charters was an exception pure and simple. That would be understandable, because the case was at least concerned with specialty, and the clause of reasonable proof could easily have been retained as mere form as detinue of charters developed out of detinue. Such an explanation rests on an evaluation of how early detinue of charters was, and it can be maintained that the forms of the writs were already sufficiently set in the 1220s for such formal extensions to have been made. Whatever the proper explanation, that exception would not appear to raise any substantial barrier to our interpretation of the clause of reasonable proof.

This kind of examination could be drawn out, but need not be. The mid-century *justicies* writs—mainly those for enforcing rights on another's free tenement—are clearly conformable to this interpretation. While there would be many people who would claim a right to water their sheep on another's property, for instance, it is not inconceivable that only those who could proffer specialty would be allowed to use the writ. Everyone else would have to proceed in some other way, perhaps by instigating a replevin situation, perhaps by accusing the other of a wrong. Thus far, then, it has been shown that the clause of reasonable proof was in fact closely related to the plaintiff's possession of specialty and that that interpretation is not unbelievable given the chronological development of the *justicies* writs.

---

[104] *Brevia Placitata*, p. 17.
[105] Ibid., pp. 19-20.

We can now focus on the vital problem of ascertaining why the *justices* writs were provided, given that they were somehow related to specialty.

It is clear that the *justices* writs were not provided primarily to give jurisdiction to the county courts. Delegation of jurisdiction, of course, may have been a secondary reason for the provision of some writs, such as the writ of customs and services. There a writ may have been necessary to bring the dispute into the county court rather than into the seignorial court. The writ actually provided for that purpose, however, need not have been in *justices* form with the clause of reasonable proof. That clause indicates a more specific intention than mere delegation of jurisdiction. A similar point can be made with debt. One could argue from *Glanvill* that some form of writ was required to give the county court jurisdiction over such cases, because they were pleas that pertained to "the crown and dignity of the lord king";[106] but it seems very improbable that the county courts had a particularly restricted jurisdiction over such matters. Even were some form of writ necessary, however, once again it need not have been drawn up with the clause of reasonable proof. Although *justices* writs did, of course, at times delegate jurisdiction, that was not their primary function nor the reason for their provision.

Justices writs were, rather, provided to grant a better procedure than that which was available in county court by customary law. Unless one supposes that the king's court maintained exclusive jurisdiction over the broad range of situations covered by *justices* writs or that that range of situations had no remedy at law before the *justices* writs, the provision of better procedure is the only possible reason available. The particular superior procedure it provided must rest in part on assumptions made concerning customary procedure in county courts in cases such as debt brought by plaint in the last part of the twelfth century and specifically concerning the consequences that would follow from the proffer of specialty. Glanvill states uncompromisingly the doctrine of the king's court: the defendant would have to answer to the specialty and would not be allowed merely to deny the debt.[107] That was not a necessary legal conclusion; the legal consequences of a proffer of specialty may have been different by customary law. There specialty may only have served as a fortification of the plaintiff's case; the consequences may have been nothing more

---

[106] *Glanvill*, p.116.
[107] Ibid., p. 127.

than a requisite increase in the number of the defendant's compurgators. If there was any such difference between customary procedure
and the procedure described in *Glanvill* for the king's court, his description merits more careful attention. For Glanvill, the plaintiff's
production of a deed not only forces the defendant to answer to the
deed, it also gives the plaintiff the right to prove the deed, either by
production of identical seals acknowledged by the defendant or by
battle, preferably by one of the witnesses named in the deed.[108] Such
an aggressive posture being granted to the plaintiff in the county
court would explain the active role ascribed to the plaintiff by the
clause of reasonable proof. The reason the litigant would want a
justicies writ, at the very first, was to obtain that procedural advantage: the right to make the defendant reply specifically to the specialty,
which the plaintiff himself was able to prove valid. The *justicies* writs
would thus be an extension of the common law, not a submission of
cases to whatever customary law the county court might follow.

There is another side to the question involving the reasoning behind
the *justicies* writs. The writs did extend to the county courts the
practice of the king's court in regard to specialty. It must be asked if
this was considered a heavy burden on the county courts: whether
this was considered a legally complicated situation. The answer must
be that this royal procedure was considered very simple. In discussing
the practice of the king's court, Glanvill clearly thought that the
proffer of specialty was tantamount to a conclusion of the case. In
the unlikely event that the specialty was challenged, it could be taken
care of rather easily. Proof after specialty was mere detail. There is
here some reason to draw a parallel also with the possibility that the
justicies writs were modeled after the early writs used for Jews, where
the central fact was the chirograph. Finally, while the *manu-militari*
theory of *justicies* writs was rejected, it does state accurately the
peremptoriness of the tone of the writs. The proffer of specialty was
seen as so definitive a proof in the new procedure that the litigation
was not expected to be complicated or prolonged. That expectation
was overly optimistic: the provision of the *justicies* writs rapidly
placed the burden of a more sophisticated law on the county courts.

The Jury Rationale of the Viscontiel Writs. There is some connection between the viscontiel writs and the introduction of trial by
jury into the county courts. It does seem improbable that the granting

---

[108] Ibid., p. 127.

of jury trial was the original reason behind the *justicies* writs or behind the viscontiel writs as a whole. It would be very difficult, for instance, to frame an argument that equated *"racionabilis monstracio"* with proof by jury. But if that was not the original rationale for the writs, it may have been the reason for the provision of individual writs, and it certainly was the reason why many litigants purchased viscontiel writs.

Little is known about the use of trial by jury in the county courts. The investigation, however, would seem to have to be guided by two principles. On the one hand, one cannot extrapolate from the usages of manorial courts to the usages of county courts. On the other hand, one must be guided by the actual evidence, and that evidence is extraordinarily sparse before the end of the thirteenth century. The following sketch is therefore less than might be desired, but it is as much as can be warranted.

The use of the jury may have been introduced into the county courts as a normal method of trial by the viscontiel writs. By the 1290s it can be shown that suits of replevin begun by plaint were being settled by jury verdict.[109] Suits begun by writ were regularly so decided, and it was commonly believed that only a writ gave the sheriff the authority to force a jury to render a verdict.[110] The implication, of course, might be that only the forcing was untoward, that willing juries could render verdicts lawfully. As early as 1246 there was concern that plaints of replevin were being settled by jury verdict.[111] While that concern, if we judge by the practice in the reign

[109] CP. 52 quindene Hilary, 17 Edward I (St. Lycio v Seyton) [S.S.]; CP. 52 octave Michaelmas, 20 Edward I (Coppedoc v Barun) [S.S.]; CP. 52 octave Trinity, 21 Edward I (Tyreswell v Deyvil) [S.S.]; C. 47/75/1/27 (26 Edward I: Carpenter v Seyton) [S.S.]; CP. 52 morrow All Souls, 29 Edward I (Mortoft v Creppingge) [S.S.].

[110] Brit. Lib., Add. 31826, fol. 266v [S.S.]: a jury refusing to swear without a writ. There is some problem as to whether the writ of replevin is itself sufficient warrant. CP. 52 quindene Easter, 29 Edward I does have a *pone* in the Warwickshire writs with the *causa* clause "Quia predicti prior, Willelmus, Rogerus . . . in libero tenemento et separali pastura ipsius prioris in Warrewyk in dampno suo ibidem averia predicti Johannis secundum legem et consuetudinem regni nostri asserunt se cepisse et idem in comitatu predicto placitando clamat habere communiam pasture in tenemento predicto ut dicitur, que quidem loquela eo quod tangit liberum tenementum ut predictum est sine brevi nostro terminari non potest." Were this kind of *causa* clause frequent with *pone* writs, it would prove that even the writ of replevin was insufficient and that a regular real action was required. This, however, is the sole instance, and therefore can be treated as a clerical error—which occasionally did happen even in chancery—particularly since removals were becoming so common. See the Provisions of Westminster, c. 18.

[111] *Crown Pleas of the Wiltshire Eyre, 1249*, ed. C.A.F. Meekings, Wiltshire Archaeological and Natural History Society, vol. 16 (Devizes, 1961), p. 31.

of Edward I, failed to stop the use of the jury in plaints, it would at least indicate that the use of the jury was more acceptable when the case was begun by writ. There is no other evidence to indicate how early the jury was utilized in county court as regular procedure.

The county courts were surely very familiar with trial by jury before 1246. Juries were often taken in county court for cases which were being heard in the king's court, and the eyres made frequent use of the jury.[112] The crucial development with regard to the use of the jury in the county court was probably directly related to the abandonment of Glanvill's ideas on the trial of allegations of forgery. Early in the thirteenth century, the settled method of proof of specialty in the king's court was neither battle nor the production of other seals, but the verdict of a jury which preferably contained the witnesses named in the deed. This kind of proof by jury could conceivably have been envisaged from the first with the writs of covenant and debt in the county courts, but I would not think it probable. It would, however, be difficult to think that the jury was not in constant use in the county courts in their own litigation by 1218; the jury must have been used to settle cases of nuisance. Furthermore, if indeed the *justicies* writ of detinue of charters contained the clause of reasonable proof as a mere matter of form and, as it were, by inheritance from debt/detinue, the authorization of trial by jury would give some reason to the maintenance of the form in this writ. In short, there is no proof, but it does seem likely that sometime in the first quarter of the thirteenth century viscontiel writs became associated with the utilization of the jury in county litigation. That use constituted a further reason for plaintiff's purchase of a writ; it was also a further extension of the procedures of the common law.

The Pone *as Motivation for the Purchase of Viscontiel Writs.* A good lawyer will always leave as many options open for bettering his situation as possible; the use of a viscontiel writ left the plaintiff with optimal maneuverability. Until 1275 cases brought by plaint were not removeable; only cases brought by writ were susceptible to being removed from county court into the king's court. Since removal by *pone* nullified process and pleading on viscontiel writs, the option to remove gave the plaintiff a way to nullify errors made in pleading. The ability to remove by *pone* was thus one reason why some litigants would purchase a viscontiel writ.

[112] Below, chapter 9, n. 94.

The availability of the *pone*, however, was not a motive for the purchase of most viscontiel writs in the early thirteenth century; it was probably never the predominant reason for the purchase of viscontiel writs. The removal of viscontiel writs does not appear to have been very frequent in the early thirteenth century, with the possible exceptions of the writs of customs and services and of naifty. When the purchase of a *pone* is recorded, it is much more likely to concern a writ of right patent; it may even concern a *pone* to remove a case from one branch of the king's court to another. The *pone* did come to provide, however, the possibility of taking the case out of the county court; and it was available for most if not all viscontiel writs prior to the reign of Edward I. That opportunity was very attractive to some litigants, not only to avoid mistakes in pleadings, but also to guard against the chance that the sheriff or undersheriff might come under the influence of the defendant. The removeability of the viscontiel writ thus constituted a further reason why viscontiel writs were popular.

Viscontiel Writs and the Common Law

The relationship of the viscontiel writs to the common law was very significant; in handling viscontiel writs the county courts were acting as courts of the common law. That conclusion may be very unusual, but it is the only conclusion conformable to the facts. The writ of false judgment alone would seem to indicate that much. More-over, the most important of the early viscontiel writs were provided during the years when justices frequently acted also as sheriffs. It is unlikely that the justices, in those years in which the writs were newly provided and in which the county courts could not refer to a custom, would have allowed each county to improvise. The dislike of the justices as sheriffs could have derived partially from such imposition of procedure.

The groundwork for the viscontiel writs was completed in the reign of Henry II. The two innovations necessary to make the viscontiel writs function as a part of the common law were taken before 1189. The first was the provision of standardized viscontiel writs. As long as viscontiel writs were not standardized, they would have little impact on normal procedure and would tend to work according to customary law whenever possible. Standardized form, however, implies some standard content. That standard content was the second great innovation. In the standardized common form of the *justicies* writs there was embedded the concept that the writ was part of royal law. That decision dictated that the procedure followed in *justicies* writs would change in accordance with the law practiced in the king's court. Thus, in addition to the force of specialty, the county soon gained also trial by jury. The work was begun in the reign of Henry II. It was probably largely finished in the reign of John. It was then that the important writs of debt/detinue and covenant were provided, and it was probably also then that the jury was added to viscontiel procedure.

The viscontiel writs, by and large, reinforced the common law. While in the future the association of covenant with specialty handicapped the enforcement of contracts in the king's court, the viscontiel writs made better procedure available to a much larger number of people than the king's court could then have accommodated. The viscontiel writs were admittedly only a part, but they were indeed a part, of the reason why the common law by 1215 was perceived to be necessary and beneficial to England as a whole and not just to the king.

8

Personal Actions: The Reign of Edward I

THE REIGN of Edward I was as important for the jurisdiction in personal actions as the reign of Henry II had been for that in real actions. By the late thirteenth century, however, the court system was much different, and jurisdictional changes then appeared as the product of tortuous and technical legal decisions and legal accident. The changes involve the declining popularity of most viscontiel writs, the development of the viscontiel writ of trespass, and the limitations placed on litigation in debt and detinue. These changes were related and provide perhaps the only documentable instance of the complicated and highly technical coordination of the king's court with the lesser courts. In addition, they provide an excellent example of the untoward influence of statutory actions and the close relationship of various kinds of suits in the court of common pleas.

It is a commonplace of legal historians that litigants preferred to bring their cases into the king's court; even the plaintiff in personal actions is held to have had some fatal attraction to Westminster. That attraction is never convincingly explained; indeed, it is normally assumed that that was merely the order of things. On the contrary, however, the lower courts offered distinct advantages to litigants.

Litigation in the county courts was generally accomplished rapidly, at least in comparison to litigation in the king's court. In the court of common pleas, personal litigation might average fourteen months from initial entry to the disappearance of the case from the rolls.[1] In

[1] Taken from cases begun in CP. 40/286-91 from Cornwall and in CP. 40/286-93 from Bedfordshire. Cases were catalogued beginning with CP. 40/284 and continued through CP. 40/302. The average is perhaps a bit low, because some of the cases

Berkshire county court, however, 45 percent of cases were entered on the rolls only once; 25 percent more were entered only twice. Within six and a half months—that is, after only six entries on the rolls—90 percent of cases had been settled. Litigation could, of course, last almost forever; some few cases had been on the rolls for several years. The overwhelmingly dominant picture, however, is one of relatively rapid settlement.[2] The county courts of Bedfordshire and Cornwall both seem somewhat slower than Berkshire,[3] but Oxfordshire—judging from a very badly mutilated roll—may have been somewhat faster.[4] In none of the instances open to examination, however, can it be maintained that the court of common pleas handled litigation more rapidly than the county courts.[5]

The dispatch with which litigation was treated in the county courts derived at least in part from the pressure which could there be put on defendants. A typical case from the court of common pleas, *Buckingham v Randes*, shows that mesne procedure even at its most efficient was fairly weak. Buckingham brought his action of debt in the court of common pleas, claiming £10 from each of four defendants. The defendants were summoned for Trinity term and did not appear; they were then attached to appear the following term and essoined.

---

continued beyond CP. 40/302 and no allowance has been made for that, The sample of 171 cases includes all new cases of debt (fifty cases averaging fifteen months), detinue (five cases averaging eleven months), detinue of charters (ten cases averaging fourteen months), account (seventy-one cases averaging thirteen and a half months), and trespass, rescue, waste, prohibition, and those formed on statute (thirty-six cases averaging twelve months). Replevin cases were not included (twenty-two cases averaging ten months), because removals were often effected merely to produce delay; and when the plaintiff initiated the removal and thereafter did not appear in court to prosecute, the case was dismissed (eleven of the cases had only one entry). Covenant in land was not included for a similar reason; most cases appeared but once and did not represent actual litigation. The time involved was calculated in a manner similar to the calculations for the county rolls. An entry enrolled only once was considered to take no time. Each term was counted as one quarter of a year, so that appearance on five successive terms is counted as persistence for one full year. It should be noted that the difference between debt and trespass is about one term, the difference that theoretically would be lost in debt by beginning with summons instead of attachment.

[2] SC. 2/153/62 [S.S.].

[3] *Rolls from the Office of the Sheriff of Beds. and Bucks.*, ed. G. H. Fowler, Beds. Historical Record Society, Quarto Series, vol. 3 (Bedford, 1929), pp. 55-69; SC. 2/161/74, mm. 1-11 [S.S.].

[4] C. 47/37/19.

[5] The *Summa Magna* (*Radulphi de Hengham Summae*, ed. W. H. Dunham [Cambridge, 1932], p. 9) indicates that litigation in county court is faster: "[comitatus] ubi celerior litis habetur determinatio quam in banco." *Brevia Placitata*, ed. G. J. Turner, Selden Society, vol. 66 (London, 1947), p. 1, indicates that removal hastens a plea, as it would, of course, when the presiding officer was biased. That statement, however, does not need to indicate generally that pleas in county court were dilatory.

The following six return days (one and a quarter years) they were attached and failed to appear, so that their pledges forfeited the amount pledged. Those forfeits amounted to a relatively small sum for each defendant. Term by term and for each defendant the forfeits were (1) 5d, 6d, 10d, 6s. 8d, 5d, 6d (total: 9s. 4d); (2) 5d, 5d, 10d, 20d, 5d, 5d (total: 4s. 2d); (3) 5d, 10d, 12d, 40d, 5d, 6d (total: 6s. 6d); (4) 5d, 6d, 6d, 40d, 5d, 6d (total: 5s. 8d).[6] The pledges were seldom for large amounts, even when the alleged debt was much greater; and the amount pledged did not constantly increase during the process. A modern, of course, would see that the penalties amounted to much less than taking out a similar loan at 5 percent interest and would happily consent to interminable attachments. Nevertheless, such attachments were ordinary in the court of common pleas; they were also effective at least at times.

In the county courts matters were somewhat differently arranged. Since sometime in the reign of Edward I, defendants there were punished less severely for the individual default: 4d or 6d or, in the case of Berkshire county court, at times, 12d. In most counties, however, that penalty would be inflicted thirteen times each year, thus equalling the pressure that was normally applied by the court of common pleas. For the smaller claims which were common in the county in the fourteenth century, the forfeits were comparatively severe; defendants were consequently rather more anxious to appear to defend themselves. That level of pledge, therefore, was a very efficient rate for the prosecution of small debts, and no more inefficient for the prosecution of large debts than the procedure of the court of common pleas. Before and for part of the reign of Edward I, county procedure had been rather more efficient for the prosecution of large debts. Then pledges forfeited more, usually 1s, sometimes as much as 40d or 6s. 8d.[7] That level of forfeiture, coinciding with the fre-

[6] CP. 40/286, m. 61d; CP. 40/288, m. 18; CP. 40/290, m. 47d; CP. 40/292, m. 13; CP. 40/292, m. 324; CP. 40/293, m. 63; CP. 40/294, m. 32; CP. 40/295, m. 22d. The case simply disappears from the rolls. The case is typical in the sense that this level of pledge is typical; many cases were not as successful in obtaining a distraint and pledge every successive return day, so that the forfeitures over the course of a year would amount to even less.

[7] See the accounts in W. A. Morris, *The Early English County Court*, University of California Publications in History, vol. 14, no. 2 (Berkeley, 1926), pp. 197-230. Although few of those entries were for defaults, the fourteenth-century rolls show that the rate of pledge and the rate for amercements and licenses to concord were the same. The few defaults in those early accounts would indicate the same for the thirteenth century. The date for the lowering of the level of amercements and distraints cannot be determined precisely, because of the paucity of surviving sheriff's accounts from the reign of Edward I and the way the few extant accounts record the profits.

quency with which they would have been levied, would have produced a very efficient mesne procedure in handling even substantial debts. The court of common pleas, then, had no advantage over the county courts in the level of pressure that could be brought to bear on defendants in personal actions by forfeitures for defaults.

The only procedural advantages in the king's court in personal actions did not involve pledges at all. In the court of common pleas both *capias* and exigent procedure were available in account and trespass and, later on, in almost all other personal actions. *Capias* amounted to arrest of the defendant so that he could be produced in court. It was most frequently used against bailiffs and against subsidiary defendants who possessed nothing whereby they could be distrained and whose presence was not necessary for successful prosecution of the plea. In the latter case, the sheriff usually ignored the directive. Only in exceptional cases, therefore, would *capias* procedure have lured plaintiffs into the king's court. By 1377, the time of the Berkshire county court rolls, *capias* procedure was even available in county courts when the case had been originated by writ.[8] Exigent procedure may have been somewhat more important for litigants. It allowed a defendant who refused to appear in court to be outlawed after proclamation in four successive sessions of the county court—or five sessions if at the fourth his presence was promised at the fifth.[9] This procedure, denying the outlaw access to the courts until he submitted himself to justice, was usually successful, if only in the long term. Nevertheless, it was not used frequently. Exigent procedure never became available for normal litigation being prosecuted in the county court itself, even though the proclamations and the declaration of outlawry had to be done in the county courts. Exigent and *capias* procedures would thus have constituted an attraction to a few plaintiffs in difficult circumstances, but would not have influenced the jurisdiction in personal actions generally.

The court of common pleas was not even superior to the county courts in methods of trial. The choice between compurgation and jury in a personal plea was not determined by the venue of the case as much as by the proof the plaintiff had to offer. If he had a writing to prove the debt, he could purchase a viscontiel writ or a regular

[8] SC. 2/153/62, m. 1. Michael Dalton, *The Office and Authority of Sheriffs* (London, 1682), p. 163, forbids *capias* for viscontiel debt.

[9] It seems that very soon—perhaps even in the reign of Edward I—it came to be felt that a person was due five proclamations anyway; one gets the impression that a member of the court would often mainpern the defendant simply to allow him the further opportunity to come forward. One indication of this is the few outlawries proclaimed after only four sessions.

returnable writ; in either situation his proffer of the writing would bar the defendant from compurgation. On the other hand, if the plaintiff had no writing, the trial of the case would be by compurgation in the court of common pleas, just as it would be in the county court. In the court of common pleas, of course, the defendant could choose to put himself on a jury instead of waging his law, but that option available for the defendant was not one which would persuade the plaintiff to litigate in the king's court. The court of common pleas would have been attractive to plaintiffs in situations for which no viscontiel writ was available, as in the various forms of trespass before 1278; after 1278, however, the court of common pleas should have been no more attractive even in trespass cases than the county courts, if methods of trial only are being considered. Compurgation was probably not even an obviously poor method of trial in the lower courts. In the court of common pleas, however, ordinary compurgation, as in debt, could well have been suspect even this early, and was certainly considered an easier proof than the jury: Westminster was far away from the local community which provided the social sentiment to reinforce the moral qualms about perjury. In the county and other lower courts, however, a defendant would be less likely to find compurgators who would swear without adequate forethought. The formality of compurgation, moreover, made it more acceptable to the plaintiff, because any hesitation or minor flaw in the oath was sufficient reason for the defendant's proof to fail. Compurgation would remain, reinforced by societal expectations and moral pressure, a sufficient force to bring most litigants to terms even before trial. The court of common pleas was thus not markedly superior, and in compurgation was markedly inferior to the county courts in methods of trial, except in regard to trespass before 1278 and other special actions not available in viscontiel forms.

The county court should, then, have been preferred to the court of common pleas for the prosecution of most personal litigation. The process was usually no weaker; the methods of trial were the same and in certain cases were even more reliable. Litigation in the court of common pleas, moreover, required greater expense, first in the expenses of travelling to Westminster (knights of the shire going to parliament were allowed 4s a day), then in hiring counsel, who were more expensive in the king's court than in the county courts. Any transfer of jurisdiction would thus have been a hardship on litigants. Nor is there anything to show that the court of common pleas was purposely striving for a larger caseload. One might suppose, then, that viscontiel writs remained a popular device and that litigation in county courts was varied and fairly important throughout the fourteenth century. The documents, however, suggest precisely the opposite conclusion.

The court rolls for fourteenth and early fifteenth century county courts indicate that litigation during that time tended increasingly to be initiated by plaint and for lesser matters, even though the county courts continued to have a very heavy caseload. From the time before 1500, only five court rolls have survived from normal county courts. Each contains enrollments for a period less than a full year, and one is so damaged as to make it impossible to derive complete figures from it. Table 8.1 lists these rolls, indicating the time periods they cover and the number of cases recorded in each roll. In 1413, Somerset county court was still a very busy court. None of the cases on that roll, however, can be shown to have been initiated by writ. In Berkshire in 1377-1378, it seems to have been the practice to enroll the viscontiel writ verbatim; in the eleven sessions, however, only two cases were initiated by writ. It is less easy to determine whether a case was initiated by writ in the Cornwall county records of 1333, but it can be shown that at least two cases were brought by writ. A further three probably were brought by writ, and it is not impossible that others were also. Cornwall however, was not a completely normal county. It had a wider jurisdiction by plaint than other counties, having preserved, for instance, a right to hold cases of mesne by plaint.[10] On the whole one is left with an impression that Cornwall

TABLE 8.1
County Caseload

County	Years	Sessions	Total Cases
Bedfordshire	1332-1333	8	69
Cornwall	1333	4	372
Oxfordshire	1378	1+	24
Berkshire	1377-1378	11	425
Somerset	1413	1	401

SOURCES: Respectively, *Rolls from the Office of the Sheriff of Beds. and Bucks.*, pp. 55-69; SC. 2/161/74; C. 47/37/19 [but taken from an ultraviolet photograph of the document when it was in better condition; the photograph has now been donated by G.D.G. Hall to the Public Record Office and is preserved there]; SC. 2/153/62; SC. 2/200/30.

[10] CP. 40/73, m. 52d (1288): "Et vicecomes modo misit recordum . . . in hec verba: Comitatus tentus apud Lostwythyel die lune in festo sanctorum Tyburtii et Valeriani. Ricardus de Dunbrathak queritur de Laurencio Basset de hoc quod idem Laurencius

was changing more slowly than other counties, but its evidence should not therefore be disregarded. Nevertheless, the court roll for Bedfordshire county court, also in 1333, is probably more representative of counties at that time. There seven cases were brought by writ, approximately 10 percent of the caseload of the court. If one can judge from these rolls, then, viscontiel writs declined in popularity in the fourteenth century; if one can judge from the apparent demand for viscontiel writs which resulted in their proliferation in the thirteenth century, viscontiel writs must have been even more popular then than they were in 1330.

The other perverse fact about county litigation in the fourteenth century is that cases other than debt and trespass came to be relatively scarce. In the later rolls there is no mention of naifty, customs and services, wardship, admeasurement of pasture or of dower, nuisance, right to land, mesne, suit to mill, account, or annuity. Table 8.2 shows the range of litigation described by the county rolls. Debt/detinue and trespass continued right through the fourteenth century to constitute the highest proportion of cases, while replevin declined after the 1330s to a relatively insignificant form of litigation. The vitality of debt and trespass must therefore be seen as one prominent feature of fourteenth-century county litigation. There is, however, even a peculiarity in the kind of debt litigation brought into the

---

eum non acquietavit de scutagio set permittit ipsum distringi per Willelmum de Hogheton ballivum de Kennelarkil per preceptum domini regis ad opus domini comitis de scutagio unius acre terre Cornubie pro qua acra terre idem Ricardus fecit homagium dicto Laurencio et reddit ei per annum duos solidos vj denarios et facit sectam ad curiam suam. Et ipse Laurencius et antecessores sui omni tempore per idem servicium versus omnes homines predictum Ricardum et antecessores suos acquietaverunt et modo idem Laurencius iniuste eum non acquietavit ad dampnum suum etc. Et inde producit sectam etc. Et Laurencius per Robertum de Wyk attornatum suum venit et petit si tenetur ei respondere desicut non ostendit titulum per quem ipsum acquietare debet. Et Ricardus venit et dicit quod omni tempore per predictum servicium de scutagio predictus Laurencius et antecessores sui ipsum acquietaverunt et hoc petit verificare per inquisicionem. Et Laurencius per attornatum suum petit iudicium expresse pro toto placito et tenet se ad suam responsionem ut supra. Unde consideratum est per totum comitatum quod idem Laurencius est indefensus. Ideo in misericordia, et Ricardus recuperet xij denarios pro dampnis suis etc. Et predicti quatuor milites quesiti si advocant predictum recordum dicunt quod sic. Et super hoc venit comes Cornubie per attornatum suum qui tenet predictum comitatum in feodo et dicit quod ipse clamat tenere huiusmodi placitum sine brevi et ipse et antecessores sui illud tenere consueverunt licet sit contra legem et communem consuetudinem Anglie. Ideo datus est eis dies hic a die sancti Michaelis in xv dies. Et tunc ostendat quare huiusmodi placitum tenere debeat. Et petit quod ab huiusmodi placitis placitandis sine brevi interim non inpediatur nec ammoveatur de eisdem placitandis ut consuevit. Et ei conceditur etc." Note that the county custom here was not presumed to take precedence to English custom but had to be defended resolutely.

TABLE 8.2
Forms of Litigation in County Courts

County	Years	Debt	Trespass	Replevin	Covenant	Detinue	Acquittance of Pledges	Mesne	Other	Unidentified
Cornwall	1333	42%	18%	26%	2%	3%	0%	5%	2%*	1%
Bedfordshire	1332-1333	55%	19%	17%	4%	1%	—	—	3%†	—
Berkshire	1377-1378	61%	25%	1%	8%	4%	0%	—	—	0%
Oxfordshire	1377-1378	[Too badly mutilated]								
Somerset	1413	68%	13%	1%	1%	2%	2%	—	—	11%‡

SOURCES: as for Table 8.1

* Detinue of charters (2); account (2); rightful bounds (3); suit to mill (1); wreck of the sea (1).

† Detinue of charters (1); bridge repair (1).

‡ In all, forty-five entries specify merely that certain adjudged damages should be levied; most appear to have been cases of debt.

county. It seems that the sums claimed in debt in the Somerset county court in 1413 usually ranged between 3s and 20s. There is no evidence that large debts were claimed there. In Bedfordshire in 1332-1333, the largest debt mentioned was 6 marks 8s. 8d.[11] Two writ files from around 1300, however, show that debts claimed then in county courts could often be for larger sums.[12] Other chance references reveal cases

[11] *Rolls from the Office of the Sheriff of Beds. and Bucks.*, p. 64.

[12] CP. 52 octave Michaelmas, 26 Edward I/octave Hilary, 28 Edward I. All sums have been converted into marks for ease in comparison; as much as possible, the following form has been followed in cataloguing the writs: County: debt claimed by writ in Michaelmas file (*causa* clause; other significant information); [writs of detinue (*causa* clause; other information)] / debt claimed by writ in Hilary file (etc.) Yorkshire: 13½ marks (no *causa* clause), 10½ marks (bias by reason of annual rent; removal successful), 7 marks 2s. 8d (bias by reason of consanguinity; endorsed "no such plea," which often meant that the plea had already been determined) / 3 marks in debt plus 20 marks in detained chattels (no *causa* clause; removal successful); Lincolnshire: 38 marks (bias by marriage; removal successful), 7½ marks (bias by in-laws; removal successful), 15 marks (bias by in-laws; removal successful) / 14 marks (bias by consanguinity; removal successful); Nottinghamshire: 20 marks (bias by annual rent; removal successful), 16 marks (bias by consanguinity; removal successful), 6 marks (bias by consanguinity; removal successful) / —; Staffordshire: 6½ marks (bias by consanguinity; "no such plea") / —; Shropshire: 8 marks 3s. 3d (bias by annual rent; removal successful), 32 marks 10s. 8d (no *causa* clause; debt composed of several smaller sums: 7½ marks, 7½ marks, 7½ marks; 3 marks; 7 marks 4s.), 106 marks 3s. 5d (no *causa* clause; composed of several smaller sums in the one writ) / —; Northamptonshire: 5 marks (bias by consanguinity; removal successful) / 30 marks (bias by consanguinity; removal successful); Herefordshire: 5½ marks (bias by con-

of debt in county courts claiming 50 marks, 80 marks, 270 marks, and even 300 marks during the reign of Edward I.[13] The perceivable differences between thirteenth and fourteenth century county courts, then, in regard to litigation, are that the later courts dealt with a narrower range of forms of litigation, fewer cases initiated by writ, and, in debt, claims for smaller sums.

These changes were the long-term results of the inquiries which produced the Hundred Rolls. On returning to England in 1274 as king, Edward I had reacted to complaints concerning, among other things, the corruption of sheriffs and bailiffs, by sending out commissioners to gather information. That information was to serve as the basis for indictments. Few of the sheriffs in the preceding decades, however, had been entirely honest during their terms—and that is far from saying that they had all been rankly corrupt—and prosecution of them all would have produced great dissatisfaction in the countryside among those who served the king, a prospect which would not have been welcome so soon after the Barons' War. Moreover, such heavy-handed tactics with sheriffs, who, after all, had probably only been following good precedent, would have made many people very reluctant to accept office. Since few prosecutions did in fact result from the Ragman Inquests, it has been assumed that nothing was done. On the contrary, like many astute rulers, Edward I—or, at least, his ministers—found it more politic to prevent future similar

---

sanguinity; "cause is not true" endorsement, which should not have been allowed) / 9 marks 4s. 10d (bias by annual rent; removal successful); Devon: 13½ marks (no *causa* clause; removal successful), 78 marks (no *causa* clause; removal successful) / —; Wiltshire: — / 24½ marks (bias by annual rent; "cause is not true" endorsement) [also a *pone* for detinue of chattels worth 10s 8d (biased by in-laws; no writ found, but parties summoned)]; Dorset: [a writ of false judgment on a case of debt brought by writ for 7 marks 12s. 8d] / —; Somerset:— / 12½ marks (no *causa* clause; removal successful); Sussex: 14 marks 7d (bias by annual rent; removal successful) / —; Huntingdonshire: 6 marks (bias by consanguinity; sheriff could find no writ which coincided with the *pone*) / —; Cambridgeshire: — / 40 marks (no *causa* clause; removal successful); Hertfordshire: — / 7½ marks (bias by consanguinity; "no such plea"); Norfolk: [a *pone* for a case of detinue of chattels valued at 19½ marks (bias by annual rent; removal successful)]. The cases which expressed no *causa* clause were those cases removed by the plaintiff from county court. In three of those cases the reason for removal was probably bias on the part of the presiding officer; they were removed approximately one month after a new sheriff had been appointed in the relevent county court. Some of the others may have been removed for a similar reason. While a plaintiff would not normally initiate a case in a prejudicial court, the court could later become prejudicial by appointment of a new sheriff, undersheriff, or clerk; a previous relationship might become known only during the case. Anyway, the range of debts claimed show that the Bedfordshire case of 1333 was for a sum which would have come at the low end of the range of litigation by writ in the reign of Edward I.

[13] CP. 40/80, m. 20d; CP. 40/79, m. 41; JUST. 1/4/1, Kent Eyre, 1293; CP. 52 quindene St. Martin, 27-28 Edward I (Sussex).

abuses than to harass past offenders who were all too often very influential. Instead of prosecution, that is, the Ragman Inquests resulted in legal reform. The jurisdiction exercised by the sheriff in county courts and by his theoretical counterparts in courts of liberties was henceforward to be limited by an increased ability on the part of litigants to remove cases into the court of common pleas.

Much litigation brought by viscontiel writ had long been removeable by the writ *pone*. The most frequent use of the *pone*, however, had been with the seignorial writs of right after they had been removed into county court by tolt. Since the use of writs of right declined during the thirteenth century, one might also have expected the use of the *pone* to decline. On the contrary, a steadily increasing use of the writ *pone* may be inferred from the fine rolls. Any statistical use of the fine rolls, of course, must be cautious; not all payments for writs were entered and even changes in terminology and methods of collecting pledged money can mislead the unwary statistician. Nevertheless, the fine rolls do suggest a larger role for the *pone*. Inspection of the rolls for the latter half of the thirteenth century suggests three periods in the use of the *pone* in those years. In the 1250s and early 1260s, using fine roll statistics which completely disregard the assizes, it seems that approximately 25 percent of the cases in the central courts had been initiated in lower courts and removed into the king's court by *pone*. Never again would removal processes supply so large a portion of the litigation in the court of common pleas. The second period runs from around 1270 to 1289, and perhaps for a few years thereafter. During this time writs *pone* accounted steadily for at least 12 percent of the payments for writs; in 1279-1281 they accounted for 17 percent. During those years, however, the number of cases coming into the king's court was increasing rapidly; the absolute number of writs *pone* mentioned in the fine rolls more than doubled. The largest increases came in the years 1274 and 1275, that is, during and shortly after the Ragman Inquests. The years from 1274 to 1281, then, seem to have been the peak period for the disruption of county litigation by the use of the *pone*, a disruption caused by the fact that the use of the *pone* annulled all pleading and process taken in the county court up to the time of the removal. Finally, in the late 1290s and on to 1327, judging from only four rolls examined, writs *pone* accounted for only from 7 percent to 9 percent of the writs mentioned.[14]

Examination of writs *pone* preserved in writ files provides a better

[14] Appendix V.

idea of the use of the *pone*. Only two writ files have been examined thoroughly for this purpose, both shortly before 1300. One of these contained sixty-six writs *pone*; the other, forty-seven. Almost half of these writs—representing accurately the number of cases removed by *pone* from all county courts and courts of liberties—were used to remove viscontiel writs of replevin into the court of common pleas: fifty-two. Other viscontiel writs were also involved: twenty-seven viscontiel writs of debt, eight of naifty, four of admeasurement of pasture, five of mesne, three of detinue, three of detinue of charters, two each of nuisance and right of way, and an example of the *pone* for both personal covenant and rightful services. Only five writs *pone* were used to remove writs of right. A comparison between the testing date of the *pone* and the corresponding writ—the two writs were, of course, sewn together—gives some idea of the length of time the case had been in county court. In the cases of replevin, the dates were often very close together; that result was to be expected. The only way to bring replevin was by initiating it in a lower court; there was no writ of replevin returnable directly to the court of common pleas. Thus many of the cases of replevin were removed from the lower courts before anything had happened there, simply because the litigants wanted to litigate in the king's court in the first place. Nevertheless, some replevin cases seem to have been in the lower courts for a respectable time: fifteen, seventeen, nineteen, twenty, and twenty-four weeks. That was long enough to show that the litigants had at least started out wanting to conclude the case in the lower courts. Still, when the plaintiffs actually had had a choice of whether to bring the writ in the lower court or in the court of common pleas, there was a longer time between testing dates. In debt, for instance, the average time between purchasing the viscontiel writ and purchasing the *pone* was twelve weeks, and the two longest periods—twelve months and twenty-eight months—were not included in calculating that average. These cases demonstrate that lower courts were still considered effective; otherwise litigants would not have purchased the viscontiel writ to begin with or at least would not thereafter have waited so long to remove the case into the court of common pleas.[15]

The reasons for removing viscontiel writs were various. When the plaintiff initiated the removal, the reason can seldom be discerned. Since removal involved delay and delay was considered a detriment

---

[15] CP. 52 octave Michaelmas, 26 Edward I; octave Hilary, 28 Edward I. Note that the *pone* by this time functions not only to remove writs of right, but also to remove cases of naifty in place of *de libertate probanda*. One writ is counted twice in above figures, since it contained a case which was both debt and detinue.

only to the plaintiff, he was allowed to remove his own case without specifying a reason to be included in the writ *pone* in the form of a *causa* clause (except when the case was actually in the court of a liberty, in which situation removal by the plaintiff was a financial injury to the lord of the court). At times, however, the reason would have been the annulment of previous process. A plaintiff who had committed himself to a jury trial on an issue which, on second thought, he regretted, would find the *pone* a convenient way to prevent the jury from delivering its verdict. The case would always be repleaded in the court of common pleas, and the plaintiff could alter his strategy, either demurring to the defendant's plea or joining issue on a different point. Even a jury verdict in county court could be annulled in this manner if judgment had not already passed. Defendants would have found the procedure advantageous for the same reasons, but they had to specify a reason for their removal, since they could obviously use the *pone* simply to delay the case. The reason they specified was not, and could not be, the procedural reason just mentioned. In most cases it was alleged bias on the part of the presiding officer—sheriff, un-dersheriff, seneschal, or bailiff—that was mentioned. That bias regularly was related either to consanguinity between the presiding officer and the opposing litigant or to an annual rent held by the presiding officer from the opposing litigant. A few times a more general hatred of the removing litigant was alleged, specifying, for instance, that he was impleading the sheriff or undersheriff in a different plea in the king's court and that that was the cause of the bias exhibited by the presiding officer.[16] Partiality on the part of the presiding officer of the various lower courts was one of the abuses complained of in 1274; it seems that the increased use of the *pone* indicated in the fine rolls in 1274 and 1275 resulted from the same concern that motivated the Ragman Inquests.

The problem of partiality could not be handled so easily. The reason for the removal expressed in the *causa* clause always contained a rider that instructed the sheriff to execute the removal only if the *causa* clause was true. A biased sheriff would not readily admit his bias or allow the case out of his court so easily. Thus, at least by the late 1290s, the sheriff was not allowed to challenge the *causa* clause when it concerned him or his undersheriff or his clerks—that is, when bias was alleged, the rider was to have no effect.[17] Removal by reason of bias thus became a sure method for a defendant to delay the plaintiff's recovery. This annulment of the effect of the rider was necessary to

[16] Above, n. 12; CP. 40/83, m. 42, 135d.
[17] Above, chapter 4, n. 24.

make the *pone* an effective tool against bias and to assure the litigants access to an impartial tribunal, but it devalued the county court in the process. The ease of removal and consequent annulment of process and pleading and jury verdict in the county court made litigating by viscontiel writ less advantageous. The viscontiel writ might assure the plaintiff of a jury, but it also made him vulnerable to useless and costly delay. This discouraging aspect to the use of viscontiel writs had probably had some effect already by 1300; at least, the declining percentage of writs *pone* in the fine rolls by 1299 would seem to indicate as much. The process, however, was not completed immediately. Patterns of litigation can prove difficult to change, particularly when, as in this case, the court involved had so many advantages over the alternative court, that is, the court of common pleas. Nevertheless, by the reign of Richard II, writ files contain very few writs *pone*; that observation fits nicely with the evidence of the county rolls in that reign, which show very few viscontiel writs. A fair hearing had been granted to litigants, but at the cost of the de facto—not the de jure—loss of writ jurisdiction by the county courts.

If the alterations in the use of the *pone* were important in changing patterns of litigation in the reign of Edward I, the related changes in the use of the writ *recordari* were more so. Prior to 1275 the *recordari* had been utilized to remove cases initiated by writ in lower courts when a record of the case was required for supervisory or other miscellaneous reasons.[18] In 1275 it was decided that a new function would be given the writ; henceforward the writ *recordari* would be used to remove plaints from the lower courts. Before 1275 plaints in lower courts could not be removed, and sheriffs and undersheriffs thus had a wide field for influencing the course of the plea. The litigants in a case brought by plaint were restricted to the county court; their only recourse was after judgment had been rendered: the cumbersome writ of false judgment.[19] The decision to allow removal

[18] Above, chapter 6 at n. 69 ff.

[19] I do not know when false judgment became available for cases brought by plaint in the county court. Early cases of false judgment concern writs of right and perhaps crown pleas. It is unlikely that in the reign of John there was any supervision of the county courts by false judgment in plaints. Before the reign of Edward I plaints of trespass were certainly subject to false judgment (JUST. 1/483, mm. 9, 9d). During the reign of Edward I plaints of debt were subject to false judgment (CP. 40/5, m. 42d), as were plaints of replevin (CP. 40/2a, mm. 20, 17d). The almost exclusive concentration of the writ of false judgment earlier in the century on writs of right, whereas later in the century viscontiel writs were also subjected to the supervision of false judgment, indicates that here too the jurisdiction of the county court was no longer as secure.

of plaints before judgment was not the result of the Parliament which produced the statutes of Westminster I, nor is there any evidence that the decision was made in the preceding Parliament, although the timing would be approximately correct. The first evidence of the new function comes from three cases removed from various county courts— Northumberland, Westmorland, and Wiltshire—into the court of common pleas early in Michaelmas term 1275.[20] This abolition of the absolute jurisdiction of county courts over the plaints initiated there inevitably raised legal difficulties, but, like the change in the use of the *pone*, was intended to guarantee litigants access to an impartial tribunal.

The writ *recordari* fast assumed its final form, completely distinct from the writ of false judgment, and came to be frequently used. Already in 1276 it seems that the four knights no longer had to bring the record in person.[21] Had they been required to come, the *recordari*, as a regular process of removal, would have put an intolerable burden on the county courts. It was therefore only necessary for the sheriff and the four knights to affix their seals to the record. Likewise, from the beginning, defendants as well as plaintiffs were allowed to remove plaints by *recordari*. Westminster II, c. 2, in 1285 provided an elaborate excuse for allowing defendants to use the *recordari* to prevent tenants from disavowing their tenancy to avoid rendering their customs and services while not actually surrendering their tenancy, but between 1276 and 1280 the defendants in at least five cases had already utilized the *recordari* to remove plaints of replevin.[22] By 1300 the *recordari* was used very frequently. Two writ files from that time yield only fifty-two *pone* writs used to remove viscontiel replevin, while there were 199 *recordari* writs used to remove plaints of replevin.[23] Likewise, *causa* clauses for the *recordari* alleging bias ap-

[20] CP. 40/11, m. 30 (Micheleye v Humfrayville); CP. 40/11, m. 63d (Berewyz v Crepping); CP. 40/11, m. 123 (Arneys v Archbishop of York). CP. 40/11, m. 13d has a *recordari* in *accedas ad hundredum* form, which should for this purpose be counted as a normal *recordari* (Cotesbrok v Gefray).

[21] CP. 40/17, m. 133: "Sussex. Preceptum fuit vicecomiti quod in pleno comitatu suo recordari faceret loquelam que fuit in eodem comitatu sine brevi regis inter Adam de Bavent et Johannem de Percy de averiis ipsius Ade captis et iniuste detentis etc. Et recordum illud haberet ad hunc diem sub sigillo suo et sigillis iiij[or] militum ex illis qui recordo illi interfuerunt. Et quod diceret prefato Ade quod esset hic ad hunc diem versus predictum Johannem inde prosecuturus si voluerit."

[22] Above, n. 21 (because the plaintiff is the litigant to be summoned); CP. 40/17, m. 123d; CP. 40/20, m. 83; CP. 40/27, m. 34; CP. 40/32, m. 23d. Since only those cases in which the removal is not effective normally appear in the plea rolls in an identifiable way, it may be presumed that there were rather more cases than these.

[23] CP. 52 octave Michaelmas, 26 Edward I; octave Hilary, 28 Edward I.

peared as early as 1280;[24] it seems that that kind of *causa* clause was probably the original kind.[25] The effect of the new function of the *recordari* in replevin was not simply to facilitate litigation; it limited the abuses inherently possible when pleas could not be removed. Nevertheless, in making such plaints removeable, plaints of replevin became subject to the same disadvantages that resulted from the greater ease in the use of the *pone*. Process, pleading, and even jury verdicts could be annulled if judgment had not been rendered; the annulment of such process was assured particularly after 1302, because then sheriffs stopped sending full records in return to the mandate.

During the 1290s the writ *recordari* as a common law removal procedure had been almost completely restricted to removing plaints of replevin—and the occasional appeal—from the lower courts; in 1275, however, chancery had made the *recordari* available for plaints of trespass and debt also. The earliest plaint of trespass which can be identified as having been removed by *recordari* into the court of common pleas was *Abbot of Leicester v Abbot of Selby*. The enrollment of that case, originally brought in the county court of Leicestershire, appeared in Michaelmas term of 1275, that is, in the same term in which the first replevin cases brought originally by plaint in lower courts were removed by *recordari*.[26] In that same term the enrollments for *Loges v Wirley*—another plaint of trespass removed

---

[24] CP. 40/32, m. 23d (Rendham v Huntingfeld [in *accedas* form]): "Quia Willelmus Turgyz capitalis clericus curie predicte qui frequenter in absencia ballivi eiusdem curie tenet placita curie illius est consanguineus predicti Mathei propter quod idem ballivus et Willelmus fovent ipsum Matheum in loquela predicta."

[25] The two writ files examined show that something less than half the *recordari* writs had *causa* clauses. Of these, fifty-nine writs had a clause not alleging bias (fifty-five had the statutory clause concerning distraint within the fee for customs and services); only thirty had clauses concerning bias (seven concerning consanguinity; twelve concerning annual rents; an unusually high ten concerning bias based ultimately on the allegation that the plaintiff was a villein of the undersheriff's patron). The large percentage concerning customs and services would not have been present before 1285, or at least not in such numbers.

[26] CP. 40/11, m. 11d: "Leyc'. Preceptum fuit vicecomiti quod in pleno comitatu suo recordari faceret loquelam que est in eodem comitatu sine brevi regis inter abbatem Leycestre et Radulphum le Provost de Quenyngburgo et Abbatem de Seleby de quadam transgressione eisdem abbati et Radulpho per predictum abbatem de Seleby illata etc. Et vicecomes misit recordum—scilicet a die sancti Martini in xv dies—set predictus abbas de Seleby non venit. Et habuit diem in banco ad hunc diem prece parcium. Ideo preceptum est vicecomiti quod distringat eum per omnes terras etc., et quod de exitibus etc., et quod habeat corpus eius hic in octabus sancti Hilarii ad respondendum predictis abbati et Radulpho de predicta transgressione etc." The membrane is dated the octave of Michaelmas. The comment concerning the quindene of St. Martin was interlined.

by *recordari*[27]—and *York v Burneton*—the first identifiable plaint of debt removed by *recordari*[28]—appears. The extension of the *recordari* for the removal of plaints thus happened simultaneously for replevin, trespass, and debt.

The extension of the *recordari* in 1275 had a far-reaching effect on both trespass and debt. Discussion of these changes normally and properly revolves around the interpretation of the Statute of Gloucester, c. 8, in 1278:

> It is likewise provided that sheriffs shall hold pleas of trespass in county courts as they used to and that no one from now on shall have a writ of trespass before justices unless he declares on oath that the goods taken away are worth at least forty shillings.[29]

The statute obviously refers to trespass and not to debt, although it will be shown that it did eventually come to influence debt litigation. The narrowest reasonable interpretation of the statute must allow that it treats of two things. First, some trespass cases which had been handled by county courts in the presumably recent past had been coming into the king's court. Such litigation was henceforward to be handled once again in the county courts. Second, and seemingly related to the first problem, trespass cases concerning goods taken and carried away which had been brought into the king's court were at times too insignificant to justify the concern of the justices. The solution for the second problem was that henceforward plaintiffs had to take an oath that the value of the goods taken away—not the damages alleged—was 40s or more. The intent of the statute obviously is thus to limit the kinds of cases that could be brought into the king's court.

The limitation that was applied in cases of trespass concerning goods and chattels taken away—a limitation drawn according to the value of the goods—was not new. Professor Milsom has already observed that early in the reign of Edward I there seems to have been such a

[27] CP. 40/11, m. 39, membrane dated 3 weeks Michaelmas. Further process: CP. 40/13, m. 66d. See also CP. 40/18, m. 52.

[28] CP. 40/11, m. 115d, in *accedas* form concerning the court of Newcastle-upon-Tyne: "de eo quod idem Henricus reddat prefato Hugoni triginta et quinque marcas quas ei debet etc., . . . tunc esset hic loquelam suam versus predictum Hugonem si voluerit etc." Further process: CP. 40/14, m. 41d.

[29] "Purveu est ensement, qe Viscuntes pleident en Cuntez les plesz de trespas auxi com il soloient estre pledez. E qe nul eit desormes bref de trespas devaunt Justices si il ne afie par fei, qe les biens enportez vaillent quarante souz al meins." The statute also required one to swear to the veracity of one's complaint of battery.

limitation and that it was enforced fairly well.[30] I have also looked at trespass cases of that period, at least those which were brought into the court of common pleas. In the years before 1275 trespass cases very often specified either the value of the goods taken away or the total value of the damages alleged. In many instances, of course, the value of both would far exceed 40s, and there were relatively few marginal instances. *Heythe v Suthwode* in 1273 is a case alleging only the taking and carrying away of goods and chattels, and they were valued at 40s.[31] There were two other similar cases that term and one case the following term which likewise specified that the goods and chattels were worth 40s.[32] When both assault and the taking away of chattels were alleged, the value of the goods was sometimes valued at less than 40s, but the damages alleged were greater than 40s.[33] Prior to 1275, then, the rule followed by chancery in issuing writs seems to have combined the elements of value of goods and value of damages. If the case concerned solely the taking away of goods and chattels, they had to be worth at least 40s, and the damages alleged—since in trespass damages included the value of the goods and chattels concerned, because those goods and chattels could not be recovered as they could be in covenant—would be rather higher than that. If the case involved both the taking away of goods and chattels and also assault, the damages alleged had to be at least 40s. There is no reason to suppose, had the situation remained as it was in 1273 and 1274, that any statute would have been required to deal with the matter; customary chancery procedures were sufficient.

The statute under consideration, however, presupposes that trespass litigation in the king's court had increased in recent years and chancery supervision of the customary rule had become ineffective; yet a cursory glance at the plea rolls of the court of common pleas in 1274 and 1277 shows no dramatic change. There were not, at least, a great many cases between 1275 and 1278 in which the goods were valued at less than 40s. It is possible, however, that the rolls do not tell the whole story. The courts themselves may have weeded out most of the cases which they considered too insignificant, sending those litigants back to the lower courts before the case was even enrolled. The fine rolls provide at least some evidence supporting such an hypothesis.

[30] S.F.C. Milsom, *Historical Foundations of the Common Law* (London, 1969), pp. 212, 247.

[31] CP. 40/2a, m. 19.

[32] CP. 40/2a, m. 20 (Peyntur v fitz John); CP. 40/2a, m. 7d (Godelawe v fitz Osbert); CP. 40/3, m. 39 (Alewaston v Somery).

[33] CP. 40/3, m. 43 (Bryan v Norton); CP. 40/3, m. 30d (Bardeswell v Colchester).

The statistics derived from the fine rolls—excerpted in Table 8.3— show that the Statute of Gloucester was directed against a real problem and achieved results. Now, while one cannot establish any precise relationship between the number of writs enrolled in the fine rolls and the number of writs actually purchased, it would seem that changes in the relative popularity of writs can be determined. Given a suffi- ciently large sample, the proportion of the total number of writs listed as trespass writs, for instance, should remain approximately the same. Large variations are sufficient grounds for cautious argument. The fine rolls are even more complicated than that, however, since they seldom specify precisely the kind of writ purchased, but rather list them in broad categories. *Pone* writs, for instance, were listed without any indication of the kind of writ they were purchased to remove (writ of right, replevin, debt, etc.). In my tables, I have not included writs of assize or of false judgment. Those writs included were de- scribed in four categories: *pone* writs, writs *ad terminum* (a general classification for any writ returnable at a specific term in the king's court, without regard to the form of action), writs of trespass (a kind of writ which could have been included in the writs *ad terminum* but which was listed separately anyway), and writs *de record'* (a difficult category to be treated later[34]). Table 8.3 indicates three important

TABLE 8.3
The Fine Rolls and Writs of Trespass

Year	Number of Trespass Writs	Percentage Change	Percentage of Total Writs
1270	8		1%
1271	4		1%
1272	10		1%
1273	112		13%
1274	201	79%	17%
1275	338	68%	25%
1276	346	2%	26%
1277			
1278	439	27%	31%
1279	273	−38%	29%
1280	199	−27%	28%
1281	160	−20%	21%
1284	152	−5%	20%

SOURCE: Appendix V. Note that the figures do not take account of writs of assize.

[34] Below, at n. 38.

changes in regard to trespass writs. The first occurred in 1273: a dramatic rise in the number of trespass writs enrolled. I consider this insignificant. Since it occurred at the beginning of the reign and changed from such a small base, the rise was probably merely a change in the method of recording. Most trespass writs in the last years of the reign of Henry III were probably enrolled as writs *ad terminum*, and the figures of 1273 and 1274 can be considered the more normal range of trespass writs. The second change was the further rise in 1275 with the subsequent increases up to the year 1278—the year of the provision of the Statute of Gloucester. That change was not merely a change in methods of recording. It undoubtedly indicates a great increase in the use of those writs described as writs of trespass, and it was an increase that resulted in statutory action. The subsequent decline in the absolute number of trespass writs recorded is not significant, since the number of writs enrolled declined as a whole, but the decline in the proportion of trespass writs does indicate that the statute stemmed the tide. In 1279 and 1280 trespass writs declined marginally in popularity, and by 1281 the situation had been returned to the status prevailing before 1275, or, at least, nearly so. The legislators in 1278 were thus dealing with a real problem—a problem which had not appeared sufficiently serious to have been dealt with in Westminster I in 1275—and provided an effective remedy.

Before 1275, then, chancery had been successful in enforcing the customary rules in trespass regarding the value of chattels and goods; in 1275 that enforcement broke down and a relatively large number of trespass cases circumvented the customary rule, resulting in an annoying problem for the king's court. That problem arose at the very time the writ *recordari* was made available to remove plaints of trespass. To prove that the *recordari* was the cause of the problem, however, one must first show that writs *recordari* could have been included in the fine roll entries as trespass writs and then show how the *recordari* would have frustrated all attempts to enforce the 40s customary rule.

The fine rolls did acknowledge a category of writ *de record'*. The easiest interpretation of this category is that it concerned writs *recordari*. It certainly was not the classification for writs of false judgment, which were listed quite specifically in their own classification. In the 1250s writs *de record'* constituted 3 percent or 4 percent of the writs counted. Between 1270 and 1289, while there were some entries *de record'*, they never constituted even 1 percent of the entries. Moreover, the absolute number of the writs enrolled as *de record'* did not even reach the numbers enrolled in the 1250s.[35] This is a sound indication that that category did not include all *recordari* writs. It can be thought, at least, that the category was used at that time only for writs *certiorari* issued to obtain a record for the court of common pleas or the king's bench from another royal justice[36] (not from the county court) or, perhaps, for writs *recordari* issued specially to obtain supplementary information from county courts concerning cases already in process in the king's courts.[37] It is thus very possible that the new kind of *recordari* writs—*recordari* writs issued to remove plaints from lower courts—were enrolled in the fine rolls under the heading in which the case being removed would have fallen had it been brought originally by a returnable writ, so that a *recordari* for a plaint of trespass would be enrolled as a writ of trespass. The *recordari* served in a sense as an original writ anyway, as the warrant by which the court of common pleas had jurisdiction in the case. At least by 1298, however, that procedure had changed. *Recordari* writs were then clearly entered as writs *de record'* and constituted something over 10 percent of the cases counted.[38] Before that time, however, and precisely when the *recordari* had just been extended in function for the removal of plaints, it is possible that the increased use of the *recordari* appeared in part under the heading of trespass writs.

It was the new use of the *recordari*, furthermore, which would have frustrated chancery enforcement of the customary 40s rule. That enforcement would have taken the form of a requirement that the plaintiff swear that the goods and chattels were worth at least 40s. In *recordari* procedure, however, it could have been the defendant who approached the chancery clerks to purchase the writ; it would have been unreasonable to make the defendant put himself on oath concerning the value of the goods. The case need not have been pleaded yet in the county court, so that the defendant would not yet have been informed of the precise value of the goods and chattels. When it was the defendant trying to remove the case, therefore, chancery enforcement of the customary rule would have been completely frustrated. In more general terms, however, the problem may have presented itself to the clerks faced with either plaintiffs or de-

[35] Appendix V.
[36] *Early Registers of Writs*, ed. Elsa de Haas and G.D.G. Hall, Selden Society, vol. 87 (London, 1970), p. 282 (R. 743).
[37] Above, chapter 6 at n. 69 ff.
[38] Appendix V.

fendants. I have argued that the *recordari* was made available for plaints primarily because there had been a governmental decision that the bias of local officials should not be allowed to work injustice. That allegation of injustice may have sufficed originally to make plaints of trespass matter for the king's court. At least when more forcible language than "taken and carried away" had been used before 1275—words such as "made off with" or "stole"—cases concerning goods and chattels of lesser values had been allowed into the court of common pleas.[39] It is likely that the allegation of bias on the part of the presiding officer—even though that would not be put into issue—made the case acceptable. *Recordari* procedure, then, at least when initiated by defendants and probably when initiated by either party, was capable of causing the breakdown of chancery enforcement of the customary jurisdictional rules in trespass; it was, moreover, the only change at that time which would have had a bearing on the problem countered by the Statute of Gloucester.

There was, in addition, another problem which would put the trespass *recordari* in bad repute. Removal of a plea was always a process which occasioned some delay and which therefore was often used by defendants merely to delay the plea. In trespass that tendency was much more serious than in replevin. In replevin, it was the defendant who most wanted the plea to be determined; as the distrainor of the animals, it was he, rather than the plaintiff, who had brought the dispute to a head. Even when the plaintiff in replevin removed the suit to the court of common pleas for the sake of delay, not much harm was done. When the plaintiff initiated the removal and did not appear in court to prosecute, the suit was quashed and the defendant received back the animals to hold once again by way of distraint. It was far different in trespass. A defendant who removed a case into the court of common pleas from county would suffer no adverse action if he did not appear on the day assigned. The justices could proceed to use the ordinary mesne procedure, but because of the fewer sessions of the king's court that mesne procedure would probably be less stringent for a while than the procedure of the county court. The justices realized this problem. Peter de Bramford, along with several others, was defendant in a case of trespass brought by plaint in the court of Bury St. Edmunds by William de Thelnitham. Bramford

---

[39] CP. 40/5, m. 18: an allegation of taking and imprisoning a man and stealing a surcoat worth 4s *contra pacem*. CP. 40/14, m. 54: an allegation of imprisonment and the stealing of goods and chattels worth 13s. 4d.

removed the case into the court of king's bench by a *recordari* in *accedas* form, and the sheriff forwarded the record. At the quindene of Michaelmas term, 1278, Thelnitham's essoiner presented himself and found that the defendants were not present. The justices, seemingly annoyed at this obvious dilatory tactic, remitted the case to the lower court, ordering the bailiff of the court to give the parties speedy justice.[40] Even here the defendants had gained delay without penalty.

In 1278, then, the Statute of Gloucester, c. 8, was provided to restrict the influx of trespass litigation, resulting, at least to a large extent, from the 1275 decision to extend the function of the writ *recordari*.[41] The action of 1278, however, was not immediately effective. The statute had only insisted that chancery would enforce the customary limitation; it did not reverse the earlier decision that the writ *recordari* would be applicable to trespass plaints. The restriction provided by the statute would only come from the purchaser's oath concerning the value of the goods and chattels. Thus, in Easter term of 1279—as soon, that is, as could be expected after the Statute of Gloucester—a new form of trespass *recordari* appeared. The new form included in the *recordari* itself the value of the goods and chattels alleged to have been taken and carried away. There is no way to tell how often this new form of writ was used, since only writs in which the sheriff failed to act can be identified in the plea

[40] KB. 27/41, m. 11d: "Adam Schot essoniator Willelmi de Thelnitham optulit se iiij die versus Petrum de Bramford, Hugonem de Bereford, Robertum le Charetter, Thomam de Ringemere, Adam Anestase, Walterum le Bever, Willelmum le Wacher, et Godefridum de Falkeham de placito quod vicecomes assumptis secum quatuor discretis et legalibus militibus de comitatu suo in propria persona sua accederet ad curiam abbatis sancti Edmundi de sancto Edmundo et in plena curia illa recordari faceret loquelam que est in eadem curia sine brevi regis inter Willelmum de Telfetham et Petrum de Bramford . . . de quadam transgressione eidem Willelmo de Telfetham per predictos Petrum . . . illata ut dicitur. Et recordum illud haberet hic ad hunc diem etc. Et vicecomes misit recordum etc. Et predicti Petrus et alii qui predictum recordum venire fecerunt non veniunt etc. Ideo remittatur recordum predictum etc. Et preceptum est ballivo etc., quod celerem justiciam partibus exhibeant etc." Bramford tried the same tactic again in KB. 27/45, m. 16d, but the bailiff properly refused to allow the case to be removed. The justices nevertheless issued a *non omittat*, but I did not find the case coming into the court of king's bench again.

[41] The statute did not speak directly about the writ *recordari* because its interest was not in the *recordari* as such, but rather in the value of the pleas of trespass that came before the justices. The statute merely stated that for any plea of trespass that came before the justices—and this would include those that came by original writ as well as those that came by *recordari*—the value of the goods and chattels taken and carried away had to be at least 40s. The statute was thus a reaffirmation of the customary rule, more comprehensive in form than a regulation of the writ *recordari* but definitely including in its possible effects a revision of *recordari* procedure.

rolls; the only known instance is *Suddon v Shelton*, in which the chattels were alleged to have been worth £7.7.-.[42] The case appeared once again in Michaelmas term, when the sheriff was once more ordered to execute the writ.[43] The new form of the *recordari*, explicitly specifying the value of the goods and chattels, was a direct result of the statute.

The new form of the *recordari*, nevertheless, had problems of its own. It had become overly precise. The sheriff could be expected to know, when presented with a *recordari* for a plaint of replevin, for instance, whether the plaint concerned chattels, a horse, or 300 sheep. After all, the sheriff had been responsible through his bailiff for replevying the animals; even if the replevy had not been successful, the plaintiff would have had to inform the sheriff of the subject of the plaint. In executing a *pone*, the sheriff could also be expected to know, for instance, that a plea of debt was for £40; the sum was included in the viscontiel writ which was retained in the sheriff's writ file while the plea was pending in the county court. In a plaint of trespass, however, the sheriff could not be expected to know more than whether or not the plaint concerned goods and chattels carried away. No more than in a plaint of replevin would he know the value of the goods until the case was almost concluded. Furthermore, the sheriff was supposed to be very precise on these matters. If the *recordari* specified that it concerned a plaint of trespass of goods taken and carried away worth £7.7.-, and the plaint was actually concerning goods worth only £6, he had to assume that the pleas were different pieces of litigation and refuse to execute the writ. In short, since the sheriff could not know the value of the goods and chattels taken away, the new form of the *recordari* was not well-conceived.

That new form of *recordari* was thus soon discontinued, and plaints of trespass could no longer be removed into the king's court from the lower courts. *Suddon v Shelton* is the last evidence of regular use of the *recordari* for plaints of trespass until the fifteenth century;[44] the cessation of the use of the *recordari* in this way undoubtedly accounts for the decline in the number of trespass writs enrolled in

[42] CP. 40/29, m. 4d: ". . . loquela que est in eadem curia sine brevi regis inter (A. et B.) de catallis ipsorum (A.) ad valenciam septem librarum et septem solidorum per prefatum (B.) captis et asportatis ut dicitur. Et recordum illud haberet hic ad hunc diem sub sigillo etc., et sigillis quatuor legalium hominum eiusdem curie ex illis. . . ." The *recordari* is in *accedas* form for the court of Eye of Edmund, earl of Cornwall.

[43] CP. 40/31, m. 29d.

[44] W. S. Holdsworth, *A History of English Law*, 14 vols. (London, 1903-1938), 2:622; *Registrum Omnium Brevium* (London, 1531), pp. 120, 120b; below, at n. 63.

the fine rolls in 1281.[45] The only examples of plaints of trespass removed into the court of common pleas later in the reign of Edward I can be attributed to the irregular activities of William de Redham, sheriff of Norfolk and Suffolk from 1290 to 1294. In 1291 he executed a *recordari* and removed *Whelvetham v. Weyland,* a plaint of trespass.[46] The *recordari* used, however, was a *recordari* for a plaint of replevin between the two mentioned parties; moreover, when the plea came to be enrolled in the court of common pleas, it was described as a plaint of replevin, not a plaint of trespass.[47] The case had undergone a transformation in the removal. In the same way, Redham allowed *Bonde v Prior of Pentney*[48] and *Frost v Peverel*[49]—both plaints of trespass—to be removed by *recordari* writs specifying plaints of replevin. In all these instances the sheriff should have refused to execute such a mandate. All other sheriffs, it seems, did refuse.[50] Between 1278 and 1281, therefore, plaints of trespass were returned to the same status they had held prior to 1275: they were subject completely to the sheriff and the county court. The only supervision possible was the writ of false judgment or, a little later, the writ of attaint.

The situation with trespass, however, was not altogether as it had been in 1274; since that time the viscontiel writ of trespass had been provided to alleviate the hardships imposed on litigants by the termination in 1278-1281 of *recordari* procedure for plaints of trespass. There is a great deal of negative evidence that the viscontiel writ of trespass was new in 1278-1279. No earlier register of writs contains such a writ.[51] Plea roll evidence points in the same direction. There

---

[45] Table 8.3.

[46] CP. 52 quindene Michaelmas, 19 Edward I [S.S.]. The *recordari* was in *accedas* form. Weyland was the purchaser of the *recordari* and alleged that the bailiff of the court of the liberty received an annuity from the plaintiff.

[47] CP. 40/90, m. 50.

[48] CP. 52 quindene Hilary, 19 Edward I [S.S.].

[49] CP. 52 quindene Hilary, 21 Edward I [S.S.].

[50] I have not seen any trespass *recordari* issued from chancery in the reign of Edward I after Suddon v Shelton. I have seen a trespass *recordari* issued specifically for a plaint of trespass early in the reign of Richard II, so that it is possible that the *recordari* had been reimplemented for trespass by that time (below, at n. 63). Nonetheless, even in that instance there were two accompanying *recordari* writs for plaints of replevin between the same parties, indicating that that plaint of trespass could have been sufficiently similar to a plaint of replevin that it would eventually be so enrolled or that it was allowed removal because it was related to the plaints of replevin removed at the same time. I have glanced through a writ file from the reign of Richard II and did not then notice any *recordari* writs.

[51] *Early Registers of Writs,* pp. cxxxii-cxxxiii.

were twenty-two actions of false judgment between 1272 and 1278 which concerned actions of trespass determined in lower courts. All twenty-two concerned plaints of trespass; not one concerned a case of trespass brought by viscontiel writ.[52] Moreover, the first two references to the viscontiel writ of trespass in the plea rolls occurred immediately after the Statute of Gloucester. In Trinity term of 1279 *de la Chaumbre v Rye* is the earliest case of false judgment on a case brought by a viscontiel writ of trespass.[53] Later, in Easter term of 1280, a case of replevin reveals a reference to *Depham v de la Snore*, an action brought by a viscontiel writ of trespass in the county court of Norfolk. That case had resulted in a concord to pay a sum of money on 6 February 1279.[54] The county court session in which the case

[52] CP. 40/2a, m. 13d (de Forz v St. Martin; in the court of Newport, Hants.); CP. 40/3, m. 18d (Scathe v Wytman; Basingstoke hundred, Hants.); CP. 40/3 (Athelwald v Wenson; Gallow hundred, Norf.); CP. 40/5, m. 27d (Heriz v Wynne; county court, Leics.); CP. 40/5, m. 71d (Forester v Cusin; Kesteven, Lincs.); CP. 40/8, m. 2d (Gardiner v Bullok; Tickhill hundred, Yorks.); CP. 40/9, m. 34d (Brathwayt v Beltoft, Kirkby Malzeard, Yorks.); CP. 40/10, m. 36 (Armestrong v Anon.; Melmerby hundred, Cumb.); CP. 40/10, m. 68 (Paulyn v Gegge; honor of Lancaster, Notts.); CP. 40/11, m. 51d (Seyton v Mauley; county court, Yorks.); CP. 40/15, m. 108 (Peschur v Chevere; Risbridge hundred, Suff.); CP. 40/17, m. 141d (Prior of Deerhurst v Countess of Gloucester and Hereford; Chadlington hundred, Oxon.); CP. 40/18, m. 53 (Karlton v Gousyl; Holderness wapentake, Yorks.); CP. 40/18, m. 58d (Attewode v fitz Roger; Holt hundred, Norf.); CP. 40/21, m. 12 (Wermesworth v Clay; Doncaster hundred, Yorks.); CP. 40/21, m. 80d (Bastard v Escudemor; Upton hundred, Wilts.); CP. 40/24, m. 42 (Craddock v Beverle; Pirehill hundred, Staffs.); CP. 40/24, m. 45d (Scaccario v Grene; Bullingdon hundred, Oxon.); CP. 40/24, m. 56 (Charneles v Abbot of Selby; county court, Lincs.); CP. 40/27, m. 4 (Prior of Frampton v Bael; Northam hundred, Devon); CP. 40/27, m. 81d (fitz Jul v Kirkeman; Rotherham, Yorks.); CP. 40/27, m. 122 (Dodemore v Bertram; Newton, Yorks.).

[53] CP. 40/30, m. 84d.

[54] CP. 40/33, m. 5d (de la Snore v Redham): "Et Willelmus venit et defendit . . . et bene cognovit quod cepit predictos equos et hoc iuste, dicit enim quod quidam Magister Thomas de Depham aliquando tulit breve domini regis versus predictum Johannem de transgressione in pleno comitatu Norf'. Et postea in eodem comitatu concordati fuerunt ita quod predictus Johannes finem fecit cum predicto magistro de quinque marcis eidem magistro Thome solvendis die lune proxima post festum Purificacionis beate Marie anno regni regis septimo. Et concessit in eodem comitatu quod si ad diem predictum in solucione predictarum quincque marcarum defecisset quod vicecomes posset eum per omnia bona sua distringere. Et quia ad diem predictum in solucione predicta defeit, predictus Willelmus tunc vicecomes distrinxit ipsum per predictos equos. Et Johannes bene cognovit quod predictus Magister Thomas aliquando implacitavit ipsum de predicta transgressione in predicto comitatu et postea concordati fuerunt extra comitatum inter amicos suos ita quod predictus Johannes finem fecit cum ipso magistro de duabus marcis et dimidia tantum eidem magistro solvendis ad predictum diem lune proxima post predictum festum Purificacionis beate Marie, ad quem diem venit cum predicta pecunia ad predictum comitatum et eam ei optulit et quod predictus magister eam accipere contradixit et quod ita fecit finem cum ipso magistro pro predictis duabus marcis et dimidia tantum nec per ipsum stetit quin eas ad predictum diem recepisset. Et offert verificare sicut curia consideraverit." A *recordari* was ordered but not entered into the rolls (CP. 40/41, m. 13d; CP. 40/45, m. 10d).

had been pleaded would have been 9 January 1279, so that the writ could not have been purchased later than 26 December 1278 and was probably purchased some days earlier. That writ must have been one of the first of the new writs of trespass issued. Thereafter the viscontiel writs of trespass appear in registers of writs—in an increasing number of forms[55] and also in actions of false judgment.[56] The viscontiel writ of trespass must then have been provided by or immediately after the Statute of Gloucester.[57]

The hardship which was meant to be alleviated by the provision of the viscontiel writs of trespass was not the primary problem of local bias, but rather a lesser problem involving proof. The remedy for curial bias in plaints of trespass was henceforward limited, as before 1275, to the writ of false judgment. Nevertheless, for a time litigants in trespass in the lower courts had been able to obtain a jury trial by using the *recordari* to remove the case into the king's court. The decision to abolish *recordari* procedure for trespass plaints eliminated this possibility, but had been aimed not against the jury trial but rather against the number of insignificant trespass cases flooding into the king's court. The option of securing a jury trial, however, was now available in replevin by use of the *recordari* and had been available for three years in trespass. The viscontiel writs therefore may have

[55] *Early Registers of Writs*, pp. cxxxii-cxxxiii.

[56] CP. 40/53, m. 44d (Teitebourne v Poskyr; county court, Devon); CP. 40/70, m. 79d (Gutteleye v Overton; honor of Winchester, Leics.); CP. 40/61, m. 59 (Benet v Lung'; Bury St. Edmunds, Suff.); CP. 40/86, m. 27 (Horshe v Kyng; Colchester, Essex); CP. 40/86, m. 245d (Atte Medwe v Messager; Middleton hundred, Kent); CP. 40/89, m. 42 (fitz Richard v Anon.; Holland, Lincs.) and other instances between CP. 40/70 and CP. 40/86.

[57] See John Beckerman, "The Forty-Shilling Jurisdictional Limit in Medieval English Personal Actions," in *Legal History Studies 1972*, ed. Dafydd Jenkins (Cardiff, 1975), p. 117, n. 16, discussing Alan Harding's findings that the statute was often copied referring to "writs of trespass" rather than "pleas of trespass." I believe the statute did not provide the viscontiel writ, but that it was closely associated to the provision. Yale University MS 60, fol. 46v introduces the trespass writs with a rendition of the substance of the statute and a specific reference to the statute. Then it goes on without reference: "Item notandum est quod omnia brevia de transgressione cuiuscumque generis fuerint placitari possunt in comitatu exceptis illis brevibus in quibus mencio est de wulneribus et de imprisonamento et de vi et armis, quia ista brevia habent terminari coram justiciariis et non in comitatu coram vicecomite quia specialiter tangit coronam." E. 13/22, m. 66: John, parson of the church of Leck, Lancs., had been impleaded by one Seyrighta de Westleye "per breve domini regis de transgressione et ibidem per consideracionem comitatus recuperavit versus eundem Johannem x s pro dampnis suis et idem Johannes nichilominus amerciatus fuit versus dominum regem ad v s, per quod idem Radulfus [de Mountjoye] prefatum Johannem distrinxit per predicta duo jumenta pro predictis x s ad opus predicte Sayrighte et pro quinque solidis ad opus domini regis. Et quia idem Johannes dicta jumenta sua noluit acquietare, eadem jumenta tam pro predictis denariis quam pro custodia eorundem jumentorum adhuc remanent irreplegiata."

been provided so that the sheriff would have sufficient warrant to make jurors take the oath and render their verdict. Alternatively, the writs may have instituted some now unknown common law procedure in regard to particularly bothersome situations. Either way, such writs relieved the king's court of a growing burden of litigation.

The relationship of the provision of viscontiel writs of trespass to the abolition of *recordari* procedure for plaints of trespass is further shown by the fact that the writ *pone* was not available for viscontiel trespass. I have seen no *pone* for viscontiel trespass issued during the reigns of Edward I and Edward II. Moreover, a rule in the register of writs early in the fourteenth century notes specifically that a *pone* could not be had for the viscontiel writ of trespass, because it could not be known in advance whether or not the damages amounted to 40s.[58] That is precisely the line of reasoning that quashed *recordari* procedure in plaints of trespass. The denial of *pone* procedure restricted viscontiel trespass to the lower courts.

The denial of *pone* procedure continued at least through the reign of Edward III, although it was not maintained with complete rigidity. A note from another fourteenth-century register of writs repeated the rule against granting the *pone* for viscontiel trespass, but it also noted two instances in which exceptions had been made. One instance was in 1342. The defendant in that case had claimed that the plaintiff was his villein. The other instance had been in 1336. The reason for that removal had been that the defendant claimed that the land on which he had cut down the trees—the wrong of which the plaintiff was complaining—was his own free tenement.[59] The note clearly

[58] *Early Registers of Writs*, p. 125: "breve vicecomitale de transgressione nullo modo habet fieri pone, quia non potest sciri quando breve de transgressione placitatur in comitatu si dampna illa attingant xl solidos et ultra." The use of damages in this context rather than the value of the goods taken and carried away seems to hearken back to the pre-1278 rule (above, at nn. 31-33); that was required by the fact that many trespass writs included other allegations besides merely the taking and carrying away of goods and chattels. Yale University MS 60, fol. 10r (temp. late Edward I) has the same note, fol. 47v makes the same general point: "Et notandum quod transgressio in comitatu non potest poni extra comitatum neque recordari si transgressio fuit per breve vel sine."

[59] Bodleian Library, Rawlinson C. 454, fol. 300r: "Nota quod omnia brevia originalia in comitatu sive in aliis curiis placitabilia exceptis brevi de transgressione et brevi de catallis et debitis quorum summa non attingunt xl solidos possunt removeri coram justiciariis. Fait assavoir qen contre cest reule 'excepto brevi de transgressione vicecomitali' que deux foich ad brief de trespass este remue: une foich par tiele cause pur ceo que le soile ou les arbres sont cressantz est le fraunc terre le demaundant et ceo fist Ed' en anno decimo, autre foith pur cest cause pur ceo que le defendant dit que le plaintif fut son villeyn et ceo fist Harleston anno xvi." I owe this reference to the late G.D.G. Hall. The register is from the 1340s. The note is dated by the mention of

regards both instances as exceptional; probably neither were regularized. Particularly in the latter case, in which the removal was made because the case concerned a free tenement, removal was decidedly unnecessary. In the 1320s the register was very clear that in such a plea of trespass—specifically one involving trees cut down—the county court had sufficient warrant in the viscontiel writ to proceed to determine the real issue.[60] In 1531 the register still claimed that county courts had such power.[61] Removal of pleas of trespass by *pone* thus continued to be considered unnecessary; exceptions were probably very rare.

There is evidence that county courts did in fact determine such real issues in trespass. *Clerc v Attewode* was a case brought by viscontiel writ of trespass in the county court of Surrey; it was pleaded on 21 April 1333. Clerc complained of trees worth 40s cut down and carried away and of hedges broken, alleging total damages therefore of £10. Attewode claimed that the trees, while planted by Clerc, had been planted on his common pasture, whereas Clerc replied that the land was his close, separate from the common pasture. The sheriff summoned a jury on that issue, and the jury stated that Attewode had indeed broken into Clerc's close, committing damages worth 40s.[62] The verdict, while not in the form of a verdict clearly in the realty, involved real matter and expressed concisely the jurors' feelings that the land was Clerc's close and not common pasture. Such a decision gave clear warning to Attewode that a real action would probably not be successful. It gave Clerc a realistic expectation that he could defend his right to the land by personal actions against all harassment and could regain the land by real actions if he was ejected. In this way viscontiel trespass early in the fourteenth century had established itself as an action mixed in nature like replevin: part personal, part real.

William de Harlaston: *Select Cases in the Court of King's Bench*, ed. G. O. Sayles, 7 vols., Selden Society, vols. 55, 57, 58, 74, 76, 82, 88 (London, 1936-1971), 6:lxxxii-lxxxiii.

[60] *Early Registers of Writs*, p. 125 (R. 71r): "Nota. Si home port bref de trespas des arbres copez et la partie en pledant cleyme purpartie en le soil, la court ad poer a terminer la roialte: e si la parole soit saunz bref ele nad my poer. Donqe en tieu plee ne puet home en nul manere avoir le recordari, pur ce qe sil soit par bref la court ad poer a terminer, e si saunz bref la partie defendra la court a pleder plus en la roialte et sil aillent avant adonqe gist bref de faux iugement." Dalton, *Office and Authority of Sheriffs*, p. 163, states that viscontiel trespass cannot handle real issues.

[61] *Registrum Omnium Brevium*, p. 120b: "Si home port brief de trespas des arbres coupes, et le partie en pledant claime propirte en le soil, la court ad poer de terminer la realte. Et si la parole soyt saunz brief, ele nad mye poiar."

[62] *Chertsey Abbey Cartularies*, Surrey Record Society, vol. 12 (London, 1958), p. 370.

After 1281 both the differences and similarities between replevin and trespass encouraged the greater use of trespass. At least into the middle of the fourteenth century there was a great difference in venue between replevin and trespass. A plea of replevin, although it always began in the lower courts, was always subject to removal procedures whether it had been initiated by plaint or by writ. Trespass, however, terminated in that court in which it had originated. Both replevin and trespass could handle disputes concerning whether a piece of land was common or several pasture, and the certainty of venue in trespass by writ would have encouraged many litigants to avoid replevin. Perhaps in the mid-fourteenth, but certainly by the fifteenth century trespass by plaint in county was made more flexible. Just as had happened in replevin in the thirteenth century, real issues were coming up occasionally in cases of trespass brought by plaint. Instead of determinedly quashing those pleas, the *recordari* was finally granted for removal of trespass plaints. It seems, however, that not all plaints were removeable. The only *causa* clauses mentioned were ones concerning villeinage and free tenements. Such issues were by definition significant; the trespass *recordari* still could not include the value of the goods taken and carried away.[63] With that increased flexibility of

---

[63] Holdsworth, *A History of English Law*, 2:622: a table of contents for a register from around the 1430s with a listing for "recordari de transgressione cum causis." University of Michigan.Law Library R337, 148-, fol. 103v: "Recordari de transgressione. Rex vicecomiti Lincoln', salutem. Precipimus tibi quod in pleno comitatu tuo recordari facias loquelam etc inter A. et B. de quadam transgressione eidem A. per prefatum B. illata ut dicitur et recordum illud habeas etc et partibus etc et habeas ibi nomina predictorum quatuor militum et hoc breve. Teste etc. Causa. Quia predictus A. placitando in comitatu predicto asseruit quod predictus B. cepit porcos ipsius A. in communi pastura sua apud S. et eos ibidem imparcavit et idem B. e contrario allegavit quod ipse porcos illos in separali solo suo ut in dampno suo et non in communi pastura ipsius A. cepit et sic capcionem illam advocavit que quidem loquela eo quod tangit liberum tenementum sicut predictum est sine brevi nostro deduci non debet. Fiat execucio etc. Causa. Quia predictus prior etc clamavit prefatam Is[abellan] esse nativam ipsius prioris et ipsum prefate Isabelle ea occasione respondere non debere ut dicitur, cuius quidem clamii probacio in eadem curia terminari non potest propter quod loquela illa in curia predicta secundum legem et consuetudinem regni nostri Anglie ulterius deduci non debet. Fiat execucio etc. Causa. Quia predictus W. placitando in curia predicta asseruit prefatum priorem cum averiis suis herbam ipsius W. in quodam loco vocato S. in villa de A. depastum fuisse conculcasse et consumpsisse quem quidem locum idem prior clamat esse liberum tenementum et solum suum proprium ut dicitur, que quidem loquela eo quod tangit liberum tenementum sicut predictum est in eadem curia sine brevi nostro ulterius deduci non debet secundum legem et consuetudinem regni nostri Anglie. Fiat execucio, etc. Et auxint cest brief ad este recorde par tiel cause pur ceo qe le soil ou les arbres fuerent cressantz fuist le frank tenement le demaundant. Si un home port brief de trespas des arbres coupez et la partie empledant cleyme propertie en le soil la courte ad poaire a terminer la roialte. Mes si la parole soit santz brief el nad mye poaire. Donqes en tiel ple ne poet home avoir recordari, pur ceo qe sil soit par brief la courte ad poaire a terminer et si sanz brief la partie defendra la

trespass, the real side of trespass was strengthened; and trespass could absorb even more of the disputes which had been resolved by replevin.

The Statute of Gloucester thus had a serious impact on the action of trespass. A customary jurisdictional rule in trespass litigation in the king's court had been obviated by the provision of greater protection against curial bias in the lower courts in the form of the writ *recordari*. That procedure of removal was used excessively—probably often for harassment and delay—and the influx of insignificant cases brought the problem rapidly to the attention of the justices and resulted in the Statute of Gloucester, c. 8. The *recordari* continued to be granted in replevin, because that action had long—at least in those cases brought by writ—been removeable by *pone* into the king's court and able to settle real issues; the irremoveability of such plaints would have created useless problems. Plaints of trespass had no such tradition in a correlative writ of trespass and were not considered actions which could handle real issues; the use of the *recordari* was thus abolished in regard to them; the customary jurisdictional rule was reinstated. The secure option of a jury trial, however, was at least given litigants with the provision of the viscontiel writs of trespass, which, since they were designed only to meet a problem in the lower courts and were subject to the same technical problems related to removal and the Statute of Gloucester, were not subject to *pone* procedure. This unique restriction of pleas to the lower courts in trespass made trespass more subject to curial bias, but it also gave litigants certain advantages. Viscontiel trespass could not be whimsically delayed by removal; it had a certain venue. Finally, in the mid-fourteenth or early fifteenth century the *recordari* was made available for a limited class of trespass plaints. Before 1275 replevin had been composed of an unremoveable set of plaints and a removeable writ. Trespass came to be composed of an unremoveable writ and a limited class of removeable plaints. It was trespass which seemed to offer the best options to litigants.

The extension of the function of the *recordari* in 1275 had almost

---

courte a empleder pluis en la roialte et sils alent avant, donqes gist brief de faux suggestion. Causa. Quia predictus I placitando in hundredo predicto asseruit se habere talem libertatem quod ipse habere debet unam faldam de collecta ovium in M. et quod nullus sine licencia sua habebit faldam ibidem aliquo tempore anni nisi a tempore autumpni usque ad festum sancti Michaelis et predictus T. levavit unam faldam in villa predicta in preiudicium ipsius I et libertatis sue predicte in qua quidem villa predictus T clamat habere faldam de ovibus suis propriis quolibet tempore anni in terris et tenementis que ipse tenet de W. in villa predicta, que quidem loquela eo quod tangit liberum tenementum etc." See also *Registrum Omnium Brevium* (1531), pp. 120, 120b.

as great an impact on the development of litigation in debt/detinue as it had on trespass. The best-known rule concerning debt/detinue litigation in the lower courts is that a viscontiel writ was required for any case in which the debt or the thing detained was worth at least 40s. That rule has until recently always been associated with the Statute of Gloucester, c. 8, but John Beckerman has rightly pointed out that that statute only concerned trespass and, moreover, only reinforced a lower limit on trespass litigation in the king's court, not an upper limit on plaint litigation in the lower courts.[64] Until now, therefore, the reason for the imposition of that rule in debt/detinue has been unknown. As with trespass, the answer lies in the relationship between litigation in the king's court and litigation in the lower courts formed by the *pone* and *recordari*.

Whereas before 1275 there was a customary limit on trespass litigation in the king's court, it does not seem that the justices were ever very strict about a jurisdictional limitation in debt/detinue before the 1290s. In 1273 there was certainly a vague sense that 40s was the proper minimum sum for a case in debt/detinue in the court of common pleas. *Basinges v Marechal*,[65] *Richard v Bispayn*,[66] and *Basyng v Ku*[67] were all cases of debt or detinue claiming precisely 40s. At the same time, however, Agnes atte Parrok sued the executors of Henry de Inghram for only 37½s;[68] the following term *Kybbeworth v Thurlington* has the plaintiff suing a dozen defendants for several small sums, the total of which amounted to only 33s. 2d.[69] There were, of course, many cases for sums worth far more than 40s. The mixture of cases precisely at 40s with cases for smaller sums probably indicates the vague feeling in chancery that 40s was an appropriate minimum jurisdiction, but that that jurisdictional limitation was not rigid.

When the writ *recordari* was made available in 1275 for plaints of debt/detinue, it did not create the problems that the trespass *recordari* did. The use of the *recordari* for plaints of debt seems to have been very limited. There were, of course, already viscontiel writs of debt and detinue, and their availability would probably have made the use of the *recordari* less attractive. It had been made available for avoid-

[64] Beckerman, "The Forty-Shilling Limit," pp. 111-17.
[65] CP. 40/3, m. 19.
[66] CP. 40/3, m. 25d.
[67] CP. 40/3, m. 20d.
[68] CP. 40/3, m. 8d.
[69] CP. 40/5, m. 51.

ance of bias; there was no lure of a trial by jury as there was in trespass. The first documentable instance of the *recordari* used for debt/detinue came in Michaelmas term 1275: *York v Burneton*. That case would have caused no problem with any jurisdictional rule, for it concerned a debt of 35 marks claimed in the court of Newcastle-upon-Tyne.[70] It is unlikely that many cases concerning lesser debts were removed into the king's court; certainly they did not elicit the immediate response by statute that had been forthcoming in trespass. It is not surprising, therefore, that *Abyndon v Russel*, a case of debt brought by viscontiel writ in the county court of Berkshire for only 26s. 8d, was removed into the court of common pleas by *pone* in 1281.[71] The court of common pleas still had no strict minimum jurisdictional rule in debt/detinue.

It was not long, however, before the justices did impose such a jurisdictional rule in debt/detinue; that rule set the minimum at 40s, apparently deriving the figure from the related rule in trespass or from that vague feeling of the proper jurisdiction of the court of common pleas that can be shown even before 1275. The best indication of this new rule came in 1290: *Gapeton v Prior of Leighs*. The case came originally into the court of Lothingland hundred, Suffolk; and the prior wanted to remove the case into the court of common pleas, because he was litigating with the bailiff of the hundred court and suspected that the bailiff was therefore favoring the plaintiff. He used a *recordari* that specified that the debt was for 40s—a form of *recordari* which would allow the chancery to supervise the jurisdiction of the court of common pleas.[72] When the parties appeared in court, however, the plaintiff argued that the plea was for only 33s. 4d and that the justices should not acknowledge so humble a plea. It is noteworthy that the plaintiff did not seek to quash the *recordari* itself on the grounds that it did not agree with the plaint but went straight to challenging the case on jurisdictional grounds. The justices agreed with the plaintiff in considering it too humble a case for the justices

---

[70] CP. 40/11, m. 115d (CP. 40/14, m. 41d).

[71] CP. 40/41, m. 45.

[72] It would seem that this form would run afoul the same difficulties that the trespass *recordari* that specified the value of the goods taken and carried away had in 1281. It is possible, however, that sheriffs were required to have some kind of specification in plaints. In replevin sheriffs were expected to know that it was an action of replevin concerning 330 sheep; in trespass they were expected to know that it was a plaint of trespass concerning goods taken and carried away; in the same way they might be expected to know that it was a case of debt for 40s. Knowing in trespass that the goods taken and carried away were worth 40s is going further than that, since it asks for two items of specification.

to handle and returned the case to the hundred court.[73] At least by that time, then, the court of common pleas had a firm rule that its minimum jurisdiction in debt/detinue was 40s.

During the time that there was no strict jurisdictional minimum in debt/detinue in the court of common pleas, there was no jurisdictional rule setting a maximum for plaints of debt/detinue in the lower courts. The precise origins of the rule are difficult to date. Certainly no statute imposed such a limitation on the lower courts. The court rolls of lower courts are likewise of little use in determining the date, since few court rolls are extant from the 1270s and 1280s and before; those that are extant seldom note the amount of the debt claimed or whether the case was brought by writ or by plaint. Investigation thus must be somewhat more indirect. The only evidence of the litigation in lower courts sufficiently precise at that early date comes from actions of false judgment in the king's court. This data, together with the traits of litigation produced by the 40s rule and the first direct mentions of the rule itself allow fairly precise determination of the rule that limited the "natural" plaint litigation of the lower courts in the important areas of debt and detinue.

Cases of debt and detinue on which actions of false judgment were brought in the court of common pleas indicate that lower courts still

---

[73] CP. 40/83, m. 135d: "Suff'. Preceptum fuit vicecomiti quod assumptis secum quatuor discretis et legalibus militibus de comitatu suo in propria persona accederet ad dimidium hundredum Johannis de Balliolo de Ludinglond et in dimidio hundredo illo recordari faceret loquelam que fuit in eodem dimidio hundredo sine brevi regis inter Rogerum de Gapeton et priorem de Legh et fratrem Willelmum de Donemore [de] debito quadraginta solidorum quod idem Rogerus a prefatis priore et Willelmo exigit. Et recordum illud haberet hic ad hunc diem sub sigillo etc. Et partibus eundem diem prefigeret etc. Quia predictus prior in curia regis coram ipso domino rege implacitat Ricardum de Aldewantt, ballivum dimidii hundredi predicti, qui tenet placita eiusdem dimidii hundredi de quadam transgressione eidem priori per prefatum Ricardum illata etc., propter quod idem ballivus fovet predictum Rogerum in loquela predicta etc. Fiat execucio istius brevis si causa sit vera et predicti prior et Willelmus hoc petant et aliter non. Et predictus Rogerus et similiter predicti prior et frater Willelmus per attornatos suos veniunt et Rogerus dicit quod loquela ista venit hic ad suggestionem predicti prioris. Et dicit quod ipse in predicto dimidio hundredo implacitavit ipsum priorem de triginta et tribus solidis et quatuor denariis tantum. Et de hoc ponit se super recordum dimidii hundredi predicti, unde petit iudicium si curia ista de tam exili debito habeat cognoscere etc. Et quia convictum est per predictum recordum quod vicecomes modo misit hic quod placitum in predicto dimidio hundredo fuit tantum de triginta et tribus solidis et quatuor denariis nec curia ista debet cognoscere de tam exili debito, consideratum est quod redeant ad predictum dimidium hundredum etc. Et prior quia per falsam suggestionem oneravit curiam etc., ideo ipse in misericordia." The record sent by the sheriff has not survived. Yale University MS 60, fol. 84r (temp. late Edward I) has the note "Sciendum quod nullum debitum quod est minus quam xl s potest placitari in banco, set in comitatu." That note disappeared before the Bodleian register "R" of 1318-1320.

considered themselves competent to handle plaints of debt/detinue for 40s or more as late as 1291. Between 1272 and 1291 there were fifty-four cases of false judgment concerning debt or detinue in lower courts. Twenty-five of these cases had been brought by writ in the lower courts and were concerned with amounts of 40s or more.[74] Fourteen more concerned cases brought by plaint in the lower courts for debts or for things detained worth less than 40s.[75] These thirty-nine actions indicate that there were reasons other than violations of a 40s rule for bringing actions of false judgment in debt/detinue. The

[74] CP. 40/17, m. 51 (Anon. v Ralee; county court, Devon; debt of 20 marks); CP. 40/17, m. 136d (Rotindin v Fleming; county court, Leics.; debt of £10); CP. 40/18, m. 55 (Hertford v Bynetre; court of Hatfield, Herts.; debt of 50s); CP. 40/28, m. 38d (Wyteford v Coston; county court, Worcs.; debt of 25 marks); CP. 40/33, m. 22d (Harecurt v Sonninges; county court, Beds.; debt of 10 marks); CP. 40/39, m. 60d (Edefeld v Abbot of St. Peter, Gloucester; county court, Glos.; debt of 33½ marks); CP. 40/49, m. 39d (Grumenhull v Mauveysin; county court, Lancs.; debt of 24 marks 3s. 4½d); CP. 40/51, m. 57 (Malewyn v Perham; county court, Wilts.; debt of 8 marks); CP. 40/52, m. 32 (Gemldale v de Alta Ripa; county court, Yorks.; debt of 10 marks); CP. 40/53, m. 11d (Schot v Stretdley; county court, Notts.; detinue of chattels worth 14 marks); CP. 40/55, m. 20 (Schaldford v Vincent; county court, Essex; debt of 110s); CP. 40/58, m. 5 (Langedene v Prouz; county court, Devon; debt of 12 marks); CP. 40/59, m. 68 (Carpenter v Gyssiche; court of Newport, Isle of Wight; debt of 19 marks); CP. 40/60, m. 137d (Abbot of Revesby v Trehampton; county court, Lincs.; debt of 6 marks); CP. 40/63, m. 8 (Abbot of St. Augustine, Canterbury v Huntingfeud; county court, Kent; debt of 8 marks); CP. 40/67, m. 18d (Podderigge v Lowe; county court, Devon; debt of 100s); CP. 40/70, m. 98 (Sampson v Burton; county court, Rutland; debt of 100s); CP. 40/70, m. 94 (Burne v Mosewelle; court of Canterbury, Kent; debt of 9½ marks); CP. 40/72, m. 3 (Cobeldyck v Pecche; court of Holland, Lincs.; debt of 40s); CP. 40/76, m. 18d (Gorges v Bracebrigg; county court, Warw.; debt of 5 marks); CP. 40/79, m. 41 (Trelosk v de Campo Arnulphi; county court, Devon; debt of 80 marks); CP. 40/80, m. 20d (Wylenby v Sees; court of south trithing, Lincs.; debt of 50 marks); CP. 40/83, m. 158 (Burgeys v Cherbesund; county court, Kent; debt of 40s); CP. 40/90, m. 62 (Houton v Nel; court of Lincoln, Lincs.; debt of 9 marks, 6s); CP. 40/91, m. 46d (Espicer v Boulton; court of Carlisle, Cumb.; debt of 100s).

[75] CP. 40/15, m. 86 (Denham v Shotford; court of Hoxne hundred, Suff.; debt of 30s); CP. 40/24, m. 45d (Chiselhampton v Scaccario; court of Bullingdon hundred, Oxon.; debt of 17s. 3/4d); CP. 40/41, m. 64 (Bould v Codding; court of Forehoe hundred, Norf.; detinue of 3½ quarters of barley worth 14s); CP. 40/44, m. 63d (Upton v Vicar of Chalfont; county court, Bucks.; debt of 23s); CP. 40/47, m. 84d (Godwyne v Godsire; court of Blofield hundred, Norf.; detinue of chattels worth 2s); CP. 40/47, m. 97d (Melkhog v Waleys; court of Newington, Kent; debt of 6s); CP. 40/59, m. 33d (Keu v Braham; county court, Northants.; detinue of chattels worth 2 marks); CP. 40/69, m. 81 (Trewynt v Billou; court of Redlegan, Corn.; debt of 27s); CP. 40/73, m. 9 (Prior of Walsingham v Corlu; court of Little Walsingham, Norf.; debt of 38s); CP. 40/73, m. 27 (Fenne v Ede; court of Boston, Lincs.; debt of 5s); CP. 40/80, m. 106d (Prior of Woburn v Hervy; court of Holt hundred; debt of 20s); CP. 40/81, m. 25 (Wyngeford v Leyston; court of the honor of Eye, Suff.; debt of 11s); CP. 40/82, m. 41 (Hawys v Boydin; court of Fenny Newbold, Warw.; detinue of chattels worth 10s); CP. 40/83, m. 158 (Middelton v Kep; court of Hevingham, Norf.; debt of 20s).

remaining fourteen actions of false judgment, however, concerned debts worth 40s or more claimed originally in the lower courts by plaint. Of these, four had been brought by merchants and thus are irrelevant, since merchants were exempt from the later 40s rule.[76] The remaining ten cases, however, are prima facie evidence that lower courts were still willing to handle plaints of debt/detinue in excess of 40s.[77] Further evidence for that point comes from the fact that the chancery seems to have had no objection to issuing a *recordari* in 1283 for a case brought by plaint in the county court of Cornwall for a debt of 60 marks.[78] Plaint litigation in debt/detinue in the lower courts was not yet limited in the 1280s.

One of the most certain indications of a 40s jurisdictional rule is the appearance of plaints of debt claiming only 39s. 11d or 39s. 11½d. That figure is improbable for a debt unless the plaintiff was seeking to avoid prosecution by writ. Moreover, such plaints often occurred in clusters between the same parties, indicating that one large debt had been broken up into several smaller debts. None of the false judgment cases before 1292 were for that peculiar amount, although several were for the more normal sum of 40s.[79] Furthermore, all the instances of the 39s. 11d plaint which are usually cited come from fourteenth-century rolls. The earliest evidence for such plaints that I have been able to find is a false judgment case from Trinity term 1292: *Curpel v Martyn.*[80] Thereafter, such pleas find their way reg-

[76] CP. 40/11, m. 39d (Wermund and Aeria v Abbot of Louth Park; court of Boston, Lincs.; debt of £100 and 14 sacks and 20 stones of wool worth 217 marks); CP. 40/52, m. 13d (Carpenter v Lo; court of Stamford, Lincs.; debt of 8 marks); CP. 40/55, m. 42 (Molyns v Bretaldon; court of Lincoln, Lincs.; debt of £16); CP. 40/62, m. 50 (Bonavel v le Moyne; court of Stamford, Lincs.; debt of £55/2/10).

[77] CP. 40/5, m. 42d (Passelewe v Lousemere; court of Cirencester, Glos.; debt of 6 marks); CP. 40/9, m. 26d (Cordel v Taverner; court of Castle Acre, Surrey; debt of 10 marks); CP. 40/14, m. 2 (Hautebyn v Wolleward; court of Exeter, Devon; detinue of wine worth 40 marks); CP. 40/39, m. 48d (Crowe v Cokesford; court of honor of Eye, Suff.; detinue of chattels worth 9 marks); CP. 40/49, m. 18 (Surlingham v Gernemuth; court of Great Yarmouth, Norf.; debt of 8 marks); CP. 40/52, m. 64 (Totebygge v Longeville; court of Southampton, Hants.; debt of 100s); CP. 40/52, m. 55d (Couper v Ryght; court of Bromley, Midd.; detinue of chattels worth 40s); CP. 40/52, m. 56d (Clerk v Rower; court of Gloucester, Glos.; debt of £36); CP. 40/73, m. 11d (Choldesworth v Attemere; court of Plympton, Devon; debt of 40s. 9d); CP. 40/90, m. 123 (Sengham v Metringham; county court of Kent; detinue of wine worth 40s).

[78] CP. 40/49, m. 49 (Littlebir' v St. Constantino).

[79] Above, n. 74.

[80] CP. 40/95, m. 18d: "Norf'. Preceptum fuit vicecomiti quod assumptis secum quatuor legalibus militibus de comitatu suo in propria persona accederet ad hundredum abbatis de Rameseye de Clakelose et in pleno hundredo illo recordari faceret loquelam que fuit in eodem hundredo sine brevi regis inter Johannem Curpel et Nicholaum

ularly into actions of false judgment. This trait of litigation, then, would not date the 40s rule prior to 1292.

That jurisdictional rule had at least been considered prior to 1292, however, because it was specifically mentioned in connection with the merchants' exemption from its effects. The tradition that merchants were allowed to prosecute by plaint for any sum is said to have resulted from the delay and actual loss which would otherwise have resulted from the merchants' itinerant life. The earliest mention of that exemption came in *Bonavel v le Moyne*, a case of false judgment on a plaint of debt for £55.2.10 in the court of Stamford, Lincolnshire. At Stamford in 1286 the defendant had claimed that he was not obliged to answer the plaintiff unless he was prosecuted by writ, because the plea exceeded 40s. The plaintiff responded with a very clear assertion of the merchants' exemption from the rule, and the court ruled in his favor. Even so, the court hesitated to execute the judgment. The plaintiff therefore obtained a royal writ commanding execution of the judgment, and the writ specified both that the case was brought by plaint and that the claim was for £55.2.10. Thereafter, the defendant accused the court of a false judgment. When the parties and the four men of the court of Stamford came into the court of common pleas pursuant to the writ of false judgment, there were further problems. The four men testified that the record was correct, so that, had the rule been clearly accepted at that time, judgment would have been rendered quickly in their favor. The four men, however, left the court in contempt, obviously fearing that judgment would be given against them. On another day they reappeared and objected expressly that merchants had always pleaded without writ concerning any debt in their court. The justices, still undecided, appointed a further day for judgment. Stamford, however, still considered the justices inclined against them. They thus pursued a policy of delay, one or another of the four men failing to appear as each successive day in court arrived. The case was thus pending from 1286 to the end of 1290, when it disappeared from the rolls without judgment rendered.[81]

Martyn de debito triginta et novem solidorum undecim denariorum et unius oboli quod idem Johannes a prefato Nicholao exigit, unde idem Nicholaus queritur falsum sibi factum fuisse iudicium in eodem hundredo. Et recordum illud haberet hic ad hunc diem sub sigillo suo et per quatuor legales.homines eiusdem hundredi ex illis qui recordo illi interfuerunt et summoneret predictum Johannem quod esset hic ad hunc diem etc., audiendum recordum illud.'' CP. 40/92, m. 143d (Lyulf v Pedwardyn) concerns the execution of a judgment in a case of debt for 39s. 4d in the court of Meon (Mene?), Herefordshire. That sum, however, might well indicate the real debt, whereas 39s. 11½d is the classic case for evasion of the jurisdictional rule.

[81] CP. 40/62, m. 50; CP. 40/64, m. 40d (the pleading and process until the departure

A similar issue, however, was decided rapidly in favor of the court of Boston, Lincolnshire, in 1293.[82] It would thus seem that the merchants' exemption was not accepted until 1293. That conclusion is reinforced by an incident in *Stavere v Scot*, a plaint of debt for £10 brought between merchants in the court of King's Lynn, Norfolk. Among the reasons which Scot adduced to further his allegation of false judgment in the king's court was the 40s rule, that that court did not have the authority to handle such a plea without a royal writ. Stavere commented that he had not made that objection during the original case—that in itself might be taken to indicate that the rule was very new—and that merchants were exempt from that rule anyway.[83] Thus the exemption of the merchants and the 40s rule itself

in contempt of court; for this entry see *Select Cases Concerning the Law Merchant*, ed. H. Hall, 3 vols., Selden Society, vols. 23, 46, 49 [London, 1908-1932], 2:42-43); CP. 40/67, m. 70d; CP. 40/69, m. 49d; CP. 40/70, m. 59d; CP. 40/78, m. 76; CP. 40/80, m. 42 (Walter Norman, one of the four men, was here reported dead; the justices ordered another man chosen in his place); CP. 40/83, m. 63d. The court involved in this case belonged to the abbot of Peterborough; John de Warenne's court in Stamford was also beleaguered with such problems (below, chapter 9 at n. 8).

[82] CP. 40/98, m. 21 (Oston v Eyton). This was a case of debt brought by plaint for £16. Eleven suitors of the court came "et dicunt quod Willelmus de Ros habet duas curias in villa de Sancto Botulpho: unam, videlicet, curiam baronis que tenetur de tribus septimanis in tres septimanas, de qua curia ipsi sunt sectatores; et aliam curiam que tenetur tempore nundinarum sancti Botulphi, que regitur et tenetur per consuetudines et consideracionem mercatorum extraneorum transeuntium. Et dicunt quod loquela illa quam predictus Radulphus modo petit recordari placitata fuit in curia illa que tenetur per mercatores ad morem et consuetudinem ipsorum. Et petunt iudicium de brevi isto quod impetratur in communi forma ac si processus loquele predicte agitatus fuisset in predicta curia que tenetur de tribus septimanis in tres septimanas. Et Radulphus non potest hoc dedicere et petit licenciam recedendi de brevi suo. Et habet. Ideo predicti sectatores inde sine die etc." (See also CP. 40/93, m. 9d.) This was a recently changed policy, not merely a procedural challenge. The same objection had been made in Carpenter v Lo by the sheriff: "accessit ad predictam curiam ad faciendum recordum, et curia predicta nullum recordum sibi facere voluit asserens quod predictum iudicium factum fuit tempore nundinarum per mercatores extraneos et non per sectatores curie et sectatores predicte curie nullum (recordum) facere voluerunt." The sheriff nonetheless was ordered to have them record the plea: CP. 40/52, m. 13d. Process continued in the plea for some time while the suitors rightly refused to record a plea they had not heard: CP. 40/53, m. 13d; CP. 40/55, m. 12d; CP. 40/57, m. 13d. Another attempt was made to correct the situation on CP. 40/59, m. 9d when the sheriff returned "quod nulli sunt sectatores Johannis de Warenna comitis Surr' de Stamford." Process continued even then, however: CP. 40/60, m. 88d. Oston v Eyton, above, thus represents a clear exclusion of the merchants' courts from the common law system not clearly acknowledged before.

[83] CP. 40/105, m. 124d: "Dicit eciam quod nulla curia auctoritatem habet placitandi aliqua placita debiti ultra debitum quadraginta solidorum sine brevi regis etc., . . . [And then the defence to this challenge:] Et ad hoc quod predictus Adam dicit sibi falsum factum fuisse iudicium in hoc quod curia predicta tenuit predictum placitum de predictis decem libris sine brevi regis etc., dicit quod de huiusmodi calumpnia non

had been considered as early as 1286, but no firm decision was made before 1291-1293.

The best method for determining when the rule came into effect, however, is by tracing the origins of the writ of prohibition, which allowed defendants to produce in the lower court a royal order to quash such a case heard by plaint for a debt worth 40s or more. Any serious intent to impose a jurisdictional rule on lower courts would require such a writ, since those lower courts, on the basis of pre-scriptive jurisdiction, would have tended to continue hearing plaints in excess of 40s. Such a writ makes its way into the printed registers of writs only in the 1320s.[84] The earliest appearance of the prohibition in the plea rolls of the court of common pleas comes somewhat earlier, in 1296: *Gobaud v Prior Spalding*. The prohibition there concerned a case of debt brought by plaint for 100s in the prior's own court at Spalding. The prohibition had been presented to the prior on 18 March 1295. In the court of common pleas it was thereafter alleged that the prior had entertained the plea against the custom of the realm and in contempt of the royal prohibition. The prior in his defense replied that he was not obliged to answer such an allegation. A writ based on such a prohibition, he said, was a new writ, newly conceived, and never up to that time used in chancery; nor, he maintained, was the writ founded on the common law or on statute. The case was adjourned for judgment but simply disappeared.[85] Such pleading, however, is sufficient proof that the writ of prohibition for such cases was relatively new and that the 40s rule was still relatively recent in origin. The prohibition reappeared in the rolls of the court of common pleas in 1300[86] and was incorporated into the register that is now in print. The latest date that can be set to the origins of the 40s rule for plaints of debt/detinue in lower courts is thus 18 March 1295.

A basic chronology for the development of the relevant rules for debt/detinue can thus be constructed. Sometime after 1281 and before 1290 the court of common pleas adopted a lower limit to its jurisdiction in debt/detinue, influenced partly by what had been considered proper

---

fit mencio etc., et nichilominus dicit quod secundum legem mercatoriam et racione libertatis burgensium Lenn' per cartas regis Anglie concesse et usitate curia predicta auctoritatem habuit cognoscendi in predicto placito sine brevi regis inter burgenses etc." There was no further argument on that point.

[84] *Early Registers of Writs*, p. 223 (R. 487-489). (R. 490 is an attachment upon a violation of the 40s rule.)

[85] Appendix VI.

[86] CP. 40/133, m. 166 (Draper v Bykenore and Heyberere); the defendants in the case were the king's bailiffs of Gloucester.

prior to 1275, partly by the rule which had been reinforced by the Statute of Gloucester for the other major branch of personal actions, trespass. By 1286 there had been serious consideration of requiring writs in lower courts for all claims in debt/detinue amounting to at least 40s. The Statute of Wales of that year, which contained a similar provision for Welsh counties, can be seen as a further indication of the thought of English justices.[87] In 1291 that rule was finally accepted, along with the corollary that merchants were not bound to abide by the limitation to plaint jurisdictions in the lower courts. Immediately ordinary litigants who wanted to evade the restrictions imposed by the rule began bringing multiple suits for sums of 39s. 11½d, thus avoiding the possibility that the case could be removed into the court of common pleas by *pone*. At least as soon as four years later chancery was issuing writs of prohibition for plaints of debt/detinue of or exceeding 40s.

The chronology indicates a relationship between the jurisdictional rules in the king's court and the jurisdictional rules in the lower courts. The logic of the new rules was predicated upon the use of the *recordari*. Prior to 1275 plaints had not been removeable from the lower courts. In 1275 plaints of replevin, trespass, and debt/detinue were made removeable with the newly revised *recordari* writ. Plaints of replevin continued to be removeable, because of the real implications of that action. Plaints of trespass removed by *recordari*, however, made impossible chancery's enforcement of a customary jurisdictional rule in the king's court, so that in 1278 the Statute of Gloucester reinforced that rule. The reinforcement made the *recordari* unworkable for plaints of trespass, so that the writ was no longer available after about 1280. By then, however, writs of viscontiel trespass had been made available to alleviate the hardships imposed on litigants by the withdrawal of the *recordari* for trespass, although those writs were unusual in not being subject to *pone* procedure. That oddity was the reason why there was never any upper limit to plaint jurisdiction in trespass in the lower courts.[88] Debt by plaint was a totally different matter. The jurisdictional rules in the court of common pleas had not been very strict for pleas of debt/detinue, and the introduction of the *recordari* procedure did not result in a great influx of cases of debt/detinue from the lower courts, largely because viscontiel writs of debt/detinue were already available. Debt/detinue was

---

[87] cc. 6, 9. Note that in Wales also the lower limit of the central court corresponded with an upper limit in the lower courts.

[88] Beckerman, "The Forty-Shilling Limit."

therefore not a problem which required the drastic solution applied to trespass in the Statute of Gloucester. Lesser cases of debt, however, were a nuisance, and the justices of the court of common pleas by 1290 had decided that cases of debt/detinue were to be subjected to a jurisdictional rule requiring those pleas concerning amounts of less than 40s to be excluded from the jurisdiction of the court of common pleas. The 40s jurisdictional rule in the court of common pleas automatically excluded the removal of any plaint of debt or writ of debt for less than 40s. Any plaint of debt or writ of debt for 40s or more, however, would still have been removeable. As in trespass, nevertheless, it was impossible to know the value of a plaint of debt when the defendant was the party initiating the removal[89] and difficult for the sheriff even when the plaintiff was removing the plea. With a viscontiel writ of debt, the amount of the debt was specified in the original writ itself, thus eliminating the problem. To have allowed plaints of debt to be brought for large sums, therefore, would have been to allow plaintiffs claiming large debts the power of denying to their defendants the ability to remove such an important case out of a court they might find very prejudicial to themselves. Such a right, however, had become firmly established since 1275; the only exception was trespass and that exception was seen as the result of statutory action, a part of the now unique essence of trespass. The only way, then, to insure both the jurisdictional rule of the court of common pleas and the right of the defendant to an impartial court was to insist that every plea of debt or detinue claiming 40s or more and brought in a lower court had to be brought by writ. The 40s limit concerning debt/detinue plaints in lower courts was thus necessitated by the interaction of a 40s jurisdictional limit in the court of common pleas with a firm commitment since 1275 to provide impartial justice even in cases originated by plaint and with the vagaries of the procedure required by the *recordari* writ.

The way in which these problems came before the justices is a matter of some speculation, but it is possible that the main factor was personal involvement. In Trinity term of 1291 one John de Metringham brought a writ of false judgment against the county court of Cambridgeshire. He had been the defendant in a plaint of detinue brought by one William de Sengham claiming a cask of wine worth 40s. This was precisely the situation the requirement of a writ in cases of debt/detinue worth 40s or more was designed to prevent.

[89] Above, before n. 39.

The case was worth 40s and was thus worthy to be considered by the court of common pleas. The defendant thought he had been wronged and probably thought that even before the case had been concluded. If he had tried to purchase a *recordari* to remove the plaint, however—and there is no evidence whether or not he did attempt to purchase a *recordari*—it would have been denied him. Just as in trespass, the defendant would not be able to assert the value of the case; because of the jurisdictional limit recently decided upon by the justices in debt/detinue, the *recordari* had become unworkable for debt/detinue. Metringham thus had to let the judgment go against him and make use of the more serious and cumbersome writ of false judgment. This situation put the problem in a very clear form before the justices. It is just possible, even, that it concerned one of the justices. John de Mettingham had only recently been made chief justice of the court of common pleas. It is conceivable that he was the defendant himself and had faced and recognized the difficulties of the rules.[90] There could have been no more persuasive advocate for the introduction of the 40s rule for lower courts. Even if "Metringham" must be taken to refer to Metheringham in Lincolnshire rather than Mettingham in Suffolk, that case comes at the right time and is likely to have been the catalyst for the imposition of the rule.

This new rule regulating plaint jurisdiction in the lower courts in debt/detinue changed one of the oldest rules of viscontiel debt. The old procedure determined the plaintiff's choice as to whether he ought to purchase a viscontiel writ of debt. The plaintiff who wanted to make use of reasonable proof—*racionabilis monstracio*—in the form of a writing or tally would need a writ; that writ enabled him to force the defendant to answer to the proof and barred him from simply making his law on the obligation. In many cases, therefore, the writ would obviate the necessity of proof other than the deed; when necessary, trial could be had in the form of a jury—including witnesses mentioned in the deed itself—to tell whether or not the writing was a forgery. That old and rational structure was demolished when any case of debt required a writ when it claimed 40s or more, regardless of the kind of proof the plaintiff could proffer. Henceforward, as in the court of common pleas, proof in viscontiel debt had to be determined by the course of the proceedings. If the plaintiff could put forward a deed, the proof could be by jury and compurgation could

[90] CP. 40/90, m. 123; CP. 40/96, m. 99. The form "Metringham" is used consistently in both entries. Those two entries are in the rolls of Trinity term 1291 and Michaelmas term 1292.

be avoided; if the plaintiff had no deed, however, he would still have to use a viscontiel writ for cases concerning 40s or more. In that latter case, proof would often take the form of compurgation. This hypothesis certainly explains the confusion on the force of the words "as he shall reasonably be able to show" in the case brought on a viscontiel writ of debt in 1298.[91] It would also show how those words came to be included in the writ and then became mere form.

The introduction of *recordari* procedure for plaints of replevin, trespass, and debt/detinue in 1275 went far beyond the mere alteration in the form of the *recordari* writ. It was, first of all, a clear commitment by the government of Edward I to put an end to the corruption— or, better, to the opportunities for corruption—which was coming to light from the Ragman Inquests. Prior to 1275 only cases begun by viscontiel or seignorial writs were considered open to royal intervention prior to judgment. After 1275 any allegation of injustice would be sufficient to bring a case into the king's court even before judgment rendered. This commitment to impartial justice was substantial even with the subsequent revisions which enforced the traditional limits of minimum jurisdiction in the court of common pleas. Furthermore, the alteration of the *recordari* drastically changed the nature of three of the most important actions in the county courts. Plaints of replevin were no longer restricted to issues in the personalty and thus became more useful to litigants, although more open to useless delay. Trespass was reinforced in the lower courts by the provision of the viscontiel writs of trespass and acquired a new, valuable, and unique characteristic in not being subject to any removal procedure at all. In the long term, this advantage made trespass more useful than replevin in the lower courts and retained for trespass a position a little beyond the realm of strictly personal issues in the fringes of the realm of realty. For debt and detinue, the complicated series of events following the provision of the *recordari* meant the end of the utility of prosecution of large debts in most lower courts. There was little attraction to prosecuting large debts in lower courts when the case could easily be removed after jury verdict or failure of law into the king's court to begin again with mesne procedure. Before 1275 removal procedure even by *pone* had not been utilized all that frequently; after 1275 it soon became a matter of course; nor could one even avoid removal by prosecuting by plaint, because of the 40s plaint restriction. Only courts such as borough courts whose inhabitants could claim that they

---

[91] Above, chapter 7 at n. 64.

should be prosecuted only locally continued to find local litigation for large sums useful. For county courts as such, finally, the introduction of the *recordari* and the greater availability of the *pone* since 1274-1275 initiated a process which reduced them from substantial courts handling a wide variety of cases by writ and many cases concerning important matters by plaint to courts which, except in trespass, were in practice normally used only for relatively small debts and seldom for cases initiated by writ.[92] These changes certainly account for the jurisdiction of the county courts revealed in the extant fourteenth-century plea rolls; they also show the changes in the county courts which comprised the local counterpart to the great increase in the importance of the court of common pleas in the reign of Edward I.

[92] The *recordari* remained available for covenant (*Early Registers of Writs*, p. 232 [R. 528]; Holdsworth, *History of English Law*, 2:625; *Registrum Omnium Brevium*, p. 166 [for a personal covenant]), but they must have been infrequently used in the reign of Edward I, because I have not noted any. Covenant brought by plaint was not restricted by a 40s limit in lower courts; the only writ of prohibition for such cases was a writ for plaints of covenant which were more properly plaints of debt sued in the form of covenant to evade the 40s debt/detinue rule: *Registrum Omnium Brevium*, p. 146. In the seventeenth century Dalton, *Office and Authority of Sheriffs*, p. 163, talks about a 40s limit in trespass and covenant brought by viscontiel writ and refers to a prohibition; but on p. 162 he also notes that viscontiel trespass can claim £20 or more in damages. His evidence is thus unreliable.

9

County,
Courts, and
Country

⚶

THE STATUS of the county courts in the thirteenth century in England was defined not only by the cases which came before them, but also by the relationship of the county courts to feudal courts, liberties, courts of the ancient demesne, and the king's court and Parliament. The counties' relationships to feudal courts—summarized in large part by the process of tolt[1]—and to the king's court—summarized in the processes demanded by the writs of false judgment, *pone, recordari*, and several other lesser processes of removal[2]—have already been treated to some degree. Just as important in shaping the county courts, however, were the alterations in the functioning of the courts of liberties and of the ancient demesne. The controversy over the franchise of return of writs in the thirteenth century defined the relationship between the county courts and the courts of liberties; the separation of the ancient demesne from county jurisdiction excluded portions of the county completely from the overall supervision of the county courts. Finally, Parliament was in part built upon the vitality of the county courts, and the development of Parliament allocated to the county courts the function of electing representatives, an allocation of duties which did not appear particularly important compared with the rest of the functions of the county courts at that time but which became without doubt the most important function of the county courts.

The franchise of return of writs was a major source of controversy between holders of liberties and the king in the latter half of the

---

[1] Above, chapter 6, n. 8 ff.
[2] Above, chapter 6.

263

thirteenth century. That franchise was considered one of the high franchises, one which granted to the holder the exercise of important governmental functions within his liberty. Between 1250 and 1258 under Henry III and then again under Edward I between 1278 and 1294, the king and his lawyers made an ambitious attempt to regularize the vast array of privileges, often held merely by long usage, possessed by the boroughs, petty aristocrats, and magnates throughout England. This effort was directed expressly against usurpation and was guided by the theory that all governmental functions belonged ultimately to the king and had to be exercised as a delegation of his authority. Those who exercised such functions—who claimed to hold franchises—were thus called upon to justify their possession through cases of *quo warranto*.[3] Undoubtedly the best proof of rightful possession of a franchise was a royal charter that expressly granted the holder or his ancestor the right claimed. It was on this point that investigation into the franchise of return of writs encountered its most serious obstacle: the phrase "return of writs" had been infrequent prior to 1250 and had seldom been used in royal charters.[4] The meaning of the phrase and its relationship to similar grants made before 1250 thus caused major problems for the courts; modern-day historians find the problem equally confusing.

The franchise of return of writs, by current interpretation, allowed the holder of a liberty to execute within his liberty those orders conveyed by writ to the sheriff which otherwise the sheriff or his bailiffs would have been obliged to execute. The process which embodied the franchise was in large part a clerical one. Upon receipt of a royal writ which required execution within a liberty, the sheriff's clerk was to make out a transcription of the writ. That transcription was known as a "return." The return was transmitted to the bailiff of the liberty, while the writ itself was retained in the sheriff's office. The bailiff of the liberty was then required to execute the contents of the return and notify the sheriff of his actions. The bailiff's report was then written onto the dorse of the writ, and the writ was returned to the king's court. The franchise of return of writs thus was the right to execute royal mandates within one's own liberty.[5]

It was the clerical part of this process that was unique to the fran-

---

[3] Donald W. Sutherland, *Quo Warranto Proceedings in the Reign of Edward I, 1278-1294* (Oxford, 1963), pp. 16-31; Michael Clanchy, "The Franchise of Return of Writs," *Transactions of the Royal Historical Society* 17 (1967):59-82.

[4] Clanchy, "Return of Writs," pp. 62-63, 81.

[5] Ibid., pp. 62-63; Henry of Bracton, p. 169 would lead one to a similar conclusion.

chise of return of writs, not the exclusion of the sheriff and his ministers. Some liberties could claim prescriptive right from time immemorial to exclude the sheriff. That claim by long usage was based ultimately on political realities; some lords were so powerful that a sheriff could not assemble the force necessary to intrude himself into the liberty. Many liberties, however, could claim the right to exclude the sheriff by virtue of a charter that contained the ancient *non intromittat* clause, a clause designed specifically to exclude the sheriff from a liberty. In 1252, however, the *non intromittat* clause was held to be insufficient warrant for a franchise of return of writs.[6] Perhaps the decision was based on a very real distinction between the relatively new franchise of return of writs and the right conferred by a *non intromittat* grant. The latter was negative in formulation; the former described a particular process. Return of writs was thus at least somewhat more specific than a *non intromittat* clause; the former became conceivable only after the innovations concerning writs made during the reign of Henry II.[7]

The new franchise and the old grant, however, were so close in meaning that the rejection of the grant as warrant for the franchise was bound to cause dissension, as did the royal claim that prescription would likewise be insufficient warrant for a valid title. The importance which was placed on the franchise of return of writs can best be illustrated by the efforts of the earl of Warenne to retain that franchise for his liberty of Stamford, even though the source of the difficulty here rested on grounds other than prescription or the insufficiency of a *non intromittat* clause.[8] Already in 1275 the sheriff of Lincolnshire reported that he had been prevented from entering Stamford to execute a distraint.[9] Again in 1276 the sheriff was ordered to take a jury in Stamford to determine *Damel v Weledon*, a case in the court of common pleas. He had responded that he could not gain entry to the town. In a subsequent writ he became much more specific. He told the justices that if he had to enter Stamford to execute the writ he would need a force of 5,000 men, that is, he would have to enter the town by overwhelming military force.[10] In 1277 Warenne received

[6] Clanchy, "Return of Writs," p. 65.
[7] See also below, after n. 28.
[8] Clanchy, "Return of Writs," p. 70.
[9] Ibid., p. 71.
[10] CP. 40/18, m. 19: "si debet predictam villam ingredi ad execucionem huius precepti faciendam oportet ipsum habere circiter quinque milia homines nec habuit spacium post receptionem huius brevis ad predictam villam cum posse comitatus accedere. Ideo ipse [the sheriff] in misericordia, et amerciatur ad xx libras." The amercement of the

a stay of such harassment until the next Parliament,[11] but in Hilary term of 1279 the matter had still not been resolved. The sheriff of Lincolnshire had been ordered by a *non omittas* writ—that form of writ used when a bailiff of a liberty would not execute the writ; it ordered the sheriff to execute the mandate notwithstanding the liberty—that he take sufficient force with him to execute a writ in *Albe v Convers*. He replied that he could not enter the town, because the bailiffs of the earl claimed to have the franchise of return of writs and that issue had not yet been discussed before the king.[12] *Non omittas* writs concerning Stamford were thereafter issued but not executed until 1281.[13] In that year the earl's claim came before the eyre of Lincolnshire and, after several adjournments, was rejected.[14] His resistance to the sheriff had been costly; at least, his acknowledgment of a debt of 1,582½ marks to the merchants of Lucca in quittance of all his other debts to them in 1282 would argue a considerable depletion of his resources.[15] Nor was Warenne the only lord actively resisting the authority of the sheriffs. In 1283 the sheriff of Herefordshire was ordered to deliver seisin of two messuages of land and the advowson of half a church to Roger de Mikelfeud. He replied that he had sent the constable and the porter of the castle of Hereford

---

sheriff, of course, was putting him under a great deal of pressure to execute a writ that it would have taken a military expedition to accomplish. See also Clanchy, "Return of Writs," p. 71, for a citation of a writ *distringas* that the sheriff was unable to execute in Stamford at about the same time.

[11] Clanchy, "Return of Writs," p. 71.

[12] CP. 40/28, m. 47d: "et vicecomes nichil inde fecit set mandavit quod ballivi comitis Warenne predicte ville non permittunt ipsum predictam execucionem facere, eo quod clamant habere returnum brevium et non dum est discussum coram rege utrum debent illud habere vel non." The entry also indicates that the sheriff was amerced again, but it does not indicate the sum. That was not the only writ that the sheriff was unable to execute in Stamford at the time: CP. 40/28, m. 71 (Coyse v Toch; the writ had ordered him to take sufficient posse, but he had neglected to do anything); CP. 40/28, m. 26d (Prioress of St. Michael outside Stamford v Cordewaner; return as with Coyse v Toch); CP. 40/28, m. 6d (Assefordeby v Eston; "mandavit quod ballivi comitis Warenne de Staumford non permittunt ipsum ingredi predictam villam ad aliquam execucionem inde faciendam"). See also Statute of Westminster II, c. 39.

[13] CP. 40/31, mm. 73, 91, 92; CP. 40/32, mm. 28, 37, 56; CP. 40/33, mm. 24d, 30, 32d, 41d, 68d, 82; CP. 40/34, m. 58d; CP. 40/36, mm. 12, 37, 91, 100. These references were just noted in passing; there are probably more instances which I did not notice.

[14] Clanchy, "Return of Writs," p. 71.

[15] CP. 40/45, m. 39. The merchants were Boruncinus Gwalteri, Richard Guidicionis, and Henry de Podio; the repayment was over the period of two years, the first four payments being 250 marks each, the last two, 300 marks and 282½ marks respectively. This evidence about Warenne's activity in Stamford lends some credence to the story of Warenne's presentation of his rusty sword as evidence for his franchises: see Clanchy, "Return of Writs," pp. 74-75.

with Mikelfeud to execute the writ, but they had been met by Simon Basset, constable of Theobald de Verdun, with 200 footmen who would not allow them to execute the mandate. The sheriff was therefore ordered to take the *posse comitatus* with him to execute the writ.[16] Similarly, the bailiff of the earl of Lincoln resisted the attempts of the sheriff of Yorkshire to enter the liberty of Osgoldcross,[17] and the bishops of Lincoln and Salisbury were said to be putting up resistance to the sheriffs also.[18] If the king was capable of preventing sheriffs from issuing returns of writs to liberties, the nobles, on their side, were capable of preventing royal mandates from being executed within their territories.

The conflict over the return of writs, however, was not concerned exclusively with returnable writs. Perhaps the situation would not have been so volatile had it only concerned the right of acting as executor for writs initiating litigation in the king's court. Just as important as the treatment of returnable writs was the handling of the summonses of the exchequer, but even here it is difficult to see any great difference between the *non intromittas* clause and the franchise of return of writs. The ambiguity arose with viscontiel writs. Only very exceptional lords would maintain that their courts were equal to the king's court. Most lords were thus willing to admit that returnable writs should at least be executed, even if they disagreed on the *way* in which they should be executed. There is, in short, no evidence that there was any demand that large numbers of cases should be transferred from the king's court to the courts of liberties. It was much more possible, however, for lords to consider their courts equal to the county courts, and it was at this point that the conflict over the franchise of return of writs began to involve jurisdiction over cases and the resulting financial perquisites.

One way of conceiving of the franchise as related to the return of viscontiel writs subordinated the courts of liberties to the county courts as much as liberties were subordinated to the king's court. The

[16] CP. 40/49, m. 12 (Mikelfeud v Verhz [?]): "vicecomes mandavit [quod] misit constabularium et portarium castri Hereford apud Pyzon cum dicto Rogero de Mikelfeud, qui ibidem invenerunt Simonem Basset constabularium Theobaldi de Verdoun de Welbell cum ducentis peditibus qui nec moram in manerio nec aliquam execucionem brevis domini regis facere permiserunt." The sheriff was ordered to arrest and hold anyone found resisting him in further execution of that writ. The defendant in this case had acknowledged the plaintiff's right, so that the dispute with the sheriff was precisely on the point of who should execute the order.

[17] CP. 40/54, m. 78 (Stapelton v Earl of Lincoln).

[18] Clanchy, "Return of Writs," p. 74.

process dictated by such a conceptualization of the franchise demanded that the sheriff and county court retain jurisdiction over the plea. The viscontiel writ itself would not, then, be returned, but only the orders for the process which derived from hearing and determining the plea. The bailiff of the liberty in this process would indeed be only the executor of mandates from the sheriff. These mandates, although they were not transcriptions of a writ or of any other document, could still have been described as returns of a writ.[19] While "return" could mean "transcription,"[20] its full meaning in this con-

---

[19] JUST. 1/1022, m. 3 (Lytleton v Abbot of Evesham), in which a sheriff's order to a liberty pursuant to a case not originated by writ at all is called a return: "et abbas respondit pro se et aliis et bene defendit omnem iniuriam, capcionem, et detentionem. Et revera bene cognoscit quod capere fecit predicta averia et iuste, quia dicit quod quidam Petrus de Litleton tenet quoddam tenementum in Litleton quod est de feodo ipsius abbatis et infra libertatem suam de Evesham ubi nullus ballivus domini regis ingredietur, et dicit quod idem Petrus occasione predicti tenementi sui debet sectam ad comitatum Wygorn'. Et quia idem Petrus fecit defaltam ad comitatum vicecomes Wygorn' mandavit ballivis libertatis ipsius abbatis per returnum brevis sui quod eis inde venit quod distringerent ipsum pro defalta predicte secte, eo quod nullus vicecomes intrare potest in libertatem illam ad districciones vel attachiamenta facienda per defectum ipsius abbatis vel ballivorum suorum." It is possible, of course, that suit is here thought of as the necessity to attend the county when necessary to answer a case brought against one, i.e., as being subject to county jurisdiction. If that is so, the case could well have been brought by writ; that hypothesis would make the word usage more sensible.

[20] Clanchy, "Return of Writs," p. 63. A good example of this kind of meaning is E. 13/18, m. 27d: "Norf'. Johannes Page, clericus vicecomitis Norf', attachiatur ad respondendum Ricardo filio Johannis de placito transgressionis et unde queritur quod cum idem Ricardus quoddam breve regis ad capiendam terram cuiusdam Nicholai Bukkesbyri in manum regis pro defalta quam idem Nicholaus fecit in curia regis coram justiciariis de Banco impetrasset et illud idem breve prefato Johanni liberasset exigendo ab eo billam iuxta statutum regis etc., idem Johannes nullam billam ei facere volebat, immo maliciose returnavit coram prefatis justiciariis ad diem in brevi illo contentum quod breve illud adeo tarde venit quod exequi non potuit ad dampnum suum viginti marcarum. Et predictus Johannes venit per attornatum suum et bene cognovit quod predictus Ricardus tale breve sibi deferebat, cuius returnum fecit ballivo de Taverham et illud liberavit prefato Ricardo ad deferendum prefato ballivo qui execucionem inde facere debebat. Et postmodum, quia idem ballivus significavit prefato Johanni quod predictus Nicholaus non habuit terras nec tenementa in ballia sua, idem Johannes iterato liberavit prefato Ricardo quoddam aliud returnum eiusdem brevis ballivo de Fleg' in cuius ballia prefatus Ricardus asserebat prefatum Nicholaum terras et tenementa habuisse ad faciendam inde debitam execucionem. Et quia predictus Ricardus illud returnum paululum ante diem in brevi suo contentum prefato ballivo de Taverham deferebat, idem ballivus returnum suum fecit prefato Johanni quod returnum predicti brevis adeo tarde sibi venit quod illud exequi non potuit et sic prefatus Johannes exposuit et significavit curie regis returnum suum secundum quod predictus ballivus de Taverham sibi retornaverat et quod nullam transgressionem ei fecit petit quod inquiratur. Et predictus Ricardus dicit quod prefatus Johannes non liberavit sibi aliquod retornum ad deferendum ballivo de Taverham seu ballivo de Flegg, sed quod maliciose retornavit coram prefatis justiciariis predictum breve ita tarde sibi venit quod illud exequi non potuit, et hoc petit similiter quod inquiratur.

text would be the allocation of a duty to another to whom the duty belonged as of right, a "giving back," a "return." This process would clearly make the courts of liberties subordinate to the county courts.

On the other hand, a return which was made of the writ itself would confer jurisdiction on the liberty, a much different result from that produced by the mere return of process. The form of such a return would be as follows:

> Sheriff to the bailiff, greetings. I have received a mandate of the lord king in these words: "Edward, by the grace of God king etc., to the sheriff of Hampshire, greetings. We command you to justice B. that justly etc., he render to A. twenty shillings which he owes him, as he says, as he shall reasonably be able to show that he ought to render to him, that we hear no further complaint thereof for want of justice. Witness etc." And therefore I order you to execute that mandate fully.[21]

That return—artificially constructed, since I have no example of a return made with a viscontiel writ—would obviously transfer the jurisdiction in the case to the court of the liberty. The sheriff would retain the original viscontiel writ, because it was addressed to him and he was principally responsible for its execution. Furthermore, if a *pone* issued out of chancery, there would be no problem in removing the case. The sheriff needed only to inform the parties, inform the liberty, and send the original writ with the *pone* to the king's court.[22] This conceptualization of the franchise of return of writs would insist that viscontiel writs be returned in physically the same manner as returnable writs, even though that return would have a rather different effect: a complete transfer of jurisdiction from one court to another. This kind of process would make the court of the liberty much more like an equal of the county court and, at the same time, would give the lord the amercements which would arise from the plea.

There is no doubt that lords wanted their liberties to have a return of writs which would transfer pleading and the right to determine the case, not merely execution of process. In 1189 Northampton was

[21] This form is composed of a standard viscontiel writ of debt together with the formula used in JUST. 1/466, m. 2d: "Vicecomes ballivo salutem. Mandatum domini regis in hec verba recepi: . . . . Et ideo tibi mando quod mandatum istud plenarie exequeris."

[22] JUST. 1/4/1, Kent eyre, 1293, (Abbot of Boxley v Tyleman) in which the sheriff responded that there was no such plea in the liberty but was able to forward the writ anyway. This did not apply, of course, when the plea was by writ of right: CP. 52 octave Hilary, 28 Edward I, Dorset (Marchaunt v Cros), "set aliud breve est breve de recto patens et remanet penes petentes."

amerced 30 marks because it had heard "pleas which pertained to the sheriff by writs directed to the sheriff."[23] In 1219 a bailiff of a liberty claimed a case of admeasurement of dower which was pending in the county court of Cambridgeshire and received jurisdiction over the case for his liberty.[24] In 1226 a jury reported that the sheriffs of Norfolk and Suffolk were accustomed to send returns of writs close to the bailiffs of the bishop of Ely of various hundreds in those counties and that by those returns "the bailiffs held those pleas in the hundreds, as well as pleas of animals taken" and seemingly all viscontiel pleas in general.[25] In 1255 the men of Shrewsbury, in claiming the franchise of return of writs, specified that they were accustomed to have return of all writs *justicies*.[26] In 1268 the bishop of Durham claimed that he and his predecessors had been accustomed to plead in the liberty of Howden all pleas which pertained to the sheriff except for the pleas of the crown, until William le Latymer by the actions of Richard de Vescy, his undersheriff, had withdrawn the return of writs from Howden as the result of a dispute between Vescy and the bailiff of the liberty.[27] In 1280 the countess of Albemarle claimed to

[23] *PR, 1 Richard I*, p. 43: "quod tenuerat placita que pertinebant ad vicecomitem per brevia directa vicecomiti."

[24] *CRR*, 8:21. Another case of admeasurement of dower from the late 1250s: JUST. 1/1185: "Jurata dicit quod revera predictus Willelmus tulit breve domini regis vicecomiti Buck' de amensuracione dotis predicte Johanne, ita quod idem vicecomes fecit returnum brevis domini regis ballivis honoris Peverel, eo quod dos ipsius Johanne fuit infra libertatem predicti honoris. Et dicit quod idem ballivus summoneri fecit predictos Robertum et Johannem adinteresse amensuracionem faciendam, non venerunt predicti Robertus et Johanna ita quod idem ballivus per sacramentum proborum et legalium hominum de visneto illo amensurari fecit omnia tenementa que iidem Robertus et Johanna tenent in dotem ipsius Johanne in comitatu isto."

[25] William Dugdale, *Monasticon Anglicanum*, 6 vols. in 8 (London, 1817-1830), 1:489: "tali usus fuit libertate quod vicecomes Norfolch et Suffolch misit retorna brevium clausorum ballivis episcopi de praedictis hundredis et ipsi per retorna illa tenuerunt placita infra omnia predicta hundreda, et similiter de averiis captis et de placitis quas vicecomes potuit tenere."

[26] *RH*, 2:78.

[27] JUST. 1/1050, m. 54 (Bishop of Durham v Latymer): "habere debeant et hucusque habere consueverunt omnia placita que ad vicecomitem pertinent in omnibus terris et tenementis suis infra comitatum Ebor'." The verdict in the case: "prefatus episcopus et predecessores sui omnia placita que ad vicecomites pertinent placitare exceptis placitis corone secundum tenorem carte domini Ricardi regis et confirmacionem domini regis nunc usi sunt placitare infra libertatem de Hoveden a tempore quo predicte carte impetrate fuerunt tam tempore predicti Willelmi le Latymer vicecomitis quam temporibus aliorum vicecomitum usque ad festum sancti Johannis Baptiste anno regni domini regis nunc l, quod idem Willelmus le Latymer vicecomes per Ricardum de Vescy subvicecomitem suum retraxit returnum brevium de predicta libertate de Hoveden, eo quod contencio tunc erat inter dictum Ricardum de Vescy et Thomam de Metham tunc ballivum predicte libertatis de Hoveden. Dicunt eciam quod predicti episcopi solebant habere returnum brevium domini regis a tempore impetracionis predictorum cartarum usque ad predictum festum sancti Johannis Baptiste."

have the franchise of return of writs for the Isle of Wight. The jury's verdict in the case reported that since the provision of the return of writs—*postquam returnum brevium provisum fuit*—the countess and her ancestors had pleaded all the pleas which the sheriff pleaded in the county court. Before the return was provided, the jury thought they had pleaded the same cases by plaint.[28] The jury was undoubtedly historically correct; the problems with writs would have arisen only after one needed a writ to prosecute certain kinds of pleas. As they became necessary, the liberties would of course attempt to retain their jurisdiction by having the writs sent to them.

This interpretation of the franchise of return of writs sheds light on the reasons why the old *non intromittat* clause in charters was deemed insufficient for the franchise. To the extent that the franchise of return of writs was interpreted as involving a delegation of jurisdiction—or to the extent that the proper interpretation was unclear— to that extent the old *non intromittat* clause would be ambiguous. The *non intromittat* clause would be sufficiently honored with the minimal return of writs, by returns that only ordered procedure, while the case was actually heard in the county court. It would have been very difficult for lawyers to have derived a delegation of jurisdiction from a *non intromittat* clause.

In the first half of the century the fuller return of viscontiel writs was often the accepted procedure. In 1230 the sheriff of Berkshire was ordered to make his returns to Abingdon Abbey according to the tenor of the writ.[29] In 1233 the king granted the bishop of Ely the return of writs in his hundreds in Norfolk and Suffolk, specifically mentioning that the bishop would have all pleas which the sheriff could plead as sheriff or by virtue of the king's writ by return of the writ to those hundreds.[30] In 1241 the sheriff of Kent was ordered to make the return of all royal writs to Christ Church Canterbury in the same form in which they were directed to him.[31] By royal orders

---

[28] KB. 27/53, m. 21 (Rex v Countess of Albemarle): "predicta comitissa et antecessores sui postquam returnum brevium provisum fuit semper habuerunt returnum brevium et placitaverunt placita eorundem brevium que vicecomes placitant in comitatu, et antequam returnum aliquod fuit provisum antecessores eiusdem comitisse placitaverunt eadem placita per billas. Et dicunt quod vicecomes aliquando per commissum et defectum dominorum distrinxit ipsos dominos de veniendo ad comitatum suum, set dicunt quod nunquam venerunt in comitatum ad aliquam responcionem faciendam set semper statum suum calumpniaverunt et sic in calumpniando etc., ponere fecerunt per breve regis illam loquelam coram justiciariis de banco."

[29] *Calendar of the Charter Rolls, 1226-1516*, prepared under the superintendence of the Deputy Keeper of the Records, 6 vols. (London, 1903-1927), 1:121.

[30] Ibid., 1:183.

[31] *CR, 1237-1242*, p. 300: "in eadem forma in qua ei diriguntur."

and grants, by jury verdicts and claims, then, the form of return of writs which transferred jurisdiction seems to have been normal.

There were, however, at least two instances in which the narrower interpretation of the franchise was chosen. In 1249 the sheriff of Hampshire was ordered to allow the Isle of Wight the return of writs as it concerned the making of summonses and attachments while the heir to the liberty was underage, but retaining for the king all the pleas which arose from those writs.[32] This, however, would seem to have been a special case, partly because it was mentioned particularly, partly because a jury later indicated that viscontiel pleas were pleaded in the Isle of Wight, not in the county court.[33]

The other instance in which the narrower interpretation was chosen comes from a final concord between the bishop of Worcester and William Beauchamp, earl of Warwick and hereditary sheriff of Worcestershire, in 1258. Henry III had granted the bishop the right to hold in his court all pleas of replevin—pleas of refusal of gage—arising in his Worcestershire lands and fees and in the lands and fees of the prior of Worcester.[34] This grant would have demanded a return of jurisdiction, even though it was not a grant of the franchise of return of writs. Beauchamp had disputed the bishop's right to pleas of replevin, so their respective rights were defined in a final concord. The bishop was acknowledged to have the right to all the pleas of replevin (except those in which he was a litigant) and to the amercements made in his court pursuant to those pleas, as had been granted by the king. Replevin was thus to be returned in the manner advocated by the liberties, but only as the result of a separate grant. The wider issue of the bishop's franchise of return of writs was treated in the restricted manner which would be in the king's interest. Beauchamp bound himself to make two kinds of returns: returns of pleas and returns of summonses of the Exchequer. The return of pleas was immediately explained by the determination of the most important

[32] CR, 1247-1251, p. 209. See Rotuli de Oblatis, p. 235.

[33] Above, n. 28.

[34] Registrum Prioratus Beate Mariae Wigorniensis, ed. William H. Hale, Camden Society, vol. 91 (London, 1865), fols. 162b-63a; also transcribed, in a rather different manner, in Dugdale, Monasticon Anglicanum, 1:611-12. Perplexingly, Helen Cam, The Hundred and the Hundred Rolls (London, 1930), p. 180, cites this as an instance in which the bailiff of a liberty was allowed to hold all the pleas that the sheriff held in the county court; the fine went to great lengths to prevent that very conclusion. It seems that around 1250 the franchise of return of writs did not include the return of writs of replevin (CR, 1247-1251, p. 510) because special authorization was required for such pleas, and the same apparently was true with the bishop of Worcester in 1251 (ibid., p. 567). See also ibid., p. 535.

point in any discussion of the franchise of return of writs: the locus of jurisdiction. It was specified that no pleas pertaining to the sheriff would be heard in the bishop's court except pleas of replevin and that the sheriff and the county court retained the right to execute process upon such pleas in the county court if the bishop's bailiff failed to act.[35] The precautions concerning interference in the bishop's liberty pursuant to process ordered for cases in the king's court was mentioned only after matters touching viscontiel pleas had been disposed of; returnable writs, after all, were to a great extent taken care of by the traditional *non intromittat* clause. The special concern in this fine arose because the bishop was to have different kinds of returns in different cases, and the full return in replevin was necessitated not by the franchise of return of writs but by the grant of the king made separately. This narrower interpretation was obviously the less influential opinion. The greater number of instances demanding full returns would only allow the final concord to show that there was still sufficient ambiguity to argue for a more royalist position.

There seems to have been no ambiguity at all in the reign of Edward I: the franchise of return of writs demanded a process which would transfer jurisdiction in cases brought by viscontiel writ to the courts of liberties. *Justicies*, *facias*, and *audias* writs were all subject to the procedure of return of writs in such a way that they were heard and determined in the courts of liberties. For the writs *justicies* there are many viscontiel writs of debt which can be shown to have been heard in liberties,[36] and at least some examples of account,[37] detinue,[38] mesne,[39]

[35] *Registrum Prioratus Beate Mariae Wigorniensis*, fols. 160b–62b; below, n. 55.

[36] CP. 40/18, m. 55 (Hertford v Bynetre; court of Hatfield, Herts.; lord: bishop of Ely; 1276); CP. 40/59, m. 68 (Carpenter v Gyssiche; court of the Isle of Wight; lord: countess of Albemarle; 1285); CP. 40/86, m. 70d (Bourne v Bourne; court of Canterbury, Kent; lord: archbishop of Canterbury; 1290, with it noted specifically in the writ that the case was in that court *per returnum brevis*); CP. 52 quindene Michaelmas, 19 Edward I (Remerston v Executors of Sartine; court of Northampton; lord: king; 1291; "*per returnum brevis*"); CP. 52 quindene Easter, 24 Edward I (Ludrik v Executors of Segrave; court of Leicester; lord: Edmund, earl of Lancaster; 1296; "*per returnum brevis*"); CP. 52 octave Michaelmas, 26 Edward I (Executors of Venur v Attebrigge; court of Lincoln; lord: king; 1298). See also *Early Registers of Writs*, ed. Elsa de Haas and G.D.G. Hall, Selden Society, vol. 87 (London, 1970), p. 159 (R. 212).

[37] CP. 40/21, m. 17 (Abbot of Dorchester v Bassemore; court of Dorchester, Oxfordshire; lord: bishop of Lincoln; 1277); CP. 40/34, m. 10d (Grey v Blund; court of honor of Leicester; 1280).

[38] CP. 40/78, m. 20d (Elys v Bercher; court of Thame hundred, Oxon.; lord: the bishop of Lincoln; 1289). For detinue of charters, see *Early Registers of Writs*, p. 157 (R. 195).

[39] CP. 52 octave Hilary, 21 Edward I (Cokeman v Hercy; court of Well wapentake, Lincolnshire; lord: bishop of Lincoln; 1292).

and covenant.[40] The *facias* writs could likewise be heard in the courts of liberties; examples are available for admeasurement of pasture[41] and replevin.[42] Perhaps even more surprising is the fact that *audias* writs were also returned to liberties, but both writs of nuisance[43] and writs of viscontiel trespass[44] were returned to liberties to be heard in those courts. Even *ne vexes* was returned to a liberty to be heard and determined there.[45] Since these examples survive merely because of the incidence of removals or of accusations of false judgment, it would seem a necessary conclusion that during the reign of Edward I all viscontiel writs were subject to determination in the courts of liberties, despite the fact that they were addressed to the sheriff.[46] It is rea-

[40] CP. 40/95, m. 106d (Sutton v Warde; court of Ripon, Ebor.; lord: archbishop of York; 1292; *"per returnum brevis"*); CP. 40/32, m. 78d (Bradewell v Templer; court of Slaughter, Glos.; lord: abbot of Fecamp; 1280).

[41] CP. 40/72, m. 63d (Penne v Mortimer; court of Bampton hundred, Oxon.; lord: William de Valence; 1288; *"per returnum brevium"*).

[42] CP. 40/23, m. 12 (Besile v Hengesteye; court of Bampton hundred, Oxon.; lord: William de Valence; 1278); CP. 40/29, m. 4d (Abbot of Eynsham v Lusa; court of Slaughter, Glos.; lord: abbot of Fecamp; 1279); JUST. 4, Kent Eyre, 1293 (Abbot of Boxley v Tyleman: "Nulla est loquela in comitatu inter partes predictas tamen retornavi tam istud breve quam breve originale seneschallo libertatis archiepiscopi Cant', qui respondit quod nulla loquela est coram eo inter partes predictas." The original writ, however, was nevertheless attached to the *pone* in the writ file. The response may have indicated that the plea had been partially or completely determined.) CP. 52 octave Hilary, 28 Edward I (Lamberd v Lyndeseye; court of Bolingbroke, Lincs.; lord: earl of Lincoln; 1300; *"per returnum brevium"*); CP. 52 octave Michaelmas, 26 Edward I (Spyking v Lyndeby; court of Well wapentake, Lincs.; lord: bishop of Lincoln; 1300; "quia predictus Stephanus [Spyking] omnia tenementa sua tenet de Olivero episcopo Lincoln' propter quod nulla tenementa sua tenet de Olivero episcopo Lincoln' propter quod Willelmus de Cokerington ballivus ipsius episcopi de Wapentachio de Wellewapentachio coram quo predicta loquela pendet in eodem wapentachio per returnum brevis nostri fovet predictum Stephanum in loquela predicta ut dicitur"). *Early Registers of Writs*, p. 156 (R. 193).

[43] CP. 40/5, m. 104 (Waukelin v Brademore; court of Kingston, Surrey; lord: king; 1274).

[44] CP. 40/86, m. 245d (Atte Medwe v Messager; court of Middleton, Kent; lord: king; 1290; *"per returnum brevium"*); CP. 40/86, m. 27 (Horshe v Kyng; court of Colchester, Essex; lord: king; 1290).

[45] CP. 40/79, m. 38 (Cok v fitz William; court of Mitford hundred, Norf.; lord: bishop of Ely; 1289; "loquela est in comitatu etc., et returnatur per vicecomitem ballivis libertatis episcopi Eliensis de hundredo de Mitford ubi loquela illa adhuc pendet inter eos.") Brit. Lib. Add. 31826, fol. 65v: "Quant le bref fut en cunte si fut le bref returne en le hundred de Mutford par la reson de la fraunchise de Ely, en quel hundred cesti Robert cunta vers ly; Roger en affermant sun dreyt de services avantdis tendi syute e derene, ou Robert se mist en la grant assise nostre seignur le Roy, le quel etc., e desicum Roger granta a cel houre le tenement cum le franc tenement Robert e ly suffri mettre sey en assise cum franc home de sun franc tenement e en sa presence, demandoms jugement si ore pusez avenir de dire qe ceo est vostre vilnage."

[46] Michael Dalton, *The Office and Authority of Sheriffs* (London, 1682), p. 163, would indicate that the franchise was reinterpreted: "Also upon a *justicies* [by which Dalton meant any writ that could bring a case into the county court] the sheriff cannot

sonable to hypothesize that the ambiguity in the interpretation of the franchise of return of writs as regards viscontiel writs was resolved in a manner more favorable to the liberties during the Barons' War, when many sheriffs were particularly subject to the baronial interests.

The heated confrontations concerning the execution of returnable writs resulted from measures taken to preserve the status of liberties and to put them in a stronger bargaining position. There can be no doubt, of course, that the right to execute returnable writs was felt to be very important to the status of a liberty. The regular intrusion of the sheriff's officials would have undermined a lord's actual control over his men; power must be not only theoretically acknowledged, it must actually be wielded. The wielding of power, even if it was only by delegation, reinforced control. It was thus important to the lords of liberties that their bailiffs be the ones who would normally execute process on returnable writs. The possibility of losing jurisdiction, however, was even more sensitive. Jurisdiction over cases was a necessary element of power. It insured a lord's dependants that they could receive impartial justice without worrying that their personal allegiance would be a hindrance in vital litigation. If they were always subject to justice in the county court, really effective control over men would be difficult to insure, particularly in times of conflict, armed or unarmed. Denial of execution of process, however, was the only countermeasure available. As long as the king was determined to deny their rights to power, then, the lords of liberties were prepared to debilitate the power of royal courts by refusing to allow execution of process. This naturally resulted in the statutory concerns for proper execution of process.[47] Finally in 1290 the matter was resolved in the requisite manner. Prescription was admitted as valid title for the franchise. The *non intromittat* clause in a charter, however, continued to cause problems, because it was less precise in process than the franchise and because it did not give any title whatsoever to jurisdiction.[48]

Not every type of procedure was returned to the courts of liberties. The most lasting exception to the franchise of return of writs involved outlawry. Neither the king's court nor the courts of hundreds or

---

make his precept or warrant to the bailiff of a franchise, neither may he suffer him to have conusance, neither may any other hold plea by force of a *justicies* directed to the sherife but onely the sherife himselfe." He cites 24 Henry VI, so that one might think the system of returns I argue for would have lasted at least through the fourteenth century.

[47] Statute of Westminster II, c. 39; Clanchy, "Return of Writs," pp. 72-74.
[48] Clanchy, "Return of Writs," p. 76.

liberties could outlaw people. Both criminal outlawry and the exigent procedure ordered by the king's court thus had to take place in the county courts themselves and could not be returned to the relevant liberty.[49] The other major exception to the franchise was the *recordari in accedas* form.[50] The *recordari*, of course, was meant to remove cases brought by plaint from the county courts; when written in the *accedas* form it was used to remove cases brought by plaint from courts of liberties. These writs commanded the sheriff to go to one of the hundred courts or a court of a liberty in his own person: *in propria persona*. He took with him four knights of the county and in the designated lower court saw to it that, as in a normal *recordari*, a certain case brought by plaint was recorded for removal into the king's court. The record was then sealed with the sheriff's seal and the seals of four men of the court and forwarded to the king's court. Regular return procedure, of course, would have let the sheriff merely order the bailiff of the liberty to record the case; but the writ was specific in charging the sheriff to go in person to the court.[51] At the same time, removing a case from a liberty was a more serious matter than removing a case from a county court. The king owned the county courts, so that it was thought that no financial injury was done anyone in removing a case from such a court. A removal from county court only delayed the plaintiff in receiving his justice. Removal from the court of a liberty, however, meant that the lord of the court was deprived of the financial proceeds of hearing and determining a case. Thus, the litigant who initiated the removal from a liberty, whether plaintiff or defendant, had to specify a valid reason necessitating the removal; in county courts only the defendant had to specify a reason when removing a case.[52] Finally, the writ of false judgment concerning

[49] Appendix VII.

[50] *Early Registers of Writs*, p. 161 (R. 216): "Rex vicecomiti salutem. Precipimus tibi quod assumptis tecum quatuor discretis et legalibus militibus de comitatu tuo in propria persona tua accedas ad curiam R. de N. et in plena curia illa recordari facias loquelam que est in eadem curia sine brevi nostro inter A. et B. de averiis ipsius A. captis etc. ut dicitur. Et recordum illud habeas etc. sub sigillis quatuor legalium hominum eiusdem curie ex illis qui recordo illi interfuerint. Et partibus eundem diem prefigas etc."

[51] CP. 52 quindene Easter, 27 Edward I (Acre v Abbot of Wendling; court of Castleacre, Norf.; 1299); CP. 52 three weeks Easter, 27 Edward I (Wace v Prioress of Redlingfield; court of Eye, Suff.) The sheriff at times sent his undersheriff (CP. 52 quindene Michaelmas, 19 Edward I: the suitors refused to record the case for him; Lung v Vavasur), but the justices of the Bench considered even that incorrect: CP. 40/138, m. 89d (Osgoteby v Pontefract: the sheriff replied that he had sent his undersheriff, and the justices ordered him to go in person).

[52] *Early Registers of Writs*, pp. 161 (R. 216r), 125 (R. 70r).

a case in a liberty could not be returned; it also was framed in the *accedas* form and was older than the *accedas recordari*, although it had less effect on the courts of liberties.[53]

The most important limitation of the franchise of return of writs, however, was not the process which could not be returned to the liberty, but rather the continuing supervision over the case exercised by the sheriff. The writ had been addressed to him and he was thus primarily responsible for seeing that justice was done. Bailiffs of liberties, also, were sworn to fidelity to the king.[54] In 1258 when Beauchamp agreed to make returns to the liberty of the bishop of Worcester, he specified that the returns were to be made to the bishop's bailiff who had sworn fidelity to the king.[55] The bailiffs of the liberties were thus not obligated solely to their lord. It was, therefore, a delict when they failed to execute an order made by the sheriff. In the fine between Beauchamp and the bishop of Worcester, the sheriff's continuing authority within the liberty was clearly defined. In replevin, the sole instance in which the jurisdiction of the plea was to be transferred to the bishop's liberty, the sheriff would command the bailiff in open county court to replevy the animals or goods if he had received word that that had not already been done. If the bailiff had not acted by the next county session, he would send his own bailiff—undoubtedly the bailiff itinerant—into the liberty by judgment of the county court to replevy the animals; the case in such circumstances would begin in the county court but would be subject to claim of court by the bishop's bailiff.[56] Likewise, if the bishop was a defendant in replevin, the jurisdiction remained with the county court, and the bailiff was only ordered to execute the process. If he refused to do so or was unable to act against his lord, the sheriff—once again by judgment of the county court—was to send his own bailiff into the

[53] Most actions of false judgment are issued against the county courts, the courts of boroughs, or the courts of ancient demesne manors. The action of false judgment could not have had a great deal of influence in liberties.

[54] *CRR*, 9:37: "ballivus ipsius episcopi de illo hundredo fidelitatem fecit domino regi." Cam, *Hundred*, pp. 54-55; 144-45.

[55] *Registrum Prioratus Beatae Mariae Wigorniensis*, fol. 161b: "Concessit predictus Willelmus pro se et heredibus suis quod ipsi de caetero faciant ballivo hundredi predicti episcopi et successorum suorum jurato regis et praesentato in pleno comitatu per litteras episcopi patentes vel per ejus senescallum retornum de omnibus brevibus feoda, terras, et libertates episcopi et successorum suorum et prioris Wygorniae et ecclesiae Wygorniae tangentibus tam de placitis quam de summonitionibus scaccarii domini regis de verbo ad verbum plenarie sub sigillo suo si praesens fuerit vel sub sigillo sui subvicecomitis si absens fuerit."

[56] Ibid., fol. 161a. See also the Statute of Marlborough, c. 21.

liberty for execution of the viscontiel mandate.[57] Moreover, on all other pleas in the county court, a judgment of the county court was sufficient warrant for the sheriff to send his own bailiffs into the liberty to execute the process without regard to the liberty, after the bailiff of the liberty had failed to execute the process ordered.[58] The same kind of intervention could take place when a bailiff of the liberty failed to execute the process ordered by a returnable writ; the relevant court in such a case, however, was the king's court, and the order of the court for the sheriff to enter the liberty would be embodied in a *non omittas* clause in the succeeding writ.[59] The sheriff and the county court, thus, by the oath of the bailiff of the liberty and by the retention of the writ itself kept also a residual jurisdiction in cases brought by viscontiel writ and, probably by the theory that all jurisdiction was delegated, sustained a continuing supervision of process within the liberty.

There are only a few extant examples of sheriffs exercising this supervision over liberties; the scarcity is a function of the limitations on documenting any county procedure, however, and should probably not be taken to indicate that this kind of activity was uncommon. Around 1294 the abbot of Hales brought a viscontiel writ of debt to the sheriff of Gloucestershire against John de Stokewelle, a resident of the liberty of the abbot of Westminster. The sheriff made the return of the writ to the bailiff of the liberty, who failed to act on several occasions. The fact that the bailiff failed to act on several occasions, whereas no further return is mentioned to have been made by the sheriff, would seem to indicate that the jurisdiction itself had been transferred. The county court, because of the negligence of the bailiff of the liberty, thus ordered the sheriff to enter the liberty. The sheriff's itinerating bailiff therefore distrained Stokewelle by four

---

[57] *Registrum Prioratus Beate Mariae Wigorniensis*, fol. 161b.

[58] Ibid., fol. 162a: "Ita quod occasione dicti returni nulla brevia ad predictum vicecomitem pertinentia in curia episcopi placitentur occasione istius finis, nisi brevia de placito vetiti namii quae idem episcopus et successores sui in curia sua placitabant, exceptis brevibus placiti vetiti namii tangentibus personam ipsius episcopi et successorum suorum quae debent placitari sicut predictum est. Et si ballivi episcopi in execucione returnorum brevium ad vicecomitem pertinentium negligentes extiterint, et de hoc sufficienter et manifeste constiterit, tunc vicecomes vice regis per considerationem comitatus et coronatorum propter defectum episcopi ea exequatur."

[59] Ibid., fols. 162a-62b: If the bailiffs are negligent with returnable writs, "Tunc in judicium eorum ad quos principale placitum pertinebit vel judices scaccarii et non aliter dictus vicecomes hujusmodi mandata propter defectum episcopi et ballivorum suorum secundum consuetudinem regni ea exequatur." Clanchy, "Return of Writs," pp. 61-63; 73-74.

oxen, which were imparked, as was proper, within the liberty. Stoke-welle, however, broke into the park and took his beasts back, so that the itinerating bailiff by judgment of the county court distrained him by a horse found in the suburb of Gloucester. Stokewelle managed to regain possession of the horse also. The county court then ordered that Stokewelle be attached by his body; when he resisted *vi et armis* the bailiff raised the hue and cry, seized him, and had him imprisoned.[60] In a similar manner, in 1292, Richard de la Folye wanted to implead the prior of St. Swithun in a plaint of replevin. He made his plaint to the sheriff, who ordered the bailiff of the prior's liberty to replevy the animals and attach the prior. The bailiff, having received the mandate, refused to act. The sheriff repeated the order and set a deadline for the bailiff's completion of what was required. The bailiff had not acted by that time, so the sheriff by sending one of his own men tried to make the bailiff of the liberty execute his duties. The bailiff, however, wholly refused to act, and the county court judged that the sheriff should enter the liberty, deliver the animals, and attach the prior.[61] The franchise of return of writs was thus not a complete alienation of jurisdiction, but merely a delegation conditional upon efficient handling of the case.

The conditional nature of the jurisdiction conferred by the franchise of return of writs is perhaps clarified by the fact that return of writs was not always a franchise. The five regional courts of Lincolnshire— the three trithings in the north, Kesteven, and Holland[62]—each had return of writs. *Bageney v fitz Agnes* is a case of mesne brought by viscontiel writ which was determined in the court of Holland around 1290.[63] In 1291 *fitz Richard v Anon.*, a case of viscontiel trespass, was specified to have been in the court of Holland by return of writ.[64] *Boys v Cirly*, a case of viscontiel account, was said in 1301 to be in the court of Kesteven by return of writ,[65] and there are several instances of viscontiel trespass in Kesteven.[66] Moreover, endorsements

[60] E. 13/20, m. 5.

[61] CP. 52 three weeks Easter, 20 Edward I [S.S.].

[62] Above, chapter 1, at n. 101.

[63] CP. 52 quindene Trinity, 19 Edward I [S.S.].

[64] CP. 40/89, m. 42.

[65] CP. 52 morrow All Souls, 29 Edward I: "Quia Henricus de Fenton subvicecomes comitatus predicti qui tenet placita wapentachii nostri decem wapentachiorum de Ane-castre coram quo loquela illa pendet per returnum brevis nostri est consanguineus predicti Johannis [Boys] propter quod idem subvicecomes fovet predicto Johanni in loquela predicta ut dicitur."

[66] Henry Stepy, Henry le Keu, and David de Fletewyk each prosecuted William Mortimer in the court of Ancaster: CP. 52 month Easter, 28 Edward I.

on writs in the writ files of the court of common pleas reveal cases of admeasurement of pasture in the south trithing[67] and in the west trithing[68] and cases of viscontiel debt in the west trithing,[69] Holland,[70] and Kesteven.[71] The jurisdiction of the regional courts, however, was not exclusive. The county court of Lincolnshire was able to entertain pleas by writ which apparently could have been returned to the regional courts.[72] Perhaps jurisdiction was determined by whether both or only one of the litigants was resident in the region. At any rate, it is hard to imagine royal courts of that nature, even with the privilege of return of writs, having any absolute jurisdiction.

The processes connected with the franchise of return of writs certainly made the county courts somewhat less important. Courts of liberties gained a recognized right to try cases by viscontiel writ; that gave them the power in turn to use jury process and hear cases concerned with certain types of documents. Such cases would otherwise often have come into the county courts. As courts, liberties were restricted, of course, by the same events as county courts, so that their plaint jurisdiction was hampered by the introduction of the expanded *recordari*—in *accedas* form—in 1275,[73] and their jurisdiction in writs was qualified by the subjection of writs to more frequent removals by *pone*.[74] While removal procedures were important for limiting the liberties, they nevertheless operated primarily through the sheriff, not through the county courts. The county courts, however, were not reduced to a position merely equal to the courts of liberties. They did have an absolute monopoly on outlawry.[75] Furthermore, cases involving the lord of the liberty himself often came before the county; and the county had a residual jurisdiction over pleas in the courts of liberties. The county courts were still the primary courts in each county, but to a certain extent the county had

---

[67] CP. 52 octave Michaelmas, 26 Edward I (Joye v Allesee).

[68] CP. 52 octave Michaelmas, 26 Edward I (Fitz Ervisius v Makerel).

[69] CP. 52 octave Michaelmas, 26 Edward I (Tathewell v Sandale).

[70] CP. 52 quindene Easter, 29 Edward I (Marchaunt v Berford).

[71] CP. 52 octave Hilary, 28 Edward I (Noble v Executors of Quayle).

[72] CP. 52 octave Michaelmas, 26 Edward 1 (Motekau v Prior of Bullington, admeasurement of pasture; Tathewell v Newmarket, debt), CP. 52 quindene Easter, 29 Edward I (Prior of Sempringham v de la More, admeasurement of pasture) have cases brought by writ that were pleaded in the couny court of Lincolnshire; all could have been pleaded in regional courts, since all five regional courts had return of writs.

[73] Above, chapter 8, at n. 20.

[74] Above, chapter 8, at n. 14.

[75] Appendix VII.

become internally decentralized, while the increased links between lower courts and the king's court were now channelled more and more through the sheriff himself and not through his court.

The county courts could not claim quite as much control over the manors of the ancient demesne as they could over the courts of liberties. The courts of the ancient demesne were created by the exclusion of certain royal manors from the benefit of the common law writs.[76] The king, like any other lord, protected the tenants of his manors and their customs, but he did this, as was royal habit, by granting them use of several writs not available for lands outside the ancient demesne. Moreover, these procedures remained available even when the manor was held by a private lord. The little writ of right close is easily the best known of the writs available to tenants of the ancient demesne; it was the only writ available for normal inter-party litigation concerning land rights. Its development presents something of a contrast to the development of the writ of right patent, which still into the early thirteenth century preserved some flexibility in pleading and proof, although soon thereafter it hardened and became inflexible.[77] The little writ of right close was ultimately flexible and

[76] R. S. Hoyt, *The Royal Demesne in English Constitutional History: 1066-1272* (Ithaca, 1950), pp. 171-208. See also Marjorie McIntosh, "The Privileged Villeins of the English Ancient Demesne," *Viator* 7 (1976):1-34, a study of one ancient demesne manor (Havering) which indicates that some manors of the ancient demesne had access to common law writs and courts for a period, but that access was withdrawn in the 1230s (before 1236).

[77] S.F.C. Milsom, *The Legal Framework of English Feudalism* (Cambridge, 1976), pp. 96-101. His pessimism about discovering the form of early writs—particularly concerning the inclusion of the *ingressum*—is perhaps marginally overdrawn. While finding the *ingressum* in the plea rolls may not be proof that the word was in the writ, the *Rotuli de Oblatis* at times gives what seem to be excerpts of the writs paid for: p. 55 ("in quod feudum non habuit Jollanus ingressum nisi per ipsam Aliciam"), p. 334 ("in quam non habet ingressum nisi per Hubertum quondam archiepiscopum Cant' qui ipsum Willelmum injuste et sine iudicio dissaisivit dum idem Radulphum fuit in custodia ipsius archiepiscopi ut dicitur"), p. 340 ("in quam non habuit ingressum nisi per canonicos de Messenden qui in eam nullum habuerunt ingressum nisi per Willelmum filium Gaufridi qui eam habuit in custodia ut dicitur"), p. 378 ("in quod idem Radulphus non habet ingressum nisi per Thomam de Veyn fratrem suum cui ipsa illud dimisit ad firmam ad terminum qui preteriit ut dicitur et nisi fecerit quod sit coram justiciariis domini regis apud Westm' ab octabus sancti Johannis Baptiste in tres septimanis ostensurus quare non fecerit"), p. 502 ("in quod non habet ingressum nisi per Philippum de Columbariis quondam virum ipsius Matillidis qui eidem Radulpho feodum illud dedit, cui ipsa Matillidis in vita sua contradicere non potuit. Habet precipe . . .") In the fine rolls the earliest mention of a "precipe de ingressu" is in C. 60/23, m. 1: "Abbatissa Ebrulf dat domino regi xx s pro habendo quodam precipe de ingressu coram justiciariis versus plures. Et mandatum est vicecomiti Oxon' quod capiat etc." [1225].

was used to initiate litigation in most common law forms of real litigation: right, entry, dower, and the assizes.[78] It was not, however, a common law writ of right, and so could not be removed into the county court by tolt.[79] Such a restriction meant also that the little writ of right close was not subject to *pone* procedure.[80]

The other major writ available for tenants of the ancient demesne— but only when the manor was not held immediately by the king— was the writ *monstraverunt*, which was issued in three forms. That writ, when addressed to the private lord who was holding an ancient demesne manor, looked much like a *ne vexes*, in that it forbade the lord from exacting more customs and services than the tenants had been accustomed to render. Nevertheless, whereas a *ne vexes* incorporated in itself the warrant for the sheriff to supervise the plea if the lord refused to comply, the *monstraverunt* only contained the threat that the sheriff would be ordered to act if compliance was not forthcoming.[81] The second kind of writ *monstraverunt* was that order, addressed to the sheriff, recounting the order given by the first writ and ordering the sheriff to see to it that the lord did not exact more than the accustomed services. A note in the registers seems to compare these two forms, describing the first as a writ giving peace, the other as a writ giving justice.[82] There is no reason to think that the second form of *monstraverunt* did not originate a case in the county court. A third kind of *monstraverunt* was possible, however, and it began a case directly in the king's court after the lord had failed to comply

---

[78] CP. 40/30, m. 10d (Swarbrond v de la Haye; pleaded in the form of a *de racionabili parte*); CP. 40/253, m. 80d (But v But; pleaded in the form of an assize of novel disseisin); CP. 40/109, m. 106 (a case pleaded in the form of a writ of entry).

[79] Tolt procedure was disputed in fitz Turgisius v le Tieis, *CRR*, 9:80-81 (1220), but it seems that tolt procedure was effective at that time anyway. It is conceivable that tolt was allowed up until the time ancient demesne tenants were definitively denied access to common law courts. If that is true, the subtraction of the proceeds of ancient demesne manors from the sheriff's account would correspond nicely with the loss of county control over ancient demesne manors. Some support is given this idea in Hoyt, *Royal Demesne*, p. 214, no. 9 (JUST. 1/864, m. 2). In that case the county court of Surrey was clearly in seisin of the plea from the ancient demesne. The case in JUST. 1/775, m. 10d (Hoyt, *Royal Demesne*, p. 216), however, was quashed because the *pone* purchased to remove the case supposed the case to have been in the county court, whereas it had not been.

[80] Hoyt, *Royal Demesne*, p. 216.

[81] *Early Registers of Writs*, p. 46 (CC. 41).

[82] Ibid., p. 47 (CC. 42): "Si autem homines de huiusmodi veteribus dominicis domini regis per huiusmodi brevia pacem vel iusticiam consequi non possunt per vicecomitem nec alio modo . . ." These first two forms were perhaps combined to produce the writ of right *ne iniuste vexes*, a writ patent, which gave jurisdiction, as in the second form, to the sheriff (p. 114 [R. 28]).

with the prohibition contained in the original *monstraverunt*.[83] Of the three forms, then, the first seems to have been a prohibition; the other two, alternate forms for initiating litigation. The little writ of right close and the *monstraverunt*, then, provided the privileged tenants of the ancient demesne with the protection of their real rights; litigation in the personalty was probably handled by plaint.

The tenants of the ancient demesne, however, also had access to the king's court in a manner which completely bypassed the county court. The writ of false judgment was available for cases initiated by the little writ of right close and terminated by judgment in the courts of the ancient demesne.[84] Such a writ demanded the participation of the sheriff and four knights of the county, but made no use of the county court as such. The *recordari*, in *accedas* form, was also made available in 1275 for the courts of the ancient demesne; it made possible removal of cases initiated in the courts of the ancient demesne. Unlike the *recordari* for the courts of liberties, however, the *accedas recordari* for the ancient demesne applied not to plaints but to real actions initiated by the little writ of right close. It made possible the removal of real litigation directly into the king's court, without demanding first the use of tolt to remove the case into the county court.[85] The reasons for removal were similar to those for other cases

[83] Ibid., p. 47 (CC. 43).

[84] KB. 27/41, m. 19d (Stalkere v Stalkere); CP. 40/30, m. 10d (Swarbrond v de la Haye); *Early Registers of Writs*, p. 45 (CC. 37). This had not always been so, *Rotuli Litterarum Clausarum*, ed. Thomas D. Hardy, 2 vols., Record Commission (London, 1833, 1844), 1:539: a viscontiel false judgment inquiry through a verdict of three manors on a fourth.

[85] CP. 40/11, m. 13 (de la Sale v de la Brome): "Preceptum fuit vicecomiti quod assumptis secum quatuor discretis et legalibus militibus de comitatu suo in propria persona [sua] accederet ad curiam prioris sancti Swithini Winton de Berton et in plena curia illa recordari faceret loquelam que est in eadem curia per breve regis de recto inter Johannem de la Sale petentem et Johannem de la Brome tenentem de uno messuagio et duabus virgatis terre et dimidio cum pertinenciis in Ovinton. Et recordum illud haberet hic ad hunc diem sub sigillo suo et per quatuor legales milites eiusdem curie ex illis qui recordo illi interfuerunt. Et quod partibus eundem diem prefigeret quod essent hic ad hunc diem auditure recordum illud et inde processure prout de iure fuerit procedendum." This is removal because of the omission of the words alleging false judgment and the specific reference to proceeding on in the case. The writ still was not fully developed as a process of removal at this point, however, because the four knights were supposed to come also, although one might wonder if an ancient demesne manor court would have four suitors who were knights. The form was obviously just not well thought out yet. CP. 40/11, m. 15d (Clerk v Beaumond) seems a bit better, although earlier, but it was not recorded in so full a form. See also CP. 40/13, m. 64d (Waleys v fitz Walter) and CP. 40/15, m. 99 (de la Lake v de la Cokeshete), in which finally the record was to be sent under the seals of the sheriff and four men, but even there the sheriff said he had delivered the record to the four

in other courts and often concerned bias on the part of the bailiffs.[86] More serious problems, however, could arise. Tenants of the ancient demesne were entitled to use the jury, but at times there were an insufficient number of jurors to determine the case. In such a situation the litigants were denied right because of the insufficiency of the court, and such a case was rightly allowed to be removed into the king's court.[87] The *recordari* and the writ of false judgment thus provided for situations in which the ancient demesne court was biased or insufficient.

The county court also retained some plaint litigation from the courts of the ancient demesne to accompany the second form of the writ *monstraverunt*, the only writ that involved the ancient demesne with the county courts. These plaints were received into the county courts because replevin was considered a crown plea. Thus, in 1291 Robert Moryn brought a plaint of replevin against Robert Bardolf and Nicholas le Serjaunt in the county court of Nottinghamshire. Bardolf objected that the place where the horse was said to have been taken was of the ancient demesne of the lord king where no writ ran except the little writ of right. Since that area was an area at special law, he thought that the case should not come before a court that administered the common law ("*si illud quod est ad legem specialem debeat terminari in ista curia que est ad legem communem*"). Moryn made the objection which would probably have defeated most liberties, that Bardolf was lord of the manor and should not be both judge and party to the dispute; and he then maintained that this kind of case was never held in the ancient demesne court of Car Colston. The parties demurred on the point, and at the next session the county court of Nottinghamshire ruled that always until that time the tenants of the

---

men. They were therefore ordered to be distrained to come to testify concerning the record. The form seems to have been finalized by CP. 40/17, m. 90 (Berewe v Caldeford), and CP. 40/18, m. 31d (Benacre v Barage) finally specified that the case was brought *per parvum breve de recto.*

[86] CP. 40/253, m. 80d (But v But). This, of course, brought an end to the peculiar situation noted by Maitland (F. Pollock and F. W. Maitland, *The History of English Law before the Time of Edward I,* 2 vols., 2nd ed. [Cambridge, 1968], 1:386) that the lord of the manor would be both judge and party.

[87] CP. 40/199, m. 3 (fitz Roger v Bule): "Quia predicti Petrus, Alicia, et Agnes que fuit uxor Willelmi in placitando in curia predicta posuerunt se in inquisicionem inde secundum consuetudinem manerii predicti capiendam et pro eo quod non sunt tot sectatores eiusdem curie quot ad inquisicionem predictam sufficiunt loquela illa in eadem curia terminari seu justicia partibus ibidem inde fieri non potest etc." The record of the case finally appeared in CP. 40/206, mm. 169, 169d, where it is recorded that there had been only five men to put on the jury. The suit was for a messuage and virgate of land with appurtenances in Geddington, Northants.

ancient demesne had pleaded in the county court all pleas of replevin—of gages denied—and that the king was in seisin of the pleas through the sheriff. Judgment was therefore rendered in favor of Moryn, who recovered his damages of 20s. Thereafter Bardolf had the case removed after judgment rendered by *recordari*—surprising in itself—and not by writ of false judgment. Since no trace of it has been discovered in the plea rolls, however, it is likely that the judgment was allowed to stand.[88] As early as 1238, at least, sheriffs had been ordered to retain jurisdiction over pleas of replevin and not to allow them to come before ancient demesne hundreds.[89] While the immediate rationale may have been that replevin was a crown plea, the effect of the decision resembled that obtained by the *monstraverunt* in that the county court supervised disputes in the ancient demesne concerning customs and services. Thus the county court could entertain litigation brought by *monstraverunt* in its viscontiel form, by—apparently—the writ of replevin, and, at least by the 1290s, by plaint of replevin. Except for these limited instances and probably also for some matters concerning outlawry, the county courts had no jurisdiction within the ancient demesne, at least after the 1230s.

In regard to those courts within the confines of the county which were not as highly privileged as the courts of the ancient demesne and the courts of liberties with the franchise of return of writs, the county courts retained a decisive superiority. Such lesser courts could only entertain litigation by plaint, and so were rapidly restricted to cases of small debts and wrongs in which the litigants did not want a jury trial. Plaintiffs who wanted to sue by writ a party normally answerable in one of these lesser courts would have to bring the defendant into the county court or the king's court—or the court of the relevant liberty. Moreover, the lesser court itself could at times be called into the county court. In cases of replevin concerning dis-

[88] CP. 52 quindene John the Baptist, 19 Edward I (Notts. [S.S.]): "Quia idem Robertus Bardolf insufficienter respondet querele predicti Roberti Moryn eo quod semper hucusque tenentes de antiquis dominicis domini regis placitaverunt in comitatu omnia placita namii vetiti et rex est in seisinam per vicecomitem de talibus placitis consideratum est per iudicium comitatus quod idem Robertus Bardolf recuperet dampna sua etc." CP. 40/90, m. 87 (Moryn v Bardolf) is a very similar plea, even with an exception relating to the ancient demesne, but the place of the taking and the animals taken vary between the two cases. [S.S.]

[89] CR, 1237-1242, p. 74: "Precipimus tibi quod omnibus de ballia tua qui dominica hundreda nostra habent in custodia scire facias et firmiter inhibeas ex parte nostra ne aliquis ipsorum in hundredis predictis aliquod placitum teneat de namiis captis et vetitis contra vadium et plegium set omnia hujusmodi placita ad comitatum veniant et ibidem deducantur coram vicecomite et comitatu secundum legem terre."

traints for services that were not admitted by the tenant, Bracton states that the lord and distrainor could vouch his court concerning the judgment. The judgment in such a case was, of course, illegal; the county court acted "so that the judgment (might) be emended."[90] Something like this process was still alive in the reign of Edward I, although the use of the *recordari* in *accedas* form was probably obviating most instances of lesser courts appearing in county to avow their judgments. In 1292 Thomas de Leukenore and his wife avowed a distraint and vouched their court in the county court of Oxfordshire. The free men of their court accordingly came and warranted them, explaining that the plaintiff had taken responsibility for William de Freteville, who had thereafter been accused of beating one Roger Dawe. The hue and cry had been raised, and the plaintiff had been summoned to have his mainpernor in court, but he had defaulted and had therefore been distrained.[91] Again in 1292, the court of Hugh de Fraxino avowed its judgment in the county court of Herefordshire; it had ruled that Richard de la Were should be distrained for refusing to swear fealty and perform suit of court.[92] In 1295 three parceners of Ellel vouched their court in the county court of Lancashire concerning a distraint made upon one who denied owing suit to their mill and had defaulted at court after summons. The suitors of the court accordingly avowed the judgment in county court, and the plaintiff objected, once again, that since she denied the service the distraint had been made outside their fee. The case was removed from the county court then by *recordari*.[93] The county courts, on the other hand, were never vouched to explain county judgments in one of the lower courts. The county courts, by the process of litigants vouching their courts, were actively involved in the supervision of the lower courts. In regard to such courts, then, the county courts were clearly superior courts.

By the reign of Edward I county courts had a fairly well-defined position as the superior courts of the counties. They had a limited jurisdiction in the manors of the ancient demesne and a somewhat broader but still restricted jurisdiction in those liberties with the franchise of the return of writs. In regard to liberties without the

[90] Bracton, 2:447.

[91] CP. 52 three weeks Easter, 20 Edward I (Bernewell v Leukenore [S.S.]): "Et liberi homines eiusdem curie presentes eis warantizant et dicunt quod . . ."

[92] JUST. 4, Hereford Eyre, 1292 (Franceys v Fraxino [S.S.]).

[93] CP. 52 three weeks Easter, 23 Edward I (Ellale v Holand [S.S.]): "Et sectatores eiusdem hallemoti venerunt et bene advocant consideracionem predictam."

franchise of the return of writs and in regard to royal hundreds, the county courts still retained broad powers of jurisdiction, although it remains unclear how the venue of a case was actually determined when there would seem to have been a choice.

The relationship between county courts and the king's court changed as much during the thirteenth century as that between county courts and the lesser courts of the county. Up until the reign of Edward I, the county courts had been used at times as an integral part of the king's court. The king's court, for instance, had a continuing problem with jury trials. Jurors were presumed to be witnesses or at least to have the facts of the case available to them, so that they had to come from the geographical area most relevant to the issue joined in pleading: the area in which the land in question was situated, the place where the contract had been made, etc. The justices could not merely summon twelve impartial residents of Middlesex, but rather had to summon jurors, say, from Northumberland. Bringing jurors from such a distance was difficult, burdensome, and expensive; but it was done. It was not, however, unusual before 1285 for the parties to agree that the jury should be taken before the sheriff and coroners in open county court.[94] The sheriff and coroners were familiar with jury process, and taking the jury in the locality in that manner avoided a great deal of expense.[95] While that would seem to have been good procedure, the king's court seldom used it after 1285. Instead, the sheriff was ordered to assemble a jury at Westminster on a specific day, unless before (*nisi prius*) that day one of the king's justices could preside over the jury in the countryside. Justices purposely toured the countryside between terms precisely to take those jury verdicts. That system was known as the *nisi prius* system of trying issues pleaded in the king's court.[96] The reason for the change is not known. Perhaps corruption was suspected, or the sheriffs simply had too many other things to do in county court. It is even possible that the king's justices were expected to be more sophisticated than the sheriffs and

---

[94] *CRR*, 12:318; 13:256-57; 14:95, 228-29, 272-73; 15:21, 29, 143, 168, 170, 240, 242, 244, 295, 312, 319, 332, 380, etc. CP. 52 octave John the Baptist, 4 Edward I (Gloc.; Heref.); CP. 52 three weeks Hilary, 4 Edward I (Leic.).

[95] *Cartulary of the Abbey of Eynsham*, ed. H. E. Salter, 2 vols., Oxford Historical Society, vols. 49, 50 (Oxford, 1906, 1908), 1:199: "concessum fuit ibidem ut xij legales homines eligerentur ad inquisicionem faciendam, et ob expensas vitandas ad comitatum Oxon' fieret inquisicio per sacramentum supradictorum xij: et quicquid illi dicerent mitteretur apud West' in xv dies post octabas Trinitatis sigillis eorum sigillatum. Et sic factum est."

[96] Statute of Westminster II, c. 30; Pollock and Maitland, *History of English Law*, 1:202, n. 5.

make the taking of verdicts more than the mechanical placing of a question to a jury. Whatever the reason, the effect of the change was to eliminate the county court as a normal arm of the king's court in the trial of a vast number of cases. Another wedge was thus driven between the county courts and the king's court, each functioning more and more without reference to the other.

There was, however, a continuing ability of chancery to interfere in litigation in the county courts. This interference was partly embodied in the writs *pone* and *recordari*. Those writs, bought from chancery, simply removed a case pending before a county court into the king's court. Interference, however, was not always so stark. The writ of prohibition enabled litigants to stay procedure in county courts either temporarily or permanently. Good examples of the prohibition are those purchased to stay procedure in county courts brought by plaint for claims of debt for 40s or more or brought by plaint for any plea of detinue of charters.[97] Cases which were stayed only temporarily—for example, because the defendant was in the king's service—could be put back in motion by the writ *de procedendo*.[98] After process and pleading and even proof, if a county was tempted to delay judgment by reason of malice or ignorance, the writ *de recordo et judicio faciendo* was available as early as the 1220s to order the county court to go to judgment in accord with the process.[99] Even after judgment, if the sheriff was dilatory in executing the judgment, the victorious litigant could obtain a royal mandate to make the sheriff put the judgment into effect: the writ *de execucione judicii*.[100] Even if the county court rendered a manifestly wrong judgment, the litigant could obtain redress by purchasing the writ of false judgment. Moreover, the chancery could intervene not only in the process of litigation, but also in the attendance of court. From 1234 the king had taken a firm stand that suitors could appoint attorneys to claim pleas and to perform suit; that right could be enforced by royal writ, as could the right to appoint an attorney to represent one in litigation.[101] The

[97] Above, chapter 8 at n. 84; W. S. Holdsworth, *A History of English Law*, 14 vols. (London, 1903-1938), 2:625.

[98] *Early Registers of Writs*, pp. 20 (CA. 8), 64 (CC. 101), 168 (R. 245). The first writ is for land and does not reappear in the later registers. The last two are for naifty.

[99] Ibid., pp. 14 (Hib. 42), 20 (CA. 7), 41 (CC. 24), 120 (R. 50). In each instance the case concerned land, so that from the registers one might well think the writ issued only for cases in the right.

[100] Ibid., pp. 116 (R. 34), 226 (R. 501). The cases concerned involve both land and debts.

[101] *CR, 1231-1234*, p. 551: "Scias quod per commune consilium regni nostri provisum est quod quilibet liber homo qui sectas debet nobis in comitatibus, hundredis,

chancery thus exerted the king's continuing and overriding authority on the county courts.

The eyres, like chancery, were disruptive influences on county litigation and became more disruptive during the thirteenth century. The eyre was a special session of the king's court relating to a single county. It was deputed to handle all the outstanding cases in the king's court with respect to that county and, furthermore, to inquire into the king's rights in that county and the working of the royal officials. The problems regarding the relationship between eyre and county court concern the cases already in the county court at the time the eyre came into the county. Those litigants involved in cases brought in the county court by writ found that they had a choice between removing the case into the eyre and leaving the case in the county. Had viscontiel writs been automatically brought before the justices, one would have expected to find a rather large number of viscontiel writs in eyre writ files. In the writ file for the Berkshire eyre of 1248, however, there are only five properly viscontiel writs.[102] Three of those pleas were brought into the eyre by purchase of a *pone*, and the plea had been in the county court of Berkshire.[103] These were not unusual instances; pleas had to be specifically removed from county court to be placed before justices in eyre.[104] The process was not automatic. Many litigants would not want to remove their pleas into the eyre; after the eyre the cases would have been automatically adjourned either before justices in eyre in another county or before the justices of the court of common pleas. They could not be remanded

---

wapentaciis et aliis curiis nostris libere faciat attornatum suum coram ballivo nostro ad sectam illam faciendam et curias domini sui et libertates exigendas et ad loquelas prosequendas et defendendas pro dominis suis motas in comitatibus, hundredis, wapentaciis et aliis curiis nostris sine litteris nostris. See *Early Registers of Writs*, pp. xcix, n. 6; 248-49 (R. 600-605). The earliest example I have seen is from 1212, *Rotuli Litterarum Clausarum*, 1:126: "Rex vicecomiti Cumb' etc. . . . Precipimus eciam tibi quod recipias loco [Ranulfi de Bonekil'] attornatum suum quem atornaverit ad sequendum comitatum et placita et faciendum sectas et servicia que pertinent ad terram suam defendendam quam habet in ballia tua. Hec autem ei concessimus ob amorem et peticionem dilecti et fidelis nostri Alexandri filii regis Scott'." See also *CR, 1231-1234*, pp. 307, 546, 548. The attorneys to do suit probably had a great deal to do with increasing professionalization of the county courts.

[102] *The Roll and Writ File of the Berkshire Eyre of 1248*, ed. M. T. Clanchy, Selden Society, vol. 90 (London, 1973), p. lxx (writs a38, a54, a161, a228, and a207). A *ne vexes* apparently should have been there but was not; I do not include writs of right as genuinely viscontiel writs.

[103] Ibid., pp. 413-14 (a38 and a39), 419-20 (a54 and a55), and 489, 497 (a213 and a228). Writ a161 was adjourned into the eyre from another county; writ a207, for which there is no *pone*, may have previously been in the court of common pleas.

[104] C. 60/33, mm. 2, 3 (18 Henry III).

back to the county court. Early in the century, then, those litigants who chose not to remove their writs into the eyre—thereby annulling process and pleading—would simply leave their cases in the county court. That option, however, also involved hardship. The county court was not supposed to meet to hear pleas during the eyre, except in regard to pleas of right and appeals.[105] All cases of debt, detinue, covenant, account, annuity, mesne, customs and services, et cetera, which had been brought by viscontiel writ would therefore be delayed until the conclusion of the eyre. Through most of the thirteenth century, eyres lasted a few weeks only: the Berkshire eyre of 1248 lasted from 15 June to 24 July.[106] Such a delay would be little hardship for any litigant. As the caseload of the court of common pleas increased, however, the number of cases which the eyre had to deal with also increased, so that the last eyres in 1329-1331 lasted many months. A year's delay would have been intolerable, and that elimination of the county court as a venue for litigation for long periods must have contributed to the unpopularity of the eyres.

If viscontiel writs were not automatically removed before the justices in eyre, it is certain that plaints remained in the county court during the eyre. Before 1275 and the remodeling of the *recordari*, plaints could not be called even into the court of common pleas. The eyre, of course, did handle some plaints; but there is no evidence at all that those plaints had been removed from the county court. They were supposed to be plaints that had arisen since the eyre began. Furthermore, in neither the early nor the late eyres can one find the multitude of claims for debts of only a few shillings. Such insignificant pleas would have constituted the primary burden on the justices had they been automatically brought into the eyre from the county court. Moreover, at the end of the eyre they would have been adjourned perhaps into the court of common pleas. Neither justices nor litigants had any wish for all the plaints in the county court to be removed before justices. It must be presumed, however, that after 1275 plaints could be removed by *recordari* into the eyre, if only by removing them first into the court of common pleas. Litigants prosecuting by plaint, however, had no choice in most cases; as the length of the

---

[105] *The Eyre of Kent of 6 and 7 Edward II*, ed. F. W. Maitland, L. W. Vernon Harcourt, and W. C. Bolland, 3 vols., Selden Society, vols. 24, 27, 29 (London, 1909-1913), 1:7: "nule court ne counte ne fust tenuz en le dit countee durant leyre sinoun par resoun de plee de terre, & ceo par bref de droit patent ou de apels en countee." The rule probably applied before the reign of Edward I, but I have no proof.

[106] *The Roll and Writ File of the Berkshire Eyre*, p. xciv.

eyre grew, justice was necessarily denied them for longer and longer periods. The eyre came to be a great disruption in the settlement of a vast number of disputes; its suspension of county and hundred courts constituted a heavy burden to be borne by the countryside.

Finally, there remain only the varied links between the county courts and Parliament. In the realm of jurisdiction, of course, there was no direct rivalry. Developments in the relationship between county courts and the king's court, however, could have long-lasting implications for Parliament, the king's highest court. G. O. Sayles has pointed out that in 1275 bills were allowed for the first time to be presented in Parliament;[107] the bill or petition was to be fundamental in the process developed for legislating. There is a year book style report, hitherto unknown, which relates the preliminary hearing given one bill probably from the 1290s.

> In a plaint of imprisonment [brought] by bill which was avowed at the Guildhall for certain reasons before the same R. Brabazon [royal justice], he spoke in this way to the plaintiff: "You ought not to have put forward such a bill to parliament to bother the king and his council of earls and barons; rather you ought to complain of such a thing to the sheriff of this town and, if he does not give you justice, then to the mayor. And if he does not give you justice, then you ought to come to us in this way and not before, because prior to that we have no reason to hold such a plea." And he asked him afterwards if he had already sued this plea before the sheriff or the mayor. The plaintiff said that he had not, because he thought that they would not want to hold right to him. *Roubury*. "And would it be right for us to withhold their jurisdiction from them because of your thought? No." And he was told to return to their court and, if they did not give him justice, that he should come back to them.[108]

[107] G. O. Sayles, *The King's Parliament of England* (London, 1975), p. 76.

[108] Brit. Lib., Add. 31826, fol. 381r: "En une pleinte de enprisonment par bille que fut avowe a la Gyhall par certein cause devant eodem R. Brabazon, si dit il al pleintiff: 'Tel bille ne dussez vous point aver bote avant al parlement a travailler le rey e sun cunseil de cuntes e de baruns, eintz vous dussez de tel chose pleindre al vicont de ceste vile e pus, sil ne vous feit point de dreit, al meir. E si ne vous feit point de dreit, adonke si dussez vous venir a nous e nun pas avant, qe avant si naverums point de achesun a tenir tel plai.' E ly demanda pus sil unqe avant cel tens sui cel ple devant le vicont ou le meire. Qui dixit quod non, que il quidoit qe eus ne ly vodreint point tenir a dreit. *Roubury.* 'E serreit coe resun que pur vostre quider que nous tendrums e eus lur jurisdiction? Qe non.' E dit ly fut que il returnast a lur curt, e sil ne li feisent point de dreit que il venist a eus." "Roubury" would seem to have been Gilbert Rothbury, who was clerk of the council from 1290 to 1295 (when he was made a justice) and clerk of Parliament from 1290: Sayles, *The King's Parliament of England*, p. 80. The mention of Rothbury and Brabazon together narrows the date down no further than between 1290 and a little after 1307, but the context of the case in the volume seems to be 1290s.

The introduction of bill procedure into that branch of the king's court—Parliament—was supplemental to other procedures. The king, of course, could submit matters for consideration on his own initiative. Errors in the king's bench could be corrected in Parliament, and cases which were already in the king's court and which were proving too complex to determine without full discussion could be adjourned into Parliament. Writs had even been available at times to bring cases straight before the king's council.[109] The acceptance of bills on private initiative, however, was a great extension of the activity of Parliament. If this report can be considered representative, the bills which would be accepted would fall within that broad category that provoked so much concern: those cases in which there had been default of right. The bill functioned as a *recordari* and was approved by the auditors. The opening up of the king's court in 1275 to give fuller justice even in problems in which there was no warrant by writ extended both to the court of common pleas and to the court of Parliament. To that extent, Parliament functioned as a supervisory body over the lower courts.

Parliament supervised the lower courts in a more direct way also; the changes in the law practiced in the county courts were increasingly legislated in Parliament. This would often, of course, be by generalization from the situation found in an individual bill. County courts had long been subject to royal changes in law. The earliest example of such changes was the assize of essoins of 1170.[110] The provision of the *pone* and the writ *de libertate probanda* as well as the provision of the viscontiel writs as a whole represent royal alterations in the way justice was meted out in the county courts. Extant cases from even early in the thirteenth century show that county courts were more likely to be concerned with customs of the realm rather than with county custom.[111] The most prominent exceptions to this statement were the counties of Cheshire, Durham, and Kent. Cheshire and Durham, of course, were very high liberties and became palatine

---

[109] C. 60/50, m. 1: "Willelmus Bardulf dat unam marcam pro uno brevi ad terminum habendo coram consilio regis," "Thomas de Barlowe dat xx s pro uno brevi de gratia habendo coram consilio regis," [1252-123]. C. 60/70, n. 26: "Johannes Haket dat dimidiam marcam pro uno brevi de transgressione habendo coram consilio regis, et mandatum est vicecomiti Suthampton'," "Willelmus de Bechehampton dat dimidiam marcam pro consimili brevi coram consilio regis habendo, et mandatum est vicecomiti Suthampton." These, of course, were very unusual entries.

[110] *Pleas before the King or His Justices*, ed. D. M. Stenton, 4 vols., Selden Society, vols. 67, 68, 83, 84 (London, 1948-1967), 1:153-54.

[111] Lorna E. M. Walker, "Some Aspects of Local Jurisdiction in the 12th and 13th Centuries" (Master's thesis, University of London, 1958), pp. 264-67, with the references there cited.

courts. Kent perversely maintained a few of its customs against the custom of the realm even though it was not a liberty.[112] Nevertheless, it was the only county to do so. County courts abided by the Magna Carta,[113] and the statutes passed in Parliament were regularly referred to in litigation in the county courts.[114] The county courts were thus definitely subject to the regulation of the king and the king in Parliament.

The county courts were also constituent parts of Parliament; the knights of the shire were selected in open county court. Such selections were nothing new for county courts. Long before they were required to select such representatives, they had been required to elect coroners and other local officials.[115] Selection, whether of local officials or of representatives, seems to have been done normally by those who ordinarily made judgments in the county courts, at least in the thirteenth and for most of the fourteenth century.[116] As it were, they made a judgment as to who would be sent to bind the county in treating with the king in Parliament. Liberties were not excluded from this selection, just as they were probably not rigorously excluded from the making of judgments. The writs *de expensis*, which provided for the remuneration of the costs incurred by the representatives, directed the expenses of the knights of the shire to be levied from

[112] JUST. 1/367, m. 19 (fitz John v Romenal): "dicit quod consuetudo comitatus istius talis est quod, si tenens alicuius in servicio defecerit et servicium illud detinuerit per unum annum et unum diem et super hoc convincatur, quod licet domino suo tenementum illud ingredi et illud in manu sua tenere quousque ei satisfactum fuerit de predicto servicio et de areragiis secundum consuetudinem Kancie"; m. 47 (Barrok v Teppe): "Et totus comitatus recordatur quod sexsus femellus etatis quatuordecim annorum potest feoffare quemcumque pro voluntate sua de terra gavelykind. Et feoffamentum huiusmodi bonum et stabile [est] secundum consuetudinem comitatus Kancie."

[113] Brit. Lib., Add. 31826, fol. 261v: "Rauf dit qe nent somons. Examinato ballivo, qui testabatur quod sic, *Boydin*: 'Oportet dicere per cuius testimonium propter magnam cartam' " [S.S.].

[114] CP. 52 three weeks Easter, 23 Edward I (Faber v Clayton): "Cepit equum suum, inparcavit in quadam domo sub cumulo contra formam statuti domini regis nuper editi et ibidem iniuste detinuit contra [vadium et] plegios per quod dictus equus obiit racione minus rigide inparcacionis, unde dicit quod deterioratus est et dampnum habet ad valenciam ij m" [S.S.]. CP. 40/102, m. 49d (Engayne v Chaumberleyn): "Et Willelmus Engayne petit iudicium de defalta eiusdem Johannis et dicit quod essonium non iacet quia prius essoniatus fuit de eodem placito unde inquisicio ut patet in comitatu precedenti. Et consideratum est per totum comitatum quod inquisicio capiatur pro defalta ipsius Johannis per statutum apud Westmonasterium ultimo editum quod inde expressam facit mencionem" [Westminster II, c. 27].

[115] Cam, *Hundred*, p. 113.

[116] T.F.T. Plucknett, "Parliament," in *Historical Studies of the English Parliament*, ed. E. B. Fryde and Edward Miller, vol. 1 (Cambridge, 1970), p. 217; Pollock and Maitland, *History of English Law*, 1:543, n. 1. Representatives seem not to have been selected particularly at meetings of the general county court.

the areas of the county both inside and outside of liberties.[117] It was, thus, the body of seneschals and bailiffs who normally elected the knights of the shire. Only later in the fourteenth century did the selection of knights of the shire become a matter of greater concern. It was provided in a general way in 1372 that sheriffs and practicing lawyers should not be selected as knights of the shire;[118] and in the fifteenth century measures were taken to insure that lesser individuals would not participate in the selection.[119] It was, finally, only in the seventeenth century that some sheriffs found that the ordinary setting of the county court was not a suitable place for the election of the representatives; then a special session of the county court was scheduled at a different and more spacious venue.[120] The practice of having the knights of the shire elected in the open county court, however, became the most important prerogative of the county courts. Together with the representatives of the boroughs, the representatives of the shire chosen in county court came to form the House of Commons.

The county courts were able to function for the county as a whole in such a manner only because of long practice, familiarity with representation, and the jurisdiction of the county itself. County courts had long been called upon to send representatives to the king's court, and the performance of those representatives was binding on the county as a whole. The best example of such a practice is the procedure initiated by the writ of false judgment. The county was required to send four knights with the record; those knights were obliged to deliver the record and even to alter the record if it was not accurate. Faulty performance from those knights would result in an amercement of the county as a whole.[121] Common action of the county was

[117] *Registrum Omnium Brevium* (London, 1531), p. 192: "Rex vicecomiti salutem. Precipimus tibi quod de communitate comitatus predicti tam infra libertates quam extra, civitatibus et burgis de quibus cives et burgenses ad parliamentum nostrum apud W. die lunae proxime ante festum omnium sanctorum ultimo preterito summoneri fecimus venerunt duntaxat exceptis, habere facias J. de S. et W. de B. militibus comitatus predicti, pro communitate eiusdem comitatus ad parliamentum praedictum venientibus, decem et novem libras et quatuor solidos, pro expensis suis veniendo ad parliamentum praedictum, ibidem morando et exinde ad propria redeundo pro xlviij diebus, utroque praedictorum J. et W. capiente per diem quatuor solidos. Teste etc."

[118] *Rotuli Parliamentorum*, 6 vols. (London, 1767), 2:310; K. L. Wood-Legh, "Sheriffs, Lawyers, and Belted Knights in the Parliaments of Edward III," *EHR* 46 (1931):372-88.

[119] The legislation is treated in Alan Rogers, "The Lincolnshire County Court in the Fifteenth Century," *Lincolnshire History and Archaeology* 1 (1966):64-69. His interpretation of the decline of the seneschals is faulty.

[120] Above, chapter 1 at n. 83.

[121] Above, chapter 3 at n. 29.

possible even in litigation: the county could sue and be sued. There survive examples of the county suing a former sheriff for misuse of buildings constructed from a general levy on the county[122] and of a county court being sued for the expenses due its representatives.[123] At times, certain members of the county committed themselves in matters concerning the county as a whole.[124] Such common actions made representation a viable course, and Helen Cam has documented the development of representation of local units made possible by such needs.[125] It should be noted precisely, however, that the county

[122] E. 13/17, m. 27d: "Willelmus Burdet qui sequitur pro rege et pro communitate totius comitatus Leyc' venit coram etc., et queritur pro rege quod cum Willelmus de Boyville tempore quo fuit vicecomes predicti comitatus [1288-1290] levasset quandam colectam de hominibus predicti comitatus per certos receptatores ad hoc per eundem Willelmum assignatos, videlicet, de quolibet homine tenente unam carucatam terre duodecim denarios, ad quandam prisonam in villa Leycestre ad opus domini regis construendam, idem tamen Willelmus domos et edificia de predicta colecta ad prisonam predictam provisa et constructa tanquam liberum tenementum sibi appropriavit ad dampnum regis etc." The county, of course, would have been under pressure to provide further funds, so that its position as plaintiff was probably not merely nominal.

[123] CP. 52 quindene St. Martin, 29 Edward I: "Edwardus dei gratia rex . . . vicecomiti Derby, salutem. Precipe communitati comitatus Derby quod iuste et sine dilatione reddat Galfrido de Gresely et Radulpho de Freschervill triginta libras quas eis debet et iniuste detinet ut dicunt. Et nisi fecerit et predicti Galfridus et Radulphus fecerint te securum de clameo suo prosequendo tunc summoneas per bonos summonitores predictam communitatem quod sit coram iusticiariis nostris apud Ebor' a die sancti Martini in xv dies ostensura quare non fecerit. Et habeas ibi summonitores et hoc breve. Teste me ipso apud Donypas xvj die Octobris anno regni nostri vicesimo nono." Part of the endorsement made on the writ at issue was "per cancellarium pro militibus [qui] venerunt ad parliamenta regis." Normally, representatives would sue the sheriff of the county, since the writ de expensis empowered him to levy the money from the county; if he did not, he was guilty of ignoring the writ. Some good examples of such prosecutions are de la Bere & Holewell v Aylesbury, KB. 27/288, m. 145; Braybrok v le Baud, E. 13/32, m. 12.

[124] E. 13/2, m. 4d: "Willelmus de Bello Campo optulit etc., versus Johannem de Erkalewe, Johannem filium Hugonis, Johannem filium Aeri, et Roberti Corbet de hoc quod tenentur coram etc., ad hunc diem ad audiendam inquisicionem faciendam per Hugonem de Wlonkelowe et alios contentos in brevi liberos et legales homines de comitatu Salop si iidem Johannes et alii debent predicto Willelmo quadraginta quatuor marcas pro quodam promisso quod ei fecerunt pro toto comitatu predicto ad quedam negocia in curia regis expedienda dictum comitatum tangencia sicut recognoverunt coram Leonino de Rammesle subvicecomiti dicti comitatus die jovis proxima ante festum sancti Hillarii anno regni domini Henrici regis lv in pleno comitatu ut dictus Willelmus dicit vel non ut predicti Johannes et alii dicunt, ita quod loquela que inde fuit coram baronis de scacario tempore eiusdem Henrici regis inter eundem Willelmum et predictos Johannes et alios esset in eodem statu in quo fuit a die sancti Michaelis anno predicti regis Henrici lvi quando prefati Johannes et alii posuerunt se in inquisicionem predictam et predictus Willelmus similiter." Earlier examples of such actions are available, mainly in regard to influencing the appointment of a sheriff.

[125] Helen Cam, "The Theory and Practice of Representation in Medieval England," in Historical Studies of the English Parliament, ed. Fryde and Miller, vol. 1, p. 262-78.

court was very much a representative body in itself. The representation involved came from the subordination of one individual to another; lords could represent their men—their court—at county; a lord could even have a representative attend in his stead in the person of his seneschal or even his bailiff.[126] By the mid-thirteenth century the county court was long familiar with representation. Moreover, its jurisdiction gave it a varied but real control over the other curial units in the county. The boroughs were perhaps the most immune from the sheriff and the county court, and many of them later developed into counties themselves.[127] They had managed to preserve special forms of land tenure,[128] and they were recognized as distinct from the county when they were allowed to send their own representatives. The county court, however, was the obvious unit to represent the rest of the county. In fact, almost as much as in language, the county court (comitatus) was the county (comitatus).

The precise relationship of the county courts to the other courts both inside and outside the county itself thus changed during the thirteenth century, but not to the extent that it lost its position of preeminence in the county. The most significant of those changes involved the evolution of the franchise of return of writs, which finally resulted in restricting the inhabitants of many liberties from pleading in the county courts, even in cases of replevin brought by writ. In those liberties, however, as well as in the courts of the ancient demesne and the lesser courts, the county court retained a supervisory jurisdiction, despite the growing definitions of ancient demesne privileges and the effects of the various uses of the recordari. That superior position in the county persisted even after 1300; that position, together with the practices forced on the county court as a whole for the preceding century and a half, had made the county court the embodiment of the community of the county. Indeed, there would have been no county community were it not for the unifying action of the sheriff in the county court. That curial community was the unit that took its place in Parliament as one of the constituent parts of the community of the realm.

[126] Above, chapter 5, n. 1 ff.

[127] *Bristol Charters, 1155-1373*, ed. N. D. Harding, 3 vols., Bristol Record Society, vols. 1, 11, 12 (Bristol, 1930-1947), 1:142 [1373]; W. Hudson and J. C. Tingey, *The Records of the City of Norwich*, 2 vols. (Norwich, 1906-1910), 1:31 [1404].

[128] Pollock and Maitland, *History of English Law*, 1:645.

10

Conclusion

THE HISTORY of the county courts of medieval England has usually been described in terms of their importance as courts: that from the twelfth to the nineteenth century the county courts declined in proportion to the king's court's increase in activity and importance. Whatever the merits of such a long-term view, it is certainly better to choose a more limited perspective. From the twelfth to the fourteenth century the most helpful theme is that of curial integration: the degree to which the various courts in England were bound together into a legal system. Curial integration was not an ideal espoused by royal officials, so that it was not a goal pursued single-mindedly. Some innovations furthered integration, while other contemporary actions tended to dissolve the bonds that unified the courts. Overall, legal processes and personnel tended to bind the courts together increasingly until the end of the thirteenth century; thereafter, the courts of the liberties, the county courts, and the king's court functioned increasingly in isolation from each other.

Legal processes were the most important factors in unifying the courts. The basic innovations in this area occurred during the reign of Henry II. Prior to that time royal mandates had initiated legal cases in county courts, but in the 1170s or 1180s standardized viscontiel writs were made available. The hypothesis underlying any system of standardized writs is that some remedy has been determined for all those who meet a certain set of conditions which define a litigious situation. There were relatively few varieties of viscontiel writs in the twelfth century, but their provision inaugurated a communality of specialized legal processes that made one county court more similar to another. As the number of viscontiel writs grew during the thirteenth century, they initiated a larger share of any county's litigation and increased the communality of the law practiced in county courts.

This spread of similar procedure initiated by royal writ affected not only the county courts, but also the courts of liberties. At first seemingly by common consent concerning judicial privileges of great lords and then by the processes and royal authorization embodied in the franchise of return of writs, viscontiel writs found their way into the lower courts of the county. Since the long-term tendency—pursued not by intention but piecemeal by adaptation and jurisprudential "accident"—was for all important disputes to be initiated by writ, by 1290 the most valuable cases in liberties as in county courts were initiated by writ and governed by the rules dictated by those royal mandates.

This spread of common practice did not spring from a void or proceed merely from the working of viscontiel writs. The process of tolt preserved the ancient superiority of the county court and its duty to provide a fair hearing for those dangerous cases which might result otherwise in violence: real litigation. Tolt limited the control of lords and feudal courts, so that only the rare liberty was exempted completely from the supervisory jurisdiction of the county courts. The action of false judgment sought to insure likewise that the county courts would not be unlimited in their activities, but would rather be subject to severe penalties for unjust judgments. The standard for justice, moreover, was the practice of the king's court; only in special instances could county custom supersede the common law. That standard was reinforced by legislation which regulated even the complex matter of essoins for county courts. Tolt, false judgment, and legislation laid the foundation for the viscontiel writs by reinforcing the preeminence of the county courts in the county as well as by subordinating the county courts to the standards and practice of the king's court.

The provision of the viscontiel writs was accompanied, perhaps immediately, by the provision of the writ *pone*. The viscontiel writs were to be instruments to delegate a case, not to alienate jurisdiction over it. The continuing ability of either party to remove the case into the king's court was a powerful assertion of a relationship between the various levels of court, not just a relationship between the issuing body—chancery—and both courts. Whereas in the writ of false judgment the county was perceived much as an independent individual who had committed a serious wrong, the provision of the *pone* demonstrated that the king's court itself had a responsibility for those cases begun in the county courts—or the courts of liberties—by viscontiel writ. If something was unsatisfactory, the case could be brought before justices without penalizing the lower court. The county court was not a judicial organ completely separate from the king's court;

as noted in *Fleta*, when a case was brought by writ into the county court the sheriff was acting something like a justice. The county court functioned in the manner of a county court, but as a limited king's court; that shared nature was embodied in the *pone*, which allowed the king's court extensive interference in county court litigation even before judgment rendered. The conditional delegation and nonpunitive supervisory procedure provided by Henry II in the form of the viscontiel writs and the *pone* are necessities for any aggregation of courts to be called a legal system.

In many ways the king's court treated the county courts as mere extensions of itself. When returnable writs were still fairly new, it was thought best that gage and pledges should be secured in open county court. The elaborate process for gaining trial by grand assize assumed that very often the mise would be made in county court, and the form of that mise would be the form—put forward by the tenant but approved by the county—which would be put to the knights of the assize. The perplexing problems of the possibility that assize litigation could supersede a determination even by battle in a lower court and of correlative cases being pursued in different courts necessitated the writ *recordari*, which provided a procedure to coordinate the activities of the wide varieties of secular courts in England. The county courts also remained the body in which people were exacted to outlawry and declared outlaws; that procedure—exigent procedure—constituted the most coercive procedure available to the king's court in personal litigation. Even in such an ordinary matter as a jury trial, the king's court relied upon the county court as the forum for its trials during most of the thirteenth century. The county courts were also relied upon for publicity. Statutes were read there, and proclamations required in the course of litigation were made in the county courts. The workings of the king's court, in short, were often formed by and molded around the existence of the county courts.

After the provision of the first viscontiel writs and the writ *pone* in the reign of Henry II, the most striking procedural innovation integrating the courts occurred in 1275: the transformation of the *recordari* into a procedure for the removal of plaints. The step taken then, of course, was too extensive; the initial provision had to be restricted first between 1278 and 1281 and then again around 1292. Nevertheless, it made even plaints in county courts a royal responsibility which was ongoing and could not be fulfilled by merely punishing wrongs. Removal is by definition a declaration of conditional delegation. Even cases not begun by royal mandate were now matters for continuing supervision by the justices. Moreover, until 1302 this transformation enlarged the record-bearing capability of the lower courts. Pleading and process, perhaps even jury verdicts taken before removal, could be accepted by the king's court. Finally, the complicated interaction of county litigation with king's court jurisdictional rules which resulted in the 40s limitation on plaint litigation in debt/detinue in the lower courts reveal a court system, not a mere aggregation of courts. It is in such procedures and interactions, rather than in the punitive procedures activated by the writ of false judgment, that the normal relationship of the county court to the king's court at that time can best be seen.

Legal processes were probably more important than legal personnel in the formation of the English legal system of the thirteenth century, but the personnel still constituted a major link between the king's court and the county courts. The most basic and lasting bond between the king's court and the county courts in matters of personnel was the body of executive officials: the sheriff and his staff. The king's court did not develop by setting up its own, new body of officials to execute procedure and judgments. It utilized the officials already in existence and serving the king directly by executing his commands and indirectly by serving the county and hundred courts. The same people who distrained a debtor who owed £500 and was being prosecuted in the court of common pleas distrained the peasant who owed 40d and was being prosecuted in the hundred court. The basic procedures and standards demanded of these men could not vary much between the courts. That communality of personnel limited the degree to which the different levels of courts could develop in isolation.

In the twelfth century, and for a period in the thirteenth, the people who were appointed sheriff played an important role in unifying the courts. For a time under Henry I a large percentage of sheriffs were also *curiales*.[1] Such a situation would have greatly facilitated implementation of royal decisions. Furthermore, immediately after the succession of Henry II and then again during the 1180s and through into the thirteenth century, that overlap between central and local officials reappeared. Some sheriffs were royal justices, who were transferred from county to county. As sheriffs they could and probably were expected to leave a royal imprint on administration and the functioning of the courts, because it was during this time that

[1] C. Warren Hollister and John Baldwin, "The Rise of Administrative Kingship," *AHR* 83 (1978):882-87.

the law was being transformed by the introduction of standardized writs and the king's court was so relying on the lower courts for a large part of their procedures. Right through the thirteenth century it was not unusual for a sheriff to serve successively in different counties. This interchangeability must have promoted the increasing similarity in the administration of the various counties. The sheriff was always the most influential person in determining the way in which the county court was going to function. The fact that the sheriff was not limited to being taken only from local men but was rather at times first a royal justice and then a sheriff from another county made the courts more responsive to royal wishes and increasingly uniform in the law they administered.

The final factor in curial integration was undoubtedly important and can be traced neither to royal action nor to royal intent. Had suitors been the only judges in the county courts, it is conceivable that the various courts would have retained a significant amount of local custom. Even in the twelfth century, however, the most important sector of the county, the great lords, would normally have been represented by seneschal or bailiff. These individuals were often so involved in law and legal administration that they can fairly be called professional lawyers. They administered and presided over the feudal courts and the courts of liberties; they were judges in the county courts; and in the king's court they represented their lords as attorneys, since they were the most trusted and legally knowledgeable men at the lord's disposal. As attorneys in the king's court they would have absorbed new ideas of precision in pleading which they would carry with them to their practice in the county courts and demand from local pleaders in the courts over which they presided. It is possible that at the time the king's court was forming as a national court and before there was any exclusive group of people permitted to plead in the court of common pleas the process may have worked the other way around: the king's court may at times have been influenced by legal standards in the county courts carried by attorneys who pleaded their cases. Not all pleaders in the county courts functioned as seneschals in the liberties and attorneys in the king's court, but there were a sufficient number of them to make the legal profession itself a living bond between the various levels of courts. Just as much as were the removal procedures, the degree to which lawyers could and did function in all the various courts is an extremely strong demonstration that the courts of England in the thirteenth century were integrated into a legal system. That system, achieved by legal procedures which bound the courts together and by legal personnel shared by the courts, can best be symbolized in the institution of Parliament.

The integration of courts achieved in the thirteenth century was not a lasting achievement. Since the building of a legal system was not intended or necessarily even recognized but is rather only a present-day construct placed on the development of legal institutions, the bonds that united the courts were soon broken or even served to isolate the courts one from the other during the fourteenth and fifteenth centuries. The decisive role in this process was once again played by the processes of removal. The viscontiel writs had insured that there was a communality of jurisdiction between the lower courts and the king's court. The procedures initiated by the writs *pone* and *recordari* had initially bound the courts together. While the transformation of the *recordari* initially made replevin more useful, in the long term, as removal became even easier, it made prosecution of plaints of replevin in lower courts often futile. Removal became a matter of course. Likewise, the transformation of the *recordari*, through a complex and unexpected series of events, resulted in the 40s limit on the prosecution for debts by plaint in the lower courts. The greater use of the *pone*, of course, increasingly made prosecution in the lower courts by viscontiel writs of either replevin or debt seem futile. The defendant could annul both pleading and process simply by removing the case at the last moment. The use of the *pone* in a similar way discouraged plaintiffs from using the other viscontiel writs even to initiate a case in the lower courts which they actually intended to have determined there. By the 1330s litigants—except in borough courts, where privileges kept litigation within the borough—had sufficiently deserted the viscontiel writs that there was little left of any common jurisdiction. The writs *pone* and *recordari*, in the last analysis, resulted in a de facto, although not a de jure, reduction of the jurisdiction of the county courts to minor debts.

This decline in the utility of most viscontiel writs had been preceded by a decline in the utility of seignorial writs. The introduction of the petty assizes in the reign of Henry II and the development of the writs of entry had made it possible to determine most real disputes without resorting to the writ of right patent and the feudal court. Moreover, rules concerning disseisins made the lord ever less amenable to adjudicate such a dispute. When litigants did finally resort to a writ of right patent, removal by tolt and *pone*—seemingly uttered in one breath with no thought that removal by tolt would not be followed by further removal by *pone*—became normal. The common jurisdiction in real litigation thus also disappeared, at least in the upper reaches of realty. In addition to the elimination of that communality, the effective elimination of the county court's ability to determine such cases made those courts somewhat less public. Prior to the middle of the thirteenth century, a conclusion to a real action in the county court would often result in a public agreement. Such an agreement made in court had some power, because further litigation concerning the same land but perhaps a different dispute was expected likewise to come before the county. As the writ of right patent fell out of use, so too did such public agreements concerning realty made in the county courts.[2] Their place was taken, naturally enough, by the final concord made in the king's court.

There were spheres of litigation in which the county court was not restricted. The transformation of the *recordari* and the Statute of Gloucester resulted in an action of trespass by viscontiel writ which was isolated from the king's court. The isolation was, of course, not complete. Actions by viscontiel writs of trespass were still subject to

[2] Some examples from cartularies: *The Chartulary of the Priory of St. Pancras of Lewes*, ed. L. F. Salzman, 2 vols., Sussex Record Society, vols. 38, 40 (Lewes, 1932, 1934), 1:144, 2:43; *A Cartulary of Buckland Priory in the County of Somerset*, ed. F. W. Weaver, Somerset Record Society, vol. 25 (London, 1909), pp. 37, 128-29, 179; *The Sandford Cartulary*, ed. Agnes M. Leys, 2 vols., Oxfordshire Record Society, vols. 19, 22 (Oxford, 1938, 1941), 1:92; *Cartulary of Worcester Cathedral Priory*, ed. R. R. Darlington (London, 1968), pp. 124, 181; *Two Cartularies of the Augustinian Priory of Bruton and the Cluniac Priory of Montacute in the County of Somerset*, Somerset Record Society, vol. 8 (London, 1894), p. 171; *The Thame Cartulary*, ed. H. E. Salter, 2 vols., Oxfordshire Record Society, vols. 25, 26 (Oxford, 1947-1948), p. 79; *The Great Chartulary of Glastonbury*, ed. Aelred Watkin, 3 vols., Somerset Record Society, vols. 59, 63, 64 (Frome, 1944-1956), p. 375; *The Burton Chartulary*, ed. G. Wrottesley, William Salt Archaeological Society, vol. 5 (London, 1884), pp. 48-49; *Cartulary of Canonsleigh Abbey*, ed. Vera C. M. London, Devon and Cornwall Record Society, n.s., vol. 8 (Torquay, 1965), pp. 4-5; *Cartulary of Darley Abbey*, ed. R. R. Darlington (Kendal, 1945), p. 356; *St. Benet of Holme, 1020-1210*, ed. J. R. West, 2 vols., Norfolk Record Society, vols. 2, 3 (London, 1932), p. 120; *The Cartulary of St. Michael's Mount*, ed. P. L. Hull, Devon and Cornwall Record Society, n.s., vol. 5 (Torquay, 1962), p. 42; *Registrum Antiquissimum*, ed. C. W. Forster and Kathleen Major, 10 vols., Lincoln Record Society, vols. 27, 29, 32, 34, 41, 42, 46, 51, 62, 67 (Lincoln, 1931-1973), 2:313; *Cartulary of the Abbey of Eynsham*, ed. H. E. Salter, 2 vols., Oxford Historical Society, vols. 49, 50 (Oxford, 1906, 1908), 1:95, 115; *Chartulary of St. John of Pontefract*, ed. Richard Holmes, 2 vols., Yorkshire Archaeological Society, vols. 25, 30 (Leeds, 1899, 1902), 2:417; "The Chartulary of Dieulacres Abbey," ed. G. Wrottesley, *Collections for a History of Staffordshire*, William Salt Archaeological Society, n.s., vol. 9 (London, 1906), p. 346; *The Stone Chartulary*, ed. G. Wrottesley, William Salt Archaeological Society, vol. 6 (London, 1885), pp. 8, 11. Some late examples: *Calendar of Charters and Documents Relating to Selborne and Its Priory*, ed. W. Dunn Macray, 2 vols., Hampshire Record Society, vols. 4, 9 (London, 1891-1894), 1:58 (1264-1269), 82 (1270).

the action of false judgment and later on to the action of attaint.[3] Neither method of supervision, however, would have been undertaken frequently. Likewise, neither the plaint of trespass nor the plaint of covenant were subjected to a 40s limit.[4] The *recordari* remained available for covenant, but, as far as I have been able to see, was little used in the first few decades of the fourteenth century. The *recordari* later on became available for trespass, but only in a limited number of situations. It is improbable that these few ties would make it possible to refer to English courts in the fifteenth century as a legal system. The lower courts were by and large either restricted to lesser matters or isolated from the impact of the king's court.

The decrease in the importance of the lower courts and the elimination of areas of common jurisdiction were accompanied by a lessening of the binding influence of court personnel. The king's court and the county courts, of course, both continued to use the sheriff and his bailiffs and clerks. The sheriffs of the fourteenth century, however, were more clearly men of the county in which they served. Their terms were generally shorter, and sheriffs often served more than one term, although almost never in different counties. The subordination of the county courts was taken for granted; there was no need for a wasteful expenditure of the time of a royal justice or a skilled official in a court with such a limited jurisdiction. Use of central officials in local offices would never again be related to the importance of the jurisdiction of the county court.

There is reason also to think that the whole structure of the legal profession changed as did the relations between the courts. While there was a substantial similarity in at least part of the jurisdictions of the lower courts and the king's court, no better attorney might be imagined than a county pleader. When that similarity disappeared, county pleaders would not only usually be involved in less important cases, they would also be less familiar with the kinds of actions they would have met in the king's court. Moreover, Margaret Hastings found that clerks of the king's court in the fifteenth century often functioned as attorneys,[5] a situation one would not expect to find

[3] W. S. Holdsworth, *A History of English Law*, 14 vols. (London, 1903-1938), 2:622; *Registrum Omnium Brevium* (1531), p. 122.

[4] Ibid., p. 146 does have a prohibition for a plaint of covenant, but the plaint of covenant (specified as worth £10) is specified to be one which should properly have been sued in debt. This prohibition was thus not meant to extend the 40s limit to covenant, but only to prevent litigants from avoiding that rule in debt by framing debts as broken covenants.

[5] Margaret Hastings, *The Court of Common Pleas in Fifteenth Century England* (Ithaca, 1947), p. 111.

very often around 1300. A further indication of this change is the drastic decline in legal fees between 1300 and 1450. In 1293 an attorney was paid 16s to prosecute a case of trespass in the court of common pleas; in 1292 a different attorney was paid 10s to prosecute a case of land in the same court.[6] In lower courts, of course, annuities for pleaders ranged from 6s. 8d to 20s. In the court of king's bench in 1280 one pleader was retained for 10 marks.[7] In short, at the end of the thirteenth century everything would seem to indicate that legal practice, evaluated case by case, was very lucrative. As late as 1380 an apprentice was hired as counsel in an assize of novel disseisin for, allegedly, 46s. 8d in money and 30s in kind. Although the apprentice denied that he had received that much, this case would at least indicate that fees were something like they had been at the beginning of the century.[8] Then, in 1452 a year book report yields the information that 40d was an acceptable fee for a sergeant, whereas 20d was sufficient for an attorney.[9] The next year Richard Alfray was accused of maintenance. He objected that, at the time of the case concerned, he had been at Greys Inn and was a man learned in the law of the land. He explained that he had been retained as counsel in the action for a fee of 40d and was therefore not guilty of maintenance.[10] This substantial decline in legal fees is difficult to explain. Whatever the explanation, however, it would make it unlikely that lawyers would find it profitable to make frequent trips between Westminster and Staffordshire or Cornwall. The king's court must have gained its own permanent and exclusive staff, so that the binding effect of the sharing of lawyers noted in the thirteenth and fourteenth centuries must have disappeared in the fifteenth century.

Certain of the bonds between the courts remained; the integration between the courts in the fifteenth century, however, was no longer an integration between units which were at least similar in jurisdiction. In the fifteenth century the courts were very dissimilar in jurisdiction. In the king's court the county courts no longer seemed of much importance and were only considered when exigent procedure was required or when the odd *pone* or *recordari* brought a case into court. In a similar way, the lower courts functioned without much explicit reference to the king's court. If one only considered the reg-

---

[6] Robert C. Palmer, "The Origins of the Legal Profession in England," *Irish Jurist* 11 (1976):137-38.

[7] *Select Cases in the Court of King's Bench*, ed. G. O. Sayles, 7 vols., Selden Society, vols. 55, 57, 58, 74, 76, 82, 88 (London, 1936-1971), 1:67-68, 80-81.

[8] CP. 40/481, m. 102.

[9] YB. Mich. 31 Henry VI.

[10] CP. 40/774, m. 313.

ister of writs, fifteenth-century courts might still have seemed a system. Most of the viscontiel writs were still there. The *pone* and the *recordari* were still listed. Jurisdictions, nonetheless, had changed and remained restricted precisely because the old removal procedures were still available. The instruments that had integrated the courts of England—focusing locally in the county courts and joining in the king's court—survived and insured the overarching importance of the king's court. During the twelfth and thirteenth centuries the courts had had a symbiotic relationship; by the middle of the fourteenth century the king's court had appropriated almost every jurisdiction of significance from the county courts.

Appendices

I. The Dates of County Days

Since county sessions tended to retain their place in an archetypical lunar calendar—both in relationship to other county courts and to the particular day of the week—it is possible to determine whether a given day was the occasion of a session of a particular county court. Such a determination may help explain the circumstances of such events as trespasses and financial or real transactions. If it is determined that both the date and the place (see Appendix II) of the event under consideration coincided with a county session, it remains, of course, a prudential decision as to whether the two events were actually related.

The normal dates for county sessions are recorded in the table in the form of four or six week numbers, that is, their normal position in the lunar calendar month or, for those counties which met six-weekly, in a six-week calendar. The numbers for dates from 1414 to 1624 are taken directly from J. J. Alexander, "The Dates of County Days," *BIHR* 3 (1925-1926):93. I have excluded his figures for Monmouthshire, the Welsh counties, and the new city and borough counties, because they fall outside the scope of this work and mostly in the sixteenth and seventeenth centuries. Alexander derived his data from dates on the returns of members of Parliament and worked with something over 1,100 dates. The figures for the thirteenth and fourteenth centuries are my own, derived from over 1,500 dates preserved in accounts, outlawries, and county court cases. From the reign of Edward I into the seventeenth century, county sessions corresponded to the predicted date about 90 percent of the time. In the latter part of the reign of Henry III, predictability is less accurate; and such figures as are noted for that time are footnoted. Prior to the middle of the thirteenth century the figures are of no provable value.

To determine whether a given date probably corresponded with a session of a given county, the position of that date on the archetypical lunar calendar must be determined. The process for the conversion from a normal date into a four or six weeks number is here regarded as a purely mechanical process and is contained in more detail in Alexander's "The Dates of County Days." The process requires the division of the sum of four separately derived figures.

TABLE A.1
County Days

County	Day	Henry III	1290-1320	ca. 1414	ca. 1442	ca. 1472	ca. 1545	ca. 1584	ca. 1624
					Four or Six-Weeks Number				
Beds	Mo		16	16	16	2^t	16	16	16
Berks	We/Mo	18^a	18	18	18	18	[23]	23	23
Bucks	We		11	11	11	25^s	11	[11]	11
Cambs	Th	5^b	19	19	19	19	[5]	5	[5]
Ches	Tu/Mo	Var.	Var.^n				23	[16]	[16]
Corn	Mo		2	2	[2]	2	2	[2]	[2]
Cumb	Tu*	10^c	10	[10]	[10]	[10]	24	[24]	24
Derb	Th	19^d	5	5	5	5	5	[5]	5
Devon	Tu	10^e	17	17	17	17	17	[17]	17
Dors	Mo		16	16	16	16	16	16	16
Essex	Tu	3^f	10	10	10	10	24	24	24
Glos	Mo/We		16^o	9	9	9	[23]	[23]	[25]^w
Hants	Mo		2	2	9	9	[23]	23	23
Heref	Sa		7	7	23^s	21^t	[21]	21	21
Herts	Th	12^f	26	26	7	5^u	19	19	19
Hunts	Sa		28	28	26	21^u	[7]	[7]	7
Kent	Mo	2/23/16^g	23^p	16	28	2^t	23	23	23
Lancs	Mo		S23	S23	16	S23	S16	2^v	9
Leics	Th		26	26	S23	26	26	[26]	26
Lincs	Mo	S16^h	S30	S30	26	S16	[S23]	9^v	9
Midd	Th		19	19	S16	5^t	12	[12]	12
Norf	Mo	9/2^i	2	2	19	2	9	9	9
Northants	Th		5	5	[2]	26^t	[26]	26	26
Northumb	Th*	S12^j	S12	[S12]	5	S12	no date	[12]^v	26

Notts	Mo	16^d	2	2	2	2	2	2	2
Oxon	Th/Tu/We	5^a	5	5	5	5	[24]	24	25
Rut	Th*		12	12	12	[26]	26	[26]	26
Salop	(Tu)/Th	(24)^k	26	26	26	26	26	[26]	[26]
Som	Mo		9	9	9	9	9	9	9
Staffs	Th		5	5	5	5	5	5	5
Suff	(Tu)/Mo	(24)/16/9^l	9	9	[9]	[9]	16	16	16
Surrey	We		11	11	11	11	11	11	[11]
Sussex	Th		19	19	19	19	[19]	[19]	19
Warw	Mo		2	2	2	2	2	2	[2]
Westm	Th*		12	12	12	12	5	[19]	19
Wilts	Tu	24^m	24	24	24	24	24	3	3
Worcs	We		18^q	25	25	25	[18]	18	[18]
Yorks	Mo		S16^r	S16	S16	S16	[S16]	2^v	2

NOTE: The apparatus for the table is as follows:

* a continuing irregularity in county court schedule despite an overall adherence to a particular day.

[ ] a four or six-weeks number not derived strictly from the year indicated in the column, but from the next closest year.

( ) a result derived from very few figures, the number of which will appear in a footnote.

Var. a variable schedule with no overall adherence to any four or six-weeks number. This occurred only in Cheshire, which, however, met consistently on Tuesdays.

a CRR, 12:220, on the basis of only two consecutive sessions.

b CRR, 12:220, on the basis of only two consecutive sessions.

c E. 199/7/1 (1227-1228).

d E. 370/5/77, 79 (1264-1265). When there was any irregularity at this time in the session of either Nottinghamshire or Derbyshire—that occurred four times in 1264-1265—it affected both counties, making them 23 and 26 respectively. The reason for the joint effect was that they shared the same sheriff, who seems to have insisted on holding both county sessions in the same week.

e E. 370/5/25 (1259).

f E. 370/5/30 (1259). For Hertfordshire in 1212, see CRR, 6:275.

Notes (cont'd)

g JUST. 1/361, m. 51 (1253), four consecutive sessions on day 2; E. 370/5/36 (1259) sessions on day 23, despite some irregularity; E. 370/5/38 (1264-1265) consistent adherence to day 16. CP. 40/9, m. 51 [S.S.] has Kent on a 23 schedule again in 1274. It thus seems that Kent felt fairly free to change the day on which it met until into the middle of the reign of Edward I.

h E. 370/5/45 (1258); Registrum Antiquissimum, 2:313 (1229).

i E. 370/9/22 (1264-1265); E. 370/5/71 (1266-1267). The change took place 9 May 1267.

j E. 101/505/10 (1258-1259). The schedule was still very irregular; only five of the nine sessions listed were on day S12; others were on days S5, S19, or S40.

k E. 370/6/10 (1239-1240), the dates are derived from a sheriff's account which is very probably but not certainly concerning Shropshire, since after those dates it lists amercements also for Staffordshire.

l E. 370/6/11, dated by Morris, Early English County Courts, p. 91, n. 10, as 1369-1370 is clearly 1258-1259. It shows Suffolk meeting six out of ten times on Tuesdays, but at times also on Saturday, Sunday, or Wednesday. All the Tuesdays were day 24, and the other dates were in close proximity. E. 370/9/22 (1264-1265) shows Suffolk meeting consistently on Monday and day 16. E. 370/5/71 (1266-1267) shows the change from day 16 to day 9 on 16 May 1267, thus coinciding with the change in Norfolk.

m CRR, 11:348, based on three of five sessions meeting on day 24; the other sessions were on day 3 and day 17.

n Meeting on Tuesdays but at irregular intervals with no discernable four- or six-weeks number as late as 1341: Chester 29/50, mm. 13-14, which records a case which lasted from Aug 1339 to Nov 1341 with the dates of all the sessions.

o Gloucestershire changed from day 16 (C. 88/6, mm. 20, 32) to day 9 (C. 88/7, m. 22) between 18 Feb 1320 and 19 Jan 1323.

p Kent met on day 23 at least as late as 1374: C. 88/46/36. See also C. 88/36/2; C. 88/37/18.

q Worcestershire met on day 18 at least until 28 Sept 1323: C. 88/7, m . 10.

r E. 370/6/23 (1258-1259).

s The change occurred in 1422 (Alexander, "The Dates of County Days").

t The change occurred in 1461 (ibid.).

u The change occurred in 1471 (ibid.).

v 2 Edward VI, c. 25 (1548).

w The change occurred in 1603 (Alexander, "The Dates of County Days").

For any given date, such as 7 Dec 1340, those four figures are

1. The *net year-number*: the year of the date less 1100 (Thus 1340 − 1100 = 240)
2. The *leap year-number*: one-fourth of the net year number, omitting fractions (240 divided by 4 = 60)
3. The *month-number*: the number which corresponds to the date's month in the following table:

Jan: 1 [0]	Apr: 7	July: 14	Oct: 22
Feb: 4 [3]	May: 9	Aug: 17	Nov: 25
Mar: 4	June: 12	Sept: 20	Dec: 27

   The bracketed numbers for Jan and Feb are used when the date occurs in leap year (for 7 Dec 1340, Dec = 27).
4. The *day-number* of the date (for 7 Dec 1340, 7).

The sum of these four figures for the sample date of 7 Dec 1340 is thus 240 + 60 + 27 +7 = 334. That sum is then divided by 28 (the number of days in a lunar month), yielding a *quotient* (here, 11) and a *remainder* (here, 26). That remainder is the four-weeks number. If there is no remainder, it is taken to be 28. For 7 Dec 1340, the four-weeks number is thus 26. If the event under consideration took place in Leicester on 7 Dec 1340 it can be assumed with high probability—referring both to the table below (which shows that Leicestershire county court met on days falling on the 26th day of the archetypical lunar calendar) and to Appendix II—that the county court session was being held at the same time and in near proximity.

If the county was one which met every six weeks, further calculations in addition to those above must be made. It involves a further division of another summation. The same sample date, 7 Dec 1340, will be used, and the above calculations are assumed to have been done already, yielding both the quotient (11) and the remainder, which was the four-weeks number (26). The further summation concerns three figures:

1. the *quotient* derived above (11)
2. the *month-position* of the date in the solar calendar, that is, Jan: 1; Feb: 2; March: 3; etc. (for 7 Dec 1340, December = 12)
3. the sum of the digits of the year under consideration (for 7 Dec 1340, 1 + 3 +4 +0 = 8).

The sum required is thus 11 + 12 + 8 = 31. That sum is then divided by 3, yielding a remainder of either 0, 1 or 2. If the remainder is 0, the six-weeks number coincides with the previously derived four-weeks number. If the remainder is 1, the six-weeks number is 28 more or 14 less than the previously derived four-weeks number. If the remainder is 2, the six-weeks number is 14 more than the four-weeks number previously derived.

For 7 Dec 1340 the division of 31 by 3 yields a remainder of 1. The six-weeks number is thus obtained by subtracting 14 from 26, yielding the six-weeks number 12. To distinguish it from a four-weeks number, it is written as S12. (The same result would be obtained by adding 28 and making adjustments for the six-week calendar, since the sum would then be 54, or 12 days into the next six-week "month.") If the event under consideration took place at Newcastle-upon-Tyne on 7 Dec 1340, it is somewhat probable that it took place on the same day and in the same place as the county session, although Northumberland, as the table indicates, was rather more irregular than other counties and, according to Appendix II, met—albeit very rarely—elsewhere than Newcastle-upon-Tyne.

Further examples can be found in Alexander's article.

II. County Venue

TABLE A.2

County	Venue	County	Venue
Beds	Bedford (Leighton Buzzard)[1]	Leics	Leicester
		Lincs	Lincoln
Berks	*	Norf	Norwich
Bucks	*	Northants	Northampton
Cambs	Cambridge	Northumb	Newcastle-upon-Tyne
Ches	Chester		(Morpath,[4] Warkworth[5])
Corn	*	Notts	Nottingham
Cumb	Carlisle	Oxon	Oxford
Derb	Derby	Rut	*
Devon	Exeter	Salop	Shrewsbury
Dorset	Dorchester[2]	Som	Somerton,[6] Ilchester,[7]
Durham	Durham[3]		(Glastonbury)[8]
Essex	*	Staffs	Stafford
Glos	Gloucester	Suff	Ipswich
Hants	Winchester	Surrey	Leatherhead,[9] Guildford[10]
Heref	Hereford	Sussex	*
Herts	*	Warw	Warwick
Hunts	Huntingdon	Westm	Appleby[11]
Kent	*	Wilts	Wilton,[12] (Devizes)[13]
Lancs	Lancaster	Worcs	Worcester
		Yorks	York

NOTE: The apparatus for the table is as follows:

* Counties that had a more complicated venue pattern; they are treated specially in Chapter 1.

Venues in parenthesis are exceptional and need not indicate normal practice. Only exceptional venues, venues difficult to document, and venues that changed are footnoted.

[1] E. 370/5/1: on 29 Jan 1475 and 21 May 1475, my only references to such a venue; probably not a thirteenth- or fourteenth-century venue.

[2] C. 88/16, m. 48: 1342.

³ JUST. 1/266, m. 7d, my only reference.

⁴ C. 219/12: two parliamentary elections held at Morpath, one on 12 Nov 1421; my only references.

⁵ CRR, 5:59: 3 Feb 1156; CRR, 11:413: "debebit ire ad comitatum apud Wercwurth sive Novum Castrum." The two references together make it possible that Warkworth was a regular or great county venue.

⁶ County town from sometime in the 1280s to the 1360s; see VCH, Somerset, 3:185.

⁷ County town prior to the 1280s and from sometime between 1366 and 1371 on to 1846, see ibid.

⁸ A Feodary of Glastonbury Abbey, ed. F. W. Weaver, Somerset Record Society, vol. 26 (London, 1910), p. 66: on 16 Aug. 1309; my only reference.

⁹ Chertsey Abbey Cartularies, Surrey Record Society, vol. 12 (London, 1958), 2:97; my only reference.

¹⁰ CR, 1261-1264, p. 134: from before 1262 and thereafter.

¹¹ C. 88/16, m. 39: in 1344; C. 88/15, m. 18: in 1342.

¹² C. 88/4, m. 36: in 1307; C. 88/7, m. 15: in 1323.

¹³ CIM, 1:no. 1211, Devizes and Marlborough listed as possible alternative venues to Wilton; Register of Malmesbury Abbey, ed. J. S. Brewer, 2 vols., Rerum Brittanicarum medii aevi scriptores, vol. 72 (London, 1879), 1:459: a session at Devizes 9 March 1189; VCH, Wiltshire, 6:16: venue for a time in the seventeenth century.

III. Cheshire County Court Memorandum

Memorandum: quod quesitum fuit per justiciarium ad hunc comitatum a iudicatoribus et sectatoribus comitatus predicti quare, cum comitatus predictus sit tenendus per justiciarium et officium justiciarii alibi per totam Angliam est in omnibus placitis coram eisdem per se ipsos dare iudicia et consideraciones in eisdem, ipsi clamant vices justiciarii supplere in iudiciis et consideracionibus faciendis, quod non apparet iuri consonum, et qualiter et quo modo.

Qui dicunt quod ipsi et antecessores sui iudicatores et sectatores comitatus predicti a tempore quo non extat memoria iudicia et consideraciones comitatus predicti hucusque reddiderunt et fecerunt tam in placitis corone quam aliis quibuscumque, hoc excepto quod si aliquis minister domini regis transgressus fuerit erga dominum comitem seu regem qui pro tempore fuerit comes Cestrie in aliquo iudicet eum justiciarius qui pro tempore fuerit prout viderit expedire, et quod terras et tenementa sua tenent per servicium predictum.

Et quod isto modo procedendum est in iudiciis reddendis: si discensio aliquis fuerit inter eos in iudicio reddendo, habebunt diem de avisamento usque ad proximum comitatum, et si necesse fuerit per tres comitatus ad plus. Et tunc, si non concordant, fiat iudicium secundum consideracionem maioris partis iudicatorum et sectatorum predictorum. Et quod iudicatores primo dicunt illud quod sibi videtur de iudicio, et sectatores postea consenciunt vel contradicunt. Et sic ad ultimum dabitur iudicium secundum maiorem partem eorundem ut predictum est.

Et dicunt quod, si aliquod falsum iudicium dent inter se in aliquo placito comitatus predicti, dominus rex ad sectam suam propriam vel alicuius alterius partis faciat venire recordum et processum predictum coram ipso domino rege vel justiciariis suis per breve suum. Habebunt diem ad supervidendum recordum et processum predictum per tres comitatus post adventum brevis et de inter se consulendo si quid fuerit emendandum et emendent. Et tunc mandabunt recordum et processum ad curiam et non aliter. Et, si inveniatur aliquid erroneum in iudicio predicto per justiciarios predictos et illud coram eisdem revocetur et adnulletur, dabunt domino regi pro falso iudicio illo centum libras et sic quociens aliquod falsum iudicium reddiderunt in aliquo placito ad cicius quod huiusmodi revocetur et adnulletur. Et quod ipsi et antecessores sui semper hucusque consuetudine ista usi sunt et gavisi etc.

—Chester 29/37, m. 10.

IV. Writs Pleadable in County Courts

TABLE A.3

Writ	Glanvill	Hib. 1220s	CA. Pre-1236	CC. 1260s	R. 1320s[a]	1430s[b]	1531[c]
Acceptance of Homage and Relief	—	—	—	—	457	—	—
Account	—	—	—	133r	418	97	135
Acquittance of Pledges	—*	43	32	121a	512	114b	158
Admeasurement of Dower	vi.18	19	—	145	595	123b	171
Admeasurement of Pasture	xii.13	33	20	166	463	113	156b
Aid to Distrain Villeins	—	—	—	135	249	61b	87b
Annual Rent	—	—	—	142a	476	115	158b
Closing of Courtyard	—	—	—	124r	446	111b	155
Covenant Real	—	49	36	153	527	117b	167
Personal	—	36	25	—	532	—	—
Customs and Services	ix.9	38	27	149	522	115	159
Debt	—*	38r	—	143a	478	100	139
Detinue	—	38r	27r	146a	516	100	139
Detinue of Charters	—	—	—	147	515	115b	159b
Dower in the Right	vi.5	—	—	6	16/17	2b	3
House Repair	—	—	—	—	468	—	153b
Levying of Tallage	—	—	—	—	250	—	—
Mesne	—	47	33	140	471	116	160
Monstraverunt	—	—	—	—	475	—	—
Naifty	xii.11	30	17	100	244	61	87
Ne Vexes	xii.10	37	26	13	28	3	4
Nuisance, Viscontiel	—	—	55	—	658	147b	199
Quod Permittat	—	—	—	—	—	—	—
Drawing of Water	—	—	—	125	447	—	—

TABLE A.3 (*cont'd.*)

Writ	Glanvill	Hib. 1220s	CA. Pre-1236	CC. 1260s	R. 1320s[a]	1430s[b]	1531[c]
Common Fishery	—	—	—	131/133r	—	—	—
Common of Pasture	—	—	—	134b.r	462r	112	156
Easements in Free Tenements	xii.14	—	—	—	—	—	—
Rightful Estovers	—	—	57	128	450	—	—
Free Bull or Boar	—	—	—	126	448	—	—
Free Fishery	—	—	—	132/133r	—	—	—
Milling Free of Multure	—	—	—	120a	416	111b	153b
Pasture for a Certain Number of Animals	—	—	—	—	461	112	156
Right of Way	—	—	—	130/133r	455r	—	—
Watering of Flock	—	—	—	127r	—	—	—
Repair							
Bridge	—	—	—	123a.r	443	113b	153b
Highway	—	—	—	123c	444	113b	154
Road	—	—	—	—	445	—	154
Walls and Ditches	—	—	—	123b.r	449	—	—
Replevin							
Man	—	35	—	108	236	55b	77b
Animals, Goods, Chattel	xii.12	—	21	85a	181	57	81
Restorations of Chattels in Novel Disseisin	xii.18	—	—	—	—	—	—
Return of Damages	—	—	—	—†	—	—	—
Right to Land	xii.3	1	1	1	—	—	1
Rightful Aid	—	—	34	122	251	1	1
Rightful Bounds	ix.14	32	19	137	469	113b	157b
Rightful Division	vii.7	—	—	—	—	—	—
Rightful Dower	xii.20	—	—	—	—	—	—
Rightful Part	—	—	2	2	19	2b	3b
Suit to Hundred	—	—	58	—	—	—	—

Writ	58	119a	412	111b	153
Suit to Mill	—	—			—
Trespass					
Beasts Impounded and Starved	—	—	294		93
Bull Carried Away	—	—	293		92b
Chattels Carried Away	—	—	285		92b
Charter Torn Up	—	—	288		92b
Dog Incited to Bite Man	—	—	297		92b/93
Dike Broken	—	—	290		
Free Fishery Fished	—	—	289		—
Free Fold Knocked Down	—	—	284		—
Grass Mowed and Carried Away	—	—	296		—
Horses Carried Away	—	—	292		92b
Personal Injury	—	—	292		92
Refusal to Return Pledged Chattels	—	—			
Sheep and Beasts Taken and Impounded (Statute Alleged)	—	231	—	—	92b
Sheep Carried Away	—	—	286		92
Surcoat Carried Away	—	—	291		93
Wardship					
Military tenant; Body or lands	54	155a	558		161b
Socage tenant; Body or lands	53	158b.r	—		161b

NOTE: The designations of the columns "Hib.," "CA.," "CC.," and "R." refer to four of the registers in *Early Registers of Writs;* the numbers in the columns refer to the writ number assigned in that volume. When the existence of a writ is proved merely by its mention in a rule, the number is followed by an "r." When there is more than one example for a writ, still only one of them is listed here. The "1430s" column is derived from the list in Holdsworth, *A History of English Law,* 2:617–36. At times it is unclear from his listing whether a writ is viscontiel or returnable; in such instances the appropriate space is left completely blank. The numbers refer to folios. The "1531" column is taken from *Registrum Omnium Brevium tam Originalium quam iudicialium;* the numbers refer to folios.

* Above, chapter 7 at notes 10–25 for the existence of viscontiel debt and acquittance of pledges in the reign of Henry II.

† The list in Beckerman, "The Forty-Shilling Limit," p. 116, from ca. 1300 lists the actions which can be pleaded in county courts. While not exhaustive, it does list a plea *"de dampno reddendo per breve."*

V. Preliminary Fine Roll Statistics

TABLE A.4

Year	Writs "ad terminum"	Writs "de transgressione"	Writs "pone"	Writs "de record"	Sample	Sample Change
34 H III (1250)	130 [73%]	24 [14%]	17 [10%]	6 [3%]	177	+38%
37 H III (1253)	167 [68%]	13 [5%]	55 [23%]	9 [4%]	244	+19%
44 H III (1260)	176 [60%]	25 [9%]	79 [27%]	11 [4%]	291	+88%
54 H III (1270)	453 [83%]	8 [1%]	85 [16%]	1 [0%]	547	+8%
55 H III (1271)	511 [86%]	4 [1%]	77 [13%]	0 —	592	+38%
56 H III (1272)	709 [87%]	10 [1%]	95 [12%]	0 —	814	+8%
1 Ed I (1273)	660 [75%]	112 [13%]	108 [12%]	2 [0%]	882	+34%
2 Ed I (1274)	820 [70%]	201 [17%]	152 [13%]	5 [0%]	1178	+13%
3 Ed I (1275)	811 [61%]	338 [25%]	185 [14%]	1 [0%]	1335	+1%
4 Ed I (1276)	830 [61%]	346 [26%]	171 [13%]	4 [0%]	1351	+7%
6 Ed I (1278)	818 [57%]	439 [31%]	177 [12%]	5 [0%]	1439	−34%
7 Ed I (1279)	514 [54%]	273 [29%]	165 [17%]	1 [0%]	953	−25%
8 Ed I (1280)	392 [55%]	199 [28%]	121 [17%]	1 [0%]	713	+9%
10 Ed I (1282)	479 [62%]	160 [21%]	135 [17%]	1 [0%]	775	−4%
12 Ed I (1284)	490 [66%]	152 [20%]	101 [14%]	2 [0%]	745	+17%
15 Ed I (1287)	609 [70%]	149 [17%]	111 [13%]	0 —	869	−15%
17 Ed I (1289)	434 [59%]	210 [29%]	91 [12%]	1 [0%]	736	+46%
26 Ed I (1298)	462 [43%]	385 [36%]	109 [10%]	118 [11%]	1074	+18%
27 Ed I (1299)	532 [42%]	488 [38%]	99 [8%]	151 [12%]	1270	−71%
2 Ed II (1308-09)	210 [57%]	77 [21%]	33 [9%]	46 [13%]	366	−60%
12 Ed II (1318-19)	116 [80%]	11 [8%]	11 [8%]	7 [5%]	145	−32%
19 Ed II (1325-26)	82 [83%]	6 [6%]	7 [7%]	4 [4%]	99	

NOTE: This table is preliminary in that it does not include all the years or all the writs recorded in the fine rolls; specifically excluded are writs of assize and of false judgment. The statistics must be treated with great caution. They can prove nothing. Not all writs which were sold were entered in the rolls. These statistics can only be used to indicate problems and their solutions; there are many different explanations for most of the changes which can be observed in the figures. The percentages in brackets indicate the category percentage of the sample; the sample is the total number of writs in the fine roll in these four categories. Exhaustive statistics would be of no further use; I do not intend to research for a final and full tabulation.

VI. Gobaud v Prior of Spalding

"Lincs. Clemens prior de Spaldyngg attachiatus fuit ad respondendum Johanni Gobaud de placito quare cum placita de debito in regno regis que summam quadraginta solidorum attingunt vel eam excedunt sine brevi regis placitari non debeant, idem prior sine brevi regis tenuit placitum in curia sua de Spaldyngg de debito centum solidorum quod Gomulda que fuit uxor Reginaldi le Mariner de Spaldyng, Johannes Cluny, Rogerus Richardesman et Reginaldum Chese a prefato Johanne Gobaud exigebant in eadem curia contra consuetudinem regni regis et contra prohibicionem etc. Et unde idem Johannes per attornatum suum queritur quod cum predictus prior tenuisset predictum placitum in curia sua predicta de debito predicto ac idem Johannes die veneris proxima post festum sancti Gregorii pape anno regni domini regis nunc vicesimo tercio apud Spaldyng in plena curia fori eiusdem ville in presencia Johannis de Cotoun, Simonis de Upton, et Johannis de Upton liberasset eidem priori regiam prohibicionem ne placitum illud ulterius teneret etc., idem prior spreta prohibicione illa nichilominus placitum illud tenuit in eadem curia quousque idem Johannes iudicaliter per eandem curiam in predicto debito condempnatus fuit contra consuetudinem etc., in ipsius Johannis dampnum et domini regis contemptum manifestum etc., unde dicit quod deterioratus est et dampnum habet ad valenciam decem librarum. Et unde producit sectam etc.

Et prior per attornatum suum venit et defendit vim et iniuriam etc. Et dicit quod non debet ei inde ad hoc breve respondere, quia dicit quod breve istud est quoddam novum breve de novo conceptum nec uncquam in cancellaria regis hucusque usitatum, dicit enim quod breve illud nec secundum communem legem etc., nec secundum aliquod statutum fundatum est aut ordinatum, unde petit iudicium etc.

Dies datus est eis de audiendo iudicio suo hic a die sancti Johannis Baptiste in xv dies etc." (CP. 40/112, m. 131)

The case is actually more interesting than even this pleading shows. A correlative action of replevin, Gobaud v Prior of Spalding (CP. 40/112, m. 54d), has the prior justifying his taking of Gobaud's goods in execution of the judgment on the original case of debt: "Et bene advocat capcionem viginti quarteriorum avene et quatuor quarteriorum ordei tantum etc., et iuste. Dicit enim quod ipse est dominus ville de Spaldyng et habet ibidem mercatum et omnes libertates ad mercatum pertinentes. Et dicit quod predictus Johannes tenebatur cuidam Reginaldo le Maryner in centum et uno solidis et tribus denariis de diversis contractibus inter ipsos Reginaldum et Johannem in eodem mercato factis tam in denariis sibi mutuatis quam piscibus et carnibus eidem per predictum Reginaldum venditis de quo debito predictus Johannes Gubaud eidem Reginaldo dum vixit non satisfecit etc., ita quod post mortem eiusdem Reginaldi predicti Johannes Cluny, Reginaldus Chese, et Johannes Richardesman executores testamenti ipsius Reginaldi in mercato predicto die et anno supradictis attachiati se coram ballivis predicti prioris predicti mercati etc., ad prosequendum versus predictum Johannem Gobaud ad quatuor querelas etc., sicilicet, de viginti solidis de prestito etc., ad unam querelam etc., et de triginta et septem solidis de prestito etc., ad secundam querelam, et de quindecim solidis et decem denariis ad terciam querelam etc., et de viginti et octo solidis ad quartam querelam etc. Et dicit quod ballivi ipsius prioris eisdem die et anno invenerunt predicta viginti quarteria avene et quatuor quarteria ordei in quodam batello in ripa predicta infra procinctum mercati predicti etc., et ea ceperunt nomine districcionis etc., super predictum Johannem Goubaud eo quod nullos plegios pro ipso Johanne invenire voluit ad respondendum etc. Et postea ad diem curie ibidem tente die martis proximo subsequente venerunt predicti executores et predictus Johannes etc. Et idem Johannes concessit se attachiatum per predictam districcionem etc., placitavit inde cum predictis executoribus et habuerunt diem ibidem die veneris proximo sequente etc., de audiendo iudicio suo de predicto placito etc. Ad quem diem partes venerunt etc., et iudicium ibidem contra ipsum Johannem inde redditum fuit, scilicet, quod predicti executores predictum debitum versus eum recuperarent etc. Et dicit quod [quia] predictus Johannes securitatem de predicto debito solvendo non invenit, ballivi ipsius prioris predicta viginti quarteria avene et quatuor quarteria ordei ea occasione detinuerunt quousque predictus Johannes predictum debitum solveret aut securitatem inde invenisset etc. Et quia idem Johannes infra annum et diem proximo sequentem etc., predictis executoribus non satisfecit de predicto debito etc., ballivi ipsius prioris mercati predicti secundum consuetudinem a tempore cuius non extat memoria ibidem usitatam predicta avenam et ordeum liberaverunt predictis executoribus per racionabile precium post predictos annum et diem in allocacionem debiti predicti etc., qua quidem libertate et consuetudine huiusmodi placita in mercato predicto tenendi et execuciones inde in forma predicta faciendi etc., idem prior et omnes predecessores sui quondam priores de Spaldyng hactenus usi sunt a tempore cuius non extat memoria etc." Gobaud countered with two interesting arguments: (1) "quod nulla placita pertinent ad mercatum etc., nisi tantum de transgressionibus et contractibus factis in mercato inter easdem personas superstites etc., et hoc ad eundem diem mercati quo huiusmodi contractus et transgressiones fieri contigerint in eodem mercato etc., et ex quo predictus prior cognovit quod tenuit predictum placitum in mercato suo racione mercati inter predictos executores et predictum Johannem et sit inter diversas personas etc., et ad alium diem mercati quam ad diem quo predicti contractus inter predictum testatorem dum vixit et predictum Johannem Gobaud facti fuerunt etc., petit iudicium etc." and (2) "dicit eciam quod cum predictus prior cognovit quod ipse per ballivos suos post predictos annum et diem liberavit predicta catalla predictis executoribus in forma predicta et hoc secundum consuetudines mercati sui predicti que quidem consuetudo de catallis tali modo liberandis est lex mercatoria et consuetudo nundinarum inter mercatores et non consuetudo mercati etc., petit iudicium etc." Unfortunately, judgment was not delivered on these pleadings, but they show a time of necessarily sharper definitions in the different roles and powers of courts.

VII. Crown Pleas

Crown Pleas have been mentioned only in passing in this book, partly because my research has turned up relatively little new in regard to the crown pleas, partly because the subject has already been covered by R. Hunnisett in *The Medieval Coroner* in about as much detail as can be hoped for. Some few words are required, however, to delineate the role of the county courts in criminal matters, because otherwise the county courts would be presented here as a forum merely for normal civil litigation.

County courts from the reign of Henry II to the middle of the fourteenth century had a limited role in the prosecution of criminal matters. The county courts, like many courts of liberties, could execute the thief caught in the act, although it would find itself in such a position rather less frequently than many other courts. It likewise had a role in the preservation of the peace, since it had a jurisdiction over beatings, brawls, assaults, and petty theft. Such things, however, were not crown pleas; they would be tried merely as trespasses or wrongs and would conclude in damages, not judgment in life and limb. Such things, that is, were treated merely as violations of the sheriff's peace. More serious matters, such as woundings, could only be prosecuted in the king's court if the plaintiff wanted to proceed by trespass and receive damages; those more serious offences were violations of the king's peace and were outside the civil jurisdiction of the county courts.

The one area in which the county courts remained concerned with crown pleas after Magna Carta in a litigious context was the appeal of felony. The appeal of felony was an old and formal process initiated by plaint (or, increasingly, by writ of the king's court) by the wronged person or his next of kin against the person named (appealed) of the homicide, rape, mayhem, et cetera. When the plaint was lodged, the appellant would often be required to show his wounds or her bloodied garments to the coroners before the county court. The accused was then obliged to appear in county to defend himself. If he could not be found, he was formally called or exacted to four— or, if he was mainperned at the fourth session, five—sessions of the county court. If he still did not appear, he was outlawed. If he appeared, trial would be by battle; if the accused lost, he was hanged. The appeal was thus a private prosecution of felony, in which the county courts normally had the only local jurisdiction.

Private prosecution of felony was open to obvious abuse; the prosecution of appeals in the county courts was thus supervised by the king's court. Supervision was accomplished mainly through removal. As early as the 1260s a writ for removal of an appeal appears in the printed registers of writs in a *venire facias* form, thus ordering the sheriff to make to come before the justices the appeal between named individuals together with the attachments and all other matters touching the appeal.[1] Later on, a *recordari* form also appeared, but only for obtaining further information when the record sent by the *venire facias* writ was insufficient.[2] The *venire facias* form was first printed with a *causa* clause explaining that the plaintiff was predetermining the outlawry by detaining the accused in the prison of a liberty so that he could not appear in county to defend himself. By 1272 removal by reason of the bias of one of the coroners was already allowed, since the coroners had primary responsibility for the appeals, not the sheriff.[3] Such supervision would have been merely occasional. While it did embody the royal determination that county courts not have an absolute jurisdiction in such things, these removals would not have radically changed the jurisdiction of the county courts in practice.

Royal justices, however, did not like the appeal and discouraged its use whenever possible. They almost systematically quashed appeals which came before them, allowing improbable exceptions to the count, and thereafter continuing the case on behalf of the king. That kind of nonsuiting of the plaintiff tended to treat the appeal rather like an indictment. Plaintiffs, moreover, would often have preferred an action of trespass, which at least yielded damages. Some plaintiffs, of course, would have preferred vengeance; a further few would have preferred the appeal in cases of larceny, when they wanted return of the specific goods. On the whole, however, the appeal was made an unrewarding and inefficient process. It would attract only those who desired vengeance more than compensation or who were concerned about the indictment process being subverted.

A further evidence for the discouragement of the appeal is the regularization of removal in cases involving the death of a man. My first notation concerning this regularization comes from 1292, but I suspect it occurred a few years prior to that. The rule decided upon was that in such cases the county court could not proclaim outlawry without obtaining a warrant from the king's court. The case was therefore to be removed into the court of common pleas, where the accused would have the opportunity to appear and defend himself in an impartial court. If he did not appear, the case was sent back to the county court, which proceeded to proclaim outlawry. This rule was embodied in a *causa* clause and decidedly limited the county courts' capability to determine cases brought before it on its own authority.

The process, limitations, and formulaic nature of the appeal is best demonstrated by retailing a case in translation: *Rempeston v Luterel*.

---

[1] *Early Registers of Writs*, ed. Elsa de Haas and G.D.G. Hall, Selden Society, vol. 87 (London, 1970), pp. 66-67 (CC. 111).

[2] Ibid., p. 333 (J. 97). The form was not always so clear; it could get very verbose and descriptive: CP. 52 octave Michaelmas, 28 Edward I (Lancs.) [S.S.].

[3] R. F. Hunnisett, *The Medieval Coroner* (Cambridge, 1961), p. 64.

[The writ *venire facias* for removal of the appeal:]

King . . . to the sheriff of Nottinghamshire, greetings. We order you to make the appeal which Cecilia, who was the wife of Thomas de Rempeston, makes in your county court against John son of Alexander Luterel concerning the death of the abovesaid Thomas, late her husband, come before our justices at Westminster on the morrow of the purification of the blessed Mary with the attachments and all other corroborative evidences touching that appeal. And tell the aforementioned Cecilia to be there to prosecute the abovesaid John thereof if she shall want. And have there this writ. Witnessed by me myself at Newcastle-upon-Tyne the 26th day of December in the 21st year of our reign. Because the abovesaid appeal cannot be determined in a lesser court than before us or our justices according to the law and custom of our kingdom. Suwell.

[The record attached thereto:]

At the county court of Nottinghamshire held the Monday the morrow of St. Matthew the apostle in the 20th year of the reign of King Edward [22 September 1292]:

Cecilia who was the wife of Thomas de Rempeston appeals John son of Alexander Luterel of this that the same John on the Thursday next before the birth of blessed Mary [4 September 1292] one half hour before prime in the 20th year came into the field of Edwalton near Plumtree in a certain place which is called Edwalton More and there assaulted the abovesaid Thomas her husband feloniously as a felon and by premeditated assault and dragged him from his horse and threw him to the earth and afterwards took his sword [from his scabbard?] and struck the abovesaid Thomas on the crown of the head and gave him a certain wound eight fingers long, two fingers wide, and, in depth, right to the brain. That assault and that felony the abovesaid John did wickedly and feloniously as a felon and by premeditated assault on the abovesaid Thomas her husband, whereof he died in her arms. And that felony and assault the abovesaid Cecelia is ready to prove against the abovesaid John as the king's court shall have considered that a woman ought to prove against a felon. Pledges of the abovesaid Cecelia for prosecuting: Peter, reeve of Stanton, and Richard, reeve of the same place.

At the county court of Nottinghamshire held the Monday next after the feast of St. Luke the evangelist in the 20th year [20 October 1292]:

Cecilia who was the wife of Thomas de Rempeston follows her appeal against John son of Alexander Luterel for the death of Thomas her husband the first time. And John, called the first time, does not come.

At the county court of Nottinghamshire held the Monday next before the feast of St. Edmund, king, in the abovesaid year [17 November 1292]:

Cecilia who was the wife of Thomas de Rempeston follows her appeal against John son of Alexander Luterel for the death of Thomas her husband the second time. And John, called the second time, does not come.

At the county court of Nottinghamshire held the Monday next after the feast of St. Lucy, virgin, in the 21st year [15 December 1292]:

Cecilia who was the wife of Thomas de Rempeston follows her appeal against John son of Alexander Luterel for the death of Thomas her husband the third time. And John, called the third time, does not come.

At the county court of Nottinghamshire held the Monday of the vigil of St. Hilary in the 21st year [12 January 1292]:

Cecilia who was the wife of Thomas de Rempeston follows her appeal against John son of Alexander Luterel for the death of Thomas her husband for the fourth time, and the appeal is removed by the writ of the lord king directed to the sheriff together with all corroborative evidences touching the said appeal before the justices of the Bench on the morrow of the Purification according to the tenor of the writ.

The plea was then transcribed verbatim into the plea rolls of the court of common pleas, with the following addition:

> And Cecilia comes, and John does not come. Therefore let the above-said appeal etc., be remitted to the abovesaid county court etc. And it is remitted etc., with all etc. And the sheriff and coroners are ordered to proceed [to outlawry] etc.[4]

Apparently county courts would not proceed to outlawry in cases concerning the death of a man without such an order to proceed in the fourteenth century. In effect, the county court needed a writ to determine such a plea.

More important than the appeal itself was that part of the process called exigent procedure: the exactions in the county court that finally terminated in outlawry. That process could take place only in the county courts and was used by the king's court. Cases of appeal and trespass brought in the king's court could utilize this process when the defendant could not be found. The county court was ordered to initiate the process by the writ *exigere facias*. The county courts were thus utilized as an extension of the king's court for purposes of mesne procedure in cases which were not in county court and would not be determined there, similar to the use of the county courts by the king's court for the taking of juries during the thirteenth century. The use of exigent procedure for cases of appeal and trespass in the king's court cannot be considered unusual; those cases could be seen to have outlawry as a natural penalty for the recalcitrant defendant. The use of exigent procedure,

---

[4] CP. 52 morrow of the Purification, 21 Edward I; CP. 40/98, m. 81 [S.S.].

however, was soon extended to actions of account and then, later on, more generally, even to actions of debt. This wider use, however, was only for litigants in the king's court. The county courts were never allowed to use exigent procedure for their own cases except in appeals, and that use even was limited by removal. Since the appeal declined in utility as an action rapidly during the thirteenth century, exigent procedure stood more and more as a separate entity, cut off from any litigious context in the county courts.

Exigent procedure had a lasting impact on the county courts. Its seriousness demanded that county court sessions be predictable; otherwise a defendant could be fraudulently outlawed by holding the county court at an improper time or venue. The use of outlawry by the king's court was thus probably the primary force in binding the county courts to their rigid schedule. Also, as exigent procedure was extended to an increasing number of actions in the king's court, it came to be the primary bond between the county courts and the king's court and to take a more important position in the way the county court was seen. In this way the crown pleas of the county courts became one of its major responsibilities. It was a major responsibility, however, which had little affect on county litigation.

Glossary
of Legal Terms and
Latin Words

(The following glossary is not intended to provide exhaustive or definitive meanings for words. Terms in small capitals are cross-references to separate entries in the Glossary.)

Advowson: the right to nominate to the bishop the person to be appointed to a church or benefice, such as to the position of parish priest of a specific church.

Amercement: a monetary penalty, discretionary in amount, imposed by the justices on a litigant. Literally, the party was "at the mercy" of the king.

Ancient Demesne: those estates which came to be seen in the thirteenth century and thereafter as pertaining particularly and inalienably to the Crown; a manor was technically part of the ancient demesne if it was listed in Domesday Book as having been a royal manor prior to the Conquest.

Appeal: *not* a review procedure, but a private prosecution by victims or their closest relative for wrongs done, including prominantly the prosecution for very serious wrongs, such as homicide, rape, robbery, and arson.

Assize: (1) an enactment or ordinance, usually from the reign of Henry II; (2) certain legal processes thus provided; and (3) the particular kind of panel of sworn men utilized in such a legal process.

Grand Assize: a sworn panel summoned by a judicial writ and used as an alternative to trial by battle in disputes about real property, which determined ultimate right to the land.

Judicial Assizes: those assizes begun by judicial writ and derivative from pleas of gage, MORT DANCESTOR, or darrein presentment.

Petty Assizes: the traditional generic designation for the assizes begun by original writs; they are characterized by the form of the original writ which both specified the questions to be put to the panel and also ordered that panel to be assembled. The petty assizes were novel disseisin, MORT DANCESTOR, utrum, and darrein presentment.

327

Assumpsit: a particular form of trespass on the case utilized to initiate disputes which were contractual in nature; the word means "he undertook" and the wrong alleged is that he failed to perform.

Attachment: a form of MESNE procedure by which a defendant's person or chattels were seized and held to procure his appearance in court.

Attaint: a legal action undertaken by a defeated litigant against the jury of a previous case. The accusation is that that jury had made a false oath.

Attorney: a litigant's representative who was capable of functioning as the litigant in a particular suit, a substitute for the litigant. His function should be contrasted with that of the PLEADER.

General Attorney: an attorney with the capacity of representing his client in all and sundry cases and capable also of appointing further an attorney for the client in a particular case.

Audias Writs: those VISCONTIEL WRITS whose central operative word was "you should hear"; viscontiel writs of nuisance and trespass.

Avow: (1) in pleading, the litigant avowed by accepting for himself the form in which the pleader had pleaded; (2) in REPLEVIN, a defendant avowed by acknowledging that he took the goods or chattels as the plaintiff alleged; the avowry was normally followed by a justification of the taking.

Bailiff: (1) for a royal hundred, the sheriff's official responsible for the execution of all royal commands made to the sheriff pertaining to that hundred and likewise responsible for the execution of process relating to his hundred from the county and the hundred court; (2) for a LIBERTY, the official responsible to both the sheriff and the lord of the liberty; his functions included those of the bailiff of a royal hundred but also extended to presiding over the liberty court and representing his lord; (3) for a manor court, a lord's official, often supervised by the lord's SENESCHAL, responsible for representing the lord's interests in the region and managing the manor.

Bailiff Itinerant: the royal bailiff who, as an officer of the sheriff, was responsible for executing the sheriff's duties which pertained to an area, such as a LIBERTY, which was not served by a royal bailiff and whose liberty bailiff defaulted in performance.

Bench: a designation for that branch of the king's court known as the court of common pleas.

Bill of Receipt: a written acknowledgment by the sheriff or his officer that he had received a particular writ on a certain day.

Capias: a form of MESNE process whereby the sheriff was ordered to imprison the defendant so that he could be brought into court to answer a plaintiff in litigation.

Causa Clause: in a WRIT PONE or RECORDARI, the clause inserted toward the end of the writ which specified the reason which justified the removal of the case from the lower court into the king's court.

Champerty: the undertaking at one's own expense of another's SUIT in return for receiving part of the subject in dispute.

Chirographer: the official of the king's court responsible for drawing up final concords.

Common: as opposed to several, that which was open to use by qualified members of a community and could not be restricted to one individual's use.

Compurgation: a form of legal proof by the oath of the prover together with a specified number of oath-helpers.

Coram non judice: "before one not a judge"; the description of proceedings taken before one not properly authorized to hear the plea.

Coram Rege: "before the king"; a designation of the king's court which theoretically met before the king himself; the king's bench.

Count: the formal opening statement in court putting forth the claimant's case.

Debet, in the: a phrase alluding to the fact that the writ contained only the word *"debet"* ("he ought") and not *"debet et solet"* ("he ought and is accustomed to"), indicating that the plaintiff was not relying on his own SEISIN.

Demurrer: in pleading, resting the plea on an issue of law, so that the case would be decided by the justices instead of by proof, as by jury or COMPURGATION.

Distraint: things taken either to assure performance of an obligation or attendance at court; in either case, the things taken are held and not confiscated.

Distringas Writs: those few VISCONTIEL WRITS whose central operative word was "you should distrain"; writs relating to repair of bridges, roads, etc.

Dower: the widow's tenure of a portion of her husband's land and tenements for the duration of her life.

Entry, Writ of: a writ which originated in the king's court litigation about real property related to a particular flaw in the tenant's title.

Escheat: (1) the reversion of land by default of heirs to the lord, however conceived; (2) a similar reversion upon an act by the tenant which entails forfeiture.

Essoin: an excuse for nonattendance at court by either litigant.

Essoiner: the person sent by the litigant to cast the essoin.

Exigent Procedure: county court procedure which solemnly summoned or "exacted" a person to appear in court to defend himself in a plea; in default of appearance, exigent procedure terminated in outlawry.

Eyre: that temporary branch of the king's court composed of justices sent out to an individual county there to hear and determine all pleas pertaining to the king's court from that county and to investigate local officials.

Facias Writs: those VISCONTIEL WRITS whose central operative word was "you should make"; writs characterized by some executive procedure demanded from the sheriff.

Farm: a preagreed sum of money to be paid by an official to his lord as the income from any revenue producing unit; the sum would be sufficiently less than the actual worth of the unit to allow the official a profit.

Fine; Final Concord: not a monetary penalty, but a particularly solemn form of written agreement concerning land tenure, a copy of which was retained by the king's court.

Forinsec: (1) in regard to a summons, a summons pertaining to a person who resided outside the territorial jurisdiction of the court; (2) in regard to tenures, a tenure concerning lands or tenements outside the jurisdiction of the communal court; (3) in regard to services, services due to one other than one's immediate lord, as to the king.

Franchise: a governmental right possessed by an individual or community by delegation, such right excluding the normal operation of royal officials.

Free Alms: an ecclesiastical tenure characterized by services of a spiritual nature, such as prayer; a particular way, but not the only way, in which land could be held by the church.

Gaol Delivery: a special commission to justices or others to try those detained in gaol for criminal offences.

Itinerant Justices: royal justices specially deputed to go on circuit through several counties on either specific or general commissions.

Judge: one who gives judgments in lower courts, to be distinguished from royal justices (who gave judgments in the king's court), from SUITORS, and from presiding officers of courts.

Judicial Writs: those RETURNABLE WRITS which did not originate litigation but rather which issued from the courts to continue litigation already pending.

Juste Deduci Facias: "cause [him] to be treated justly"; a clause characteristic of the AUDIAS WRITS and the writ of REPLEVIN.

Justicies Writs: those VISCONTIEL WRITS whose central operative word was "you should justice."

De Libertate Probanda: the writ used by one alleged to be a villein to remove the case into the king's court there to assert his freedom; "concerning proof of freedom."

Liberty: generally, the territorial unit covered by a particular FRANCHISE.

Mainpernors: those who take over the custody of a person under arrest and undertake to produce him in court when required.

Manu-Militari: "by military hand"; in regard to a command, a command which is purely executive.

Mesne: "middle"

Mesne Procedure: that court procedure required to bring the parties—usually the defendants—into court.

Mesne Tenants: in a feudal hierarchy of tenant in demesne (the tenant on the land), tenant in service (the lord of the tenant in demesne), and the chief lord (the lord of the tenant in service), the mesne tenant is the middle tenant: the tenant in service. More generally the mesne is anyone with right to the land who has both a man for the land and also a lord.

Mise: in "mise of the grand assize," that form in which the tenant of the land put himself on the GRAND ASSIZE; the mise could be either general (who has greater right?) or special (does one have greater right to hold it in demesne than the other to hold it of him?).

Mort Dancestor: an ASSIZE which protected the inheritance of land from parents, siblings, aunts, and uncles.

Naifty: a VISCONTIEL WRIT for claiming one as one's villein.

Nisi Feceris Clause: the clause in writs of right patent which specified that "if [the addressed lord] does not do" the thing ordered, the sheriff will; the threat was a reference to TOLT procedure.

Nisi Prius Procedure: a procedure formalized in 1285 for taking jury verdicts, whereby the sheriff was ordered to assemble a jury and to have it at Westminster at a certain time "unless before" that time a justice on circuit arrived in the county to take the jury verdict locally.

Non Intromittat Clause: a clause in royal grants specifying that the sheriff "should not meddle" in the affairs of the LIBERTY.

Non Omittas Writ: a writ issued after the bailiff of a LIBERTY had failed to execute a previous writ; it specified that the sheriff "should not omit" to execute the order by reason of the liberty.

Nonsuit: dismissal of a suit for failure by the plaintiff to prosecute either by default or by inability to bring the case to issue.

Nuisance, Writ of: a class of writ, some VISCONTIEL, some RETURNABLE, which complained of damage done to the plaintiff's free tenement by an action of the defendant outside of the plaintiff's tenement.

Original Writs: those WRITS which initiated litigation.

Oyer: "to hear"

> *Oyer* and *Terminer*: a commission "to hear and to determine" a case.

Parcener: one of the cotenants of an inheritance.

Personal Actions: those legal remedies which dealt solely with wrongs and obligations, thus not determining rights to real property.

Pipe Rolls: a series of royal records recording debts owed and payments made to the king; the records were made in the Exchequer.

Plaint: a complaint or bill; in regard to litigation, a suit which was brought not by a royal writ purchased from chancery but by an oral or written complaint submitted by the plaintiff directly to the court.

Pleader: one who undertook a litigant's oral argument in court but who was auxiliary to and not a substitute for the litigant.

Pone: the WRIT which ordered the removal of a case originally brought by writ and pending in a lower court from that lower court into the king's court.

Portmansmote: a court of merchants.

Posse Comitatus: "the [military] might of the county"; that body of men in the county who owed allegiance to the king and could be called upon as the last resort to execute a royal order.

Precipe: in general, all those RETURNABLE WRITS which began with the word "command"; in particular, a shorthand designation for the *precipe* writ of right as distinct from the seignorial writ of right patent.

Prescription: title acquired by long and continued usage.

Questus Est Mihi: "[A certain person] has complained to me"; the initial clause in the AUDIAS WRITS and in the writ of novel disseisin.

Quod Permittat: a class of writs, some RETURNABLE, some JUSTICIES viscontiel, which concerned the enforcement of rights relating to the lands of others.

Quod Plenum Rectum Teneas: "that you hold full right [to the claimant]"; the central command of the writ of right patent.

Quo Warranto: "by what warrant"; the phrase often used to inquire into the basis of a person's claim to possession of land or governmental privileges.

Racionabilis: "reasonable" or "rightful" (adj.)
   Racionabilis Demonstracio: "reasonable showing"
   Racionabilis Monstracio: "reasonable showing"
   Racionabiliter Monstrare: "reasonably to show"
   Racionabiliter: "reasonably" or "rightfully" (adv.)

Recordari Writs: in this book, not a false judgment writ, but rather that writ which ordered the sheriff to have recorded a plea which was in the county court; after 1275 the writ was particularly associated with the removal of cases begun by PLAINT.

   Accedas Recordari: a *recordari* writ adapted for application to cases in courts of LIBERTIES.

Registers of Writs: transcriptions made of the file used in chancery as a pattern for drafting writs.

Remainder: that interest in land held by a third party to a grant, that is, by persons who are neither the grantor or his heirs nor the direct grantee or his heirs, but rather a specified third party or his heirs to whom the land would remain after the term of the grant to the grantee expired and before the land reverted to the grantor's line.

   Remainderman: one whose interest in a tenement is a remainder.

Renable Demunstrance: "reasonable showing"

Replegiari Facias: "you should make to be replevied [to the plaintiff his animals]"; the initial command in the writ of REPLEVIN.

Replevin: litigation nominally concerning the taking and unjust detention of goods or chattels, in which it is expected that the defendant's justification will be the actual matter in dispute.

Return of Writs: that FRANCHISE by which a LIBERTY can claim the right to execute those orders to the sheriff which pertain to the liberty and to have jurisdiction over the viscontiel pleas which would otherwise be held in county court.

Returnable Writs: those writs which both commanded an action and demanded a report; these writs originated and continued litigation in the king's court.

Right, Action of: any of those remedies which purported to give an ultimate determination of a suit; normally used in reference to those actions concerning lands and tenements which could determine in battle or the GRAND ASSIZE.

Scire Facias: "you should make [the defendant] know": an order to the sheriff to notify a defendant that he would be subject to an executive order (as the levying of a debt) unless he appeared in court to show reason why it should not be so ordered.

Seignorial Writs: those writs addressed to a lord, not to the sheriff; often called writs patent.

Seisin: lawful possession; originally associated closely with the origin of the tenant's title beginning in a lord's acceptance, finally concerned only with the tenant's tenure having some color of right.

Seneschal: steward; the major legal and administrative officer of a lord; the superior of a lord's BAILIFFS.

Serjeanty: that tenure characterized by lesser military services.

Several: as opposed to COMMON, that which was appropriated to an individual and thus not part of the common land.

Sicut Pluries: "as many times"; that form of writ which issued after a writ SICUT PRIUS, noting that the particular command being made to the sheriff had been made to him many times before.

Sicut Prius: "as before"; that form of writ which issued after a royal command had not been executed.

Sicut Racionabiliter Monstrare Poterit: "as he shall reasonably be able to show"; the conditional clause characteristic of the JUSTICIES WRITS.

Socage Tenure: the normal free small-holder's tenure characterized by moderate rents and fealty but not homage, so that the socager's lord was not entitled to military incidents like marriage and wardship.

Specialty: a deed or TALLY under seal.

Suit: the witnesses produced by a plaintiff to reinforce his claim so that the court would require the defendant to respond.

Suit to Court: that form of service for a tenement which obliged the tenant to attend court (county, hundred, liberty, feudal), theoretically to render judgments and give counsel.

Suit to Mill: a tenant's obligation to have his grain ground at a particular mill.

Suitor: (1) in general, one obliged to render any kind of SUIT; (2) in Cheshire, specifically, a person who not only owed SUIT to a court but who was also a subordinate member of the court and inferior to the JUDGES; (3) for most counties, in this book, the word used to denote those obliged to attend court without implying thereby that they attended in person.

333

Surcharge: excessive use.

Tallage: a discretionary taxation by a lord of his unfree tenants or by the king of the ANCIENT DEMESNE and boroughs.

Tally: an accounting device utilizing a wooden stick which was notched in a traditional manner, written on, and then split, leaving both pieces identically notched according to the amount owed; the tally could also be sealed; single piece (i.e. not split) tallies were also often used.

Testificare Racionabiliter: "to testify reasonably."

Tolt: that process by which a plea initiated by a writ of right patent was removed from a lord's court for default of justice and brought into the county court.

Tourn: the sheriff's circuit around his county twice a year to have recorded presentable offences and to take the VIEW OF FRANKPLEDGE.

Trespass: in general, a wrong of any nature, normally a nonfelonious wrong.

Trithing: a regional division in Yorkshire and the northern half of Lincolnshire midway between county and WAPENTAKE.

Venire Facias: "you should make to come"; the key phrase in the writ which ordered the sheriff to assemble a panel to form a jury.

Vi et Armis: "with force and arms": one of the key phrases in a RETURNABLE WRIT of trespass, although it was not uniformly present in such writs.

View of Frankpledge: the inspection of the frankpledge groups—groups of the lesser and unfree men pledged to produce each other in court if accused of a crime—to insure that all were pledged who ought to be.

Viscontiel Writs: those original writs which initiated litigation theoretically before the sheriff in county court.

Vouch to Warranty: the calling of the seller or grantor into court to stand by his sale or grant and make good by exchange that transaction if he had not been in a position to sell or grant.

Wager of Law: the promise and pledge to prove one's assertion by COMPURGATION.

Wapentake: for all practical purposes, the equivalent in northern counties of hundred courts.

Wardship: in regard to a military tenant, the right of the lord to custody of the tenant's body and/or lands until the heir's majority; in regard to a SOCAGE TENANT, the right of the closest relative incapable of inheriting to the custody.

Words of Court: a standard, formal, and general defense made by the defendant before his more particular defense; in theory, it seems to have been a general defense against the allegations as they would have been offensive to the court and the lord of the court prior to the defense against the plaintiff.

Writ: a written order under seal, whether it began litigation or not, whether it was addressed to the sheriff or not.

Writ of Course: one of the standardized writs for which no special authorization was required for issuance.

Bibliography

of Books and Documents

Cited in the Notes

ф

I. Manuscript Sources

Bodleian Library Rawlinson C. 454. Register of Writs.

British Library Additional 5925. Reports of Cases.

British Library Additional 28024. Registers of Charters and Title-deeds of the Family of Beauchamp, Earls of Warwick.

British Library Additional 31826. Reports of Cases.

British Library Lansdowne 564. Registers of Writs; Reports of Cases.

Lincoln's Inn Hale 137(1). Reports of Cases.

Lincoln's Inn Hale 188. Reports of Cases.

Lincoln's Inn Miscellaneous 87. Reports of Cases.

Public Record Office

    C. 47. Chancery Miscellanea.

    C. 60. Patent Rolls.

    C. 88. Records on Exigent Procedure for Pardons.

    C. 219. Returns for Members of Parliament.

    Chester 3/3. Inquisitions Post Mortem (Chester and Flint).

    Chester 29. Plea Rolls of the Palatinate of Chester.

    Chester 30. Plea Rolls of the Welsh County of Flint.

    CP. 25. Feet of Fines.

    CP. 40. Plea Rolls of the Court of Common Pleas.

    CP. 52. Writ Files of the Court of Common Pleas.

    DL. 30. Court Rolls from the Duchy of Lancaster.

    E. 13. Pleas Rolls of the Exchequer of Pleas.

    E. 101. Accounts Various.

    E. 164/21. Miscellaneous Books. Series I. Cartulary of Coventry Priory.

    E. 179. Subsidy Rolls.

    E. 368. Memoranda Rolls (L.T.R.)

    E. 370. Miscellaneous Rolls (L.T.R.)

    JUST. 1. Eyre Rolls, Assize Rolls, etc.

JUST. 3. Gaol Delivery Rolls.

JUST. 4. Writ Files of Eyres, Assizes, etc.

KB. 26. *Curia Regis* Rolls.

KB. 27. Plea Rolls of the Court of King's Bench.

SC. 2. Court Rolls.

SC. 6. Ministers' Accounts.

University of Michigan Law Library, R337, 148-?. Register of Writs.

Yale University MS 60. Register of Writs.

II. Printed Sources

Accounts of the Chamberlains and Other Officers of the County of Chester, 1301-1360. Edited by R. Stewart-Brown. Publications of The Record Society, vol. 59. London, 1910.

Anglo-Saxon Charters. Edited by A. J. Robertson. Cambridge, 1956.

Book of Fees, Commonly Called "Testa de Nevill." Prepared under the superintendence of the Deputy Keeper of the Records. 3 vols. London, 1920-1931.

Borough Customs. Edited by Mary Bateson. 2 vols. Publications of the Selden Society, vols. 18, 21. London, 1904, 1906.

Bracton, Henry of, *De Legibus et Consuetudinibus Angliae.* Edited by G. E. Woodbine, translated by S. E. Thorne. 4 vols. to date. Published in Association with the Selden Society. Cambridge, Mass., and London, 1968-.

Bracton's Note Book. Edited by F. W. Maitland. 3 vols. London, 1887.

Brevia Placitata. Edited by G. J. Turner. Publications of the Selden Society, vol. 66. London, 1947.

Bristol Charters, 1155-1373. Edited by N. D. Harding. 3 vols. Publications of the Bristol Record Society, vols. 1, 11, 12. Bristol, 1930-1947.

British Borough Charters, 1216-1307. Edited by Adolphus Ballard and James Tait. 2 vols. Cambridge, 1923.

Britton. Edited by F. M. Nichols. 2 vols. Oxford, 1865.

The Burton Chartulary. Edited by G. Wrottesley. Publications of the William Salt Archaeological Society, vol. 5. London, 1884.

Calendar of Charters and Documents Relating to Selborne and Its Priory. Edited by W. Dunn Macray. 2 vols. Publications of the Hampshire Record Society, vols. 4, 9. London, 1891, 1894.

Calendar of Close Rolls. Edward I-Edward III. Prepared under the superintendence of the Deputy Keeper of the Records. 23 vols. London, 1892-1913.

Calendar of County Court, City Court, and Eyre Rolls of Chester. Edited by R. Stewart-Brown. Publications of the Chetham Society, n.s., vol. 84. Aberdeen, 1925.

Calendar of Fine Rolls. 1272-1485. Prepared under the superintendence of the Deputy Keeper of the Records. 21 vols. London, 1911-1961.

Calendar of Inquisitions Miscellaneous. 1219-1422. Prepared under the superintendence of the Deputy Keeper of the Records. 7 vols. London, 1916-1968.

Calendar of Inquisitions Post Mortem. Henry III-Richard II. Prepared under the superintendence of the Deputy Keeper of the Records. 16 vols. London, 1904-1974.

Calendar of Liberate Rolls. Henry III. Prepared under the superintendence of the Deputy Keeper of the Records. 6 vols. London, 1916-1964.

Calendar of Patent Rolls. Henry III-Richard III. Prepared under the superintendence of the Deputy Keeper of the Records. 52 vols. London, 1893-1916.

Calendar of the Charter Rolls. 1226-1516. Prepared under the superintendence of the Deputy Keeper of the Records. 6 vols. London, 1903-1927.

The Caption of Seisin of the Duchy of Cornwall (1337). Edited by P. L. Hull. Publications of the Devon and Cornwall Record Society, n.s., vol. 17. Exeter, 1971.

Cartularium Monasterii de Rameseia. Edited by W. H. Hart and Ponsonby Lyons. 3 vols. Rerum Brittanicarum medii aevi scriptores, vol. 79. London, 1884-1893.

Cartularium Prioratus de Gyseburne Ebor' Dioeceseos. Edited by W. Brown. 2 vols. Publications of the Surtees Society, vols. 86, 88. Durham, 1889-1891.

Cartulary and Historical Notes of the Cistercian Abbey of Flaxley, otherwise called Dene Abbey. Edited by A. W. Crawley-Boevey. Exeter, 1887.

A Cartulary of Buckland Priory in the County of Somerset. Edited by F. W. Weaver. Publications of the Somerset Record Society, vol. 25. London, 1909.

Cartulary of Canonsleigh Abbey. Edited by Vera C. M. London. Publications of the Devon and Cornwall Record Society, n.s., vol. 8. Torquay, 1965.

Cartulary of Darley Abbey. Edited by R. R. Darlington. Kendal, 1945.

The Cartulary of St. Michael's Mount. Edited by P. L. Hull. Publications of the Devon and Cornwall Record Society, n.s., vol. 5. Torquay, 1962.

Cartulary of the Abbey of Eynsham. Edited by H. E. Salter. 2 vols. Publications of the Oxford Historical Society, vols. 49, 50. Oxford, 1906, 1908.

Cartulary of Tutbury Priory. Edited by Avrom Saltman. Publications of the Staffordshire Record Society, 4th s., vol. 4. Kendal, 1962.

Cartulary of Worcester Cathedral Priory. Edited by R. R. Darlington. London, 1968.

Casus Placitorum. Edited by W. H. Dunham. Publications of the Selden Society, vol. 69. London, 1950.

"The Chartulary of Dieulacres Abbey." Edited by G. Wrottesley. In *Collections for a History of Staffordshire,* William Salt Archaeological Society, n.s., vol. 9. London, 1906.

Chartulary of St. John of Pontefract. Edited by Richard Holmes. 2 vols. Yorkshire Archaeological Society, vols. 25, 30. Leeds, 1899, 1902.

The Chartulary of the Priory of St. Pancras of Lewes. Edited by L. F. Salzman. 2 vols. Publications of the Sussex Record Society, vols. 38, 40. Lewes, 1932-1934.

Chartulary or Register of the Abbey of Saint Werburgh, Chester. Edited by James Tait. 2 vols. Publications of the Chetham Society, vols. 79, 82. Manchester, 1920-1923.

Chertsey Abbey Cartularies. Publications of the Surrey Record Society, vol. 12. London, 1958.

Chronicon Monasterii de Abingdon. Edited by Joseph Stevenson. 2 vols. Rerum Brittanicarum medii aevi scriptores, vol. 2. London, 1858.

Civil Pleas of the Wiltshire Eyre, 1249. Edited by M. T. Clanchy. Publications of the Wiltshire Record Society, vol. 26. Devizes, 1970.

Close Rolls: Henry III. Prepared under the superintendence of the Deputy Keeper of the Records. 14 vols. London, 1902-1938.

The Court Baron. Precedents of Pleading in Manorial and Other Courts. Edited by F. W. Maitland. Publications of the Selden Society, vol. 4. London, 1890.

Crown Pleas of the Wiltshire Eyre, 1249. Edited by C.A.F. Meekings. Publications of the Wiltshire Archaeological and Natural History Society, vol. 16. Devizes, 1961.

Curia Regis Rolls. Prepared under the superintendence of the Deputy Keeper of the Records. 16 vols. London, 1922-1979.

Domesday Book seu liber censualis Willelmi Primi Regis Angliae. Edited by A. Farley. 2 vols. London, 1783.

Earliest Lincolnshire Assize Rolls, 1202-1209. Edited by Doris M. Stenton. Publications of the Lincolnshire Record Society, vol. 22. Lincoln, 1926.

Earliest Northamptonshire Assize Rolls. Edited by D. M. Stenton. Publications of the Northamptonshire Record Society, vol. 5. Lincoln and London, 1930.

Early Registers of Writs. Edited by Elsa de Haas and G.D.G. Hall. Publications of the Selden Society, vol. 87. London, 1970.

Early Yorkshire Charters. Edited by William Farrer. 4 vols. Edinburgh, 1914.

English Historical Documents. General editor, David C. Douglas. 12 vols. New York, 1955-1977.

The Eyre of Kent of 6 and 7 Edward II. Edited by F. W. Maitland, L. W. Vernon Harcourt, and W. C. Bolland. 3 vols. Publications of the Selden Society, vols. 24, 27, 29. London, 1909-1913.

The Eyre of London, 14 Edward II (A.D. 1321). Edited by Helen M. Cam. 2 vols. Publications of the Selden Society, vols. 85, 86. London, 1968-1969.

A Feodary of Glastonbury Abbey. Edited by F. W. Weaver. Publications of the Somerset Record Society, vol. 26. London, 1910.

Feudal Aids. Prepared under the superintendence of the Deputy Keeper of the Records. 6 vols. London, 1890-1920.

Fleta: Commentarius Juris Anglicani. Edited by H. G. Richardson and G. O. Sayles. 2 vols. Publications of the Selden Society, vols. 72, 89. London, 1953-1972.

Gloucestershire Subsidy Roll, 1 Edward III. Anonomous transcription preserved at the Public Record Office, London.

The Great Chartulary of Glastonbury. Edited by Aelred Watkin. 3 vols. Publications of the Somerset Record Society, vols. 59, 63, 64. Frome, 1944-1956.

The Great Roll of the Pipe. 59 vols. Publications of the Pipe Roll Society. London, 1883-1962.

Lancashire Inquests, Extents, and Feudal Aids. Edited by William Farrer. 3 vols. Publications of The Record Society, vols. 48, 54, 70. Liverpool, 1903-1915.

The Laws of the Kings of England from Edmund to Henry I. Edited by A. J. Robertson. Cambridge, 1925.

Lay Subsidy Roll for the County of Worcester, 1 Edward III. Edited by F. J. Eld. Publications of the Worcestershire Historical Society. Oxford, 1895.

Lay Subsidy Roll for Warwickshire, 6 Edward III. Edited by W. F. Carter. Publications of the Dugdale Society, vol. 6. London, 1926.

The Ledger Book of Vale Royal Abbey. Edited by John Brounbill. Publications of The Record Society, vol. 68. Edinburgh, 1914.

Leges Henrici Primi. Edited by L. J. Downer. Oxford, 1972.

Liber Memorandorum Ecclesie de Bernewelle. Edited by J. W. Clark. Cambridge, 1907.

Luffield Priory Charters. Edited by G. R. Elvey. Publications of the Northamptonshire Record Society, vols. 22, 26. Oxford, 1968-1975.

Magnum Rotulum Scaccarii vel Magnum Rotulum Pipae, 31 Henry I. Edited by Joseph Hunter. London, 1929.

Mamecestre. Edited by John Harland. 3 vols. Publications of the Chetham Society, vols. 53, 56, 58. Manchester, 1859-1863.

A Middlewich Chartulary Compiled by William Vernon in the Seventeenth Century. Edited by Joan Varley and James Tait. 2 vols. Publications of the Chetham Society, vols. 105, 108. Manchester, 1941-1944.

Placita Anglo-Normannica. Edited by Melville M. Bigelow. London, 1879.

Placita de Quo Warranto Temporibus Edw. I, II, & III in Curia Receptae Scaccarij Westm. Asservata. Record Commission. London, 1818.

Pleas before the King or His Justices. Edited by Doris M. Stenton. 4 vols. Publications of the Selden Society, vols. 67, 68, 83, 84. London, 1948-1967.

Radulphi de Hengham Summae. Edited by W. H. Dunham. Cambridge, 1932.

Red Book of Worcester. Edited by Marjory Hollings. Publications of the Worcestershire Historical Society. London, 1934-1937.

Register of Malmesbury Abbey. Edited by J. S. Brewer. 2 vols. Rerum Brittanicarum medii aevi scriptores, vol. 72. London, 1879.

Registrum Antiquissimum of the Cathedral Church of Lincoln. Edited by C. W. Foster and Kathleen Major. 10 vols. Publications of the Lincoln Record Society, vols. 27, 29, 32, 34, 41, 42, 46, 51, 62, 67. Lincoln, 1931-1973.

Registrum Omnium Brevium tam Originalium quam Judicalium. London, 1531.

Registrum Prioratus Beate Mariae Wigorniensis. Edited by William H. Hale. Publications of the Camden Society, vol. 91. London, 1865.

The Roll and Writ File of the Berkshire Eyre of 1248. Edited by M. T. Clanchy. Publications of the Selden Society, vol. 90. London, 1973.

Rolls from the Office of the Sheriff of Beds. and Bucks., 1332-1334. Edited by G. H. Fowler. Publications of the Beds. Historical Record Society, Quarto Series, vol. 3. Bedford, 1929.

Rolls of the Justices in Eyre for Gloucestershire, Warwickshire, and Staffordshire, 1221, 1222. Edited by D. M. Stenton. Publications of the Selden Society, vol. 59. London, 1940.

Rolls of the Justices in Eyre for Lincolnshire, 1218-9, and Worcestershire, 1221. Edited by Doris M. Stenton. Publications of the Selden Society, vol. 53. London, 1934.

Rolls of the King's Court in the Reign of King Richard the First. Publications of the Pipe Roll Society, vol. 14. London, 1891.

Rotuli Curiae Regis. Edited by Francis Palgrave. 2 vols. Record Commission. London, 1835.

Rotuli de Oblatis et Finibus in Turri Londinensi Asservati, Tempore Regis Johannis. Edited by Thomas Duffus Hardy. London, 1835.

Rotuli Hundredorum. 2 vols. Record Commission. London, 1812, 1813.

Rotuli Litterarum Clausarum, 1204-1224. Edited by Thomas D. Hardy. 2 vols. Record Commission. London, 1833-1844.

Rotuli Parliamentorum. 6 vols. London, 1767.

Rotuli Scaccarii Normanniae sub Regibus Anglie. Edited by Thomas Stapleton. 2 vols. London, 1840.

Royal Writs in England from the Conquest to Glanvill, Studies in the Early History of the Common Law. Edited by R. C. Van Caenegem. Publications of the Selden Society, vol. 77. London, 1959.

Rufford Charters. Edited by C. J. Holdsworth. 2 vols. Publications of the Thoroton Record Society, vols. 29, 30. Nottingham, 1972, 1974.

St. Benet of Holme, 1020-1210. Edited by J. R. West. 2 vols. Publications of the Norfolk Record Society, vols. 2, 3. London, 1932.

The Sandford Cartulary. Edited by Agnes M. Leys. 2 vols. Publications of the Oxfordshire Record Society, vols. 19, 22. Oxford, 1938, 1941.

Select Cases Concerning the Law Merchant. Edited by H. Hall. 3 vols. Publications of the Selden Society, vols. 23, 46, 49. London, 1908-1932.

Select Cases in the Court of King's Bench. Edited by G. O. Sayles. 7 vols. Publications of the Selden Society, vols. 55, 57, 58, 74, 76, 82, 88. London, 1936-1971.

Select Charters Illustrative of English Constitutional History. Edited by William Stubbs. 8th ed. Oxford, 1900.

Select Pleas in Manorial and Other Seignorial Courts. Edited by F. W. Maitland. Publications of the Selden Society, vol. 2. London, 1888.

Selected Rolls of the Chester City Courts. Edited by A. Hopkins. Publications of the Chetham Society, 3d series, vol. 2. Manchester, 1950.

Some Court Rolls of the Lordships, Wapentakes, and Demesne Manors of Thomas, Earl of Lancaster. Edited by William Farrer. Publications of The Record Society, vol. 41. n.p., 1901.

Somersetshire Pleas from the Rolls of the Itinerant Justices. Edited by Charles Chadwyck-Healey. 2 vols. Publications of the Somerset Record Society, vols. 11, 36. London, 1897, 1923.

The Stone Chartulary. Edited by G. Wrottesley. Publications of the William Salt Archaeological Society, vol. 6. London, 1885.

The Stoneleigh Leger Book. Edited by R. H. Hilton. Publications of the Dugdale Society, vol. 24. Oxford, 1960.

The Thame Cartulary. Edited by H. E. Salter. 2 vols. Publications of the Oxfordshire Record Society, vols. 25, 26. Oxford, 1947-1948.

Three Early Assize Rolls for the County of Northumberland. Edited by William Page. Publications of the Surtees Society, vol. 88. Durham, 1891.

Tractatus de legibus et consuetudinibus regni Anglie qui Glanvilla vocatur. Edited by G.D.G. Hall. London, 1965.

Two Cartularies of the Augustinian Priory of Bruton and the Cluniac Priory of Montacute in the County of Somerset. Publications of the Somerset Record Society, vol. 8. London, 1894.

Two Chartularies of the Priory of St Peter at Bath. Edited by William Hunt. Publications of the Somerset Record Society, vol. 7. London, 1893.

Warwickshire Feet of Fines. Edited by Ethel Stokes and Lucy Drucker. Publications of the Dugdale Society, vol. 15. London, 1939.

Year Books of 4 Edward II. Edited by G. J. Turner. Publications of the Selden Society, vol. 26. London, 1911.

III. Secondary Sources

Alexander, J. J. "The Dates of County Days." *Bulletin of the Institute of Historical Research* 3 (1925-1926): 89-95.

———. "Dates of Early County Elections." *English Historical Review* 40 (1925): 1-12.

Alexander, James W. "New Evidence of the Palatine of Chester." *English Historical Review* 85 (1970): 715-29.

Ault, W. O. *Private Jurisdictions in England.* New Haven, 1923.

Baker, J. H. *An Introduction to English Legal History.* London, 1979.

Barraclough, Geoffrey. "The Earldom and County Palatine of Chester." *Transactions of the Historical Society of Lancashire and Cheshire* 103 (1951): 23-59.

Beckerman, John. "The Forty-Shilling Jurisdictional Limit in Medieval English Personal Actions." In *Legal History Studies 1972,* edited by Dafydd Jenkins. Cardiff, 1975.

Brand, Paul. A. "*Hengham Magna*: A Thirteenth-Century English Common Law Treatise and Its Composition." *Irish Jurist* 11 (1976): 147-69.

Bridgeman, C.G.O. "The Burton Abbey Twelfth-Century Surveys." In *Collections for a History of Staffordshire.* Publications of the William Salt Archaeological Society, n.s., vol. 9. London, 1918.

The British Library. *General Catalogue of Printed Books.* 263 vols. London, 1958-1966.

Broune, John. *The History of the Metropolitan Church of St. Peter, York.* 2 vols. York, 1847.

Cam, Helen. "An East Anglian Shire-Moot of Stephen's Reign, 1148-1153." *English Historical Review* 39 (1924): 568-71.

————. *The Hundred and the Hundred Rolls.* London, 1930.

————. *Law-Finders and Law-Makers.* London, 1962.

————. "The Theory and Practice of Representation in Medieval England." In *Historical Studies of the English Parliament,* edited by E. B. Fryde and Edward Miller, vol. 1. Cambridge, 1970.

Carpenter, D. A. "The Decline of the Curial Sheriff in England, 1194-1258." *English Historical Review* 91 (1976): 1-32.

Clanchy, Michael. "The Franchise of Return of Writs." *Transactions of the Royal Historical Society* 17 (1967): 59-82.

Cronne, H. A. *The Borough of Warwick in the Middle Ages.* Dugdale Occasional Papers, no. 10. Oxford, 1954.

Dalton, Michael. *The Office and Authority of Sheriffs.* London, 1682.

Dugdale, William. *Monasticon Anglicanum.* 6 vols. in 8. London, 1817-1830.

English Place Name Society. *Survey of English Place Names.* 53 vols. Cambridge, 1924-1980.

Hall, G.D.G. Review of *Royal Writs.* Edited by R. C. Van Caenegem. *English Historical Review* 76 (1961): 316-19.

Hastings, Margaret. *The Court of Common Pleas in the Fifteenth Century.* Ithaca, 1947.

Holdsworth, W. S. *A History of English Law.* 14 vols. London, 1903-1938.

Hollister, C. Warren, and Baldwin, John. "The Rise of Administrative Kingship: Henry I and Philip Augustus." *American Historical Review* 83 (1978): 867-905.

Hoyt, R. S. *The Royal Demesne in English Constitutional History*: 1066-1272. Ithaca, 1950.

Hudson, W., and Tingey, J. C. *The Records of the City of Norwich*. 2 vols. Norwich, 1906-1910.

Hunnisett, R. F. *The Medieval Coroner*. Cambridge, 1961.

Hurnard, Naomi D. "The Jury of Presentment and the Assize of Clarendon." *English Historical Review* 56 (1941): 374-410.

Hyams, Paul R. "The Proof of Villein Status in the Common Law." *English Historical Review* 89 (1974): 721-49.

Lapsley, G. T. "Buzones." *English Historical Review* 47 (1932): 177-93, 545-67.

———. "The Court, Record and Roll of the County in the Thirteenth Century." *Law Quarterly Review* 51 (1935): 299-326.

———. *Crown, Community and Parliament in the Later Middle Ages*. Edited by Helen Cam and Geoffrey Barraclough. Oxford, 1951.

Liebermann, Felix. *Die Gesetze der Angelsachsen*. 3 vols. Halle an der Saale, 1898-1916.

List of Sheriffs for England and Wales. 1898. Reprint. New York, 1963.

Loyn, H. R. "Anglo-Saxon Stamford." In *The Making of Stamford*, edited by Alan Rogers. Leicester, 1965.

McIntosh, Marjorie. "The Privileged Villeins of the English Ancient Demesne." *Viator* 7 (1976): 1-34.

Members of Parliament. 3 vols. London, 1878-1891.

Mills, Mabel H. "The Medieval Shire House." In *Studies Presented to Sir Hilary Jenkinson*, edited by J. Conway Davies. London, 1957.

Milsom, S.F.C. *Historical Foundations of the Common Law*. London, 1969.

———. *The Legal Framework of English Feudalism*. Cambridge, 1976.

Morris, W. A. *The Early English County Court: An Historical Treatise with Illustrative Documents*. University of California Publications in History, vol. 14, no. 2. Berkeley, 1926.

———. *The Medieval English Sheriff to 1300*. Manchester, 1927.

Palmer, Robert C. "County Year Book Reports: The Professional Lawyer in the Medieval County Court." *English Historical Review* 91 (1976): 776-801.

———. "The Feudal Framework of English Law." *Michigan Law Review* 79 (1981): 1130-1164.

———. "The Origins of the Legal Profession in England." *Irish Jurist* 11 (1976): 126-47.

Plucknett, T.F.T. "Parliament." In *Historical Studies of the English Parliament*, edited by E. B. Fryde and Edward Miller, vol. 1. Cambridge, 1970.

Pollock, F., and Maitland, F. W. *The History of English Law before the Time of Edward I*. 2 vols. 2nd. Cambridge, 1968.

Putnam, Bertha H. *The Place in Legal History of Sir William Shareshull, Chief Justice of the King's Bench, 1350-1361*. Cambridge, 1950.

Revised Medieval Latin Word-List. Prepared by R. E. Latham. London, 1965.

Richardson, H. G., and Sayles, G. O. *The Governance of Medieval England from the Conquest to the Magna Carta.* Edinburgh, 1963.

Rogers, Alan. "The Lincolnshire County Court in the Fifteenth Century." *Lincolnshire History and Archaeology* 1 (1966): 64-78.

———. "Medieval Stamford." In *The Making of Stamford*, edited by Alan Rogers. Leicester, 1965.

Sayles, G. O. *The King's Parliament of England.* London, 1975.

Simpson, A.W.B. *A History of the Common Law of Contract.* Oxford, 1975.

Stenton, Doris M. *English Justice between the Norman Conquest and the Great Charter, 1066-1215.* London, 1965.

Stewart-Brown, R. *The Serjeants of the Peace in Medieval England and Wales.* Manchester, 1936.

Sutherland, Donald W. *The Assize of Novel Disseisin.* Oxford, 1973.

———. *Quo Warranto Proceedings in the Reign of Edward I, 1278-1294.* Oxford, 1963.

Thorne, S. E. "Notes on Courts of Record in England." *West Virginia Law Quarterly* 40 (1934): 346-59.

The Victoria History of the Counties of England. 163 vols.

Walker, Lorna E. M. "Some Aspects of Local Jurisdiction in the 12th and 13th Centuries, with Special Reference to Private and County Courts." Master's thesis, University of London, 1958.

Wood-Legh, K. L. "Sheriffs, Lawyers, and Belted Knights in the Parliaments of Edward III." *English Historical Review* 46 (1931): 372-88.

Index

Robert C. Palmer is a Junior Fellow of the Michigan Society of Fellows at the University of Michigan Law School.

Library of Congress Cataloging in Publication Data

Palmer, Robert C., 1947-
The county courts of medieval England, 1150-1350.
Bibliography: p.
Includes index.
1. County courts—Great Britain—History. I. Title.
KD6972.P34   347.42'021   81-47939
              344.2072   AACR2
       ISBN 0-691-05341-3